The Faces of Clio

The Faces of Clio

*An Anthology
of Classics
in Historical Writing
from Ancient Times
to the Present*

Robert Stinson

Nelson-Hall nh Chicago

LIBRARY OF CONGRESS CATALOGING-IN-PUBLICATION DATA

Stinson, Robert.
  The faces of Clio.

  Includes index.
  1. World history. I. Title.
  D6.S765 1986   909   86-12569
  ISBN 0-8304-1040-6

Manufactured in the United States of America

10 9 8 7 6 5 4 3 2 1

The paper in this book is pH neutral (acid-free).

CONTENTS

Every student learns sooner or later that writing history involves deciding not just what to say but also what not to say, for the historian offers up not the past but a selection from the past. What fact can represent many facts? What is important to the argument, to reader interest? What is unnecessary, beclouding?

The task is the same for the historian who creates an anthology of historians; hence, the first thing students should know about this book is that more has been left out from the work of even the legitimately "classic" historians than has been put in. By including certain figures and excluding others who, in some other scheme, might have a claim to inclusion, I have implicitly decided what is important or not in the history of historical writing. My book is a selection, which means, spare as it is, it is a kind of interpretation.

First, it is a selection of writers. Some names are obvious and, like Herodotus and Thucydides, would be on anyone's list of twenty great writers. Others—William Bradford comes to mind—are less obvious. Does his *Of Plymouth Plantation* (c.1640) sufficiently represent Reformation historiography? If a reasonably immediate influence on other writers is a criterion for inclusion, will Bradford do, especially since his account of England and New England in the seventeenth century was not published until the mid-nineteenth century? While my introductory comments on Bradford in chapter 9 place him in the stream of historiography, I should say that, for me, Bradford does double duty: he illustrates some aspects of the revival of a fully Christian point of view in historical writing, even if his work does not have a place in the heated polemics of the Reformation, and he marks the beginning of an American historiography, a pattern that can be followed skeletally from him to Francis Parkman, Frederick Jackson Turner, Charles Beard, and others.

But the point remains, and students may like to discuss at some length not just who is here but who is not and yet ought to be. My answer to the first question will be clear enough from the introductions to each chapter. As to the second question, who is not here, I am as happy to be second-guessed as I am happy with my selection as it stands.

Second, this book involves a selection of themes, for the history of historical writing, like any history, has flowed in many channels, and a brief anthology, to have any coherence, can follow only a few of them. I was especially conscious of rather arbitrarily reducing historiography to one theme as I read the rich complexity of nineteenth- and twentieth-century historical writing. Another editor might have focused on the contributions of Marxist historiography and the ideological debates that have attended their appearance, whereas I have included only an excerpt from Karl Marx's own *Eighteenth Brumaire of Louis Bonaparte* (1852). Yet another might choose to illustrate the development of the comparative history of civilization by including selections from the massive works of Oswald Spengler, Arnold Toynbee, or William MacNeil. Or one might include something from Samuel Eliot Morison or Barbara Tuchman to point up the persistence of brilliant narrative history.

My own choice has been to illustrate the development of *historicism* from Leopold von Ranke to Lucien Febvre and the growing conflict between historicism and history as a social science. My introduction to chapter 11 on Ranke and the long note on historicism on page 294 are statements of one side in the conflict, while the comments on Crane Brinton and William Aydelotte in chapters 19 and 20 introduce the other side.

In any case, my selection of the last several historical works has to do with historicism and social science largely to the exclusion of other themes that, I am fully aware, are no less real and important.

It is also worth noting that all my authors are historians, people who are known by the history they wrote. That has meant excluding philosophers like Augustine of Hippo and Wilhelm Dilthey. Yet, who was more central to the development of Christian history than St. Augustine? Who saw the implications of historicism better than Dilthey? My thought, however, was that while philosophers of history are well represented in some very good books—think of Fritz Stern, editor, *Varieties of History,* Hans Meyerhoff, editor, *The Philosophy of History in Our Time,* and Patrick Gardiner, editor, *Theories of History*— working historians are to be found chiefly in their hundreds of volumes on library shelves and are not as easy to sample for an overview. In any case, my anthology shows not so much how historians thought history should be written as it does how they actually wrote it. I have not reprinted (as Stern does in *Varieties of History*) Leopold von Ranke's famous preface to the *History of the Latin and Teutonic Peoples*—a manifesto about historical study—but rather a chapter from the middle of Ranke's *History of the Popes.* Students will find that some of what Ranke says explicitly in his manifesto is *implicit* in his actual history. Indeed, a question readers should ask as they read and discuss each selection is, What must the writer's philosophy of history be if he can write history *this* way?

The introduction to each chapter offers some basic biographical information on each historian, a description of his leading characteristics as an historian, a little background information about the subject he is writing on, and a few hints about what to look for in the excerpt itself. Beyond this, I have made a little attempt to compare and connect some figures with the ones that come immediately before and after them, but such comments provide only a minimal sense of continuity and are hardly definitive. I am assuming that students will read *The Faces of Clio* as a supplement to listening to lectures on the history of history or to reading in books like Harry Elmer Barnes's *A History of Historical Writing* and others among those listed in the bibliography of general works below.

I hope, too, that what students read here will spark their interest enough to read more deeply in the classic works from which my excerpts have been taken, for historical writing is a rich literature that students, I think, will be happy to discover.

I wish to thank my colleagues, Mary Faith Carson, Howard Cox, Dennis Glew, and Janet Loengard, for reading parts of the manuscript. If errors and misjudgments remain, they are mine. Ruth D'Aleo of Reeves Library located hard-to-find editions of the classic historians. Thanks also to Catherine Cruciani, Jean Hunter, Mickey Ortiz, and Jean Siska, who typed these pages in several drafts. Finally, I am grateful to Moravian College for providing me a sabbatical leave during which most of this book was composed, and I also thank the Faculty Development and Research Committee for a grant to cover some of the project's costs.

Bibliography

Barnes, Harry Elmer. *A History of Historical Writing*. 2d rev. ed. New York, 1962.

Breisach, Ernst. *Historiography: Ancient, Medieval, and Modern*. Chicago, 1983.

Butterfield, Herbert. "Historiography." In *Dictionary of the History of Ideas, Studies of Selected Pivotal Ideas,* vol. 2, edited by Philip P. Wiener. New York, 1973.

Collingwood, R. G. *The Idea of History*. New York and London, 1946.

Conkin, Paul, and Roland Stromberg. *The Heritage and Challenge of History*. New York, 1972.

Fitzsimons, Matthew; Alfred G. Pundt; and Charles E. Nowell. *The Development of Historiography*. Harrisburg, Pa., 1954.

Fitzsimons, M. A. *The Past Recaptured: Great Historians and the History of History*. Notre Dame and London, 1983.

Hay, Denys. *Annalists and Historians: Western Historiography from the Eighth to the Eighteenth Centuries*. London, 1977.

Manuel, Frank. *Shapes of Philosophical History*. Stanford, Calif., 1965.

Mazlish, Bruce. *The Riddle of History: The Great Speculators from Vico to Freud*. New York, 1966.

Schevill, Ferdinand. *Six Historians*. Chicago, 1956.

Shotwell, James T. *An Introduction to the History of History*. New York, 1922.

Tholfsen, T. R. *Historical Thinking: An Introduction*. New York, 1969.

Thompson, James Westfall. *A History of Historical Writing*. 2 vols. New York, 1942.

Wish, Harvey. *The American Historian: A Social-Intellectual History of the Writing of the American Past*. New York, 1960.

CHAPTER 1

"*The Succession Narrative*"

(c. Tenth Century B.C.)

The Israelites were the first "history conscious" people in the ancient world, and a very early text instructed them to recite their history in the very prayers they offered to Yahweh:

> A wandering Aramean was my father; and he went down into Egypt and sojourned there, few in number; and there he became a nation, great, mighty, and populous. And the Egyptians treated us harshly, and afflicted us, and laid upon us hard bondage. Then we cried to the Lord the God of our fathers, and the Lord heard our voice, and saw our affliction, our toil, and our oppression; and the Lord brought us out of Egypt with a mighty hand and an outstretched arm, with great terror, with signs and wonders; and he brought us into this place and gave us this land, a land flowing with milk and honey. (Deuteronomy 26:5–9)

This historical confession of faith is unlike anything found among the ancient Assyrians or Egyptians, who kept sparse records of isolated events or made lists of their kings, but who possessed no sense of history as having continuity, direction, or meaning.

The so-called "Succession Narrative," excerpted here from the Second Book of Samuel 9–20, is generally recognized as the finest piece of ancient Hebrew historical writing. It deals with the emergence of the hereditary monarchy in Israel and the question of who should succeed King David. The narrative satisfies even modern readers in its complex representation of characters and events, in its realistic distribution of praise and blame, and in its interpretation of events according to a comprehensive theme.

Concerning its author we know very little, not even his name. Some scholars believe he is Abiathar the priest, but whoever wrote the "Succession Narrative" must have been an intimate of the king's court in Jerusalem, for the text shows he knew many private details about David's family. His history may date from the time of King Solomon (c. 960–922 B.C.), David's son by Bathsheba, who took the throne following David's often troubled reign.

Below is the account of Absalom's rebellion, which, since the historian devoted so much space to it, must have been the most serious of all challenges to David's authority. As David sought to transform the Hebrew tribal

1

confederacy into a more centralized monarchy, internecine warfare broke out. A conflict within the king's own family spread to divisions within the larger Israelite community as Absalom, one of David's sons, raised an army to overthrow his father.

Take note of the historian's characterizations, especially that of David. The whole "Succession Narrative" represents him as winsome, generous, and just, but also remembers him as an adulterer and murderer. Observe, too, how the writer selects events to develop religious and political themes: the connection between sin and suffering and the problem of monarchical succession. And read the story of Absalom for narrative technique. The historian shifts skillfully between public and private affairs, but major turns in the story are evoked as the personal experience of the king or his son. Thus, David's evacuation of Jerusalem occurs as a series of significant personal encounters, and Absalom's tactical error in the final conflict is drawn out as a choice between actions argued by rival counselors. Then the historian carefully slows his story's pace at the point where David receives news of the battle's outcome.

13 NOW AB'SALOM, David's son, had a beautiful sister, whose name was Tamar; and after a time Amnon, David's son, loved her. And Amnon was so tormented that he made himself ill because of his sister Tamar; for she was a virgin, and it seemed impossible to Amnon to do anything to her. But Amnon had a friend, whose name was Jon'adab, the son of Shim'e-ah, David's brother; and Jon'adab was a very crafty man. And he said to him, "O son of the king, why are you so haggard morning after morning? Will you not tell me?" Amnon said to him, "I love Tamar, my brother Ab'salom's sister." Jon'adab said to him. "Lie down on your bed, and pretend to be ill; and when your father comes to see you, say to him, 'Let my sister Tamar come and give me bread to eat, and prepare the food in my sight, that I may see it, and eat it from her hand.'" So Amnon lay down, and pretended to be ill; and when the king came to see him, Amnon said to the king, "Pray let my sister Tamar come and make a couple of cakes in my sight, that I may eat from her hand."

Then David sent home to Tamar, saying, "Go to your brother Amnon's house, and prepare food for him." So Tamar went to her brother Amnon's house, where he was lying down. And she took dough, and kneaded it, and made cakes in his sight, and baked the cakes. And she took the pan and emptied it out before him, but he refused to eat. And Amnon said, "Send out every one from me." So every one went out from him. Then Amnon said to Tamar, "Bring the food into the chamber, that I may eat from your hand." And Tamar took the cakes she had made, and brought them into the chamber to Amnon her brother. But when she brought them near him to eat, he took hold of her, and said to her, "Come, lie with me, my sister." She answered him, "No, my brother, do not force me; for such a thing is not done in Israel; do not do this wanton folly. As for me, where could I carry my shame? And as for you, you would be as one of the wanton fools in Israel. Now therefore, I pray you, speak to the king; for he will not withhold me from you." But he would not listen to her; and being stronger than she, he forced her, and lay with her.

Then Anmon hated her with very great hatred; so that the hatred with which he hated her was greater than the love with which he had loved her. And Amnon said to her, "Arise, be gone." But she said to him, "No, my brother; for this wrong in sending me away is greater than the other which you did to me." But he would not listen to her. He called the young man who served him and said, "Put this woman out of my presence, and bolt the door after her." Now she was wearing a long robe with sleeves; for thus were the virgin daughters of the king clad of old. So his servant put her out, and bolted the door after her. And Tamar put ashes on her head, and rent the long-sleeved robe which she wore; and she laid her hand on her head, and went away, crying aloud as she went.

And her brother Ab'salom said to her, "Has Amnon your brother been with you? Now hold your peace, my sister; he is your brother; do not take this to heart." So Tamar dwelt, a desolate woman, in her brother Ab'salom's house. When King David heard of all these things, he was very angry. But Ab'salom spoke to Amnon neither good nor bad; for Ab'salom hated Amnon, because he had forced his sister Tamar.

After two full years Ab'salom had sheepshearers at Ba'al-ha'zor, which is near E'phraim, and Ab'salom invited all the king's sons. And Ab'salom came to the king, and said, "Behold, your servant has sheepshearers; pray let the king and his servants go with your servant." But the king said to Ab'salom, "No, my son, let us not all go, lest we be burdensome to you." He pressed him, but he would not go but gave him his blessing. Then Ab'salom said, "If not, pray let my brother Amnon go with us." And the king said to him, "Why should he go with you?" But Ab'salom pressed him until he let Amnon and all the king's sons go with him. Then Ab'salom commanded his servants, "Mark when Amnon's heart is merry with wine, and when I say to you, 'Strike Amnon,' then kill him. Fear not; have I not commanded you? Be courageous and be valiant." So the servants of Ab'salom did to Amnon as Ab'salom had commanded. Then all the king's sons arose, and each mounted his mule and fled.

While they were on the way, tidings came to David, "Ab'salom has slain all the king's sons, and not one of them is left." Then the king arose, and rent his garments, and lay on the earth; and all his servants who were standing by rent their garments. But Jon'adab the son of Shim'e-ah, David's brother, said, "Let not my lord suppose that they have killed all the young men the king's sons, for Amnon alone is dead, for by the command of Ab'salom this has been determined from the day he forced his sister Tamar. Now therefore let not my lord the king so take it to heart as to suppose that all the king's sons are dead; for Amnon alone is dead."

But Ab'salom fled. And the young man who kept the watch lifted up his eyes, and looked, and behold, many people were coming from the Horona'im road by the side of the mountain. And Jon'adab said to the king, "Behold, the king's sons have come; as your servant said, so it has come about." And as soon as he had finished speaking, behold, the king's sons came, and lifted up their voice and wept; and the king also and all his servants wept very bitterly.

But Ab'salom fled, and went to Talmai the son of Ammi'hud, king of Geshur. And David mourned for his son day after day. So Ab'salom fled, and went to Geshur, and was there three years. And the spirit of the king longed to go forth to Ab'salom; for he was comforted about Amnon, seeing he was dead.

14 Now Jo'ab the son of Zeru'iah perceived that the king's heart went out to Ab'salom. And Jo'ab sent to Teko'a, and fetched from there a wise woman, and said to her, "Pretend to be a mourner, and put on mourning garments; do not anoint yourself with oil, but behave like a woman who has been mourning many days for the dead; and go to the king, and speak thus to him." So Jo'ab put the words in her mouth.

When the woman of Teko'a came to the king, she fell on her face to the ground, and did obeisance, and said, "Help, O king." And the king said to her, "What is your trouble?" She answered, "Alas, I am a widow; my husband is dead. And your handmaid had two sons, and they quarreled with one another in the field; there was no one to part them, and one struck the other and killed him. And now the whole family has risen against your handmaid, and they say, "Give up the man who struck his brother, that we may kill him for the life of his brother whom he slew'; and so they would destroy the heir also. Thus they would quench my coal which is left, and leave to my husband neither name nor remnant upon the face of the earth."

Then the king said to the woman, "Go to your house, and I will give orders concerning you." And the woman of Teko'a said to the king, "On me be the guilt, my lord the king, and on my father's house; let the king and his throne be guiltless." The king said, "If anyone says anything to you, bring him to me, and he shall never touch you again." Then she said, "Pray let the king invoke the LORD your God, that the avenger of blood slay no more, and my son be not destroyed." He said, "As the LORD lives, not one hair of your son shall fall to the ground."

Then the woman said, "Pray let your handmaid speak a word to my lord the king." He said, "Speak." And the woman said, "Why then have you planned such a thing against the people of God? For in giving this decision the king convicts himself, inasmuch as the king does not bring his banished one home again. We must all die, we are like water spilt on the ground, which cannot be gathered up again; but God will not take away the life of him who devises means not to keep his banished one an outcast. Now I have come to say this to my lord the king because the people have made me afraid; and your handmaid thought, 'I will speak to the king; it may be that the king will perform the request of his servant. For the king will hear, and deliver his servant from the hand of the man who would destroy me and my son together from the heritage of God.' And your handmaid thought, 'The word of my lord the king will set me at rest'; for my lord the king is like the angel of God to discern good and evil. The LORD your God be with you!"

Then the king answered the woman, "Do not hide from me anything I ask you." And the woman said, "Let my lord the king speak." The king said, "Is the hand of Jo'ab with you in all this?" The woman answered and said, "As surely as you live, my lord the king, one cannot turn to the right hand or to the left from anything that my lord the king has said. It was your servant Jo'ab who bade me; it was he who put all these words in the mouth of your handmaid. In order to change the course of affairs your servant Jo'ab did this. But my lord has wisdom like the wisdom of the angel of God to know all things that are on the earth."

Then the king said to Jo'ab, "Behold now, I grant this; go, bring back the young man Ab'salom." And Jo'ab fell on his face to the ground, and did obeisance, and blessed the king; and Jo'ab said, "Today your servant knows that I have found favor in your sight, my lord the king, in that the king has granted the request of his servant." So Jo'ab arose and went to Geshur, and brought Ab'salom to Jerusalem. And the king said, "Let him dwell apart in his own house; he is not to come into my presence." So Ab'salom dwelt apart in his own house, and did not come into the king's presence.

Now in all Israel there was no one so much to be praised for his beauty as Ab'salom; from the sole of his foot to the crown of his head there was no blemish in him. And when he cut the hair of his head (for at the end of every year he used to cut it; when it was heavy on him, he cut it), he weighed the hair of his head, two hundred shekels by the king's weight.

There were born to Ab′salom three sons, and one daughter whose name was Tamar; she was a beautiful woman.

So Ab′salom dwelt two full years in Jerusalem, without coming into the king's presence. Then Ab′salom sent for Jo′ab, to send him to the king; but Jo′ab would not come to him. And he sent a second time, but Jo′ab would not come. Then he said to his servants, "See, Jo′ab's field is next to mine, and he has barley there; go and set it on fire." So Ab′salom's servants set the field on fire. Then Jo′ab arose and went to Ab′salom at his house, and said to him, "Why have your servants set my field on fire?" Ab′salom answered Jo′ab, "Behold, I sent word to you, 'Come here, that I may send you to the king, to ask, "Why have I come from Geshur? It would be better for me to be there still." Now therefore let me go into the presence of the king; and if there is guilt in me, let him kill me.'" Then Jo′ab went to the king, and told him; and he summoned Ab′salom. So he came to the king, and bowed himself on his face to the ground before the king; and the king kissed Ab′salom.

15   After this Ab′salom got himself a chariot and horses, and fifty men to run before him. And Ab′salom used to rise early and stand beside the way of the gate; and when any man had a suit to come before the king for judgment, Ab′salom would call to him, and say, "From what city are you?" And when he said, "Your servant is of such and such a tribe in Israel," Ab′salom would say to him, "See, your claims are good and right; but there is no man deputed by the king to hear you." Ab′salom said moreover, "Oh that I were judge in the land! Then every man with a suit or cause might come to me, and I would give him justice." And whenever a man came near to do obeisance to him, he would put out his hand, and take hold of him, and kiss him. Thus Ab′salom did to all of Israel who came to the king for judgment; so Ab′salom stole the hearts of the men of Israel.

And at the end of four years Ab′salom said to the king, "Pray, let me go and pay my vow, which I have vowed to the LORD, in Hebron. For your servant vowed a vow while I dwelt at Geshur in Aram, saying, 'If the LORD will indeed bring me back to Jerusalem, then I will offer worship to the LORD.'" The king said to him, "Go in peace." So he arose, and went to Hebron. But Ab′salom sent secret messengers throughout all the tribes of Israel, saying, "As soon as you hear the sound of the trumpet then say, 'Ab′salom is king at Hebron!'" With Ab′salom went two hundred men from Jerusalem who were invited guests, and they went in their simplicity, and knew nothing. And while Ab′salom was offering the sacrifices, he sent for Ahith′ophel the Gi′lonite, David's counselor, from his city Giloh. And the conspiracy grew strong, and the people with Ab′salom kept increasing.

And a messenger came to David, saying, "The hearts of the men of

Israel have gone after Ab'salom." Then David said to all his servants who were with him at Jerusalem, "Arise, and let us flee; or else there will be no escape for us from Ab'salom; go in haste, lest he overtake us quickly, and bring down evil upon us, and smite the city with the edge of the sword." And the king's servants said to the king, "Behold, your servants are ready to do whatever my lord the king decides." So the king went forth, and all his household after him. And the king left ten concubines to keep the house. And the king went forth, and all the people after him; and they halted at the last house. And all his servants passed by him; and all the Cher'ethites, and all the Pel'ethites, and all the six hundred Gittites who had followed him from Gath, passed on before the king.

Then the king said to It'tai the Gittite, "Why do you also go with us? Go back, and stay with the king; for you are a foreigner, and also an exile from your home. You came only yesterday, and shall I today make you wander about with us, seeing I go I know not where? Go back, and take your brethren with you; and may the LORD show steadfast love and faithfulness to you." But It'tai answered the king, "As the LORD lives, and as my lord the king lives, wherever my lord the king shall be, whether for death or for life, there also will your servant be." And David said to It'tai, "Go then, pass on." So It'tai the Gittite passed on, with all his men and all the little ones who were with him. And all the country wept aloud as all the people passed by, and the king crossed the brook Kidron, and all the people passed on toward the wilderness.

And Abi'athar came up, and lo, Zadok came also, with all the Levites, bearing the ark of the covenant of God; and they set down the ark of God, until the people had all passed out of the city. Then the king said to Zadok, "Carry the ark of God back into the city. If I find favor in the eyes of the LORD, he will bring me back and let me see both it and his habitation; but if he says, 'I have no pleasure in you,' behold, here I am, let him do to me what seems good to him." The king also said to Zadok the priest, "Look, go back to the city in peace, you and Abi'athar, with your two sons, Ahim'a-az your son, and Jonathan the son of Abi'athar. See, I will wait at the fords of the wilderness, until word comes from you to inform me." So Zadok and Abi'athar carried the ark of God back to Jerusalem; and they remained there.

But David went up the ascent of the Mount of Olives, weeping as he went, barefoot and with his head covered; and all the people who were with him covered their heads, and they went up, weeping as they went. And it was told David, "Ahith'ophel is among the conspirators with Ab'salom." And David said, "O LORD, I pray thee, turn the counsel of Ahith'ophel into foolishness."

When David came to the summit, where God was worshiped, behold, Hushai the Archite came to meet him with his coat rent and earth upon his head. David said to him, "If you go on with me, you will be a burden to me. But if you return to the city, and say to Ab'salom, 'I will be your servant, O king; as I have been your father's servant in time past, so now I will be your servant,' then you will defeat for me the counsel of Ahith'ophel. Are not Zadok and Abi'athar the priests with you there? So whatever you hear from the king's house, tell it to Zadok and Abi'athar the priests. Behold, their two sons are with them there, Ahim'a-az, Zadok's son, and Jonathan, Abi'athar's son; and by them you shall send to me everything you hear." So Hushai, David's friend, came into the city, just as Ab'salom was entering Jerusalem.

16   When David had passed a little beyond the summit, Ziba the servant of Mephib'osheth met him, with a couple of asses saddled, bearing two hundred loaves of bread, a hundred bunches of raisins, a hundred of summer fruits, and a skin of wine. And the king said to Ziba, "Why have you brought these?" Ziba answered, "The asses are for the king's household to ride on, the bread and summer fruit for the young men to eat, and the wine for those who faint in the wilderness to drink." And the king said, "And where is your master's son?" Ziba said to the king, "Behold, he remains in Jerusalem; for he said, 'Today the house of Israel will give me back the kingdom of my father.'" Then the king said to Ziba, "Behold, all that belonged to Mephib'osheth is now yours." And Ziba said, "I do obeisance; let me ever find favor in your sight, my lord the king."

When King David came to Bahu'rim, there came out a man of the family of the house of Saul, whose name was Shim'e-i, the son of Gera; and as he came he cursed continually. And he threw stones at David, and at all the servants of King David; and all the people and all the mighty men were on his right hand and on his left. And Shim'e-i said as he cursed, "Begone, begone, you man of blood, you worthless fellow! The LORD has avenged upon you all the blood of the house of Saul, in whose place you have reigned; and the LORD has given the kingdom into the hand of your son Ab'salom. See, your ruin is on you; for you are a man of blood."

Then Abi'shai the son of Zeru'iah said to the king, "Why should this dead dog curse my lord the king? Let me go over and take off his head." But the king said, "What have I to do with you, you sons of Zeru'iah? If he is cursing because the LORD has said to him, 'Curse David,' who then shall say, 'Why have you done so?'" And David said to Abi'shai and to all his servants, "Behold, my own son seeks my life; how much more now may this Benjaminite! Let him alone, and let him curse; for the LORD has bidden him. It may be that the LORD will look upon my affliction, and that the LORD will repay me with good for this cursing of me today." So David and his men went on the road, while Shim'e-i went along on the hillside opposite him and cursed as he went, and threw stones at him and flung dust. And the king, and all the people who were with him, arrived weary at the Jordan; and there he refreshed himself.

Now Ab'salom and all the people, the men of Israel, came to Jerusalem, and Ahith'ophel with him. And when Hushai the Archite, David's friend, came to Ab'salom, Hushai said to Ab'salom, "Long live the king! Long live the king!" And Ab'salom said to Hushai, "Is this your loyalty to your friend? Why did you not go with your friend?" And Hushai said to Ab'salom, "No; for whom the LORD and this people and all the men of Israel have chosen, his I will be, and with him I will remain. And again, whom should I serve? Should it not be his son? As I have served your father, so I will serve you."

Then Ab'salom said to Ahith'ophel, "Give your counsel; what shall we do?" Ahith'ophel said to Ab'salom, "Go in to your father's concubines, whom he has left to keep the house; and all Israel will hear that you have made yourself odious to your father, and the hands of all who are with you will be strengthened." So they pitched a tent for Ab'salom upon the roof; and Ab'salom went in to his father's concubines in the sight of all Israel. Now in those days the counsel which Ahith'ophel gave was as if one consulted the oracle of God; so was all the counsel of Ahith'ophel esteemed, both by David and Ab'salom.

17 Moreover Ahith'ophel said to Ab'salom, "Let me choose twelve thousand men, and I will set out and pursue David tonight. I will come upon him while he is weary and discouraged, and throw him into a panic; and all the people who are with him will flee. I will strike down the king only, and I will bring all the people back to you as a bride comes home to her husband. You seek the life of only one man, and all the people will be at peace." And the advice pleased Ab'salom and all the elders of Israel.

Then Ab'salom said, "Call Hushai the Archite also, and let us hear what he has to say." And when Hushai came to Ab'salom, Ab'salom said to him, "Thus has Ahith'ophel spoken; shall we do as he advises? If not, you speak." Then Hushai said to Ab'salom, "This time the counsel which Ahith'ophel has given is not good." Hushai said moreover, "You know that your father and his men are mighty men, and that they are enraged, like a bear robbed of her cubs in the field. Besides, your father is expert in war; he will not spend the night with the people. Behold, even now he has hidden himself in one of the pits, or in some other place. And when some of the people fall at the first attack, whoever hears it will say, 'There has been a slaughter among the people who follow Ab'salom.' Then even the valiant man, whose heart is like the heart of a lion, will utterly melt with fear; for all Israel knows that your father is a mighty man, and that those who are with him are valiant men. But my counsel is

10   THE FACES OF CLIO

that all Israel be gathered to you, from Dan to Beer-sheba, as the sand by the sea for multitude, and that you go to battle in person. So we shall come upon him in some place where he is to be found, and we shall light upon him as the dew falls on the ground; and of him and all the men with him not one will be left. If he withdraws into a city, then all Israel will bring ropes to that city, and we shall drag it into the valley, until not even a pebble is to be found there." And Ab'salom and all the men of Israel said, "The counsel of Hushai the Archite is better than the counsel of Ahith'ophel." For the LORD had ordained to defeat the good counsel of Ahith'ophel, so that the LORD might bring evil upon Ab'salom.

Then Hushai said to Zadok and Abi'thar the priests, "Thus and so did Ahith'ophel counsel Ab'salom and the elders of Israel; and thus and so have I counseled. Now therefore send quickly and tell David, 'Do not lodge tonight at the fords of the wilderness, but by all means pass over; lest the king and all the people who are with him be swallowed up.'" Now Jonathan and Ahim'a-az were waiting at En-ro'gel; a maidservant used to go and tell them, and they would go and tell King David; for they must not be seen entering the city. But a lad saw them, and told Ab'salom; so both of them went away quickly, and came to the house of a man at Bahu'rim, who had a well in his courtyard; and they went down into it. And the woman took and spread a covering over the well's mouth, and scattered grain upon it; and nothing was known of it. When Ab'salom's servants came to the woman at the house, they said, "Where are Ahim'a-az and Jonathan?" And the woman said to them, "They have gone over the brook of water." And when they had sought and could not find them, they returned to Jerusalem.

After they had gone, the men came up out of the well, and went and told King David. They said to David, "Arise, and go quickly over the water; for thus and so has Ahith'ophel counseled against you." Then David arose, and all the people who were with him, and they crossed the Jordan; by daybreak not one was left who had not crossed the Jordan.

When Ahith'ophel saw that his counsel was not followed, he saddled his ass, and went off home to his own city. And he set his house in order, and hanged himself; and he died, and was buried in the tomb of his father.

Then David came to Mahana'im. And Ab'salom crossed the Jordan with all the men of Israel. Now Ab'salom had set Ama'sa over the army instead of Jo'ab. Ama'sa was the son of a man named Ithra the Ish'-maelite, who had married Ab'igal the daughter of Nahash, sister of Zeru'-iah, Jo'ab's mother. And Israel and Ab'salom encamped in the land of Gilead.

When David came to Mahana'im, Shobi the son of Nahash from Rabbah of the Ammonites, and Machir the son of Am'mi-el from Lo'de-bar, and Barzil'lai the Gileadite from Ro'gelim, brought beds, basins, and earthen vessels, wheat, barley, meal, parched grain, beans and lentils, honey and curds and sheep and cheese from the herd, for David and the people with him to eat; for they said, "The people are hungry and weary and thirsty in the wilderness."

18 Then David mustered the men who were with him, and set over them commanders of thousands and commanders of hundreds. And David set forth the army, one third under the command of Jo'ab, one third under the command of Abi'shai the son of Zeru'iah, Jo'ab's brother, and one third under the command of It'tai the Gittite. And the king said to the men, "I myself will also go out with you." But the men said, "You shall not go out. For if we flee, they will not care about us. If half of us die, they will not care about us. But you are worth ten thousand of us; therefore it is better that you send us help from the city." The king said to them, "Whatever seems best to you I will do." So the king stood at the side of the gate, while all the army marched out by hundreds and by thousands. And the king ordered Jo'ab and Abi'shai and It'tai, "Deal gently for my sake with the young man Ab'salom." And all the people heard when the king gave orders to all the commanders about Ab'salom.

So the army went out into the field against Israel; and the battle was fought in the forest of E'phraim. And the men of Israel were defeated there by the servants of David, and the slaughter there was great on that day, twenty thousand men. The battle spread over the face of all the country; and the forest devoured more people that day than the sword.

And Ab'salom chanced to meet the servants of David. Ab'salom was riding upon his mule, and the mule went under the thick branches of a great oak, and his head caught fast in the oak, and he was left hanging between heaven and earth, while the mule that was under him went on. And a certain man saw it, and told Jo'ab, "Behold, I saw Ab'salom hanging on an oak." Jo'ab said to the man who told him, "What, you saw him! Why then did you not strike him there to the ground? I would have been glad to give you ten pieces of silver and a girdle." But the man said to Jo'ab, "Even if I felt in my hand the weight of a thousand pieces of silver, I would not put forth my hand against the king's son; for in our hearing the king commanded you and Abi'shai and It'tai, 'For my sake protect the young man Ab'salom.' On the other hand, if I had dealt treacherously against his life (and there is nothing hidden from the king), then you yourself would have stood aloof." Jo'ab said, "I will not waste time like this with you." And he took three darts in his hand, and thrust them into the heart of Ab'salom, while he was still alive in the oak. And ten young men, Jo'ab's armor-bearers, surrounded Ab'salom and struck him, and killed him.

Then Jo'ab blew the trumpet, and the troops came back from pursuing Israel; for Jo'ab restrained them. And they took Ab'salom, and threw him into a great pit in the forest, and raised over him a very great heap of stones; and all Israel fled every one to his own home. Now Ab'salom in his lifetime had taken and set up for himself the pillar which is in the King's Valley, for he said, "I have no son to keep my name in remembrance"; he called the pillar after his own name, and it is called Ab'salom's monument to this day.

Then said Ahi'ma-az the son of Zadok, "Let me run, and carry tidings to the king that the LORD has delivered him from the power of his enemies." And Jo'ab said to him, "You are not to carry tidings today; you may carry tidings another day, but today you shall carry no tidings, because the king's son is dead." Then Jo'ab said to the Cushite, "Go, tell the king what you have seen." The Cushite bowed before Jo'ab, and ran. Then Ahi'ma-az the son of Zadok said again to Jo'ab, "Come what may, let me also run after the Cushite." And Jo'ab said, "Why will you run, my son, seeing that you will have no reward for the tidings?" "Come what may," he said, "I will run." So he said to him, "Run." Then Ahi'ma-az ran by the way of the plain, and outran the Cushite.

Now David was sitting between the two gates; and the watchman went up to the roof of the gate by the wall, and when he lifted up his eyes and looked, he saw a man running alone. And the watchman called out and told the king. And the king said, "If he is alone, there are tidings in his mouth." And he came apace, and drew near. And the watchman saw another man running; and the watchman called to the gate and said, "See, another man running alone!" The king said, "He also brings tidings." And the watchman said, "I think the running of the foremost is like the running of Ahi'ma-az the son of Zadok." And the king said, "He is a good man, and comes with good tidings."

Then Ahi'ma-az cried out to the king, "All is well." And he bowed before the king with his face to the earth, and said, "Blessed be the LORD your God, who has delivered up the men who raised their hand against my lord the king." And the king said, "Is it well with the young man Ab'-salom?" Ahi'ma-az answered, "When Jo'ab sent your servant, I saw a great tumult, but I do not know what it was." And the king said, "Turn aside, and stand here." So he turned aside, and stood still.

And behold, the Cushite came; and the Cushite said, "Good tidings for my lord the king! For the LORD has delivered you this day from the power of all who rose up against you." The king said to the Cushite, "Is it well with the young man Ab'salom?" And the Cushite answered, "May the enemies of my lord the king, and all who rise up against you for evil, be like that young man." And the king was deeply moved, and went up to the chamber over the gate, and wept; and as he went, he said, "O my son Ab'salom, my son, my son Ab'salom! Would I had died instead of you, O Ab'salom, my son, my son!"

Bibliography

Ackroyd, Peter R. "The Succession Narrative (so called)." *Interpretation,* 35 (1981): 383–96.

Alter, Robert. *The Art of Biblical Narrative.* New York, 1981.

Anderson, Bernhard W. *Understanding the Old Testament.* Englewood Cliffs, N.J., 1957.

Burrows, Millar. "Ancient Israel." In *The Idea of History in the Ancient Near East,* edited by Robert C. Dentan. New Haven, Conn., 1955.

Coates, G. W. "Parable, Fable, and Anecdote: Storytelling in the Succession Narrative." *Interpretation,* 35 (1981): 368–82.

Eliade, Mircea. *Cosmos and History: The Myth of the Eternal Return,* translated by Willard R. Trask. New York, 1959.

Moore, George Foote. *The Literature of the Old Testament.* London, 1913.

North, C. R. *The Old Testament Interpretation of History.* London, 1946.

Ostborn, Gunnar. *Yahweh's Words and Deeds: A Preliminary Study of the Old Testament Presentation of History.* Uppsala and Wiesbaden, 1952.

Pfeiffer, Robert H. "Facts and Faith in Biblical History." *Journal of Biblical Literature,* 70 (1951): 1–14.

von Rad, Gerhard. "The Beginnings of Historical Writing in Ancient Israel." In *The Problem of the Hexateuch and Other Essays,* translated by E. W. Trueman Dicken. Edinburgh, 1966.

Ramsey, George W. *The Quest for the Historical Israel.* Atlanta, Ga., 1981.

Wharton, J. A. "A Plausible Tale: Story and Theology in II Samuel 9–20, I Kings 1–2." *Interpretation,* 35 (1981): 341–54.

CHAPTER 2

Herodotus
The Persian Wars
(c. 430 B.C.)

Herodotus of Halicarnassus (c.480–425 B.C.) exhibits something of a paradox. Known and admired by his successors as the "father of history" for his great account of the Persian Wars (499–479 B.C.), he nonetheless acquired a reputation among ancient and later critics as a credulous storyteller and, some would say, a liar. The truth probably rests somewhere between these views, but Herodotus surely earned his "fatherhood" by virtue of the scale of his history. Greeks of his time had produced numerous local histories, but he was the first to write a universal history, an attempt to account for much, if not all, of the whole world's past. Though his principal theme is the war between the Greeks and Persians, which opened the fifth century B.C., his complicated narrative structure includes digressions to explain the origins and manners of the various peoples who became party to the conflict.

Herodotus was born in Halicarnassus (Bodrum in present-day Turkey), but spent much of his life in travel, exiled from his city as a result of his involvement in a failed coup against its ruler. Halicarnassus was on the path between Greek and Persian civilizations, giving Herodotus an early familiarity with both sides, but it may have been his exile, forcing him to abandon the local perspective, that prompted the idea of a broad history. Possibly he supported himself as a trader, but he also derived some income and fame as a public reader. Indeed, his chief means of "publication" were the dramatic readings he gave in Athens (where Thucydides heard him) and elsewhere in the Greek Mediterranean. Herodotus died about 425 B.C.

Herodotus' motive for writing is given in the famous opening lines of *Persian Wars:*

> These are the researches of Herodotus of Halicarnassus, which he publishes, in the hope of thereby preserving from decay the remembrance of what men have done, and of preventing the great and wonderful actions of the Greeks and the Barbarians from losing their due meed of glory; and withal to put on record what were their grounds of feud.

But he may also have wanted to record the earlier unified Greek resistance to Persia as an object lesson to his own time when Greeks were fighting Greeks in the Peloponnesian War (431–404 B.C.).

Two excerpts from Herodotus are given here, and both illustrate his characteristic methods and style. First is an account of the emergence of Cyrus as king of Persia in the mid-sixth century B.C. Cyrus stood at the head of Persian imperialism, and Herodotus offers an extended account of his origins, trying to choose carefully between competing versions he had heard. "And herein," he says, "I shall follow those Persian authorities whose object it appears to be not to magnify the exploits of Cyrus, but to relate the simple truth. I know besides three ways in which the story is told, all differing from my own narrative." Yet his account is still a folktale that borrowed from Oedipus and other Greek stories. What does the tale suggest about Herodotus' view of causation? Does destiny transcend personal actions, or are individuals responsible for what happens to them?

The second excerpt is Herodotus' account of the famous Battle of Thermopylae in 480 B.C., in which Xerxes, a later Persian king, defeated a Spartan (Herodotus says Lacedaemonian) army led by Leonidas. Herodotus' story suggests that he personally examined the battleground and tried hard to select among various explanations he had heard for certain key actions by the principals. Herodotus is generally open-minded about foreign peoples and customs, but does he betray here an anti-Persian bias?

A FTER THIS CYAXARES DIED . . . . Astyages, the son of Cyaxares, succeeded to the throne. He had a daughter who was named Mandané, concerning whom he had a wonderful dream. He dreamt that from her such a stream of water flowed forth as not only to fill his capital, but to flood the whole of Asia. This vision he laid before such of the Magi as had the gift of interpreting dreams, who expounded its meaning to him in full, whereat he was greatly terrified. On this account, when his daughter was now of ripe age, he would not give her in marriage to any of the Medes who were of suitable rank, lest the dream should be accomplished; but he married her to a Persian of good family indeed, but of a quiet temper, whom he looked on as much inferior to a Mede of even middle condition.

Thus Cambyses (for so was the Persian called) wedded Mandané, and took her to his home, after which, in the very first year, Astyages saw another vision. He fancied that a vine grew from the womb of his daughter, and overshadowed the whole of Asia. After this dream, which he sub-

Reprinted from *The History of Herodotus*, 4 vols., translated by George Rawlinson, 4th ed. (London: John Murray, 1880), 1: 236–55; 4: 162–80.

mitted also to the interpreters, he sent to Persia and fetched away Mandané, who was now with child, and was not far from her time. On her arrival he set a watch over her, intending to destroy the child to which she should give birth; for the Magian interpreters had expounded the vision to foreshow that the offspring of his daughter would reign over Asia in his stead. To guard against this, Astyages, as soon as Cyrus was born, sent for Harpagus, a man of his own house and the most faithful of the Medes, to whom he was wont to entrust all his affairs, and addressed him thus— "Harpagus, I beseech thee neglect not the business with which I am about to charge thee; neither betray thou the interests of thy lord for others' sake, lest thou bring destruction on thine own head at some future time. Take the child born of Mandané my daughter; carry him with thee to thy home and slay him there. Then bury him as thou wilt." "Oh! king," replied the other, "never in time past did Harpagus disoblige thee in anything, and be sure that through all future time he will be careful in nothing to offend. If therefore it be thy will that this thing be done, it is for me to serve thee with all diligence."

When Harpagus had thus answered, the child was given into his hands, clothed in the garb of death, and he hastened weeping to his home. There on his arrival he found his wife, to whom he told all that Astyages had said. "What then," said she, "is it now in thy heart to do?" "Not what Astyages requires," he answered; "no, he may be madder and more frantic still than he is now, but I will not be the man to work his will, or lend a helping hand to such a murder as this. Many things forbid my slaying him. In the first place the boy is my own kith and kin; and next, Astyages is old, and has no son. If then when he dies the crown should go to his daughter—that daughter whose child he now wishes to slay by my hand—what remains for me but danger of the fearfullest kind? For my own safety, indeed, the child must die; but some one belonging to Astyages must take his life, not I or mine."

So saying he sent off a messenger to fetch a certain Mitradates, one of the herdsmen of Astyages, whose pasturages he knew to be the fittest for his purpose, lying as they did among mountains infested with wild beasts. This man was married to one of the king's female slaves, whose Median name was Spaco, which is in Greek Cyno, since in the Median tongue the word "Spaca" means a bitch. The mountains, on the skirts of which his cattle grazed, lie to the north of Agbatana, towards the Euxine. That part of Media which borders on the Saspirians is an elevated tract, very mountainous, and covered with forests, while the rest of the Median territory is entirely level ground. On the arrival of the herdsman, who came at the hasty summons, Harpagus said to him—"Astyages requires thee to take this child and lay him in the wildest part of the hills, where he will be sure to die speedily. And he bade me tell thee, that if thou dost not kill the boy, but anyhow allowest him to escape, he will put thee to the most painful of deaths. I myself am appointed to see the child exposed."

The herdsman on hearing this took the child in his arms, and went back the way he had come till he had reached the folds. There, providentially, his wife, who had been expecting daily to be put to bed, had just, during the absence of her husband, been delivered of a child. Both the herdsman and his wife were uneasy on each other's account, the former fearful because his wife was so near her time, the woman alarmed because it was a new thing for her husband to be sent for by Harpagus. When therefore he came into the house upon his return, his wife, seeing him arrive so unexpectedly, was the first to speak, and begged to know why Harpagus had sent for him in such a hurry. "Wife," said he, "when I got to the town I saw and heard such things as I would to heaven I had never seen—such things as I would to heaven had never happened to our masters. Every one was weeping in Harpagus's house. It quite frightened me, but I went in. The moment I stepped inside, what should I see but a baby lying on the floor, panting and whimpering, and all covered with gold, and wrapped in clothes of such beautiful colours. Harpagus saw me, and directly ordered me to take the child in my arms and carry him off, and what was I to do with him, think you? Why, to lay him in the mountains, where the wild beasts are most plentiful. And he told me it was the king himself that ordered it to be done, and he threatened me with such dreadful things if I failed. So I took the child in my arms, and carried him along. I thought it might be the son of one of the household slaves. I did wonder certainly to see the gold and the beautiful baby clothes, and I could not think why there was such a weeping in Harpagus's house. Well, very soon, as I came along, I got at the truth. They sent a servant with me to show me the way out of the town, and to leave the baby in my hands; and he told me that the child's mother is the king's daughter Mandané, and his father Cambyses, the son of Cyrus; and that the king orders him to be killed; and look, here the child is."

With this the herdsman uncovered the infant, and showed him to his wife, who, when she saw him, and observed how fine a child and how beautiful he was, burst into tears, and clinging to the knees of her husband, besought him on no account to expose the babe; to which he answered, that it was not possible for him to do otherwise, as Harpagus would be sure to send persons to see and report to him, and he was to suffer a most cruel death if he disobeyed. Failing thus in her first attempt to persuade her husband, the woman spoke a second time, saying, "If then there is no persuading thee, and a child must needs be seen exposed upon the mountains, at least do thus. The child of which I have just been delivered is still-born; take it and lay it on the hills, and let us bring up as our own the child of the daughter of Astyages. So shalt thou not be charged with unfaithfulness to thy lord, nor shall we have managed badly for our-selves. Our dead babe will have a royal funeral, and this living child will not be deprived of life."

It seemed to the herdsman that this advice was the best under the circumstances. He therefore followed it without loss of time. The child which he had intended to put to death he gave over to his wife, and his own dead child he put in the cradle wherein he had carried the other, clothing it first in all the other's costly attire, and taking it in his arms he laid it in the wildest place of all the mountain-range. When the child had been three days exposed, leaving one of his helpers to watch the body, he started off for the city, and going straight to Harpagus's house, declared himself ready to show the corpse of the boy. Harpagus sent certain of his body-guard, on whom he had the firmest reliance, to view the body for him, and, satisfied with their seeing it, gave orders for the funeral. Thus was the herdsman's child buried, and the other child, who was afterwards known by the name of Cyrus, was taken by the herdsman's wife, and brought up under a different name.

When the boy was in his tenth year, an accident which I will now relate, caused it to be discovered who he was. He was at play one day in the village where the folds of the cattle were, along with the boys of his own age, in the street. The other boys who were playing with him chose the cowherd's son, as he was called, to be their king. He then proceeded to order them about—some he set to build him houses, others he made his guards, one of them was to be the king's eye, another had the office of carrying his messages, all had some task or other. Among the boys there was one, the son of Artembares, a Mede of distinction, who refused to do what Cyrus had set him. Cyrus told the other boys to take him into cus-tody, and when his orders were obeyed, he chastised him most severely with the whip. The son of Artembares, as soon as he was let go, full of rage at treatment so little befitting his rank, hastened to the city and com-plained bitterly to his father of what had been done to him by Cyrus. He did not, of course, say "Cyrus," by which name the boy was not yet known, but called him the son of the king's cowherd. Artembares, in the heat of his passion, went to Astyages, accompanied by his son, and made complaint of the gross injury which had been done him. Pointing to the boy's shoulders, he exclaimed, "Thus, oh! king, has thy slave, the son of a cowherd, heaped insult upon us."

At this sight and these words Astyages, wishing to avenge the son of Artembares for his father's sake, sent for the cowherd and his boy. When they came together into his presence, fixing his eyes on Cyrus, Astyages said, "Hast thou then, the son of so mean a fellow as that, dared to behave thus rudely to the son of yonder noble, one of the first in my court?" "My lord," replied the boy, "I only treated him as he deserved. I was chosen king in play by the boys of our village, because they thought me the best for it. He himself was one of the boys who chose me. All the others did according to my orders; but he refused, and made light of them, until at last he got his due reward. If for this I deserve to suffer punishment, here I am ready to submit to it."

While the boy was yet speaking Astyages was struck with a suspicion who he was. He thought he saw something in the character of his face like his own, and there was a nobleness about the answer he had made; besides which his age seemed to tally with the time when his grandchild was exposed. Astonished at all this, Astyages could not speak for a while. At last, recovering himself with difficulty, and wishing to be quit of Artembares, that he might examine the herdsman alone, he said to the former, "I promise thee, Artembares, so to settle this business that neither thou nor thy son shall have any cause to complain." Artembares retired from his presence, and the attendants, at the bidding of the king, led Cyrus into an inner apartment. Astyages then being left alone with the herdsman, inquired of him where he had got the boy, and who had given him to him; to which he made answer that the lad was his own child, begotten by himself, and that the mother who bore him was still alive, and lived with him in his house. Astyages remarked that he was very ill-advised to bring himself into such great trouble, and at the same time signed to his body-guard to lay hold of him. Then the herdsman, as they were dragging him to the rack, began at the beginning, and told the whole story exactly as it happened, without concealing anything, ending with entreaties and prayers to the king to grant him forgiveness.

Astyages, having got the truth of the matter from the herdsman, was very little further concerned about him, but with Harpagus he was exceedingly enraged. The guards were bidden to summon him into the presence, and on his appearance Astyages asked him, "By what death was it, Harpagus, that thou slewest the child of my daughter whom I gave into thy hands?" Harpagus, seeing the cowherd in the room, did not betake himself to lies, lest he should be confuted and proved false, but replied as follows:—"Sire, when thou gavest the child into my hands I instantly considered with myself how I could contrive to execute thy wishes, and yet, while guiltless of any unfaithfulness towards thee, avoid imbruing my hands in blood which was in truth thy daughter's and thine own. And this was how I contrived it. I sent for this cowherd, and gave the child over to him, telling him that by the king's orders it was to be put to death. And in this I told no lie, for thou hadst so commanded. Moreover, when I gave him the child, I enjoined him to lay it somewhere in the wilds of the mountains, and to stay near and watch till it was dead; and I threatened him with all manner of punishment if he failed. Afterwards, when he had done according to all that I commanded him, and the child had died, I sent some of the most trustworthy of my eunuchs, who viewed the body for me, and then I had the child buried. This, sire, is the simple truth, and this is the death by which the child died."

Thus Harpagus related the whole story in a plain, straightforward way; upon which Astyages, letting no sign escape him of the anger that he felt, began by repeating to him all that he had just heard from the cow-herd, and then concluded with saying, "So the boy is alive, and it is best as it is. For the child's fate was a great sorrow to me, and the reproaches of my daughter went to my heart. Truly fortune has played us a good turn in this. Go thou home then, and send thy son to be with the new comer, and to-night, as I mean to sacrifice thank-offerings for the child's safety to the gods to whom such honour is due, I look to have thee a guest at the banquet."

Harpagus, on hearing this, made obeisance, and went home rejoicing to find that his disobedience had turned out so fortunately, and that, instead of being punished, he was invited to a banquet given in honour of the happy occasion. The moment he reached home he called for his son, a youth of about thirteen, the only child of his parents, and bade him go to the palace, and do whatever Astyages should direct. Then, in the gladness of his heart, he went to his wife and told her all that had happened. Astyages, meanwhile, took the son of Harpagus, and slew him, after which he cut him in pieces, and roasted some portions before the fire, and boiled others; and when all were duly prepared, he kept them ready for use. The hour for the banquet came, and Harpagus appeared, and with him the other guests, and all sat down to the feast. Astyages and the rest of the guests had joints of meat served up to them; but on the table of Harpagus, nothing was placed except the flesh of his own son. This was all put before him, except the hands and feet and head, which were laid by themselves in a covered basket. When Harpagus seemed to have eaten his fill, Astyages called out to him to know how he had enjoyed the repast. On his reply that he enjoyed it excessively, they whose business it was brought him the basket, in which were the hands and feet and head of his son, and bade him open it, and take out what he pleased. Harpagus accordingly uncovered the basket, and saw within it the remains of his son. The sight, however, did not scare him, or rob him of his self-possession. Being asked by Astyages if he knew what beast's flesh it was that he had been eating, he answered that he knew very well, and that whatever the king did was agreeable. After this reply, he took with him such morsels of the flesh as were uneaten, and went home, intending, as I conceive, to collect the remains and bury them.

Such was the mode in which Astyages punished Harpagus: afterwards, proceeding to consider what he should do with Cyrus, his grandchild, he sent for the Magi, who formerly interpreted his dream in the way which alarmed him so much, and asked them how they had expounded it. They answered, without varying from what they had said before, that "the boy must needs be a king if he grew up, and did not die too soon." Then Astyages addressed them thus: "The boy has escaped, and lives; he has been brought up in the country, and the lads of the village where he lives have made him their king. All that kings commonly do he has done. He has had his guards, and his doorkeepers, and his messengers, and all the other usual officers. Tell me, then, to what, think you, does all this tend?" The Magi answered, "If the boy survives, and has ruled as a king without any craft or contrivance, in that case we bid thee cheer up, and feel no more alarm on his account. He will not reign a second time. For we have found even oracles sometimes fulfilled in an unimportant way; and dreams, still oftener, have wondrously mean accomplishments." "It is what I myself most incline to think," Astyages rejoined; "the boy having been already king, the dream is out, and I have nothing more to fear from him. Nevertheless, take good heed and counsel me the best you can for the safety of my house and your own interests." "Truly," said the Magi in reply, "it very much concerns our interests that thy kingdom be firmly established; for if it went to this boy it would pass into foreign hands, since he is a Perisan: and then we Medes should lose our freedom, and be quite despised by the Persians, as being foreigners. But so long as thou, our fellow-countryman, art on the throne, all manner of honours are ours, and we are even not without some share in the government. Much reason therefore have we to forecast well for thee and for thy sovereignty. If then we saw any cause for present fear, be sure we would not keep it back from thee. But truly we are persuaded that the dream has had its accomplishment in this harmless way; and so our own fears being at rest, we recommend thee to banish thine. As for the boy, our advice is, that thou send him away to Persia, to his father and mother."

Astyages heard their answer with pleasure, and calling Cyrus into his presence, said to him, "My child, I was led to do thee a wrong by a dream which has come to nothing: from that wrong thou wert saved by thy own good fortune. Go now with a light heart to Persia; I will provide thy escort. Go, and when thou gettest to thy journey's end, thou wilt behold thy father and thy mother, quite other people from Mitradates the cowherd and his wife."

With these words Astyages dismissed his grandchild. On his arrival at the house of Cambyses, he was received by his parents, who, when they learnt who he was, embraced him heartily, having always been convinced that he died almost as soon as he was born. So they asked him by what means he had chanced to escape; and he told them how that till lately he had known nothing at all about the matter, but had been mistaken—oh! so widely!—and how that he had learnt his history by the way, as he came from Media. He had been quite sure that he was the son of the king's cowherd, but on the road the king's escort had told him all the truth; and then he spoke of the cowherd's wife who had brought him up, and filled his whole talk with her praises; in all that he had to tell them about himself, it was always Cyno—Cyno was everything. So it happened that his parents, catching the name at his mouth, and wishing to persuade the Persians that there was a special providence in his preservation, spread the report that Cyrus, when he was exposed, was suckled by a bitch. This was the sole origin of the rumour.

Afterwards, when Cyrus grew to manhood, and became known as the bravest and most popular of all his compeers, Harpagus, who was bent on revenging himself upon Astyages, began to pay him court by gifts and messages. His own rank was too humble for him to hope to obtain vengeance without some foreign help. When therefore he saw Cyrus, whose wrongs were so similar to his own, growing up expressly (as it were) to be the avenger whom he needed, he set to work to procure his support and aid in the matter. He had already paved the way for his designs, by persuading, severally, the great Median nobles, whom the harsh rule of their monarch had offended, that the best plan would be to put Cyrus at their head, and dethrone Astyages. These preparations made, Harpagus, being now ready for revolt, was anxious to make known his wishes to Cyrus, who still lived in Persia; but as the roads between Media and Persia were guarded, he had to contrive a means of sending word secretly, which he did in the following way. He took a hare, and cutting open its belly without hurting the fur, he slipped in a letter containing what he wanted to say, and then carefully sewing up the paunch, he gave the hare to one of his most faithful slaves, disguising him as a hunter with nets, and sent him off to Persia to take the game as a present to Cyrus, bidding him tell Cyrus, by word of mouth, to paunch the animal himself, and let no one be present at the time.

All was done as he wished, and Cyrus, on cutting the hare open, found the letter inside, and read as follows:—"Son of Cambyses, the gods assuredly watch over thee, or never wouldst thou have passed through thy many wonderful adventures—now is the time when thou mayst avenge thyself upon Astyages, thy murderer. He willed thy death, remember; to the gods and to me thou owest that thou art still alive. I think thou art not ignorant of what he did to thee, nor of what I suffered at his hands because I committed thee to the cowherd, and did not put thee to death. Listen now to me, and obey my words, and all the empire of Astyages shall be thine. Raise the standard of revolt in Persia, and then march straight on Media. Whether Astyages appoint me to command his forces against thee, or whether he appoint any other of the princes of the Medes, all will go as thou couldst wish. They will be the first to fall away from him, and joining thy side, exert themselves to overturn his power. Be sure that on our part all is ready; wherefore do thou thy part, and that speedily."

Cyrus, on receiving the tidings contained in this letter, set himself to consider how he might best persuade the Persians to revolt. After much thought, he hit on the following as the most expedient course: he wrote what he thought proper upon a roll, and then calling an assembly of the Persians, he unfolded the roll, and read out of it that Astyages appointed him their general. "And now," said he, "since it is so, I command you to go and bring each man his reaping-hook." With these words he dismissed the assembly.

Now the Persian nation is made up of many tribes. Those which Cyrus assembled and persuaded to revolt from the Medes, were the principal ones on which all the others are dependent. These are the Pasargadae, the Maraphians, and the Maspians, of whom the Pasargadae are the noblest. The Achaemenidae, from which spring all the Perseid kings, is one of their clans. The rest of the Persian tribes are the following: the Panthialaeans, the Derusiaeans, the Germanians, who are engaged in husbandry; the Daans, the Mardians, the Dropicans, and the Sagartians, who are Nomads.

When, in obedience to the orders which they had received, the Persians came with their reaping-hooks, Cyrus led them to a tract of ground, about eighteen or twenty furlongs each way, covered with thorns, and ordered them to clear it before the day was out. They accomplished their task; upon which he issued a second order to them, to take the bath the day following, and again come to him. Meanwhile he collected together all his father's flocks, both sheep and goats, and all his oxen, and slaughtered them, and made ready to give an entertainment to the entire Persian army. Wine, too, and bread of the choicest kinds were prepared for the occasion. When the morrow came, and the Persians appeared, he bade them recline upon the grass, and enjoy themselves. After the feast was over, he requested them to tell him "which they liked best, to-day's work, or yesterday's?" They answered that "the contrast was indeed strong: yesterday brought them nothing but what was bad, to-day everything that was good." Cyrus instantly seized on their reply, and laid bare his purpose in these words: "Ye men of Persia, thus do matters stand with you. If you choose to hearken to my words, you may enjoy these and ten thousand similar delights, and never condescend to any slavish toil; but if you will not hearken, prepare yourselves for unnumbered toils as hard as yesterday's. Now therefore follow my bidding, and be free. For myself I feel that I am destined by Providence to undertake your liberation; and you, I am sure, are no whit inferior to the Medes in anything, least of all in bravery. Revolt, therefore, from Astyages, without a moment's delay."

The Persians, who had long been impatient of the Median dominion, now that they had found a leader, were delighted to shake off the yoke. Meanwhile Astyages, informed of the doings of Cyrus, sent a messenger to summon him to his presence. Cyrus replied, "Tell Astyages that I shall appear in his presence sooner than he will like." Astyages, when he received this message, instantly armed all his subjects, and, as if God had deprived him of his senses, appointed Harpagus to be their general, forgetting how greatly he had injured him. So when the two armies met and engaged, only a few of the Medes, who were not in the secret, fought; others deserted openly to the Persians; while the greater number counterfeited fear, and fled.

Astyages, on learning the shameful flight and dispersion of his army, broke out into threats against Cyrus, saying, "Cyrus shall nevertheless have no reason to rejoice"; and directly he seized the Magian interpreters, who had persuaded him to allow Cyrus to escape, and impaled them; after which, he armed all the Medes who had remained in the city, both young and old; and leading them against the Persians, fought a battle, in which he was utterly defeated, his army being destroyed, and he himself falling into the enemy's hands.

Harpagus then, seeing him a prisoner, came near, and exulted over him with many gibes and jeers. Among other cutting speeches which he made, he alluded to the supper where the flesh of his son was given him to eat, and asked Astyages to answer *him* now, how he enjoyed being a slave instead of a king? Astyages looked in his face, and asked him in return, why he claimed as his own the achievements of Cyrus? "Because," said Harpagus, "it was my letter which made him revolt, and so I am entitled to all the credit of the enterprise." Then Astyages declared, that "in that case he was at once the silliest and the most unjust of men: the silliest, if when it was in his power to put the crown on his own head, as it must assuredly have been, if the revolt was entirely his doing, he had placed it on the head of another; the most unjust, if on account of that supper he had brought slavery on the Medes. For, supposing that he was obliged to invest with another the kingly power, and not retain it himself, yet justice required that a Mede, rather than a Persian, should receive the dignity. Now, however, the Medes, who had been no parties to the wrong of which he complained, were made slaves instead of lords, and slaves moreover of those who till recently had been their subjects."

Thus after a reign of thirty-five years, Astyages lost his crown, and the Medes, in consequence of his cruelty, were brought under the rule of the Persians. Their empire over the parts of Asia beyond the Halys had lasted one hundred and twenty-eight years, except during the time when the Scythians had the dominion. Afterwards the Medes repented of their submission, and revolted from Darius, but were defeated in battle, and again reduced to subjection. Now, however, in the time of Astyages, it was the Persians who under Cyrus revolted from the Medes, and became thenceforth the rulers of Asia. Cyrus kept Astyages at his court during the remainder of his life, without doing him any further injury. Such then were the circumstances of the birth and bringing up of Cyrus, and such were the steps by which he mounted the throne. It was at a later date that he was attacked by Croesus, and overthrew him, as I have related in an earlier portion of this history. The overthrow of Croesus made him master of the whole of Asia.

. . . .

King Xerxes pitched his camp in the region of Malis called Trachinia, while on their side the Greeks occupied the straits. These straits the Greeks in general call Thermopylae (the Hot Gates); but the natives, and those who dwell in the neighbourhood, call them Pylae (the Gates). Here then the two armies took their stand; the one master of all the region lying north of Trachis, the other of the country extending southward of that place to the verge of the continent.

The Greeks who at this spot awaited the coming of Xerxes were the following:—From Sparta, three hundred men-at-arms: from Arcadia, a thousand Tegeans and Mantineans, five hundred of each people; a hundred and twenty Orchomenians, from the Arcadian Orchomenus; and a thousand from other cities: from Corinth, four hundred men: from Phlius, two hundred: and from Mycenae eighty. Such was the number from the Peloponnese. There were also present from Boeotia, seven hundred Thespians and four hundred Thebans.

Besides these troops, the Locrians of Opus and the Phocians had obeyed the call of their countrymen, and sent, the former all the force they had, the latter a thousand men. For envoys had gone from the Greeks at Thermoplyae among the Locrians and Phocians, to call on them for assistance, and to say—"They were themselves but the vanguard of the host, sent to precede the main body, which might every day be expected to follow them. The sea was in good keeping, watched by the Athenians, the Eginetans, and the rest of the fleet. There was no cause why they should fear; for after all the invader was not a god but a man; and there never had been, and never would be, a man who was not liable to misfortunes from the very day of his birth, and those misfortunes greater in proportion to his own greatness. The assailant therefore, being only a mortal, must needs fall from his glory." Thus urged, the Locrians and the Phocians had come with their troops to Trachis.

The various nations had each captains of their own under whom they served; but the one to whom all especially looked up, and who had the command of the entire force, was the Lacedaemonian, Leonidas. Now

Leonidas was the son of Anaxandridas, who was the son of Leo, who was the son of Eurycratidas, who was the son of Anaxander, who was the son of Eurycrates, who was the son of Polydôrus, who was the son of Alcamenes, who was the son of Têlecles, who was the son of Archelaüs, who was the son of Agesilaüs, who was the son of Doryssus, who was the son of Labôtas, who was the son of Echestratus, who was the son of Agis, who was the son of Eurysthenes, who was the son of Aristodêmus, who was the son of Aristomachus, who was the son of Cleodaeus, who was the son of Hyllus, who was the son of Hercules.

Leonidas had come to be king of Sparta quite unexpectedly.

Having two elder brothers, Cleomenes and Dorieus, he had no thought of ever mounting the throne. However, when Cleomenes died without male offspring, as Dorieus was likewise deceased, having perished in Sicily, the crown fell to Leonidas, who was older than Cleombrotus, the youngest of the sons of Anaxandridas, and moreover, was married to the daughter of Cleomenes. He had now come to Thermopylae, accompanied by the three hundred men which the law assigned him, whom he had himself chosen from among the citizens, and who were all of them fathers with sons living. On his way he had taken the troops from Thebes, whose number I have already mentioned, and who were under the command of Leontiades the son of Eurymachus. The reason why he made a point of taking troops from Thebes, and Thebes only, was, that the Thebans were strongly suspected of being well inclined to the Medes. Leonidas therefore called on them to come with him to the war, wishing to see whether they would comply with his demand, or openly refuse, and disclaim the Greek alliance. They, however, though their wishes leant the other way, nevertheless sent the men.

The force with Leonidas was sent forward by the Spartans in advance of their main body, that the sight of them might encourage the allies to fight, and hinder them from going over to the Medes, as it was likely they might have done had they seen that Sparta was backward. They intended presently, when they had celebrated the Carneian festival, which was what now kept them at home, to leave a garrison in Sparta, and hasten in full force to join the army. The rest of the allies also intended to act similarly; for it happened that the Olympic festival fell exactly at this same period. None of them looked to see the contest at Thermopylae decided so speedily; wherefore they were content to send forward a mere advanced guard. Such accordingly were the intentions of the allies.

The Greek forces at Thermopylae, when the Persian army drew near to the entrance of the pass, were seized with fear; and a council was held to consider about a retreat. It was the wish of the Peloponnesians generally that the army should fall back upon the Pelopennese, and there guard the Isthmus. But Leonidas, who saw with what indignation the Phocians and Locrians heard of this plan, gave his voice for remaining where they were, while they sent envoys to the several cities to ask for help, since they were too few to make a stand against an army like that of the Medes.

While this debate was going on, Xerxes sent a mounted spy to observe the Greeks, and note how many they were, and see what they were doing. He had heard, before he came out of Thessaly, that a few men were assembled at this place, and that at their head were certain Lacedaemonians, under Leonidas, a descendant of Hercules. The horseman rode up to the camp, and looked about him, but did not see the whole army; for such as were on the further side of the wall (which had been rebuilt and was now carefully guarded) it was not possible for him to behold; but he observed those on the outside, who were encamped in front of the rampart. It chanced that at this time the Lacedaemonians held the outer guard, and were seen by the spy, some of them engaged in gymnastic exercises, others combing their long hair. At this the spy greatly marvelled, but he counted their number, and when he had taken accurate note of everything, he rode back quietly; for no one pursued after him, nor paid any heed to his visit. So he returned, and told Xerxes all that he had seen.

Upon this, Xerxes, who had no means of surmising the truth—namely, that the Spartans were preparing to do or die manfully—but thought it laughable that they should be engaged in such employments, sent and called to his presence Demaratus the son of Ariston, who still remained with the army. When he appeared, Xerxes told him all that he had heard, and questioned him concerning the news, since he was anxious to understand the meaning of such behaviour on the part of the Spartans. Then Demaratus said—

"I spake to thee, O King! concerning these men long since, when we had but just begun our march upon Greece; thou, however, didst only laugh at my words, when I told thee of all this, which I saw would come to pass. Earnestly do I struggle at all times to speak truth to thee, sire; and now listen to it once more. These men have come to dispute the pass with us; and it is for this that they are now making ready. 'Tis their custom, when they are about to hazard their lives, to adorn their heads with care. Be assured, however, that if thou canst subdue the men who are here and the Lacedaemonians who remain in Sparta, there is no other nation in all the world which will venture to lift a hand in their defence. Thou hast now to deal with the first kingdom and town in Greece, and with the bravest men."

Then Xerxes, to whom what Demaratus said seemed altogether to surpass belief, asked further, "how it was possible for so small an army to contend with his?"

"O King!" Demaratus answered, "let me be treated as a liar, if matters fall not out as I say."

But Xerxes was not persuaded any the more. Four whole days he suffered to go by, expecting that the Greeks would run away. When, however, he found on the fifth that they were not gone, thinking that their firm stand was mere impudence and recklessness, he grew wroth, and sent against them the Medes and Cissians, with orders to take them alive and bring them into his presence. Then the Medes rushed forward and charged the Greeks, but fell in vast numbers: others however took the places of the slain, and would not be beaten off, though they suffered terrible losses. In this way it became clear to all, and especially to the King, that though he had plenty of combatants, he had but very few warriors. The struggle, however, continued during the whole day.

Then the Medes, having met so rough a reception, withdrew from the fight; and their place was taken by the band of Persians under Hydarnes, whom the King called his "Immortals": they, it was thought, would soon finish the business. But when they joined battle with the Greeks, 'twas with no better success than the Median detachment—things went much as before—the two armies fighting in a narrow space, and the barbarians using shorter spears than the Greeks, and having no advantage from their numbers. The Lacedaemonians fought in a way worthy of note, and showed themselves far more skilful in fight than their adversaries, often turning their backs, and making as though they were all flying away, on which the barbarians would rush after them with much noise and shouting, when the Spartans at their approach would wheel round and face their pursuers, in this way destroying vast numbers of the enemy. Some Spartans likewise fell in these encounters, but only a very few. At last the Persians, finding that all their efforts to gain the pass availed nothing, and that, whether they attacked by divisions or in any other way, it was to no purpose, withdrew to their own quarters.

During these assaults, it is said that Xerxes, who was watching the battle, thrice leaped from the throne on which he sat, in terror for his army.

Next day the combat was renewed, but with no better success on the part of the barbarians. The Greeks were so few that the barbarians hoped to find them disabled, by reason of their wounds, from offering any further resistance; and so they once more attacked them. But the Greeks were drawn up in detachments according to their cities, and bore the brunt of the battle in turns,—all except the Phocians, who had been stationed on the mountain to guard the pathway. So, when the Persians found no difference between that day and the preceding, they again retired to their quarters.

Now, as the King was in a great strait, and knew not how he should deal with the emergency, Ephialtes, the son of Eurydêmus, a man of Malis, came to him and was admitted to a conference. Stirred by the hope of receiving a rich reward at the King's hands, he had come to tell of the pathway which led across the mountain to Thermopylae; by which disclosure he brought destruction on the band of Greeks who had there withstood the barbarians. This Ephialtes afterwards, from fear of the Lacedaemonians, fled into Thessaly; and during his exile, in an assembly of the Amphictyons held at Pylae, a price was set upon his head by the Pylagorae. When some time had gone by, he returned from exile, and went to Anticyra, where he was slain by Athênades, a native of Trachis. Athênades did not slay him for his treachery, but for another reason, which I shall mention in a later part of my History: yet still the Lacedaemonians honoured him none the less. Thus then did Ephialtes perish a long time afterwards.

Besides this there is another story told, which I do not at all believe—to wit, that Onêtas the son of Phanagoras, a native of Carystus, and Corydallus, a man of Anticyra, were the persons who spoke on this matter to the King, and took the Persians across the mountain. One may guess which story is true, from the fact that the deputies of the Greeks, the Pylagorae, who must have had the best means of ascertaining the truth, did not offer the reward for the heads of Onêtas and Corydallus, but for that of Ephialtes of Trachis; and again from the flight of Ephialtes, which we know to have been on this account. Onêtas, I allow, although he was not a Malian, might have been acquainted with the path, if he had lived much in that part of the country; but as Ephialtes was the person who actually led the Persians round the mountain by the pathway, I leave his name on record as that of the man who did the deed.

Great was the joy of Xerxes on this occasion; and as he approved highly of the enterprise which Ephialtes undertook to accomplish, he forthwith sent upon the errand Hydarnes, and the Persians under him. The troops left the camp about the time of the lighting of the lamps. The pathway along which they went was first discovered by the Malians of these parts, who soon afterwards led the Thessalians by it to attack the Phocians, at the time when the Phocians fortified the pass with a wall, and so put themselves under covert from danger. And ever since, the path has always been put to an ill use by the Malians.

The course which it takes is the following:—Beginning at the Asôpus, where that stream flows through the cleft in the hills, it runs along the ridge of the mountain (which is called, like the pathway over it, Anopae), and ends at the city of Alpênus—the first Locrian town as you come from Malis—by the stone called Melampygus and the seats of the Cercopians. Here it is as narrow as at any other point.

The Persians took this path, and, crossing the Asôpus, continued their march through the whole of the night, having the mountains of Oeta on their right hand, and on their left those of Trachis. At dawn of day they found themselves close to the summit. Now the hill was guarded, as I have already said, by a thousand Phocian men-at-arms, who were placed there to defend the pathway, and at the same time to secure their own country. They had been given the guard of the mountain path, while the other Greeks defended the pass below, because they had volunteered for the service, and had pledged themselves to Leonidas to maintain the post.

The ascent of the Persians became known to the Phocians in the following manner:—During all the time that they were making their way up, the Greeks remained unconscious of it, inasmuch as the whole mountain was covered with groves of oak; but it happened that the air was very still, and the leaves which the Persians stirred with their feet made, as it was likely they would, a loud rustling, whereupon the Phocians jumped up and flew to seize their arms. In a moment the barbarians came in sight, and, perceiving men arming themselves, were greatly amazed; for they had fallen in with an enemy when they expected no opposition. Hydarnes, alarmed at the sight, and fearing lest the Phocians might be Lacedaemonians, inquired of Ephialtes to what nation those troops belonged. Ephialtes told him the exact truth, whereupon he arrayed his Persians for battle. The Phocians, galled by the showers of arrows to which they were exposed, and imagining themselves the special object of the Persian attack, fled hastily to the crest of the mountain, and there made ready to meet death; but while their mistake continued, the Persians, with Ephialtes and Hydarnes, not thinking it worth their while to delay on account of Phocians, passed on and descended the mountain with all possible speed.

The Greeks at Thermopylae received the first warning of the destruction which the dawn would bring on them from the seer Megistias, who read their fate in the victims as he was sacrificing. After this deserters came in, and brought the news that the Persians were marching round by the hills: it was still night when these men arrived. Last of all, the scouts came running down from the heights, and brought in the same accounts, when the day was just beginning to break. Then the Greeks held a council to consider what they should do, and here opinions were divided: some were strong against quitting their post, while others contended to the contrary. So when the council had broken up, part of the troops departed and went their ways homeward to their several states; part however resolved to remain, and to stand by Leonidas to the last.

It is said that Leonidas himself sent away the troops who departed, because he tendered their safety, but thought it unseemly that either he or his Spartans should quit the post which they had been especially sent to guard. For my own part, I incline to think that Leonidas gave the order, because he perceived the allies to be out of heart and unwilling to encoun-

ter the danger to which his own mind was made up. He therefore commanded them to retreat, but said that he himself could not draw back
with honour; knowing that, if he stayed, glory awaited him, and that
Sparta in that case would not lose her prosperity. For when the Spartans,
at the very beginning of the war, sent to consult the oracle concerning it,
the answer which they received from the Pythoness was, "that either
Sparta must be overthrown by the barbarians, or one of her kings must
perish." The prophecy was delivered in hexameter verse, and ran thus:—

"O ye men who dwell in the streets of broad Lacedaemon!
Either your glorious town shall be sacked by the children of Perseus
Or, in exchange, must all through the whole Laconian country
Mourn for the loss of a king, descendant of Great Hêrácles.
He cannot be withstood by the courage of bulls nor of lions,
Strive as they may; he is mighty as Jove; there is nought that shall stay
    him,
Till he have got for his prey your king, or your glorious city."

The remembrance of this answer, I think, and the wish to secure the
whole glory for the Spartans, caused Leonidas to send the allies away.
This is more likely than that they quarrelled with him, and took their
departure in such unruly fashion.

To me it seems no small argument in favour of this view, that the seer
also accompanied the army, Megistias, the Acarnanian,—said to have
been of the blood of Melampus, and the same who was led by the appearance of the victims to warn the Greeks of the danger which threatened
them,—received orders to retire (as it is certain he did) from Leonidas,
that he might escape the coming destruction. Megistias, however, though
bidden to depart, refused, and stayed with the army; but he had an only
son present with the expedition, whom he now sent away.

So the allies, when Leonidas ordered them to retire, obeyed him and
forthwith departed. Only the Thespians and the Thebans remained with
the Spartans; and of these the Thebans were kept back by Leonidas as
hostages, very much against their will. The Thespians, on the contrary,
stayed entirely of their own accord, refusing to retreat, and declaring that
they would not forsake Leonidas and his followers. So they abode with
the Spartans, and died with them. Their leader was Demophilus, the son
of Diadromes.

At sunrise Xerxes made libations, after which he waited until the time
when the forum is wont to fill, and then began his advance. Ephialtes had
instructed him thus, as the descent of the mountain is much quicker, and
the distance much shorter, than the way around the hills, and the ascent.
So the barbarians under Xerxes began to draw nigh; and the Greeks under
Leonidas, as they now went forth determined to die, advanced much further than on previous days, until they reached the more open portion of the

pass. Hitherto, they had held their station within the wall, and from this had gone forth to fight at the point where the pass was the narrowest. Now they joined battle beyond the defile, and carried slaughter among the barbarians, who fell in heaps. Behind them the captains of the squadrons, armed with whips, urged their men forward with continual blows. Many were thrust into the sea, and there perished; a still greater number were trampled to death by their own soldiers; no one heeded the dying. For the Greeks, reckless of their own safety and desperate, since they knew that, as the mountain had been crossed, their destruction was nigh at hand, exerted themselves with the most furious valour against the barbarians.

By this time the spears of the greater number were all shivered, and with their swords they hewed down the ranks of the Persians; and here, as they strove, Leonidas fell fighting bravely, together with many other famous Spartans, whose names I have taken care to learn on account of their great worthiness, as indeed I have those of all the three hundred. There fell too at the same time very many famous Persians: among them, two sons of Darius, Abrocomes and Hyperanthes, his children by Phrataguné, the daughter of Artanes. Artanes was brother of King Darius, being a son of Hystaspes, the son of Arsames; and when he gave his daughter to the King, he made him heir likewise of all his substance; for she was his only child.

Thus two brothers of Xerxes here fought and fell. And now there arose a fierce struggle between the Persians and the Lacedaemonians over the body of Leonidas, in which the Greeks four times drove back the enemy, and at last by their great bravery succeeded in bearing off the body. This combat was scarcely ended when the Persians with Ephialtes approached; and the Greeks, informed that they drew nigh, made a change in the manner of their fighting. Drawing back into the narrowest part of the pass, and retreating even behind the cross wall, they posted themselves upon a hillock, where they stood all drawn up together in one close body, except only the Thebans. The hillock whereof I speak is at the entrance of the straits, where the stone lion stands which was set up in honour of Leonidas. Here they defended themselves to the last, such as still had swords using them, and the others resisting with their hands and teeth; till the barbarians, who in part had pulled down the wall and attacked them in front, in part had gone round and now encircled them upon every side, overwhelmed and buried the remnant which was left beneath showers of missile weapons.

Thus nobly did the whole body of Lacedaemonians and Thespians behave; but nevertheless one man is said to have distinguished himself above all the rest, to wit, Diêneces the Spartan. A speech which he made before the Greeks engaged the Medes, remains on record. One of the Trachinians told him, "Such was the number of the barbarians, that when they shot forth their arrows the sun would be darkened by their multitude." Diêneces, not at all frightened at these words, but making light of the Median numbers, answered, "Our Trachinian friend brings us excellent tidings. If the Medes darken the sun, we shall have our fight in the shade." Other sayings too of a like nature are reported to have been left on record by this same person.

Next to him two brothers, Lacedaemonians, are reputed to have made themselves conspicuous: they were named Alpheus and Maro, and were the sons of Orsiphantus. There was also a Thespian who gained greater glory than any of his countrymen: he was a man called Dithyrambus, the son of Harmatidas.

The slain were buried where they fell; and in their honour, nor less in honour of those who died before Leonidas sent the allies away, an inscription was set up, which said,—

"Here did four thousand men from Pelops' land
Against three hundred myriads bravely stand."

This was in honour of all. Another was for the Spartans alone:—

"Go, stranger, and to Lacedaemon tell
That here, obeying her behests, we fell."

This was for the Lacedaemonians. The seer had the following:—

"The great Megistias' tomb you here may view,
    Whom slew the Medes, fresh from Spercheius' fords.
Well the wise seer the coming death foreknew,
    Yet scorned he to forsake his Spartan lords."

These inscriptions, and the pillars likewise, were all set up by the Amphictyons, except that in honour of Megistias, which was inscribed to him (on account of their sworn friendship) by Simonides, the son of Leôprepes.

Bibliography

Brown, Truesdell S. "Herodotus and his Profession." *American Historical Review,* 59 (July 1954): 829–43.
Bury, J. B. *The Ancient Greek Historians.* London, 1909.
Evans, J. A. S. *Herodotus.* Boston, Mass., 1982.
Glover, T. R. *Herodotus.* Berkeley, Calif., 1924.
Grant, Michael. *The Ancient Historians.* London, 1970.
How, W. W., and Wells, J. *A Commentary on Herodotus.* 2 vols. Oxford, 1964.
Lattimore, R. "The Composition of the History of Herodotus." *Classical Philology,* 53 (1958): 9–21.
Lesky, Albin. *A History of Greek Literature,* translated by James Willis and Cornelius de Heer. New York, 1966.
Meyers, J. L. *Herodotus, Father of History.* Oxford, 1953.
Momigliano, Arnaldo. "Greek Historiography." *History and Theory,* 17 (Spring 1978): 1–28.
Momigliano, Arnaldo. "The Place of Herodotus in the History of Historiography." In *Studies in Historiography.* New York, 1966.
Powell, John Enoch. *The History of Herodotus.* Cambridge, Mass., 1939.
de Selincourt, Aubrey. *The World of Herodotus.* London, 1962.

CHAPTER 3

Thucydides

The Peloponnesian War

(c.431–404 B.C.)

Thucydides (c.460–400 B.C.) was an Athenian of the generation after Herodotus. Yet he shared two characteristics with his predecessor: he was an exile, and he wrote history from a universal point of view. In the midst of the Peloponnesian War between Athens and Sparta, Thucydides was given a command in Thrace, but when he failed to hold Amphipolis, a ship-building center, against the enemy, Athens dismissed him and expelled him from the city. (Or perhaps he thought it wise not to return.) For twenty years thereafter he travelled throughout the Greek world researching and writing his history, and his broad view of the war came partly from his extensive contacts with people on both sides.

Thucydides emphasized the differences between himself and Herodotus, and he had the latter's reputation as a story-teller in mind when he wrote, "The absence of romance in my history will, I fear, detract somewhat from its interest. . . . In fine, I have written my work, not as an essay to win the applause of the moment, but as a possession for all time." *He* would write only from evidence that could survive "the most severe and detailed tests possible." Later critics have mostly adopted Thucydides' appraisal, with Leopold von Ranke (chapter 11), the nineteenth-century founder of modern historical method, renewing the praise close to our own time. Still, some scholars point out that Thucydides' narrow insistence on personal observation or immediate eyewitness accounts meant he—and later writers who used him as a model—could not go very far back in time. Herodotus, for all his seeming credulousness, could at least imagine the world with a longer past. (See, however, his "Archaeology," an account of early Greek history in Book I.)

One of the most compelling sections of Thucydides' *Peloponnesian War* is his account of the disastrous Athenian invasion of Sicily in 416 B.C. For its drama and subtle appreciation of how flawed the Athenian expectations were from the start—and despite Thucydides' doubts about his book's readability—this section rivals anything in Herodotus. He sets up his account beautifully with a debate between Athenian politicians favoring and opposing the expedition, and then offers a description of the Athenians as they set sail from Piraeus with a splendid force—larger, he says, than any the Greeks ever assembled. The excerpt below picks up the story three years later, when, having met resistance from Syracuse, Sparta's Sicilian ally, an Athenian force commanded by Nicias stood at the edge of annihilation near Syracuse itself. The speeches of the rival commanders, Nicias and Gylippus, on the eve of the last battle prepare the reader's mind for the debacle that is to come, but Thucydides also uses them to suggest that the principals were wholly conscious of *this* battle's special significance among all others in the campaign. How reliable are such speeches? In what other ways, stylistically, does Thucydides try to take his reader into the "feel" of events?

THE ATHENIANS, SEEING THEM closing up the harbour and informed of their further designs, called a council of war. The generals and colonels assembled and discussed the difficulties of the situation; the point which pressed most being that they no longer had provisions for immediate use (having sent on to Catana to tell them not to send any, in the belief that they were going away), and that they would not have any in future unless they could command the sea. They therefore determined to evacuate their upper lines, to enclose with a cross wall and garrison a small space close to the ships, only just sufficient to hold their stores and sick, and manning all the ships, seaworthy or not, with every man that could be spared from the rest of their land forces, to fight it out at sea, and if victorious, to go to Catana, if not, to burn their vessels, form in close order, and retreat by land for the nearest friendly place they could reach, Hellenic or barbarian. This was no sooner settled than carried into effect: they descended gradually from the upper lines and manned all their vessels, compelling all to go on board who were of age to be in any way of use. They thus succeeded in manning about one hundred and ten ships in all, on board of which they embarked a number of archers and darters taken from the Acarnanians and from the other foreigners, making all other provisions allowed by the nature of their plan and by the necessities which imposed it. All was now nearly ready, and Nicias, seeing the soldiery disheartened by their unprecedented and decided defeat at sea, and by reason of the scarcity of provisions eager to fight it out as soon as possible, called them all together, and first addressed them, speaking as follows:

From Thucydides, *The History of the Peloponnesian War*, translated by Richard Crawley, revised by R. C. Feetham (London: J. M. Dent, 1910, 1963), 395–411.

"Soldiers of the Athenians and of the allies, we have all an equal interest in the coming struggle, in which life and country are at stake for us quite as much as they can be for the enemy; since if our fleet wins the day, each can see his native city again, wherever that city may be. You must not lose heart, or be like men without any experience, who fail in a first essay, and ever afterwards fearfully forebode a future as disastrous. But let the Athenians among you who have already had experience of many wars, and the allies who have joined us in so many expeditions, remember the surprises of war, and with the hope that fortune will not be always against us, prepare to fight again in a manner worthy of the number which you see yourselves to be.

"Now, whatever we thought would be of service against the crush of vessels in such a narrow harbour, and against the force upon the decks of the enemy, from which we suffered before, has all been considered with the helmsmen, and, as far as our means allowed, provided. A number of archers and darters will go on board, and a multitude that we should not have employed in an action in the open sea, where our science would be crippled by the weight of the vessels; but in the present land-fight that we are forced to make from shipboard all this will be useful. We have also discovered the changes in construction that we must make to meet theirs; and against the thickness of their cheeks, which did us the greatest mischief, we have provided grappling-irons, which will prevent an assailant backing water after charging, if the soldiers on deck here do their duty; since we are absolutely compelled to fight a land battle from the fleet, and it seems to be our interest neither to back water ourselves, nor to let the enemy do so, especially as the shore, except so much of it as may be held by our troops, is hostile ground.

"You must remember this and fight on as long as you can, and must not let yourselves be driven ashore, but once alongside must make up your minds not to part company until you have swept the heavy infantry from the enemy's deck. I say this more for the heavy infantry than for the seamen, as it is more the business of the men on deck; and our land forces are even now on the whole the strongest. The sailors I advise, and at the same time implore, not to be too much daunted by their misfortunes, now that we have our decks better armed and a greater number of vessels. Bear in mind how well worth preserving is the pleasure felt by those of you who through your knowledge of our language and imitation of our manners were always considered Athenians, even though not so in reality, and as such were honoured throughout Hellas, and had your full share of the advantages of our empire, and more than your share in the respect of our subjects and in protection from ill treatment. You, therefore, with whom alone we freely share our empire, we now justly require not to betray that empire in its extremity, and in scorn of Corinthians, whom you have often conquered, and of Siceliots, none of whom so much as presumed to stand against us when our navy was in its prime, we ask you to repel them, and to show that even in sickness and disaster your skill is more than a match for the fortune and vigour of any other.

"For the Athenians among you I add once more this reflection: You left behind you no more such ships in your docks as these, no more heavy infantry in their flower; if you do aught but conquer, our enemies here will immediately sail thither, and those that are left of us at Athens will become unable to repel their home assailants, reinforced by these new allies. Here you will fall at once into the hands of the Syracusans—I need not remind you of the intentions with which you attacked them—and your countrymen at home will fall into those of the Lacedaemonians. Since the fate of both thus hangs upon this single battle, now, if ever, stand firm, and remember, each and all, that you who are now going on board are the army and navy of the Athenians, and all that is left of the state and the great name of Athens, in whose defence if any man has any advantage of skill or courage, now is the time for him to show it, and thus serve himself and save all."

After this address Nicias at once gave orders to man the ships. Meanwhile Gylippus and the Syracusans could perceive by the preparations which they saw going on that the Ahenians meant to fight at sea. They had also notice of the grappling-irons, against which they specially provided by stretching hides over the prows and much of the upper part of their vessels, in order that the irons when thrown might slip off without taking hold. All being now ready, the generals and Gylippus addressed them in the following terms:

"Syracusans and allies, the glorious character of our past achievements and the no less glorious results at issue in the coming battle are, we think, understood by most of you, or you would never have thrown yourselves with such ardour into the struggle; and if there be any one not as fully aware of the facts as he ought to be, we will declare them to him. The Athenians came to this country first to effect the conquest of Sicily, and after that, if successful, of Peloponnese and the rest of Hellas, possessing already the greatest empire yet known, of present or former times, among the Hellenes. Here for the first time they found in you men who faced their navy which made them masters everywhere; you have already defeated them in the previous sea-fights, and will in all likelihood defeat them again now. When men are once checked in what they consider their special excellence, their whole opinion of themselves suffers more than if they had not at first believed in their superiority, the unexpected shock to their pride causing them to give way more than their real strength warrants; and this is probably now the case with the Athenians.

"With us it is different. The original estimate of ourselves which gave us courage in the days of our unskilfulness has been strengthened, while the conviction superadded to it that we must be the best seamen of the time, if we have conquered the best, has given a double measure of hope to every man among us; and, for the most part, where there is greatest hope, there is also the greatest ardour for action. The means to combat us which they have tried to find in copying our armament are familiar to our warfare, and will be met by proper provisions; while they will never be able to have a number of heavy infantry on their decks, contrary to their custom, and a number of darters (born landsmen, one may say, Acarnanians and others, embarked afloat, who will not know how to discharge their weapons when they have to keep still), without hampering their vessels and falling all into confusion among themselves through fighting not according to their own tactics. For they will gain nothing by the number of their ships—I say this to those of you who may be alarmed by having to fight against odds—as a quantity of ships in a confined space will only be slower in executing the movements required, and most exposed to injury from our means of offence. Indeed, if you would know the plain truth, as we are credibly informed, the excess of their sufferings and the necessities of their present distress have made them desperate; they have no confidence in their force, but wish to try their fortune in the only way they can, and either to force their passage and sail out, or after this to retreat by land, it being impossible for them to be worse off than they are.

"The fortune of our greatest enemies having thus betrayed itself, and their disorder being what I have described, let us engage in anger, convinced that, as between adversaries, nothing is more legitimate than to claim to sate the whole wrath of one's soul in punishing the aggressor, and nothing more sweet, as the proverb has it, than the vengeance upon an enemy, which it will now be ours to take. That enemies they are and mortal enemies you all know, since they came here to enslave our country, and if successful had in reserve for our men all that is most dreadful, and for our children and wives all that is most dishonourable, and for the whole city the name which conveys the greatest reproach. None should therefore relent or think it gain if they go away without further danger to us. This they will do just the same, even if they get the victory; while if we succeed, as we may expect, in chastising them, and in handing down to all Sicily her ancient freedom strengthened and confirmed, we shall have achieved no mean triumph. And the rarest dangers are those in which failure brings little loss and success the greatest advantage."

After the above address to the soldiers on their side, the Syracusan generals and Gylippus now perceived that the Athenians were manning their ships, and immediately proceeded to man their own also. Meanwhile Nicias, appalled by the position of affairs, realizing the greatness and the nearness of the danger now that they were on the point of putting out from shore, and thinking, as men are apt to think in great crises, that when all has been done they have still something left to do, and when all has been said that they have not yet said enough, again called on the captains one by one, addressing each by his father's name and by his own, and by that of his tribe, and adjured them not to belie their own personal renown, or to obscure the hereditary virtues for which their ancestors were illustrious: he reminded them of their country, the freest of the free, and of the unfettered discretion allowed in it to all to live as they pleased; and added other arguments such as men would use at such a crisis, and which, with little alteration, are made to serve on all occasions alike—appeals to wives, children and national gods—without caring whether they are thought commonplace, but loudly invoking them in the belief that they will be of use in the consternation of the moment. Having thus admonished them, not, he felt, as he would, but as he could, Nicias withdrew and led the troops to the sea, and ranged them in as long a line as he was able, in order to aid as far as possible in sustaining the courage of the men afloat; while Demosthenes, Menander, and Euthydemus, who took the command on board, put out from their own camp and sailed straight to the barrier across the mouth of the harbour and to the passage left open, to try to force their way out.

   The Syracusans and their allies had already put out with about the same number of ships as before, a part of which kept guard at the outlet, and the remainder all round the rest of the harbour, in order to attack the Athenians on all sides at once; while the land forces held themselves in readiness at the points at which the vessels might put into the shore. The Syracusan fleet was commanded by Sicanus and Agatharchus, who had each a wing of the whole force, with Python and the Corinthians in the centre. When the rest of the Athenians came up to the barrier, with the first shock of their charge they overpowered the ships stationed there, and tried to undo the fastenings; after this, as the Syracusans and allies bore down upon them from all quarters, the action spread from the barrier over the whole harbour, and was more obstinately disputed than any of the preceding ones. On either side the rowers showed great zeal in bringing up their vessels at the boatswains' orders, and the helmsmen great skill in manœuvring, and great emulation one with another; while the ships once alongside, the soldiers on board did their best not to let the service on deck be outdone by the others; in short, every man strove to prove himself the first in his particular department. And as many ships were engaged in a small compass (for these were the largest fleets fighting in the narrowest space ever known, being together little short of two hundred), the regular attacks with the beak were few, there being no opportunity of backing water or of breaking the line; while the collisions caused by one ship chancing to run foul of another, either in flying from or attacking a third, were more frequent. So long as a vessel was coming up to the charge the men on the decks rained darts and arrows and stones upon her; but once alongside, the heavy infantry tried to board each other's vessel, fighting to hand. In many quarters also it happened, by reason of the narrow room, that a vessel was charging an enemy on one side and being charged herself on another, and that two or sometimes more ships had perforce got entangled round one, obliging the helmsmen to attend to defence here, offence there, not to one thing at once, but to many on all sides; while the huge din caused by the number of ships crashing together not only spread terror, but made the orders of the boatswains inaudible. The boatswains on either side in the discharge of their duty and in the heat of the conflict shouted incessantly orders and appeals to their men; the Athenians they urged to force the passage out, and now if ever to show their mettle and lay hold of a safe return to their country; to the Syracusans and their allies they cried that it would be glorious to prevent the escape of the enemy, and conquering, to exalt the countries that were theirs. The generals, moreover, on either side, if they saw any in any part of the battle backing ashore without being forced to do so, called out to the captain by name and asked him—the Athenians, whether they were retreating because they thought the thrice hostile shore more their own than that sea which had cost them so much labour to win; the Syracusans, whether they were flying from the flying Athenians, whom they well knew to be eager to escape in whatever way they could.

Meanwhile the two armies on shore, while victory hung in the balance, were a prey to the most agonizing and conflicting emotions; the natives thirsting for more glory than they had already won, while the invaders feared to find themselves in even worse plight than before. The all of the Athenians being set upon their fleet, their fear for the event was like nothing they had ever felt; while their view of the struggle was necessarily as chequered as the battle itself. Close to the scene of action and not all looking at the same point at once, some saw their friends victorious and took courage, and fell to calling upon heaven not to deprive them of salvation, while others who had their eyes turned upon the losers, wailed and cried aloud, and, although spectators, were more overcome than the actual combatants. Others, again, were gazing at some spot where the battle was evenly disputed; as the strife was protracted without decision, their swaying bodies reflected the agitation of their minds, and they suffered the worst agony of all, ever just within reach of safety or just on the point of destruction. In short, in that one Athenian army as long as the sea-fight remained doubtful there was every sound to be heard at once, shrieks, cheers, 'We win,' 'We lose,' and all the other manifold exclamations that a great host would necessarily utter in great peril; and with the men in the fleet it was nearly the same; until at last the Syracusans and their allies, after the battle had lasted a long while, put the Athenians to flight, and with much shouting and cheering chased them in open rout to the shore. The naval force, one one way, one another, as many as were not taken afloat, now ran ashore and rushed from on board their ships to their camp; while the army, no more divided, but carried away by one impulse, all with shrieks and groans deplored the event, and ran down, some to help the ships, others to guard what was left on their wall, while the remaining and most numerous part already began to consider how they should save themselves. Indeed, the panic of the present moment had never been surpassed. They now suffered very nearly what they had inflicted at Pylos; as then the Lacedaemonians with the loss of their fleet lost also the men who had crossed over to the island, so now the Athenians had no hope of escaping by land, without the help of some extraordinary accident.

The sea-fight having been a severe one, and many ships and lives having been lost on both sides, the victorious Syracusans and their allies now picked up their wrecks and dead, and sailed off to the city and set up a trophy. The Athenians, overwhelmed by their misfortune, never even thought of asking leave to take up their dead or wrecks, but wished to retreat that very night. Demosthenes, however, went to Nicias and gave it as his opinion that they should man the ships they had left and make another effort to force their passage out next morning; saying that they had still left more ships fit for service than the enemy, the Athenians having about sixty remaining as against less than fifty of their opponents. Nicias was quite of his mind; but when they wished to man the vessels, the sailors refused to go on board, being so utterly overcome by their defeat as no longer to believe in the possibility of success.

Accordingly they all now made up their minds to retreat by land. Meanwhile the Syracusan Hermocrates suspecting their intention, and impressed by the danger of allowing a force of that magnitude to retire by land, establish itself in some other part of Sicily, and from thence renew the war, went and stated his views to the authorities, and pointed out to them that they ought not to let the enemy get away by night, but that all the Syracusans and their allies should at once march out and block up the roads and seize and guard the passes. The authorities were entirely of his opinion, and thought that it ought to be done, but on the other hand felt sure that the people, who had given themselves over to rejoicing and were taking their ease after a great battle at sea, would not be easily brought to obey; besides, they were celebrating a festival, having on that day a sacrifice to Heracles, and most of them in their rapture at the victory had fallen to drinking at the festival, and would probably consent to anything sooner than to take up their arms and march out at that moment. For these reasons the thing appeared impracticable to the magistrates; and

Hermocrates, finding himself unable to do anything further with them, had now recourse to the following stratagem of his own. What he feared was that the Athenians might quietly get the start of them by passing the most difficult places during the night; and he therefore sent, as soon as it was dusk, some friends of his own to the camp with some horsemen who rode up within earshot and called out to some of the men, as though they were well-wishers of the Athenians, and told them to tell Nicias (who had in fact some correspondents who informed him of what went on inside the town), not to lead off the army by night as the Syracusans were guarding the roads, but to make his preparations at his leisure and to retreat by day. After saying this they departed; and their hearers informed the Athenian generals, who put off going for that night on the strength of this message, not doubting its sincerity.

Since after all they had not set out at once, they now determined to stay also the following day to give time to the soldiers to pack up as well as they could the most useful articles, and, leaving everything else behind, to start only with what was strictly necessary for their personal subsistence. Meanwhile the Syracusans and Gylippus marched out and blocked up the roads through the country by which the Athenians were likely to pass, and kept guard at the fords of the streams and rivers, posting themselves so as to receive them and stop the army where they thought best; while their fleet sailed up the beach and towed off the ships of the Athenians. Some few were burned by the Athenians themselves as they had intended; the rest the Syracusans lashed on to their own at their leisure as they had been thrown up on shore, without any one trying to stop them, and conveyed them to the town.

After this, Nicias and Demosthenes now thinking that enough had been done in the way of preparation, the removal of the army took place upon the second day after the sea-fight. It was a lamentable scene, not merely from the single circumstance that they were retreating after having lost all their ships, their great hopes gone, and themselves and the state in peril; but also in leaving the camp there were things most grievous for every eye and heart to contemplate. The dead lay unburied, and each man as he recognized a friend among them shuddered with grief and horror; while the living whom they were leaving behind, wounded or sick, were to the living far more shocking than the dead, and more to be pitied than those who had perished. These fell to entreating and bewailing until their friends knew not what to do, begging them to take them and loudly calling to each individual comrade or relative whom they could see, hanging upon the necks of their tent-fellows in the act of departure, and following as far as they could, and when their bodily strength failed them, calling again and again upon heaven and shrieking aloud as they were left behind. So that the whole army being filled with tears and distracted after this fashion found it not easy to go, even from an enemy's land, where they had already suffered evils too great for tears and in the unknown future before them feared to suffer more. Dejection and self-condemnation were also rife among them. Indeed they could only be compared to a starved-out town, and that no small one, escaping; the whole multitude upon the march being not less than forty thousand men. All carried anything they could which might be of use, and the heavy infantry and troopers, contrary to their wont, while under arms carried their own victuals, in some cases for want of servants, in others through not trusting them; as they had long been deserting and now did so in greater numbers than ever. Yet even thus they did not carry enough, as there was no longer food in the camp. Moreover their disgrace generally, and the universality of their sufferings, however to a certain extent alleviated by being borne in company, were still felt at the moment a heavy burden, especially when they contrasted the splendour and glory of their setting out with the humiliation in which it had ended. For this was by far the greatest reverse that ever befell an Hellenic army. They had come to enslave others, and were departing in fear of being enslaved themselves: they had sailed out with prayer and paeans, and now started to go back with omens directly contrary; travelling by land instead of by sea, and trusting not in their fleet but in their heavy infantry. Nevertheless the greatness of the danger still impending made all this appear tolerable.

Nicias seeing the army dejected and greatly altered, passed along the ranks and encouraged and comforted them as far as was possible under the circumstances, raising his voice still higher and higher as he went from one company to another in his earnestness, and in his anxiety that the benefit of his words might reach as many as possible:

'Athenians and allies, even in our present position we must still hope on, since men have ere now been saved from worse straits than this; and you must not condemn yourselves too severely either because of your disasters or because of your present unmerited sufferings. I myself who am not superior to any of you in strength—indeed you see how I am in my sickness—and who in the gifts of fortune am, I think, whether in private life or otherwise, the equal of any, am now exposed to the same danger as the meanest among you; and yet my life has been one of much devotion toward the gods, and of much justice and without offence toward men. I have, therefore, still a strong hope for the future, and our misfortunes do not terrify me as much as they might. Indeed we may hope that they will be lightened: our enemies have had good fortune enough; and if any of the gods was offended at our expedition, we have been already amply punished. Others before us have attacked their neighbours and have done what men will do without suffering more than they could bear; and we may now justly expect to find the gods more kind, for we have become fitter objects for their pity than their jealousy. And then look at your-selves, mark the numbers and efficiency of the heavy infantry marching in your ranks, and do not give way too much to despondency, but reflect that you are yourselves at once a city wherever you sit down, and that there is no other in Sicily that could easily resist your attack, or expel you when once established. The safety and order of the march is for yourselves to look to; the one thought of each man being that the spot on which he may be forced to fight must be conquered and held as his country and stronghold. Meanwhile we shall hasten on our way night and day alike, as our provisions are scanty; and if we can reach some friendly place of the Sicels, whom fear of the Syracusans still keeps true to us, you may forth-with consider yourselves safe. A message has been sent on to them with directions to meet us with supplies of food. To sum up, be convinced, sol-diers, that you must be brave, as there is no place near for your cowardice to take refuge in, and that if you now escape from the enemy, you may all see again what your hearts desire, while those of you who are Athenians will raise up again the great power of the state, fallen though it be. Men make the city and not walls or ships without men in them.'

As he made this address, Nicias went along the ranks, and brought back to their place any of the troops that he saw straggling out of the line; while Demosthenes did as much for his part of the army, addressing them in words very similar. The army marched in a hollow square, the division under Nicias leading, and that of Demosthenes following, the heavy in-fantry being outside and the baggage-carriers and the bulk of the army in the middle. When they arrived at the ford of the river Anapus they found drawn up a body of the Syracusans and allies, and routing these, made good their passage and pushed on, harassed by the charges of the Syracu-san horse and by the missiles of their light troops. On that day they ad-vanced about four miles and half, halting for the night upon a certain hill. On the next they started early and got on about two miles further, and descended into a place in the plain and there encamped, in order to pro-cure some eatables from the houses, as the place was inhabited, and to carry on with them water from thence, as for many furlongs in front, in the direction in which they were going, it was not plentiful. The Syracu-sans meanwhile went on and fortified the pass in front, where there was a steep hill with a rocky ravine on each side of it, called the Acraean cliff. The next day the Athenians advancing found themselves impeded by the missiles and charges of the horse and darters, both very numerous, of the Syracusans and allies; and after fighting for a long while, at length retired to the same camp, where they had no longer provisions as before, it being impossible to leave their position by reason of the cavalry.

Early next morning they started afresh and forced their way to the hill, which had been fortified, where they found before them the enemy's infantry drawn up many shields deep to defend the fortification, the pass being narrow. The Athenians assaulted the work, but were greeted by a storm of missiles from the hill, which told with the greater effect through its being a steep one, and unable to force the passage, retreated again and rested. Meanwhile occurred some claps of thunder and rain, as often happens towards autumn, which still further disheartened the Athenians, who thought all these things to be omens of their approaching ruin. While they were resting Gylippus and the Syracusans sent a part of their army to throw up works in their rear on the way by which they had advanced; however, the Athenians immediately sent some of their men and prevented them; after which they retreated more towards the plain and halted for the night. When they advanced the next day the Syracusans surrounded and attacked them on every side, and disabled many of them, falling back if the Athenians advanced and coming on if they retired, and in particular assaulting their rear, in the hope of routing them in detail, and thus striking a panic into the whole army. For a long while the Athenians persevered in this fashion, but after advancing for four or five furlongs halted to rest in the plain, the Syracusans also withdrawing to their own camp.

During the night Nicias and Demosthenes, seeing the wretched condition of their troops, now in want of every kind of necessary, and numbers of them disabled in the numerous attacks of the enemy, determined to light as many fires as possible, and to lead off the army, no longer by the same route as they had intended, but towards the sea in the opposite direction to that guarded by the Syracusans. The whole of this route was leading the army not to Catana but to the other side of Sicily, towards Camarina, Gela, and the other Hellenic and barbarian towns in that quarter. They accordingly lit a number of fires and set out by night. Now all armies, and the greatest most of all, are liable to fears and alarms, especially when they are marching by night through an enemy's country and with the enemy near; and the Athenians falling into one of these panics, the leading division, that of Nicias, kept together and got on a good way in front, while that of Demosthenes, comprising rather more than half the army, got separated and marched on in some disorder. By morning, however, they reached the sea, and getting into the Helorine road, pushed on in order to reach the river Cacyparis, and to follow the stream up through the interior, where they hoped to be met by the Sicels whom they had sent for. Arrived at the river, they found there also a Syracusan party engaged in barring the passage of the ford with a wall and a palisade, and forcing this guard, crossed the river and went on to another called the Erineus, according to the advice of their guides.

Meanwhile, when day came and the Syracusans and allies found that the Athenians were gone, most of them accused Gylippus of having let them escape on purpose, and hastily pursuing by the road which they had no difficulty in finding that they had taken, overtook them about dinner-time. They first came up with the troops under Demosthenes, who were behind and marching somewhat slowly and in disorder, owing to the night panic above referred to, and at once attacked and engaged them, the Syracusan horse surrounding them with more ease now that they were separated from the rest, and hemming them in on one spot. The division of Nicias was five or six miles on in front, as he led them more rapidly, thinking that under the circumstances their safety lay not in staying and fighting, unless obliged, but in retreating as fast as possible, and only fighting when forced to do so. On the other hand, Demosthenes was, generally speaking, harassed more incessantly, as his post in the rear left him the first exposed to the attacks of the enemy; and now, finding that the Syracusans were in pursuit, he omitted to push on, in order to form his men for battle, and so lingered until he was surrounded by his pursuers and himself and the Athenians with him placed in the most distressing position, being huddled into an enclosure with a wall all round it, a road on this side and on that, and olive-trees in great number, where missiles were showered in upon them from every quarter. This mode of attack the Syracusans had with good reason adopted in preference to fighting at close quarters, as to risk a struggle with desperate men was now more for the advantage of the Athenians than for their own; besides, their success had now become so certain that they began to spare themselves a little in order not to be cut off in the moment of victory, thinking too that, as it was, they would be able in this way to subdue and capture the enemy.

In fact, after plying the Athenians and allies all day long from every side with missiles, they at length saw that they were worn out with their wounds and other sufferings; and Gylippus and the Syracusans and their allies made a proclamation, offering their liberty to any of the islanders who chose to come over to them; and some few cities went over. Afterwards a capitulation was agreed upon for all the rest with Demosthenes, to lay down their arms on condition that no one was to be put to death either by violence or imprisonment or want of the necessaries of life. Upon this they surrendered to the number of six thousand in all, laying down all the money in their possession, which filled the hollows of four shields, and were immediately conveyed by the Syracusans to the town.

Meanwhile Nicias with his division arrived that day at the river Erineus, crossed over, and posted his army upon some high ground upon the other side. The next day the Syracusans overtook him and told him that the troops under Demosthenes had surrendered, and invited him to follow their example. Incredulous of the fact, Nicias asked for a truce to send a horseman to see, and upon the return of the messenger with the tidings that they had surrendered, sent a herald to Gylippus and the Syracusans, saying that he was ready to agree with them on behalf of the Athenians to repay whatever money the Syracusans had spent upon the war if they would let his army go; and offered until the money was paid to give Athenians as hostages, one for every talent. The Syracusans and Gylippus rejected this proposition, and attacked this division as they had the other, standing all round and plying them with missiles until the evening. Food and necessaries were as miserably wanting to the troops of Nicias as they had been to their comrades; nevertheless they watched for the quiet of the night to resume their march. But as they were taking up their arms the Syracusans perceived it and raised their paean, upon which the Athenians, finding that they were discovered, laid them down again, except about three hundred men who forced their way through the guards and went on during the night as they were able.

As soon as it was day Nicias put his army in motion, pressed, as before, by the Syracusans and their allies, pelted from every side by their missiles, and struck down by their javelins. The Athenians pushed on for the Assinarus, impelled by the attacks made upon them from every side by a numerous cavalry and the swarm of other arms, fancying that they should breathe more freely if once across the river, and driven on also by their exhaustion and craving for water. Once there they rushed in, and all order was at an end, each man wanting to cross first, and the attacks of the enemy making it difficult to cross at all; forced to huddle together, they fell against and trod down one another, some dying immediately upon the javelins, others getting entangled together and stumbling over the articles of baggage, without being able to rise again. Meanwhile the opposite bank, which was steep, was lined by the Syracusans, who showered missiles down upon the Athenians, most of them drinking greedily and heaped together in disorder in the hollow bed of the river. The Peloponnesians also came down and butchered them, especially those in the water, which was thus immediately spoiled, but which they went on drinking just the same, mud and all, bloody as it was, most even fighting to have it.

At last, when many dead now lay piled one upon another in the stream, and part of the army had been destroyed at the river, and the few that escaped from thence cut off by the cavalry, Nicias surrendered himself to Gylippus, whom he trusted more than he did the Syracusans, and told him and the Lacedaemonians to do what they liked with him, but to stop the slaughter of the soldiers. Gylippus, after this, immediately gave orders to make prisoners; upon which the rest were brought together alive, except a large number secreted by the soldiery, and a party was sent in pursuit of the three hundred who had got through the guard during the night, and who were now taken with the rest. The number of the enemy collected as public property was not considerable; but that secreted was very large, and all Sicily was filled with them, no convention having been made in their case as for those taken with Demosthenes. Besides this, a large portion were killed outright, the carnage being very great, and not exceeded by any in this Sicilian war. In the numerous other encounters upon the march, not a few also had fallen. Nevertheless many escaped, some at the moment, others served as slaves, and then ran away subsequently. These found refuge at Catana.

The Syracusans and their allies now mustered and took up the spoils and as many prisoners as they could, and went back to the city. The rest of their Athenian and allied captives were deposited in the quarries, this seeming the safest way of keeping them; but Nicias and Demosthenes were butchered, against the will of Gylippus, who thought that it would be the crown of his triumph if he could take the enemy's generals to Lacedaemon. One of them, as it happened, Demosthenes, was one of her greatest enemies, on account of the affair of the island and of Pylos; while the other, Nicias, was for the same reasons one of her greatest friends, owing to his exertions to procure the release of the prisoners by persuading the Athenians to make peace. For these reasons the Lacedaemonians felt kindly towards him; and it was in this that Nicias himself mainly confided when he surrendered to Gylippus. But some of the Syracusans who had been in correspondence with him were afraid, it was said, of his being put to the torture and troubling their success by his revelations; others, especially the Corinthians, of his escaping, as he was wealthy, by means of bribes, and living to do them further mischief; and these persuaded the allies and put him to death. This or the like was the cause of the death of a man who, of all the Hellenes in my time, least deserved such a fate, seeing that the whole course of his life had been regulated with strict attention to virtue.

The prisoners in the quarries were at first hardly treated by the Syracusans. Crowded in a narrow hole, without any roof to cover them, the heat of the sun and the stifling closeness of the air tormented them during the day, and then the nights, which came on autumnal and chilly, made them ill by the violence of the change; besides, as they had to do everything in the same place for want of room, and the bodies of those who died of their wounds or from the variation of the temperature, or from similar causes, were left heaped together one upon another, intolerable stenches arose; while hunger and thirst never ceased to afflict them, each man during eight months having only half a pint of water and a pint of corn given him daily. In short, no single suffering to be apprehended by men thrust into such a place was spared them. For some seventy days they thus lived all together, after which all, except the Athenians and any Siceliots or Italiots who had joined in the expedition, were sold. The total number of prisoners taken it would be difficult to state exactly, but it could not have been less than seven thousand.

This was the greatest Hellenic achievement of any in this war, or, in my opinion, in Hellenic history; at once most glorious to the victors, and most calamitous to the conquered. They were beaten at all points and altogether; all that they suffered was great; they were destroyed, as the saying is, with a total destruction, their fleet, their army, everything was destroyed, and few out of many returned home.

Bibliography

Adock, F. E. *Thucydides and His History.* Cambridge, 1963.

Bury, J. B. *The Ancient Greek Historians.* London, 1909.

Cochrane, Charles N. *Thucydides and the Science of History.* Oxford, 1929.

Cornford, Francis MacDonald. *Thucydides Mythistoricus.* London, 1907, 1965.

Edmunds, Lowell. *Chance and Intelligence in Thucydides.* Cambridge, Mass., 1975.

Finley, John H., Jr. *Thucydides.* Cambridge, Mass., 1942.

Gomme, A. W. et al., *An Historical Commentary on Thucydides.* 5 vols. Oxford, 1945–81.

Grant, Michael. *The Ancient Historians.* London, 1970.

Kagan, Donald. *The Peace of Nicias and the Sicilian Expedition.* Ithaca, 1981.

Kagan, Donald. "The Speeches of Thucydides in the Mytilene Debate." *Yale Classical Studies* 24 (1975): 71–95.

Lesky, Albin. *A History of Greek Literature,* translated by James Willis and Cornelius de Heer. New York, 1966.

Momigliano, Arnaldo. "Greek Historiography." *History and Theory* 17 (Spring 1978): 1–28.

CHAPTER 4

Titus Livy

The History of Rome

(c. 25 B.C.–A.D. 17)

Titus Livy's (c. 59 B.C.–A.D. 17) subject was colossal: the 744-year history of Rome from its earliest foundations to his own time. Not all the 142 books have survived; indeed, only the first 10 and books 21 through 35—a fragment— have come down to us. Yet they are enough to show why Livy was lionized as the greatest historian of his day. His account of early Rome, which included a retelling of ancient myths, and his books on the wars with Hannibal in the third century B.C. are unequalled for sheer literary brilliance. Some critics were willing to forgive his liberties with the facts and, occasionally, his simple disinterest in them, because they admired Livy's ability to think his way back into the minds of men and feel again the emotions of multitudes. Thucydides, four centuries earlier, was more careful with his sources, but where he was often drawn to the technical details of, say, a battle, Livy invariably probed for the psychology of it.

Unlike his Greek predecessors and, for that matter, later Roman historians, Livy was not a well-traveled man of the world. Born in Patavium (Padua), he lived most of his life in Rome, where he enjoyed the patronage of Augustus (27 B.C.–A.D. 14) but watched uneasily as his sponsor transformed the Roman Republic into the Roman Empire. His history was mildly "senatorial," praising the ancient republican institutions and virtues which now were but trappings in an increasingly "royal" administration. Living within the Augustan circle softened his criticism (he did not publish the last books until Augustus died), but so also did his own belief in the sheer grandeur of Roman history, his principal theme.

The two excerpts below are taken from Livy's account of the war with Hannibal. In 219 B.C. the great Carthaginian general cast aside the understanding that had for years defined Roman and African spheres of influence. In a dramatic move, Hannibal marched from Spain to the Alps and descended upon Italy with a powerful army, putting Roman resistance to rout. The Battle of Cannae in 216 B.C., which Livy narrates partly as a morality tale, was an especially decisive Roman defeat. But in the long run Rome was able to avoid further large-scale battles. Instead, Rome concentrated on isolating

Hannibal from his outside sources of supply and, in 202 B.C., challenged and defeated him once and for all in Africa.

Note the vivid detail with which Livy recreates Hannibal's crossing of the Alps. Nature itself as well as nature's wild men are invoked to defend the mountain passes. Yet Livy's detail is selective and imaginative, and for all its fullness, we cannot tell to this day exactly what route Hannibal took. Chance and deception are at the heart of the historian's account of the Battle of Cannae, and Livy pits the Roman commanders, Varro and Paullus, against each other, not just as personalities but as models of Roman rashness and Roman prudence. Paullus must die while Varro survives, but eventually Rome would remember Paullus' caution and would go on to reduce Hannibal in a war of exhaustion.

H AVING INSPIRITED THEM WITH . . . words of encouragement, Hannibal bade them refresh themselves and prepare for their march. Next day he advanced up the Rhone toward the interior of Gaul, not because this was the more direct route to the Alps, but thinking that the further he withdrew from the sea, the less likely he was to encounter the Romans, whom it was not his intention to engage till his arrival in Italy. In four days' march he reached the Island. Here the Isère and the Rhone, which pour down their waters from Alpine summits far apart, and embrace a large stretch of country, unite in one stream, and the plains between have received the name of the Island. In the neighbourhood are settled the Allobroges, a tribe even at that time inferior to none of the tribes of Gaul in resources or renown. They were then at strife. Two brothers were contending for the throne. The elder, who had previously been king, Brancus by name, was now being thrust aside by his younger brother, and a party of the younger men, who had more might than right on their side. The settlement of the feud was very opportunely referred to Hannibal, and he having thus to dispose of the kingdom restored the elder brother to power, such having been the feeling of the senate and the chiefs. For this service he was helped with supplies and an abundance of all things, clothing especially, which the notorious horrors of the cold in the Alps compelled him to provide.

Having composed the feud of the Allobroges, Hannibal marched toward the Alps, not, however, pursuing a direct course, but turning left-

Titus Livius, *Roman History*, translated by John Henry Freese, Alfred John Church, and William Jackson Brodribb (New York: D. Appleton and Company, 1898), 261–67, 334–43.

ward to the country of the Tricastini, from which again he passed to that of the Tricorii, along the extreme frontier of the Vocontii, a route at no point embarrassing till he reached the river Druentia. One of the rivers of the Alps, it is naturally far the most difficult to cross of all the streams in Gaul; for though it rushes down with a vast body of water, it is not navigable, not being confined within banks, and flowing in many channels at once, and these not always the same. Its ever-changing shallows and eddies, which make the passage perplexing even to one on foot, and the rocks and gravelly bed over which it rolls, allow no sure and safe foothold. At this time it happened to be swollen by rains, and so caused much confusion among the men as they crossed—a confusion increased by other alarms, and by their own haste and bewildered cries.

About three days after Hannibal had moved from the Rhone, the consul Publius Cornelius reached the enemy's camp with his army in order of battle, resolved to fight without a moment's delay. Seeing, however, that the lines were abandoned, and that the enemy must be too far ahead to be easily overtaken, he went back to the sea and to his ships, assured that he could thus more safely and conveniently encounter Hannibal on his descent from the Alps. But not to leave Spain, his allotted province, bare of Roman defence, he sent his brother Cneius Scipio with the largest part of his army against Hasdrubal, not merely to protect our old allies and form fresh alliances, but actually to drive Hasdrubal out of the country. Scipio himself with quite a small force returned to Genua, purposing to defend Italy with the troops encamped in the neighbourhood of the Po.

From the Druentia Hannibal marched through a country generally flat to the Alps, wholly unmolested by the Gauls in those parts. And then, though rumour which usually magnifies the unknown far beyond truth had given some anticipation of the facts, still the near sight of the mountain heights with their snows almost mingling with the sky, the rude huts perched on the rocks, cattle and beasts of burden shrivelled with cold, human beings unkempt and wild, and all things animate and inanimate stiffened with frost, with other scenes more horrible to behold than to describe, revived the terror of the soldiers.

As the vanguard was struggling up the first slopes, the mountain tribes showed themselves on the overhanging hills. Had they lain hid in some of the obscurer valleys and suddenly rushed out to the attack, they must have caused terrible panic and loss. Hannibal ordered a halt, and the Gauls were sent on to reconnoitre. When he ascertained that here there was no passage for his troops, he pitched his camp in the broadest valley he could find, where the country all around was rugged and precipitous. Then from those same Gauls, mingling and conversing with the mountaineers, whom indeed in language and manners they resembled, he learned that it was only by day that the pass was barred, and that at night all dispersed to their various dwellings. With early dawn he advanced to the foot of the hills, as if he meant to push his way by force in open day through the defiles. In this feint, preparing a movement not really intended, the day was spent, and the camp was fortified on the spot on which it had been pitched. But the moment Hannibal saw the mountaineers coming down from the hills and the outposts weakly manned, he had a multitude of fires lit for show, greater than would correspond with the number of troops in camp, and then leaving behind him the baggage with the cavalry as well as the greater part of the infantry, and taking with him some lightly armed men, the bravest he could pick, he rapidly mounted the passes and established himself on the very hills which the enemy had occupied.

At daybreak the camp was broken up and the rest of the army began to move. The mountaineers on a signal given were now gathering in force from their fortresses to one of their regular positions, when suddenly they saw the enemy, some on the heights over their heads and in possession of their own stronghold, the remainder marching through the pass. The double impression thus made on their sight and imagination held them for a brief while rooted to the earth. Soon, when they saw the hurry in the defiles, and how the army was in utter confusion from its own disorder, the horses especially being wild with fright, they thought that, could they in any way increase the panic, it would insure the enemy's destruction, and rushed down the face of the rocks they knew so well, whether along pathless steeps or obscure tracks. Then indeed both the foe and the perils of the place fought against the Carthaginians, and while every man strove for himself to get soonest out of danger, there was more struggling among the soldiers themselves than between them and the enemy. The horses were the most dangerous hindrance to the army. They were terrified and scared by the confused cries which the woods and echoing valleys further multiplied, and if they chanced to be struck and wounded, in the wildness of their terror they made fearful havoc alike among the men and the baggage of every description. The pressure, too, in the defile, each side of which was a sheer precipice, hurled numbers down to an immense depth, and among them were soldiers with their accoutrements; but it was more particularly the beasts with their burdens, which rolled down with just such a crash as a falling house.

Horrible as all this was to behold, Hannibal halted a while and kept his men in their ranks, so as not to aggravate the disorder and panic, and then, as soon as he saw a break in the line, and the danger that the army might accomplish the passage safely indeed but to no purpose, because stripped of all their baggage, he hurried down from his position on the heights and routed the enemy, but at the same time increased the confusion of his own troops. This confusion, however, was quieted in a moment when the flight of the mountaineers left the roads clear, and all soon marched through the pass not merely in peace but almost in silence. Next he took a fortress, the capital of the district, and some villages in the neighbourhood, and fed his troops for three days on the corn and cattle he had seized. In those three days he accomplished a considerable march, as there was not much hindrance from the ground or from the mountaineers, whom they had cowed at the outset.

Then they reached a canton, which, for a mountain district, was densely peopled. Here Hannibal was all but cut off, not by open fighting, but by his own peculiar arts, treachery and ambuscade. Some old men, governors of the fortresses, came to him as envoys, with assurances that warned by the salutary examples of the misfortunes of others, they preferred to make trial of the friendship rather than of the might of the Carthaginians; that thereupon they would obediently do his bidding; and they begged him to accept supplies, guides for his march, and hostages as a guarantee of their promises. Hannibal, feeling that he must not either rashly trust or slight them, lest refusal might make them open enemies, gave them a gracious answer. He accepted the offered hostages, and used the supplies which they had themselves brought to the road, but he followed the guides with his army in fighting order, not as if he was among a friendly people. His van was formed of the elephants and cavalry, while he marched himself in the rear with the main strength of the infantry, anxiously reconnoitring at every step. The moment they entered a narrow pass, dominated on one side by an overhanging height, the barbarians sprang out of their ambuscades in every direction, attacking in front and rear, discharging missiles and coming to close quarters, and rolling down huge stones upon the army. It was on the rear that the enemy pressed in greatest force. The infantry column wheeled and faced him; but it was proved beyond a doubt that, had not the rear been well strengthened, a terrible disaster would have been sustained in that pass. Even as it was, they were brought to the extremest jeopardy, and were within a hair's breadth of destruction. For while Hannibal was hesitating about sending his men into the defile because, though he could himself support the cavalry, he had no reserve in his rear for the infantry, the mountaineers rushed on his flanks, and having cut his line in half barred his advance. One night he had to pass without his cavalry and his baggage.

Next day, as the barbarians were less active in their attacks, the army was again united, and fought its way through the pass, but not without loss, which, however, fell more heavily on the beasts of burden than on the men. From this point the mountaineers became less numerous; hovering round more like brigands than soldiers, they threatened now the van, now the rear, whenever the ground gave them a chance, or stragglers in advance or behind offered an opportunity. The elephants, though it was a tedious business to drive them along the narrow precipitous passes, at least protected the troops from the enemy wherever they went, inspiring as they did, a peculiar fear in all who were unused to approach them.

On the ninth day they reached the top of the Alps, passing for the most part over trackless steeps, and by devious ways, into which they were led by the treachery of their guides. Two days they encamped on the height, and the men, worn out with hardships and fighting, were allowed to rest. Some beasts of burden too which had fallen down among the crags, found their way to the camp by following the army's track. The men were already worn out and wearied with their many miseries, when a fall of snow coming with the setting of the Pleiades added to their sufferings a terrible fear. At daybreak the march was resumed, and as the army moved wearily over ground all buried in snow, languor and despair were visibly written on every face, when Hannibal stepped to the front, and having ordered a halt on a peak which commanded a wide and distant prospect, pointed to Italy and to the plains round the Po, as they lay beneath the heights of the Alps, telling his men, "'Tis the walls not of Italy only but of Rome itself that you are now scaling. What remains," he added, "will be a smooth descent; in one, or at the most, in two battles we shall have the citadel and capital of Italy in our grasp and power."

The army then began to advance, and now even the enemy attempted nothing but some stealthy ambuscades, as opportunity offered. The remainder, however, of the march proved far more difficult than the ascent, as the Alps for the most part on the Italian side have a shorter and therefore a steeper slope. In fact the whole way was precipitous, narrow, and slippery, so much so that they could not keep themselves from falling, nor could those who had once stumbled maintain their foothold. Thus they tumbled one over another and the beasts of burden over the men.

Next they came to a much narrower pass with walls of rock so perpendicular that a light-armed soldier could hardly let himself down by feeling his way, and grasping with his hands the bushes and roots sticking out around him. The place of old was naturally precipitous, and now by a recent landslip it had broken away sheer to a depth of a thousand feet. Here the cavalry halted, as if it must be the end of their route, and Hannibal wondering what delayed the march, was told that the rock was impassable. Then he went himself to examine the spot. There seemed to be no doubt that he must lead his army round by pathless and hitherto untrodden slopes, however tedious might be the circuit. This route, however, was impracticable; for while on last season's still unmelted snow lay a fresh layer of moderate depth, where the foot of the first comer found a good hold on the soft and not very deep drift, as soon as it had been once trampled down under the march of such a host of men and beasts, they had to walk on the bare ice beneath, and the liquid mud from the melting snow. Here there was a horrible struggle. The slippery ice allowed no firm foothold, and indeed betrayed the foot all the more quickly on the slope, so that whether a man helped himself to rise by his hands or knees, his supports gave way, and he fell again. And here there were no stalks or roots to which hand or foot could cling. Thus there was incessant rolling on nothing but smooth ice or slush of snow. The beasts broke through, occasionally treading down even to the very lowest layer of snow, and when they fell, as they wildly struck out with their hoofs in their efforts to rise, they cut clean to the bottom, till many of them stuck fast in the hard and deep frozen ice, as if caught in a trap.

At last, when both men and beasts were worn out with fruitless exertion, they encamped on a height, in a spot which with the utmost difficulty they had cleared; so much snow had to be dug out and removed. The soldiers were then marched off to the work of making a road through the rock, as there only was a passage possible. Having to cut into the stone, they heaped up a huge pile of wood from great trees in the neighbourhood, which they had felled and lopped. As soon as there was strength enough in the wind to create a blaze they lighted the pile, and melted the rocks, as they heated, by pouring vinegar on them. The burning stone was cleft open with iron implements, and then they relieved the steepness of the slopes by gradual winding tracks, so that even the elephants as well as the other beasts could be let down. Four days were spent in this rocky pass, and the beasts almost perished of hunger, as the heights generally are quite bare, and such herbage as grows is buried in snow. Amid the lower slopes were valleys, sunny hills too, and streams, and woods beside them, and spots now at last more worthy to be the habitations of man. Here they sent the beasts to feed, and the men worn out with the toil of road-making, were allowed to rest. In the next three days they reached level ground, and now the country was less wild, as was also the character of the inhabitants.

Such of the whole was the march which brought them to Italy, in the fifth month, according to some authors, after leaving New Carthage, the passage of the Alps having occupied fifteen days.

· ·

It seemed to (Hannibal) that both time and place favoured a stratagem. Making his soldiers carry with them nothing but their arms, he quitted his camp, leaving it full of property both public and private. He drew up his infantry in concealment behind the hills on his left, and his cavalry on the right; and made the baggage pass up the valley between, hoping to surprise the Romans while their thoughts and hands were busied with the plunder of a camp which seemed to have been deserted by the sudden flight of its occupants. Many fires were left in the camp, intended to create the impression that he had wished to keep the consuls where they were, till he had got a long start in his retreat, just as he had deceived Fabius the year before.

When day broke, the Romans saw with astonishment, first, that the pickets were withdrawn, and then when they approached the camp, that there was an unusual stillness. As soon as they were quite certain that it was deserted, there was a rush to the headquarters of the consul, and a cry that the enemy had fled in such haste that they had abandoned their camp with the tents standing, and that to conceal their retreat, many fires had been left burning. A loud shout was set up that the consuls should at once order an advance and lead them to pursue the enemy, and forthwith plunder the camp. One of the consuls was nothing better than one of the mob of soldiers. Paulus said again and again that they must be prudent and cautious. At last, seeing no other way of holding his own against the mutineers and their leader, he sent Marius Statilius with a Lucanian troop of horse under his command to reconnoitre.

Riding up to the gates and bidding the rest remain outside the lines, Marius and two others entered the intrenchments, and after carefully surveying every point, brought back word that there was certainly some hidden danger; that the fires that had been left were on the side of the camp nearest to the Romans, the tents were open and everything of value was left perfectly accessible; that he had even seen silver strewn at random in some places along the paths, as if to invite plunder. What was calculated to restrain the soldiers from their greed of gain, only inflamed them. A shout arose that if the signal were not given they would go without their generals; but there was a general forthcoming, for Varro immediately gave the signal to start. Paulus, whose only wish was for delay, heard that the auguries of the sacred chicken did not sanction an advance, and bade the fact be communicated to Varro just as he was marching out of the camp-gates. Varro was greatly vexed, but the recent disaster of Flaminius and the famous defeat of the consul Claudius in the first Punic war, had impressed religious fears upon his mind. I may almost say that Heaven itself that day postponed rather than averted the doom that was hanging over the Romans. It so happened that while the consul was bidding the soldiers retire into the camp and they were refusing to obey him, two slave attendants, one belonging to a trooper from Formiæ and the other to a trooper from Sidicinum, who had been captured among the foragers by the Numidians when Servilius and Atilius were consuls, that day escaped to their old masters. They were brought to the consuls and told them that the whole army of Hannibal lay in ambush behind the hills. Their opportune arrival restored the authority of the consuls, though one consul, bent as he was on popularity, had by an unprincipled indulgence impaired the dignity of his office.

Hannibal saw that the Romans had indeed moved rashly, but were not yet venturing the last desperate risk, and he returned disappointed to his camp, now that his stratagem was discovered. He could not remain there many days, as provisions were running short. Every day new plans suggested themselves, not only among his troops, a miscellaneous crowd, the refuse of the world, but to the general himself. Murmurs that soon grew into loud clamours had been heard, demands for overdue pay, and complaints first of scanty rations and then of absolute famine; rumours had spread that the mercenaries, the Spaniards especially, had talked of changing sides, and Hannibal himself was said to have sometimes had thoughts of retreating into Gaul, hurrying away with his cavalry, but leaving all his infantry behind. Such being the plans discussed and such the temper prevailing in the camp, he resolved to move into Apulia, a warmer country, where the harvest would be earlier; the greater too his distance from the enemy, the more difficult would desertion be for the weaker spirits in his army. He started during the night, leaving, as he had done before, a few fires and tents to deceive the enemy. Fear of some such stratagem as before would, he hoped, keep them where they were. But when after a thorough exploration of all the country beyond the camp, and on the other side of the hills, by Statilius, the Lucanian officer mentioned already, it was reported that the hostile army had been seen in the distance, the question of pursuit was at once debated. The two consuls adhered to their former opinions, but as nearly all voted with Varro, and no one, except the ex-consul Servilius, with Paulus, the judgment of the majority prevailed, and the army moved out, to make Cannæ, for so destiny would have it, famous forever for a great Roman defeat. Hannibal had pitched his camp near that village, so as not to face the wind called Vulturnus, which, blowing across plains parched with drought, carries with it clouds of dust. The arrangement was most convenient for the camp, and was afterward found to be of similar advantage when they marshalled their troops for battle. Their own faces were turned away and the wind did but blow on their backs, while the enemy with whom they were to fight was blinded by volumes of dust.

The consuls, after duly reconnoitring the roads, followed the Carthaginians till they reached Cannæ, where they had the enemy in sight. They then intrenched and fortified two camps, separating their forces by about the same distance as before at Gereonium. The river Aufidus, which flowed near both camps, furnished water to both armies, the soldiers approaching as they most conveniently could, not, however, without some skirmishing. From the smaller camp, which had been pitched on the farther side of the Aufidus, the Romans procured water with less difficulty, as the opposite bank was not held by any hostile force. Hannibal saw his hope accomplished, that the consuls would offer battle on ground made for the action of cavalry, in which arm he was invincible. He drew up his men, and sought to provoke his foe by throwing forward his Numidian troopers. Then the Roman camp was once more disturbed by mutiny among the troops and disagreement between the consuls. Paulus taunted Varro with the rashness of Sempronius and Flaminius; Varro reproached Paulus with copying Fabius, an example attractive to timid and indolent commanders, and called both gods and men to witness that it was no fault of his if Hannibal had now a prescriptive possession of Italy. "I," said he, "have my hands tied and held fast by my colleague. My soldiers, furious and eager to fight, are stripped of their swords and arms." Paulus declared that if any disaster befell the legions recklessly thrown and betrayed into battle without deliberation or forethought, he would share all their fortunes, while holding himself free from all blame. Let Varro look to it that they whose tongues were so ready and so bold, had hands equally vigorous in the day of battle.

While they thus wasted the time in disputing rather than in deliberating, Hannibal, who had kept his lines drawn up till late in the day, called back the rest of his troops into his camp, but sent forward the Numidian cavalry across the river to attack the water-parties from the smaller of the two Roman camps. Coming on with shouting and uproar they sent the undisciplined crowd flying before they had even reached the bank, and rode on till they came on an outpost stationed before the rampart and close to the very camp-gates. So scandalous did it seem that a Roman camp should be alarmed by some irregular auxiliaries that the only circumstance which hindered the Romans from immediately crossing the river and forming their line of battle was, that the supreme command that day rested with Paulus. But the next day Varro, without consulting his colleagues, gave the signal to engage, and drawing up his forces led them across the river. Paulus followed him; he could withhold his sanction from the movement, but not his support. The river crossed, they joined to their own the forces retained by them in the smaller camp, and then formed their lines. On the right wing (the one nearer to the river) they posted the Roman cavalry and next the infantry. On the extreme flank on the left wing were the allied cavalry, next the allied infantry, side by side with the Roman legions in the centre. Slingers and other light-armed auxiliaries made up the first line. Paulus commanded the right wing; Varro the left; Geminius Servilius had charge of the centre.

At dawn, Hannibal, sending in advance his slingers and light-armed troops, crossed the river, assigning each division its position as it crossed. His Gallic and Spanish cavalry he posted near the river bank on the left wing, facing the Roman horse; the right wing was assigned to the Numidian cavalry; the centre showed a strong force of infantry, having on either side the African troops, with the Gauls and Spaniards between them.

These Africans might have been taken for a Roman force; so largely were they equipped with weapons taken at Trebia, and yet more at Trasumennus. The Gauls and Spaniards had shields of very nearly the same shape, but their swords were widely different in size and form, the Gauls having them very long and pointless, while the Spaniards, who were accustomed to assail the enemy with thrusts rather than with blows, had them short, handy, and pointed. These nations had a specially terrible appearance, so gigantic was their stature and so strange their look. The Gauls were naked above the navel; the Spaniards wore tunics of linen bordered with purple, of a whiteness marvellously dazzling. The total number of the infantry who were that day ranged in line was forty thousand, that of the cavalry ten thousand. Hasdrubal commanded the left wing; Maharbal the right; Hannibal himself, with his brother Mago, was in the centre. The sun—whether the troops were purposely so placed, or whether it was by chance—fell very conveniently sideways on both armies, the Romans facing the south, the Carthaginians the north. The wind (called Vulturnus by the natives of those parts) blew straight against the Romans and whirled clouds of dust into their faces till they could see nothing.

With a loud shout the auxiliaries charged, the light troops thus beginning the battle. Next the Gallic and Spanish horse of the left wing encountered the right wing of the Romans. The fight was not at all like a cavalry engagement; they had to meet face to face; there was no room for manœuvring, shut in as they were by the river on one side and the lines of infantry on the other. Both sides pushed straight forward till, with their horses brought to a stand and crowded together in a mass, each man seized his antagonist and strove to drag him from his seat. The struggle now became mainly a struggle of infantry; but the conflict was rather fierce than protracted. The Roman cavalry were defeated and put to flight. Just before the encounter of the cavalry came to an end the fight between the infantry began. The two sides were equal in strength and courage, as long as the Gauls and Spaniards kept their ranks unbroken; at last the Romans, after long and repeated efforts, broke, by their wedge-shaped front and deep formation, the enemy's column, which, advanced as it was from the rest of the line, was shallow and therefore weak. Pursuing the broken and rapidly retreating foe, they made their way without a halt through the rout of panic-stricken fugitives till they reached, first, the centre of the line, and then, meeting with no check, the reserves of the African troops. These had been stationed on the wings which had been somewhat retired, while the centre, where the Gauls and Spaniards had been posted, was proportionately advanced. As that column fell back, the line became level; when they pushed their retreat, they made a hollow in the centre. The Africans now overlapped on either side, and as the Romans rushed heedlessly into the intervening space, they first outflanked them and then, extending their own formation, actually hemmed in their rear. Upon this the Romans, who had fought one battle to no purpose, quitted the Gauls and Spaniards, whose rear they had been slaughtering, and began a new conflict with the Africans, a conflict unfair, not only because they were shut in with foes all around them, but because they were wearied, while the enemy was fresh and vigorous.

On the left wing of the Romans the cavalry of the allies had been posted against the Numidians. Here, too, battle had been joined, though with little spirit for a time, the first movement being a Carthaginian stratagem. Nearly five hundred Numidians who, besides their usual armour and missiles had swords hidden under their cuirasses, rode out from their own line with their shields slung behind their backs as though they had been deserters, leaped in haste from their horses and threw their shields and javelins at the feet of the Romans. They were received into the centre of the line, taken to the extreme rear, and bidden to keep their place behind. While the battle spread from place to place, they remained motionless; but as soon as all eyes and thoughts were intent on the conflict, they seized the shields which lay scattered everywhere among the piles of dead, and fell on the Roman line from the rear. They wounded the backs and legs of the men, and, while they made a great slaughter, spread far greater panic and confusion. While there was terror and flight on the right, and in the centre an obstinate resistance, though with little hope, Hasdrubal, who was in command in this quarter, withdrew the Numidians from the centre, seeing that they fought with but little spirit, and having sent them in all directions to pursue the enemy, re-enforced with the Spanish and Gallic cavalry the African troops, wearied as they now were with slaughter rather than with fighting.

Paulus was on the other side of the field. He had been seriously wounded at the very beginning of the battle by a bullet from a sling, but yet he repeatedly encountered Hannibal with a compact body of troops, and at several points restored the fortune of the day. He was protected by the Roman cavalry, who at last sent away their horses when the consul became too weak to manage his charger. Some one told Hannibal that the consul had ordered the cavalry to dismount. "He might better hand them over to me bound hand and foot," said he. The horsemen fought on foot as men were likely to fight, when, the victory of the enemy being beyond all doubt, the vanquished preferred dying where they stood to flight, and the victors, furious with those who delayed their triumph, slaughtered the foes whom they could not move. Move them, however, they did—that is, a few survivors, exhausted with wounds and fatigue. All were then scattered, and such as were able sought to recover their horses and fly. Cn. Lentulus, as he galloped by, saw the consul sitting on a stone and covered with blood. "Lucius Æmilius," he cried, "the one man whom Heaven must regard as guiltless of this day's calamity, take this horse while you have some strength left, and I am here to be with you, to lift you to the saddle, and to defend you. Do not make this defeat yet sadder by a consul's death. There are weeping and sorrow enough without this." The consul replied: "'Tis a brave thought of thine, Cn. Cornelius; but waste not the few moments you have for escaping from the enemy in fruitless pity. My public message to the senators is that they must fortify Rome and make its garrison as strong as may be before the victorious enemy arrives. My private message to Quintus Fabius is that Lucius Æmilius remembered his teaching in life and death. As for me, let me breathe my last among my slaughtered soldiers. I would not again leave my counsulship to answer for my life, nor would I stand up to accuse my colleague, and by accusing another protect my own innocence."

While they thus talked together, they were overtaken, first by a crowd of Roman fugitives and then by the enemy. These last buried the consul under a shower of javelins, not knowing who he was. Lentulus galloped off in the confusion. The Romans now fled wildly in every direction. Seven thousand men escaped into the smaller, ten thousand into the larger camp, ten thousand more into the village of Cannæ itself. These last were immediately surrounded by Carthalo and the cavalry, for no fortification protected the place. The other consul, who, whether by chance or of set purpose, had not joined any large body of fugitives, fled with about five hundred horsemen to Venusia. Forty-five thousand five hundred infantry, two thousand seven hundred cavalry, and almost as many more citizens and allies are said to have fallen. Among these were the quæstors of both consuls, Lucius Atilius and Furius Bibaculus, twenty-nine tribunes of the soldiers, not a few ex-consuls, ex-prætors, and ex-ædiles (among them Cn. Servilius and Marcus Minucius, who the year before had been the master of the horse, and consul some years before that), eighty who were either actual senators or had filled such offices as made them eligible for the senate, and who had volunteered to serve in the legions. In this battle three thousand infantry and one thousand five hundred cavalry are said to have been taken prisoners.

Such was the battle of Cannæ, as famous as the disaster at the Allia, and though less serious in its consequences, thanks to the inaction of the enemy, yet in loss of men still more ruinous and disgraceful. The flight at the Allia lost the city but saved the army; at Cannæ the consul who fled was followed by barely fifty men; with the consul who perished, perished nearly the whole army.

The two camps held a defenceless crowd with no one to command them. The occupants of the larger camp sent a messenger to their neighbours, suggesting that they should come over to them, while night still kept the enemy wrapped in the profound sleep that would follow battle and the joyous banquets of conquerors; they might then unite in one body and retreat to Canusium. Some wholly scorned the proposal. "Why," said they, "do not the men who send for us come themselves, being just as well able to effect the junction as we? The fact is that the whole space between is crowded with the enemy, and they had sooner expose the persons of others to this deadly peril than their own."

Others did not so much disapprove of the proposal as want courage to execute it. Then cried Publius Sempronius Tudilanus, a tribune of the soldiers: "Would you sooner be taken prisoners by this rapacious and cruel enemy, and have a price put on your heads and your value determined by inquiries as to whether you are Roman citizens or Latin allies, while others are winning honours out of the miseries and insults you endure? You would not suffer it if you are fellow-countrymen of the consul, Lucius Æmilius, who chose to die with honour rather than live with disgrace, and of all those gallant citizens who lie in heaps about him. Before day comes upon us, before larger forces of the enemy intercept our way, let us charge through this disorderly and undisciplined foe that clamours at our gates. Courage and the sword can force their way even through the densest enemy. Your column can as easily scatter this loose disorganized array as if it opposed no resistance. Come, then, with me, all you who wish yourselves and the commonwealth to be in safety." Saying this, he drew his sword, formed a column, and passed through the midst of the enemy. Seeing that the Numidians aimed at their right sides, which were exposed, they changed their shields to their right arms, and escaped to the number of six hundred into the greater camp, and then, having been joined by another considerable force, immediately made their way to Canusium without loss. This action among the conquered came more from the impulse which natural courage or accident supplied than from any concerted plan or any officer's generalship.

Round the victorious Hannibal crowded his officers with congratulations and entreaties that now that this mighty war was finished he should take what remained of that day and the following night for rest, and give the same to his wearied soldiers. Maharbal, the general of his cavalry, thought that there should be no pause. "Nay," he cried, "that you may know what has been achieved by this victory, you shall hold a conqueror's feast within five days in the Capitol. Pursue them; I will go before you with my cavalry, and they shall know that you are come before they know you are coming." Hannibal felt that his success was too great for him to be able to realize it at the moment. "He commended," he said, "Maharbal's zeal, but he must take time to deliberate." Maharbal replied: "Well, the gods do not give all gifts to one man. Hannibal, you know how to conquer; not how to use a conquest." That day's delay is believed to have saved Rome and its empire.

The next day, at daybreak, they issued forth to collect the spoil and to gaze upon a scene of slaughter, at which even a foe must have shuddered. Many thousands of the Roman dead lay there, foot-soldiers and horsemen as chance had thrown them together in the battle or the flight. Some were cut down by the foe as they rose covered with blood from the field of death, revived by the cold of the morning which had closed their wounds. Some, who were discovered lying alive, but with the sinews of thighs and knees divided, bared their necks and throats and begged the foe to shed what blood yet remained to them. Others were found with their heads buried in holes in the earth, and it was evident that they had made these holes for themselves, had heaped up the soil on their faces, and so suffocated themselves. Of all sights the most striking was a Numidian who lay with a dead Roman upon him; he was alive, but his ears and nose were mangled, for with hands that were powerless to grasp a weapon, the man's rage had turned to madness, and he had breathed his last while he tore his enemy with his teeth.

Till a late hour of the day Hannibal was gathering in the spoils. This done, he marched to attack the smaller camp. His first act was to throw up an earthwork, and so shut them off from the river. But the whole force, so worn out were they with toil and sleeplessness and even wounds, surrendered sooner than he had expected. It was agreed that they should give up their horses and arms, should pay for every Roman citizen three hundred "chariot" pieces, for every ally two hundred, for every slave one hundred, and that, this ransom discharged, they should depart with one garment apiece. They admitted the enemy into their camp, and were all put under arrest, the citizens and allies being kept separate. During the delay thus caused, all who had strength and courage sufficient—that is, about four thousand infantry and two hundred cavalry—escaped from the greater camp and sought refuge, some marching in column, others by twos and threes, across country, a way quite as safe, into Canusium. The camp was surrendered by the timid and disabled remainder on the same terms as the other. The booty secured was immense, and the whole of it was handed over to the troops, except the horses, the prisoners, and any silver that was found. Most of this was in the trappings of the horses; for of plate for the table they used very little, at least when on service. Hannibal then ordered that the bodies of his own dead should be brought together for burial. It is said that there were as many as eight thousand, all men of tried valour. Some writers say that the body of the Roman consul was also found after search and buried.

Bibliography

Grant, Michael, *The Ancient Historians*. London, 1970.
Laistner, M. L. W. *The Greater Roman Historians*. Berkeley, 1947.
Luce, T. J. *Livy, The Composition of His History*. Princeton, 1977.
Syme, Ronald. "History and Rome." *In Tacitus*. 2 vols. Oxford, 1958.
Syme, Ronald. *The Roman Revolution*. Oxford, 1952.
Walsh, P. G. *Livy: His Historical Aims and Methods*. Cambridge, 1966.

CHAPTER 5

Cornelius Tacitus

The Annals of Imperial Rome

(c. A.D. 117)

Cornelius Tacitus (c. A.D. 56–120) is an ancient historian whose work has an almost modern ring. His theme that the terrifying reigns of the Roman emperors who succeeded Augustus must be remembered and condemned and his stark description of the dark years from A.D. 14 to 96 seemed especially relevant to the great modern critic, Lionel Trilling, in 1942. As the United States faced the brutal regimes of Adolf Hitler and Benito Mussolini in World War II, Trilling wrote that Americans had never before then given a sympathetic reading to Tacitus' terrors, because "until recently, our political experience gave us no ground to understand what he was talking about." And perhaps the Cold War politics of our own day—at home as well as abroad—continue to invite us back to Tacitus' Rome.

Tacitus was born about A.D. 56 or 57 to a family in Rome's provincial aristocracy, perhaps in Southern France or Northern Italy. Unlike Livy, he became a public official, serving as a consul at Rome itself, probably commanding a Roman legion, and finishing his career as governor of a province in Asia Minor. Thus, when we read his accounts of politics and military affairs, we sense that he is writing from a wider experience than Livy. Three whole works and parts of two others have survived: *Agricola* (c. A.D. 98), a biography of his father-in-law; *Germania* (c. A.D. 98), a portrait of the German tribes north of the Alps; *Dialogue on Orators* (c. A.D. 102), which reveals Tacitus' interest in public declamation of history and literature; *The Histories* (c. A.D. 109), covering imperial politics from A.D. 69 to 96; and *The Annals* (c. A.D. 117), going back to the years from A.D. 14 to 68.

The Annals is Tacitus' masterpiece. He wrote it during the reign of Trajan (A.D. 98–117), a time of relief from the brutalities—which Tacitus had witnessed and survived—of Trajan's predecessors, especially Domitian (A.D. 81–96). His account is, of course, decidedly "senatorial" as he chronicles year by year the capricious willfulness and murder in Roman political society since the end of the Republic and the passing of the Senate's authority. His history, therefore, continues what one might call the ethical tradition of historical writing that had also defined the work of the ancient Hebrews and Greeks.

Two excerpts from the *Annals* are given below: the murder of Emperor Claudius by Agrippina, Nero's mother, to clear the throne for her son instead of Brittanicus, Claudius' son; and an account of Emperor Nero's excesses, including the infamous burning of Rome in A.D. 64.

Tacitus' sentences are shorter than Livy's and his style more dramatic. "In his hands," notes one scholar, Dennis Glew, "language is a weapon: sometimes a sharp pointed stiletto, at other times a slow-acting poison. But he is always poignant and eloquent." Tacitus keeps himself out of his story, seeming only to call the reader's attention to conjectures and versions of events known among contemporaries. Yet he leaves no doubt as to his own choices among them. He admits, for example, that the burning of Rome may have been an accident, but the structure of his account juxtaposes Nero's debaucheries with the conflagration. Tacitus details lust and the public celebration of lust and then writes, "A disaster followed. . . ." The emperor blamed the fire on the Christians, but Tacitus, though he had no liking for Christianity, discounts the charge implicitly by raising it only at the end of his account and only because Nero makes it, as an afterthought.

U NDER THIS GREAT BURDEN of anxiety, (Claudius) had an attack of ill-ness, and went to Sinuessa to recruit his strength with its balmy climate and salubrious waters. Thereupon, Agrippina, who had long decided on the crime and eagerly grasped at the opportunity thus offered, and did not lack instruments, deliberated on the nature of the poison to be used. The deed would be betrayed by one that was sudden and instantaneous, while if she chose a slow and lingering poison, there was a fear that Claudius, when near his end, might, on detecting the treachery, return to his love for his son. She decided on some rare compound which might derange his mind and delay death. A person skilled in such matters was selected, Locusta by name, who had lately been condemned for poisoning, and had long been retained as one of the tools of despotism. By this woman's art the poison was prepared, and it was to be administered by an eunuch, Halotus, who was accustomed to bring in and taste the dishes.

All the circumstances were subsequently so well known, that writers

From *Annals of Tacitus*, translated by Alfred John Church and William Jackson Brodribb (London: Macmillan and Co., 1895), 282–84, 374–82.

of the time have declared that the poison was infused into some mushrooms, a favourite delicacy, and its effect not at the instant perceived, from the emperor's lethargic, or intoxicated condition. His bowels too were relieved, and this seemed to have saved him. Agrippina was thoroughly dismayed. Fearing the worst, and defying the immediate obloquy of the deed, she availed herself of the complicity of Xenophon, the physician, which she had already secured. Under pretence of helping the emperor's efforts to vomit, this man, it is supposed, introduced into his throat a feather smeared with some rapid poison; for he knew that the greatest crimes are perilous in their inception, but well rewarded after their consummation.

Meanwhile the Senate was summoned, and prayers rehearsed by the consuls and priests for the emperor's recovery, though the lifeless body was being wrapped in blankets with warm applications, while all was being arranged to establish Nero on the throne. At first Agrippina, seemingly overwhelmed by grief and seeking comfort, clasped Britannicus in her embraces, called him the very image of his father, and hindered him by every possible device from leaving the chamber. She also detained his sisters, Antonia and Octavia, closed every approach to the palace with a military guard, and repeatedly gave out that the emperor's health was better, so that the soldiers might be encouraged to hope, and that the fortunate moment foretold by the astrologers might arrive.

At last, at noon on the 13th of October, the gates of the palace were suddenly thrown open, and Nero, accompanied by Burrus, went forth to the cohort which was on guard after military custom. There, at the suggestion of the commanding officer, he was hailed with joyful shouts, and set on a litter. Some, it is said, hesitated, and looked round and asked where Britannicus was; then, when there was no one to lead a resistance, they yielded to what was offered them. Nero was conveyed into the camp, and having first spoken suitably to the occasion and promised a donative after the example of his father's bounty, he was unanimously greeted as emperor. The decrees of the Senate followed the voice of the soldiers, and there was no hesitation in the provinces. Divine honours were decreed to Claudius, and his funeral rites were solemnized on the same scale as those of Augustus; for Agrippina strove to emulate the magnificence of her great-grandmother, Livia. But his will was not publicly read, as the preference of the stepson to the son might provoke a sense of wrong and angry feeling in the popular mind.

· ·

In the year of the consulship of Caius Læcanius and Marcus Licinius a yet keener impulse urged Nero to show himself frequently on the public

stage. Hitherto he had sung in private houses or gardens, during the Juve-
nile games, but these he now despised, as being but little frequented, and
on too small a scale for so fine a voice. As, however, he did not venture to
make a beginning at Rome, he chose Neapolis, because it was a Greek
city. From this as his starting-point he might cross into Achaia, and there,
winning the well-known and sacred garlands of antiquity, evoke, with increased fame, the enthusiasm of the citizens. Accordingly, a rabble of the
townsfolk was brought together, with those whom the excitement of such
an event had attracted from the neighbouring towns and colonies, and
such as followed in the emperor's train to pay him honour or for various
objects. All these, with some companies of soldiers, filled the theatre at
Neapolis.

There an incident occurred, which many thought unlucky, though to
the emperor it seemed due to the providence of auspicious deities. The
people who had been present, had quitted the theatre, and the empty
building then fell in without harm to anyone. Thereupon Nero in an elaborate ode thanked the gods, celebrating the good luck which attended the
late downfall, and as he was on his way to cross the sea of Hadria, he
rested awhile at Beneventum, where a crowded gladiatorial show was being exhibited by Vatinius. The man was one of the most conspicuously
infamous sights in the imperial court, bred, as he had been, in a shoemak-
er's shop, of a deformed person and vulgar wit, originally introduced as a
butt. After a time he grew so powerful by accusing all the best men, that in
influence, wealth, and ability to injure, he was pre-eminent even in that
bad company.

While Nero was frequently visiting the show, even amid his pleasures
there was no cessation to his crimes. For during the very same period Torquatus Silanus was forced to die, because over and above his illustrious
rank as one of the Junian family he claimed to be the great-grandson of
Augustus. Accusers were ordered to charge him with prodigality in lav-
ishing gifts, and with having no hope but in revolution. They said further
that he had nobles about him for his letters, books, and accounts, titles all
and rehearsals of supreme power. Then the most intimate of his freedmen
were put in chains and torn from him, till, knowing the doom which im-
pended, Torquatus divided the arteries in his arms. A speech from Nero
followed, as usual, which stated that though he was guilty and with good
reason distrusted his defence, he would yet have lived, had he awaited the
clemency of the judge.

Soon afterwards, giving up Achaia for the present (his reasons were
not certainly known), he returned to Rome, there dwelling in his secret
imaginations on the provinces of the east, especially Egypt. Then having
declared in a public proclamation that his absence would not be long and
that all things in the State would remain unchanged and prosperous, he

visited the temple of the Capitol for advice about his departure. There he adored the gods; then he entered also the temple of Vesta, and there feeling a sudden trembling throughout his limbs, either from terror inspired by the deity or because, from the remembrance of his crimes, he was never free from fear, he relinquished his purpose, repeatedly saying that all his plans were of less account than his love of his country. "He had seen the sad countenances of the citizens, he heard their secret complainings at the prospect of his entering on so long a journey, when they could not bear so much as his brief excursions, accustomed as they were to cheer themselves under mischances by the sight of the emperor. Hence, as in private relationships the closest ties were the strongest, so the people of Rome had the most powerful claims and must be obeyed in their wish to retain him."

These and the like sentiments suited the people, who craved amusement, and feared, always their chief anxiety, scarcity of corn, should he be absent. The Senate and leading citizens were in doubt whether to regard him as more terrible at a distance or among them. After a while, as is the way with great terrors, they thought what happened the worst alternative.

Nero, to win credit for himself of enjoying nothing so much as the capital, prepared banquets in the public places, and used the whole city, so to say, as his private house. Of these entertainments the most famous for their notorious profligacy were those furnished by Tigellinus, which I will describe as an illustration, that I may not have again and again to narrate similar extravagance. He had a raft constructed on Agrippa's lake, put the guests on board and set it in motion by other vessels towing it. These vessels glittered with gold and ivory; the crews were arranged according to age and experience in vice. Birds and beasts had been procured from remote countries, and sea monsters from the ocean. On the margin of the lake were set up brothels crowded with noble ladies, and on the opposite bank were seen naked prostitutes with obscene gestures and movements. As darkness approached, all the adjacent grove and surrounding buildings resounded with song, and shone brilliantly with lights. Nero, who polluted himself by every lawful or lawless indulgence, had not omitted a single abomination which could heighten his depravity, till a few days afterwards he stooped to marry himself to one of that filthy herd, by name Pythagoras, with all the forms of regular wedlock. The bridal veil was put over the emperor; people saw the witnesses of the ceremony, the wedding dower, the couch and the nuptial torches; everything in a word was plainly visible, which, even when a woman weds darkness hides.

A disaster followed, whether accidental or treacherously contrived by the emperor, is uncertain, as authors have given both accounts, worse, however, and more dreadful than any which have ever happened to this city by the violence of fire. It had its beginning in that part of the circus which adjoins the Palatine and Cælian hills, where, amid the shops containing inflammable wares, the conflagration both broke out and instantly became so fierce and so rapid from the wind that it seized in its grasp the entire length of the circus. For here there were no houses fenced in by solid masonry, or temples surrounded by walls, or any other obstacle to interpose delay. The blaze in its fury ran first through the level portions of the city, then rising to the hills, while it again devastated every place below them, it outstripped all preventive measures; so rapid was the mischief and so completely at its mercy the city, with those narrow winding passages and irregular streets, which characterised old Rome. Added to this were the wailings of terror-stricken women, the feebleness of age, the helpless inexperience of childhood, the crowds who sought to save themselves or others, dragging out the infirm or waiting for them, and by their hurry in the one case, by their delay in the other, aggravating the confusion. Often, while they looked behind them, they were intercepted by flames on their side or in their face. Or if they reached a refuge close at hand, when this too was seized by the fire, they found that, even places, which they had imagined to be remote, were involved in the same calamity. At last, doubting what they should avoid or whither betake themselves, they crowded the streets or flung themselves down in the fields, while some who had lost their all, even their very daily bread, and others out of love for their kinsfolk, whom they had been unable to rescue, perished, though escape was open to them. And no one dared to stop the mischief, because of incessant menaces from a number of persons who forbade the extinguishing of the flames, because again others openly hurled brands, and kept shouting that there was one who gave them authority, either seeking to plunder more freely, or obeying orders.

Nero at this time was at Antium, and did not return to Rome until the fire approached his house, which he had built to connect the palace with the gardens of Mæcenas. It could not, however, be stopped from devouring the palace, the house, and everything around it. However, to relieve the people, driven out homeless as they were, he threw open to them the Campus Martius and the public buildings of Agrippa, and even his own gardens, and raised temporary structures to receive the destitute multitude. Supplies of food were brought up from Ostia and the neighbouring towns, and the price of corn was reduced to three sesterces a peck. These acts, though popular, produced no effect, since a rumour had gone forth everywhere that, at the very time when the city was in flames, the emperor appeared on a private stage and sang of the destruction of Troy, comparing present misfortunes with the calamities of antiquity.

At last, after five days, an end was put to the conflagration at the foot of the Esquiline hill, by the destruction of all buildings on a vast space, so that the violence of the fire was met by clear ground and an open sky. But before people had laid aside their fears, the flames returned, with no less fury this second time, and especially in the spacious districts of the city. Consequently, though there was less loss of life, the temples of the gods, and the porticoes which were devoted to enjoyment, fell in a yet more widespread ruin. And to this conflagration there attached the greater infamy because it broke out on the Æmilian property of Tigellinus, and it seemed that Nero was aiming at the glory of founding a new city and calling it by his name. Rome, indeed, is divided into fourteen districts, four of which remained uninjured, three were levelled to the ground, while in the other seven were left only a few shattered, half-burnt relics of houses.

It would not be easy to enter into a computation of the private mansions, the blocks of tenements, and of the temples, which were lost. Those with the oldest ceremonial, as that dedicated by Servius Tullius to Luna, the great altar and shrine raised by the Arcadian Evander to the visibly appearing Hercules, the temple of Jupiter the Stayer, which was vowed by Romulus, Numa's royal palace, and the sanctuary of Vesta, with the tutelary deities of the Roman people, were burnt. So too were the riches acquired by our many victories, various beauties of Greek art, then again the ancient and genuine historical monuments of men of genius, and, notwithstanding the striking splendour of the restored city, old men will remember many things which could not be replaced. Some persons observed that the beginning of this conflagration was on the 19th of July, the day on which the Senones captured and fired Rome. Others have pushed a curious inquiry so far as to reduce the interval between these two conflagrations into equal numbers of years, months, and days.

Nero meanwhile availed himself of his country's desolation, and erected a mansion in which the jewels and gold, long familiar objects, quite vulgarised by our extravagance, were not so marvellous as the fields and lakes, with woods on one side to resemble a wilderness, and, on the other, open spaces and extensive views. The directors and contrivers of the work were Severus and Celer, who had the genius and the audacity to attempt by art even what nature had refused, and to fool away an emperor's resources. They had actually undertaken to sink a navigable canal from the lake Avernus to the mouths of the Tiber along a barren shore or through the face of hills, where one meets with no moisture which could supply water, except the Pomptine marshes. The rest of the country is broken rock and perfectly dry. Even if it could be cut through, the labour would be intolerable, and there would be no adequate result. Nero, however, with his love of the impossible, endeavoured to dig through the nearest hills to Avernus, and there still remain the traces of his disappointed hope.

Of Rome meanwhile, so much as was left unoccupied by his mansion, was not built up, as it had been after its burning by the Gauls, without any regularity or in any fashion, but with rows of streets according to measurement, with broad thoroughfares, with a restriction on the height of houses, with open spaces, and the further addition of colonnades, as a protection to the frontage of the blocks of tenements. These colonnades Nero promised to erect at his own expense, and to hand over the open spaces, when cleared of the debris, to the ground landlords. He also offered rewards proportioned to each person's position and property, and prescribed a period within which they were to obtain them on the completion of so many houses or blocks of building. He fixed on the marshes of Ostia for the reception of the rubbish, and arranged that the ships which had brought up corn by the Tiber, should sail down the river with cargoes of this rubbish. The buildings themselves, to a certain height, were to be solidly constructed, without wooden beams, of stone from Gabii or Alba, that material being impervious to fire. And to provide that the water which individual license had illegally appropriated, might flow in greater abundance in several places for the public use, officers were appointed, and everyone was to have in the open court the means of stopping a fire. Every building, too, was to be enclosed by its own proper wall, not by one common to others. These changes which were liked for their utility, also added beauty to the new city. Some, however, thought that its old arrangement had been more conducive to health, inasmuch as the narrow streets with the elevation of the roofs were not equally penetrated by the sun's heat, while now the open space, unsheltered by any shade, was scorched by a fiercer glow.

Such indeed were the precautions of human wisdom. The next thing was to seek means of propitiating the gods, and recourse was had to the Sibylline books, by the direction of which prayers were offered to Vulcanus, Ceres, and Proserpina. Juno, too, was entreated by the matrons, first, in the Capitol, then on the nearest part of the coast, whence water was procured to sprinkle the fane and image of the goddess. And there were sacred banquets and nightly vigils celebrated by married women. But all human efforts, all the lavish gifts of the emperor, and the propitiations of the gods, did not banish the sinister belief that the conflagration was the result of an order. Consequently, to get rid of the report, Nero fastened the guilt and inflicted the most exquisite tortures on a class hated for their abominations, called Christians by the populace. Christus, from whom the name had its origin, suffered the extreme penalty during the reign of Tiberius at the hands of one of our procurators, Pontius Pilatus, and a most mischievous superstition, thus checked for the moment, again broke out not only in Jadæa, the first source of the evil, but even in Rome, where all things hideous and shameful from every part of the world find their centre and become popular. Accordingly, an arrest was first made of all who pleaded guilty; then, upon their information, an immense multitude was convicted, not so much of the crime of firing the city, as of hatred against mankind. Mockery of every sort was added to their deaths. Covered with the skins of beasts, they were torn by dogs and perished, or were nailed to crosses, or were doomed to the flames and burnt, to serve as a nightly illumination, when daylight had expired.

Nero offered his gardens for the spectacle, and was exhibiting a show in the circus, while he mingled with the people in the dress of a charioteer or stood aloft on a car. Hence, even for criminals who deserved extreme and exemplary punishment, there arose a feeling of compassion; for it was not, as it seemed, for the public good, but to glut one man's cruelty that they were being destroyed.

Meanwhile Italy was thoroughly exhausted by contributions of money, the provinces were ruined, as also the allied nations and the free states, as they were called. Even the gods fell victims to the plunder; for the temples in Rome were despoiled and the gold carried off, which, for a triumph or a vow, the Roman people in every age had consecrated in their prosperity or their alarm. Throughout Asia and Achaia not only votive gifts, but the images of deities were seized, Acratus and Secundus Carinas having been sent into those provinces. The first was a freedman ready for any wickedness; the latter, as far as speech went, was thoroughly trained in Greek learning, but he had not imbued his heart with sound principles. Seneca, it was said, to avert from himself the obloquy of sacrilege, begged for the seclusion of a remote rural retreat, and, when it was refused, feigning ill health, as though he had a nervous ailment, would not quit his chamber. According to some writers, poison was prepared for him at Nero's command by his own freedman, whose name was Cleonicus. This Seneca avoided through the freedman's disclosure, or his own apprehension, while he used to support life on the very simple diet of wild fruits, with water from a running stream when thirst prompted.

During the same time some gladiators in the town of Præneste, who attempted to break loose, were put down by a military guard stationed on the spot to watch them, and the people, ever desirous and yet fearful of change, began at once to talk of Spartacus, and of bygone calamities. Soon afterwards, tidings of a naval disaster was received, but not from war, for never had there been so profound a peace. Nero, however, had ordered the fleet to return to Campania on a fixed day, without making any allowance for the dangers of the sea. Consequently the pilots, in spite of the fury of the waves, started from Formiæ, and while they were struggling to double the promontory of Misenum, they were dashed by a violent south-west wind on the shores of Cumæ, and lost, in all directions, a number of their triremes with some smaller vessels.

At the close of the year people talked much about prodigies, presaging impending evils. Never were lightning flashes more frequent, and a comet too appeared, for which Nero always made propitiation with noble blood. Human and other births with two heads were exposed to public view, or were discovered in those sacrifices in which it is usual to immolate victims in a pregnant condition. And in the district of Placentia, close to the road, a calf was born with its head attached to its leg. Then followed an explanation of the diviners, that another head was preparing for the world, which however would be neither mighty nor hidden, as its growth had been checked in the womb, and it had been born by the wayside.

Bibliography

Auerbach, Erich. *Mimesis, The Representation of Reality in Western Literature.* Translated by Willard R. Trask. Princeton, 1953. Pp. 33–40.

Grant, Michael. *The Ancient Historians.* London, 1970.

Laistner, M. L. W. *The Greater Roman Historians.* Berkeley, 1947.

Mendell, Clarence W. *Tacitus: The Man and His Work.* New Haven, 1957.

Syme, Ronald. *Tacitus.* 2 vols. Oxford, 1958.

Trilling, Lionel. "Tacitus Now." In *The Liberal Imagination, Essays on Literature and Society.* New York, 1950.

Walker, Bessie. *The Annals of Tacitus: A Study in the Writing of History.* Manchester, 1960.

CHAPTER 6

Venerable Bede

The Ecclesiastical History of the English People

(A.D. 731)

The world changed dramatically in the centuries following Tacitus and the Roman condemnation of Christianity. By the fourth century, Christianity became the religion of the emperors themselves, and the See of St. Peter at Rome governed a church that was spreading to the furthest extent of the empire, including Britain. Then, in the fifth century, the Roman Empire disintegrated, its constituent parts increasingly dominated by native cultures and shifting local polities. By the year 673, when the great historian Bede (673–735) was born, the Roman presence in Britain was but a memory already two and a half centuries old. Yet generations of Christian missionaries had kept the church alive in Britain to represent the growing spiritual empire still centered at Rome.

Christianity's hold was fragile. Bede's *Ecclesiastical History* tells of pagan kings who embraced and then repudiated Christianity almost overnight, and a major theme in his narrative is the running dispute between continental and Celtic Christians over the correct observance of Easter and the legitimacy of the church hierarchy. In the face of these threats, Bede's narrative takes on a sense of urgency befitting a defense of the faith.

Bede's upbringing prepared him for the defense. "Being born in the territory of that monastery," he writes at one point, referring to Jarrow on the coast of the North Sea,

> [I] was given, at seven years of age, to be educated by the most reverend Abbot Benedict, and afterwards by Ceolfrid; and spending all the remaining time of my life in that monastery, I wholly applied myself to the study of Scripture, and amidst the observance of regular discipline, and the daily care of singing in the church, I always took delight in learning, teaching and writing.

He rarely travelled outside Jarrow and seems best informed on the history of his native Northumbria. Yet his work has a broad scope, partly because churchmen who did travel supplied him with essential documents and observations from places as distant as Rome. Indeed, Bede's practice of stating his sources and copying documents verbatim makes him unique among early medieval historians. (It was in the nature of Bede's cosmology, however, to accept miracles as legitimate explanations for earthly events.)

The *Ecclesiastical History* covers Roman Britain, the coming of the Anglo-Saxons in the fifth century, and the emergence of the Heptarchy, or Seven Kingdoms of Essex, Wessex, Sussex, Kent, East Anglia, Mercia, and Northumbria. But these secular events have value only in their interaction with the English church and its missionaries. Bede's account of King Edwin's reign in Northumbria (625–633) is typical. His evocation of Edwin's personal history and character as the king contemplates conversion to Christianity is striking, and the oft-quoted metaphor of the sparrow in a banquet hall, which Edwin's counselor uses to portray the mystery of life and the afterlife, is poignant. Look, too, for Bede's awareness that however much history is in God's hands, the reconstruction of history depends upon earthly historical sources, the documents, memories, and relics that are the bare survivals of the past. Finally, Bede's chronology (which is *our* chronology)—the dating of events by year from the birth of Christ—is new. He conceived the practice and popularized it as his works spread throughout Europe.

A T THIS TIME THE NATION of the Northumbrians, that is, the nation of the Angles that live on the north side of the river Humber, with their king, Edwin, received the faith through the preaching of Paulinus, abovementioned. This Edwin, as a reward of his receiving the faith, and as an earnest of his share in the heavenly kingdom, received an increase of that which he enjoyed on earth, for he reduced under his dominion all the borders of Britain that were provinces either of the aforesaid nation, or of the Britons, a thing which no British king had ever done before; and he in like manner subjected to the English the Mevanian islands, as has been said above. The first whereof, which is to the southward, is the largest in extent, and most fruitful, containing nine hundred and sixty families, according to the English computation; the other above three hundred.

The occasion of this nation's embracing the faith was, their aforesaid king, being allied to the kings of Kent, having taken to wife Ethelberga, otherwise called Tate, daughter to King Ethelbert. He having by his ambassadors asked her in marriage of her brother Eadbald, who then reigned in Kent, was answered, "That it was not lawful to marry a Christian virgin

From Bede, *The Ecclesiastical History of the English Nation*, translated by John Stevens, edited by J. A. Giles, in *The Venerable Bede's Ecclesiastical History of England*; also *The Anglo-Saxon Chronicle* (London and New York: George Bell and Sons, 1892), 82–101, 106–7.

to a pagan husband, lest the faith and the mysteries of the heavenly King should be profaned by her cohabiting with a king that was altogether a stranger to the worship of the true God." This answer being brought to Edwin by his messengers, he promised in no manner to act in opposition to the Christian faith, which the virgin professed; but would give leave to her, and all that went with her, men or women, priests or ministers, to follow their faith and worship after the custom of the Christians. Nor did he deny, but that he would embrace the same religion, if, being examined by wise persons, it should be found more holy and more worthy of God.

Hereupon the virgin was promised, and sent to Edwin, and pursuant to what had been agreed on, Paulinus, a man beloved of God, was ordained bishop, to go with her, and by daily exhortations, and celebrating the heavenly mysteries, to confirm her and her company, lest they should be corrupted by the company of the pagans. Paulinus was ordained bishop by the Archbishop Justus, on the 21st day of July, in the year of our Lord 625, and so he came to King Edwin with the aforesaid virgin as a companion of their union in the flesh. But his mind was wholly bent upon reducing the nation to which he was sent to the knowledge of truth; according to the words of the apostle, "To espouse her to one husband, that he might present her as a chaste virgin to Christ." Being come into that province, he laboured much, not only to retain those that went with him, by the help of God, that they should not revolt from the faith, but, if he could, to convert some of the pagans to a state of grace by his preaching. But, as the apostle says, though he laboured long in the word, "The god of this world blinded the minds of them that believed not, lest the light of the glorious Gospel of Christ should shine unto them."

The next year there came into the province a certain assassin, called Eumer, sent by the king of the West-Saxons, whose name was Cuichelm, in hopes at once to deprive King Edwin of his kingdom and his life. He had a two-edged dagger, dipped in poison, to the end, that if the wound were not sufficient to kill the king, it might be performed by the venom. He came to the king on the first day of Easter, at the river Derwent, where then stood the regal city, and being admitted as if to deliver a message from his master, whilst he was in an artful manner delivering his pretended embassy, he started on a sudden, and drawing the dagger from under his garment, assaulted the king; which Lilla, the king's beloved minister, observing, having no buckler at hand to secure the king from death, interposed his own body to receive the stroke; but the wretch struck so home, that he wounded the king through the knight's body. Being then attacked on all sides with swords, he in that confusion also slew another soldier, whose name was Forthhere.

On that same holy night of Easter Sunday, the queen had brought forth to the king a daughter, called Eanfled. The king, in the presence of

Bishop Paulinus, gave thanks to his gods for the birth of his daughter; and the bishop, on the other hand, returned thanks to Christ, and endeavoured to persuade the king, that by his prayers to him he had obtained that the queen should bring forth the child in safety, and without much pain. The king, delighted with his words, promised, that in case God would grant him life and victory over the king by whom the assassin had been sent, he would cast off his idols, and serve Christ; and as a pledge that he would perform his promise, he delivered up that same daughter to Paulinus, to be consecrated to Christ. She was the first baptized of the nation of the Northumbrians, on Whitsunday, with twelve others of her family. At that time, the king, being recovered of the wound which he had received, marched with his army against the nation of the West-Saxons; and having begun the war, either slew or subdued all those that he had been informed had conspired to murder him. Returning thus victorious into his own country, he would not immediately and unadvisedly embrace the mysteries of the Christian faith, though he no longer worshipped idols, ever since he made the promise that he would serve Christ; but thought fit first at leisure to be instructed, by the venerable Paulinus, in the knowledge of faith, and to confer with such as he knew to be the wisest of his prime men, to advise what they thought was fittest to be done in that case. And being a man of extraordinary sagacity, he often sat alone by himself a long time, silent as to his tongue, but deliberating in his heart how he should proceed, and which religion he should adhere to.

At this time he received letters from Pope Boniface [IV.] exhorting him to embrace the faith, which were as follows:—
COPY OF THE LETTER OF THE HOLY AND APOSTOLIC POPE OF THE CHURCH OF ROME, BONIFACE, TO THE GLORIOUS EDWIN, KING OF THE ENGLISH.

"*To the illustrious Edwin, king of the English, Bishop Boniface, the servant of the servants of God.* Although the power of the Supreme Deity cannot be expressed by human speech, as consisting in its own greatness, and in invisible and unsearchable eternity, so that no sharpness of wit can comprehend or express it; yet in regard that the goodness of God, to give some notion of itself, having opened the doors of the heart, has mercifully, by secret inspiration, infused into the minds of men such things as he is willing shall be declared concerning himself, we have thought fit to extend our priestly care to make known to you the fulness of the Christian faith; to the end that, informing you of the Gospel of Christ, which our Saviour commanded should be preached to all nations, they might offer to you the cup of life and salvation.

"Thus the goodness of the Supreme Majesty, which, by the word of his command, made and created all things, the heaven, the earth, the sea, and all that is in them, disposing the order by which they should subsist, hath, with the counsel of his co-eternal Word, and the unity of the Holy

Spirit, formed man after his own likeness, out of the slime of the earth; and granted him such supereminent prerogative, as to place him above all others; so that, observing the command which was given him, his continuance should be to eternity. This God,—Father, Son, and Holy Ghost, which is an undivided Trinity,—mankind, from the east unto the west, by confession of faith to the saving of their souls, do worship and adore, as the Creator of all things, and their own Maker; to whom also the heights of empire, and the powers of the world, are subject, because the bestowal of all kingdoms is granted by his disposition. It hath pleased him, therefore, of his great mercy, and for the greater benefit of all his creatures, by his Holy Spirit wonderfully to kindle the cold hearts also of the nations seated at the extremities of the earth in the knowledge of himself.

"For we suppose your excellency has, from the country lying so near, fully understood what the clemency of our Redeemer has effected in the enlightening of our glorious son, King Eadbald, and the nations under his subjection; we therefore trust, with assured confidence of celestial hope, that his wonderful gift will be also conferred on you; since we understand that your illustrious consort, which is known to be a part of your body, is illuminated with the reward of eternity, through the regeneration of holy baptism. We have, therefore, taken care by these presents, with all possible affection, to exhort your illustrious selves, that, abhorring idols and their worship, and contemning the follies of temples, and the deceitful flatteries of auguries, you believe in God the Father Almighty, and his Son Jesus Christ, and the Holy Ghost, to the end that, being discharged from the bonds of captivity to the Devil, by believing you may, through the co-operating power of the holy and undivided Trinity, be partaker of the eternal life.

"How great guilt they lie under, who adhere to the pernicious superstitions and worship of idolatry, appears by the examples of the perdition of those whom they worship. Wherefore it is said of them by the Psalmist, 'All the gods of the Gentiles are devils, but the Lord made the heavens.' And again, they have eyes and do not see, they have ears and do not hear, they have noses and do not smell, they have hands and do not feel, they have feet and do not walk. Therefore they are like those that confide in them.' For how can they have any power to yield assistance, that are made for you out of corruptible matter, by the hands of your inferiors and subjects, to wit, on whom you have by human art bestowed an inanimate similitude of members? Who, unless they be moved by you, will not be able to walk; but, like a stone fixed in one place, being so formed, and having no understanding, but absorbed in insensibility, have no power of doing harm or good. We cannot, therefore, upon mature deliberation, find out how you come to be so deceived as to follow and worship those gods, to whom you yourselves have given the likeness of a body.

"It behoves you, therefore, by taking upon you the sign of the holy cross, by which the human race is redeemed, to root out of your hearts all those arts and cunning of the Devil, who is ever jealous of the works of the divine goodness, and to lay hold and break in pieces those which you have hitherto made your material gods. For the very destruction and abolition of these, which could never receive life or sense from their makers, may plainly demonstrate to you how worthless they were which you till then had worshipped, when you yourselves, who have received life from the Lord, are certainly better than they, as Almighty God has appointed you to be descended, after many ages and through many generations, from the first man whom he formed. Draw near, then, to the knowledge of Him who created you, who breathed the breath of life into you, who sent his only-begotten Son for your redemption, to cleanse you from original sin, that being delivered from the power of the Devil's wickedness, He might bestow on you a heavenly reward.

"Hear the words of the preachers, and the Gospel of God, which they declare to you, to the end that, believing, as has been said, in God the Father Almighty, and in Jesus Christ his Son, and the Holy Ghost, and the indivisible Trinity, having put to flight the sensualities of devils, and driven from you the suggestions of the venomous and deceitful enemy, and being born again by water and the Holy Ghost, you may, through his assistance and bounty, dwell in the brightness of eternal glory with Him in whom you shall believe. We have, moreover, sent you the blessing of your protector, the blessed Peter, prince of the apostles, that is, a shirt, with one gold ornament, and one garment of Ancyra, which we pray your highness to accept with the same goodwill as it is friendly intended by us."

The same pope also wrote to King Edwin's consort, Ethelberga, to this effect:—

THE COPY OF THE LETTER OF THE MOST BLESSED AND APOSTOLIC BONIFACE, POPE OF THE CITY OF ROME, TO ETHELBERGA, KING EDWIN'S QUEEN.

"*To the illustrious lady his daughter, Queen Ethelberga, Boniface, bishop, servant of the servants of God:* The goodness of our Redeemer has with much providence offered the means of salvation to the human race, which he rescued, by the shedding of his precious blood, from the bonds of captivity to the Devil: so that making his name known in divers ways to the Gentiles, they might acknowledge their Creator by embracing the mystery of the Christian faith, which thing, the mystical purification of your regeneration plainly shows to have been bestowed upon the mind of your highness by God's bounty. Our mind, therefore, has been much rejoiced in the benefit of our Lord's goodness, for that he has vouchsafed, in your conversion, to kindle a spark of the orthodox religion, by which he might the more easily inflame in his love the understanding, not only of your glorious consort, but also of all the nation that is subject to you.

"For we have been informed by those, who came to acquaint us with the laudable conversion of our illustrious son, King Eadbald, that your highness, also, having received the wonderful sacrament of the Christian faith, continually excels in the performance of works pious and acceptable to God. That you likewise carefully refrain from the worship of idols, and the deceits of temples and auguries, and having changed your devotion, are so wholly taken up with the love of your Redeemer, as never to cease lending your assistance for the propagation of the Christian faith. And our fatherly charity having earnestly inquired concerning your illustrious husband, we were given to understand, that he still served abominable idols, and would not yield obedience or give ear to the voice of the preachers. This occasioned us no small grief, for that part of your body still remained a stranger to the knowledge of the supreme and undivided Trinity. Whereupon we, in our fatherly care, did not delay to admonish your Christian highness, exhorting you, that, with the help of the Divine inspiration, you will not defer to do that which, both in season and out of season, is required of us; that with the co-operating power of our Lord and Saviour Jesus Christ, your husband also may be added to the number of Christians; to the end that you may thereby enjoy the rights of marriage in the bond of a holy and unblemished union. For it is written, 'They two shall be in one flesh.' How can it be said, that there is unity between you, if he continues a stranger to the brightness of your faith, by the interposition of dark and detestable error?

"Wherefore, applying yourself continually to prayer, do not cease to beg of the Divine Mercy the benefit of his illumination; to the end, that those whom the union of carnal affection has made in a manner but one body, may, after death, continue in perpetual union, by the bond of faith. Persist, therefore, illustrious daughter, and to the utmost of your power endeavour to soften the hardness of his heart by insinuating the Divine precepts; making him sensible how noble the mystery is which you have received by believing, and how wonderful is the reward which, by the new birth, you have merited to obtain. Inflame the coldness of his heart by the knowledge of the Holy Ghost, that by the abolition of the cold and pernicious worship of paganism, the heat of Divine faith may enlighten his understanding through your frequent exhortations; that the testimony of the holy Scripture may appear the more conspicuous, fulfilled by you, 'The unbelieving husband shall be saved by the believing wife.' For to this effect you have obtained the mercy of our Lord's goodness, that you may return with increase the fruit of faith, and the benefits entrusted in your hands; for through the assistance of His mercy we do not cease with frequent prayers to beg that you may be able to perform the same.

"Having premised thus much, in pursuance of the duty of our fatherly affection, we exhort you, that when the opportunity of a bearer shall offer, you will as soon as possible acquaint us with the success which the

Divine Power shall grant by your means in the conversion of your consort, and of the nation subject to you; to the end, that our solicitude, which earnestly expects what appertains to the salvation of you and yours, may, by hearing from you, be set at rest; and that we, discerning more fully the brightness of the Divine propitiation diffused in you, may with a joyful confession abundantly return due thanks to God, the Giver of all good things, and to St. Peter, the prince of apostles. We have, moreover, sent you the blessing of your protector, St. Peter, the prince of the apostles, that is, a silver looking-glass, and a gilt ivory comb, which we entreat your glory will receive with the same kind affection as it is known to be sent by us."

Thus the aforesaid Pope Boniface wrote for the salvation of King Edwin and his nation. But a heavenly vision, which the Divine Mercy was pleased once to reveal to this king, when he was in banishment at the court of Redwald, king of the Angles, was of no little use in urging him to embrace and understand the doctrines of salvation. Paulinus, therefore, perceiving that it was a very difficult task to incline the king's lofty mind to the humility of the way of salvation, and to embrace the mystery of the cross of life, and at the same time using both exhortation with men, and prayer to God, for his and his subjects' salvation; at length, as we may suppose, it was shown him in spirit what was the vision that had been formerly revealed to the king. Nor did he lose any time, but immediately admonished the king to perform the vow which he made, when he received the oracle, promising to put the same in execution, if he was delivered from the trouble he was at that time under, and should be advanced to the throne.

The vision was this. When Ethelfrid, his predecessor, was persecuting him, he for many years wandered in a private manner through several places and kingdoms, and at last came to Redwald, beseeching him to give him protection against the snares of his powerful persecutor. Redwald willingly admitted him, and promised to perform what he requested. But when Ethelfrid understood that he had appeared in that province, and that he and his companions were hospitably entertained by Redwald, he sent messengers to offer that king a great sum of money to murder him, but without effect. He sent a second and a third time, bidding more and more each time, and threatening to make war on him if he refused. Redwald, either terrified by his threats, or gained by his gifts, complied with his request, and promised either to kill Edwin, or to deliver him up to the ambassadors. This being observed by a trusty friend of his, he went into his chamber, where he was going to bed, for it was the first hour of the night; and calling him out, discovered what the king had promised to do with him, adding, "If, therefore, you think fit, I will this very hour conduct you out of this province, and lead you to a place where neither Redwald nor Ethelfrid shall ever find you." He an-

swered, "I thank you for your good will, yet I cannot do what you propose, or be guilty of breaking the compact I have made with so great a
king, when he has done me no harm, nor offered me any injury; but, on
the contrary, if I must die, let it rather be by his hand than by that of any
meaner person. For whither shall I now fly, when I have for so many
years been a vagabond through all the provinces of Britain, to escape the
hands of my enemies?" His friend being gone, Edwin remained alone
without, and sitting with a heavy heart before the palace, began to be
overwhelmed with many thoughts, not knowing what to do, or which
way to turn himself.

When he had remained a long time in silence, brooding over his misfortunes in anguish of mind, he, on a sudden, in the dead of night, saw
approaching a person, whose face and habit were equally strange, at
which unexpected sight he was not a little frightened. The stranger coming close up, saluted him, and asked him, "Why he sat there alone and
melancholy on a stone at that time, when all others were taking their
rest, and were fast asleep?" Edwin, in his turn, asked, "What it was to
him, whether he spent the night within doors or abroad?" The stranger,
in reply, said, "Do not think that I am ignorant of the cause of your grief,
your watching, and sitting alone without. For I know who you are, and
why you grieve, and the evils which you fear will fall upon you. But tell
me, what reward you will give the man that shall deliver you out of this
anguish, and persuade Redwald neither to do you any harm himself, nor
to deliver you up to be murdered by your enemies." Edwin replied,
"That he would give that person all that he was able for so singular a
favour." The other further added, "What if I also assure you, that you
shall overcome your enemies, and surpass in power, not only all your
own progenitors, but even all that have reigned before you over the English nation?" Edwin, encouraged by these questions, did not hesitate to
promise that he would make a suitable return to him who should so
highly oblige him. Then said the other, "But if he who foretells so much
good as is to befall you, can also give you better advice for your life and
salvation than any of your progenitors or kindred ever heard of, do you
consent to submit to him, and to follow his wholesome counsel?" Edwin
did not hesitate to promise that he would in all things follow the directions of that man who should deliver him from so many calamities, and
raise him to a throne.

Having received this answer, the person that talked to him laid his
hand on his head saying, "When this sign shall be given you, remember
this present discourse that has passed between us, and do not delay the
performance of what you now promise." Having uttered these words, he is
said to have immediately vanished, that the king might understand it was
not a man, but a spirit, that had appeared to him.

Whilst the royal youth still sat there alone, glad of the comfort he had received, but seriously considering who he was, or whence he came, that had so talked to him, his above-mentioned friend came to him, and saluting him with a pleasant countenance, "Rise," said he, "go in and compose yourself to sleep without fear; for the king's resolution is altered, and he designs to do you no harm, but rather to perform the promise which he made you; for when he had privately acquainted the queen with his intention of doing what I told you before, she dissuaded him from it, declaring it was unworthy of so great a king to sell his good friend in such distress for gold, and to sacrifice his honour, which is more valuable than all other ornaments, for the lucre of money." In short, the king did as he was advised, and not only refused to deliver up the banished man to his enemy's messengers, but assisted him to recover his kingdom. For as soon as the ambassadors were returned home, he raised a mighty army to make war on Ethelfrid; who, meeting him with much inferior forces, (for Redwald had not given him time to gather all his power,) was slain on the borders of the kingdom of Mercia, on the east side of the river that is called Idle. In this battle, Redwald's son, called Regnhere, was killed; and thus Edwin, pursuant to the oracle he had received, not only escaped the danger from the king his enemy, but, by his death, succeeded him in the throne.

King Edwin, therefore, delaying to receive the word of God at the preaching of Paulinus, and using for some time as has been said, to sit several hours alone, and seriously to ponder with himself what he was to do, and what religion he was to follow, the man of God came to him, laid his right hand on his head, and asked, "Whether he knew that sign?" The king in a trembling condition, was ready to fall down at his feet, but he raised him up, and in a familiar manner said to him, "Behold, by the help of God you have escaped the hands of the enemies whom you feared. Behold you have of his gift obtained the kingdom which you desired. Take heed not to delay that which you promised to perform; embrace the faith, and keep the precepts of Him who, delivering you from temporal adversity, has raised you to the honour of a temporal kingdom; and if, from this time forward, you shall be obedient to his will, which through me he signifies to you, he will not only deliver you from the everlasting torments of the wicked, but also make you partaker with him of his eternal kingdom in heaven."

The king, hearing these words, answered, that he was both willing and bound to receive the faith which he taught; but that he would confer about it with his principal friends and counsellors, to the end that if they also were of his opinion, they might all together be cleansed in Christ the Fountain of Life. Paulinus consenting, the king did as he said; for, holding a council with the wise men, he asked of every one in particular what he thought of the new doctrine, and the new worship that was preached? To which the chief of his own priests, Coifi, immediately answered, "O king, consider what this is which is now preached to us; for I verily declare to you, that the religion which we have hitherto professed has, as far as I can learn, no virtue in it. For none of your people has applied himself more diligently to the worship of our gods than I; and yet there are many who receive greater favours from you, and are more preferred than I, and are more prosperous in all their undertakings. Now if the gods were good for any thing, they would rather forward me, who have been more careful to serve them. It remains, therefore, that if upon examination you find those new doctrines, which are now preached to us, better and more efficacious, we immediately receive them without any delay."

Another of the king's chief men, approving of his words and exhortations, presently added: "The present life of man, O king, seems to me, in comparison of that time which is unknown to us, like to the swift flight of a sparrow through the room wherein you sit at supper in winter, with your commanders and ministers, and a good fire in the midst, whilst the storms of rain and snow prevail abroad; the sparrow, I say, flying in at one door, and immediately out at another, whilst he is within, is safe from the wintry storm; but after a short space of fair weather, he immediately vanishes out of your sight, into the dark winter from which he had emerged. So this life of man appears for a short space, but of what went before, or what is to follow, we are utterly ignorant. If, therefore, this new doctrine contains something more certain, it seems justly to deserve to be followed." The other elders and king's counsellors, by Divine inspiration, spoke to the same effect.

But Coifi added, that he wished more attentively to hear Paulinus discourse concerning the God whom he preached; which he having by the king's command performed, Coifi, hearing his words, cried out, "I have long since been sensible that there was nothing in that which we worshipped; because the more diligently I sought after truth in that worship, the less I found it. But now I freely confess, that such truth evidently appears in this preaching as can confer on us the gifts of life, of salvation, and of eternal happiness. For which reason I advise, O king, that we instantly abjure and set fire to those temples and altars which we have consecrated without reaping any benefit from them." In short, the king publicly gave his licence to Paulinus to preach the Gospel, and renouncing idolatry, declared that he received the faith of Christ: and when he inquired of the high priest who should first profane the altars and temples of their idols, with the enclosures that were about them, he answered, "I; for who can more properly than myself destroy those things which I worshipped through ignorance, for an example to all others, through the wisdom which has been given me by the true God?" Then immediately, in contempt of his former superstitions, he desired the king to furnish him with arms and a stallion; and mounting the same, he set out to destroy the idols; for it was not lawful before for the high priest either to carry arms, or to ride on any but a mare. Having, therefore, girt a sword about him, with a spear in his hand, he mounted the king's stallion and proceeded to the idols. The multitude, beholding it, concluded he was distracted; but he lost no time, for as soon as he drew near the temple he profaned the same, casting into it the spear which he held; and rejoicing in the knowledge of the worship of the true God, he commanded his companions to destroy the temple, with all its enclosures, by fire. This place where the idols were is still shown, not far from York, to the eastward, beyond the river Derwent, and is now called Godmundingham, where the high priest, by the inspiration of the true God, profaned and destroyed the altars which he had himself consecrated.

King Edwin, therefore, with all the nobility of the nation, and a large number of the common sort, received the faith, and the washing of regeneration, in the eleventh year of his reign, which is the year of the incarnation of our Lord 627, and about one hundred and eighty after the coming of the English into Britain. He was baptized at York, on the holy day of Easter, being the 12th of April, in the church of St. Peter the Apostle, which he himself had built of timber, whilst he was catechising and instructing in order to receive baptism. In that city also he appointed the see of the bishopric of his instructor and bishop, Paulinus. But as soon as he was baptized, he took care, by the direction of the same Paulinus, to build in the same place a larger and nobler church of stone, in the midst whereof that same oratory which he had first erected should be enclosed. Having, therefore, laid the foundation, he began to build the church square, encompassing the former oratory. But before the whole was raised to the proper height, the wicked assassination of the king left that work to be finished by Oswald his successor. Paulinus, for the space of six years from that time, that is, till the end of the reign of that king, by his consent and favour, preached the word of God in that country, and all that were preordained to eternal life believed and were baptized. Among whom were Osfrid and Eadfrid, King Edwin's sons, who were both born to him, whilst he was in banishment, of Quenberga, the daughter of Cearl, king of the Mercians.

Afterwards other children of his by Queen Ethelberga were baptized, viz. Ethelhun and his daughter Etheldrith, and another, Wuscfrea, a son; the first two of which were snatched out of this life whilst they were still in their white garments, and buried in the church at York. Iffi, the son of Osfrid, was also baptized, and many more noble and illustrious persons. So great was then the fervour of the faith, as is reported, and the desire of the washing of salvation among the nation of the Northumbrians, that Paulinus at a certain time coming with the king and queen to the royal country-seat, which is called Adgefrin, stayed there with them thirty-six days, fully occupied in catechising and baptizing; during which days, from morning till night, he did nothing else but instruct the people resorting from all villages and places, in Christ's saving word; and when instructed, he washed them with the water of absolution in the river Glen, which is close by. This town, under the following kings, was abandoned, and another was built instead of it, at the place called Melmin.

These things happened in the province of the Bernicians; but in that of the Deiri also, where he was wont often to be with the king, he baptized in the river Swale, which runs by the village of Cataract; for as yet oratories, or fonts, could not be made in the early infancy of the church in those parts. But he built a church in Campodonum, which afterwards the pagans, by whom King Edwin was slain, burnt, together with all the town. In the place of which the later kings built themselves a country-seat in the country called Loidis. But the altar, being of stone, escaped the fire and is still preserved in the monastery of the most reverend abbot and priest, Thridwulf, which is in Elmete wood.

Edwin was so zealous for the worship of truth, that he likewise persuaded Eorpwald, king of the East Saxons, and son of Redwald, to abandon his idolatrous superstitions, and with his whole province to receive the faith and sacraments of Christ. And indeed his father Redwald had long before been admitted to the sacrament of the Christian faith in Kent, but in vain; for on his return home, he was seduced by his wife and certain perverse teachers, and turned back from the sincerity of the faith; and thus his latter state was worse than the former; so that, like the ancient Samaritans, he seemed at the same time to serve Christ and the gods whom he had served before; and in the same temple he had an altar to sacrifice to Christ, and another small one to offer victims to devils; which temple, Aldwulf, king of that same province, who lived in our time, testifies had stood until his time, and that he had seen it when he was a boy. The aforesaid King Redwald was noble by birth, though ignoble in his actions, being the son of Tytilus, whose father was Uuffa, from whom the kings of the East Angles are called Uuffings.

Eorpwald was, not long after he had embraced the Christian faith, slain by one Richbert, a pagan; and from that time the province was under error for three years, till the crown came into the possession of Sigebert, brother to the same Eorpwald, a most Christian and learned man, who was banished, and went to live in France during his brother's life, and was there admitted to the sacraments of the faith, whereof he made it his business to cause all his province to partake as soon as he came to the throne. His exertions were much promoted by the Bishop Felix, who, coming to Honorius, the archbishop, from Burgundy, where he had been born and ordained, and having told him what he desired, he sent him to preach the word of life to the aforesaid nation of the Angles. Nor were his good wishes in vain; for the pious husbandman reaped therein a large harvest of believers, delivering all that province (according to the signification of his name, Felix) from long iniquity and infelicity, and bringing it to the faith and works of righteousness, and the gifts of everlasting happiness. He had the see of his bishopric appointed him in the city Dommoc, and having presided over the same province with pontifical authority seventeen years, he ended his days there in peace.

Paulinus also preached the word to the province of Lindsey, which is the first on the south side of the river Humber, stretching out as far as the sea; and he first converted the governor of the city of Lincoln, whose name was Blecca, with his whole family. He likewise built, in that city, a stone church of beautiful workmanship; the roof of which having either fallen through age, or been thrown down by enemies, the walls are still to be seen standing and every year some miraculous cures are wrought in that place, for the benefit of those who have faith to seek the same. In that church, Justus having departed to Christ, Paulinus consecrated Honorius bishop in his stead, as will be hereafter mentioned in its proper place. A certain abbot and priest of the monastery of Peartaneu, a man of singular veracity, whose name was Deda, in relation to the faith of this province told me that one of the oldest persons had informed him, that he himself had been baptized at noon-day, by the Bishop Paulinus, in the presence of King Edwin, with a great number of the people, in the river Trent, near the city, which in the English tongue is called Tiovulfingacestir; and he was also wont to describe the person of the same Paulinus, that he was tall of stature, a little stooping, his hair black, his visage meagre, his nose slender and aquiline, his aspect both venerable and majestic. He had also with him in the ministry, James, the deacon, a man of zeal and great fame in Christ's church, who lived even to our days.

It is reported that there was then such perfect peace in Britain, wheresoever the dominion of King Edwin extended, that, as is still proverbially said, a woman with her newborn babe might walk throughout the island, from sea to sea, without receiving any harm. That king took such care for the good of his nation, that in several places where he had seen clear springs near the highways, he caused stakes to be fixed, with brass dishes hanging at them, for the conveniency of travellers; nor durst any man touch them for any other purpose than that for which they were designed, either through the dread they had of the king, or for the affection which they bore him. His dignity was so great throughout his dominions, that his banners were not only borne before him in battle, but even in time of peace, when he rode about his cities, towns, or provinces, with his officers, the standard-bearer was wont to go before him. Also, when he walked along the streets, that sort of banner which the Romans call Tufa, and the English, Tuuf, was in like manner borne before him.

. . . .

Edwin reigned most gloriously seventeen years over the nations of the English and the Britons, six whereof, as has been said, he also was a servant in the kingdom of Christ. Cadwalla, king of the Britons, rebelled against him, being supported by Penda, a most warlike man of the royal race of the Mercians, and who from that time governed that nation twenty-two years with various success. A great battle being fought in the plain that is called Heathfield, Edwin was killed on the 12th of October, in the year of our Lord 633, being then forty-seven years of age, and all his army was either slain or dispersed. In the same war also, before him fell Osfrid, one of his sons, a warlike youth; Eanfrid, another of them, compelled by necessity, went over to King Penda, and was by him afterwards, in the reign of Oswald, slain, contrary to his oath. At this time a great slaughter was made in the church or nation of the Northumbrians; and the more so because one of the commanders, by whom it was made, was a pagan, and the other a barbarian, more cruel than a pagan; for Penda, with all the nation of the Mercians, was an idolater, and a stranger to the name of Christ; but Cadwalla, though he bore the name and professed himself a Christian, was so barbarous in his disposition and behaviour, that he neither spared the female sex, nor the innocent age of children, but with savage cruelty put them to tormenting deaths, ravaging all their country for a long time, and resolving to cut off all the race of the English within the borders of Britain. Nor did he pay any respect to the Christian religion which had newly taken root among them; it being to this day the custom of the Britons not to pay any respect to the faith and religion of the English, nor to correspond with them any more than with pagans. King Edwin's head was brought to York, and afterwards into the church of St. Peter the Apostle, which he had begun, but which his successor Oswald finished, as has been said before. It was deposited in the porch of St. Gregory, Pope, from whose disciples he had received the word of life.

The affairs of the Northumbrians being in confusion, by reason of this disaster, without any prospect of safety except in flight, Paulinus, taking with him Queen Ethelberga, whom he had before brought thither, returned into Kent by sea, and was honourably received by the Archbishop Honorius and King Eadbald. He came thither under the conduct of Bassus, a most valiant soldier of King Edwin, having with him Eanfleda, the daughter, and Wuscfrea, the son of Edwin, as also Iffi, the son of Osfrid, his son, whom afterwards the mother, for fear of Eadbald and Oswald, sent over into France to be bred up by King Dagobert, who was her friend; and there they both died in infancy, and were buried in the church with the honour due to royal children and to innocents of Christ. He also brought with him many rich goods of King Edwin, among

which were a large gold cross, and a golden chalice, dedicated to the use of
the altar, which are still preserved, and shown in the church of Canter-
bury.

Bibliography

Browne, G. F. *The Venerable Bede.* London, 1919.
Campbell, James. "Bede." In *Latin Historians,* edited by T. A. Dorey. London, 1966.
Gransden, Antonia. *Historical Writing in England, c550 to 1307.* Ithaca, 1974.
Henning, Robert W. *The Vision of History in Early Britain.* New York, 1966.
Laistner, M. L. W. *Thought and Letters in Western Europe, 500–900.* Ithaca, 1957.
Sherley-Price, Leo. Introduction to *A History of the English Church and People,* by
    Bede. Translation by Leo Sherley-Price. London, 1955.
Thompson, A. Hamilton, ed. *Bede, His Life, Times and Writings.* New York, 1966.

CHAPTER 7

Jean Froissart

Chronicles

(c.1369–1400)

Jean Froissart (c.1337–1410), the greatest historian of the late Middle Ages, wrote his account of the Hundred Years War six hundred years after Bede. The differences between them illustrate the changes in historical writing from the eighth century to the fourteenth. Bede wrote in Latin, the universal language of the church; Froissart wrote in the vernacular, in his case French. Bede defended the Catholic church and Christian ideals; Froissart celebrated the largely secular ideal of chivalry, the code of right conduct for the European aristocracy. Bede's writing is sparse and unselfconscious in its moments of literary grace; Froissart's prose is rich and expansive, the literary style of a practiced storyteller.

Froissart was born about 1337 to a merchant family at Valenciennes, which is a French city now but in Froissart's time was in the independent county of Hainault in the Netherlands. He accompanied Philippa of Hainault to England in 1361 when she married Edward III. While in her service as a clerk he was able to interview English military men concerning the war with France that had just been suspended—temporarily, as it turned out—after twenty-three years of hostilities. He also talked with French prisoners and prepared to write a history of the war, which resumed in 1367 and would eventually be known as the Hundred Years War.

On Queen Philippa's death in 1369, Froissart returned to the Continent and began writing his *Chronicles* under other patrons, most notably Guy de Blois. Some of his material came from an earlier account by Jean Le Bel, much from interviews during Froissart's own extensive travels, and some from his observations as the war continued, outlasting Froissart himself, who died about 1410.

The *Chronicles* is less valuable as a factual account of the Hundred Years War than for its portrayal of aristocratic life in the fourteenth century. One can take this view too far, of course, for much of what Froissart says is corroborated by other evidence. But he was often too willing to arrange and weigh his facts to make a good story. And because he was thoroughly wrapped up in the chivalric ideal, he missed almost entirely the large social and economic forces that, to modern historians, make the fourteenth century a turning point in Western civilization. Shifts in the economic base of political and military life and the first stirrings of nationalism pointed to the destruction of the very ideals Froissart pursued as his main theme.

The excerpts below illustrate two aspects of Froissart's chivalry. As you read his account of the Battle of Crécy (1346), note Froissart's eye for "great feats of arms," no matter whether they were those of English or French knights. Some scholars think the first part of the *Chronicles,* written under English patronage, is pro-English, while the remainder, composed under French patronage, is pro-French. But in the final analysis, Froissart admires the qualities of an aristocracy that transcends national cultures. In the well-turned morality tale of King Charles of Luxembourg and Lord Charles of Bohemia, the former represents honor and courage and the latter, cowardice and betrayal.

Froissart's account of the "Jacquerie" (1358), one of many bloody peasant revolts in the fourteenth century, shows him not the least interested in why the villeins rose. Instead, he focuses on their suppression by French *and* English knights acting in concert.

T HE KING OF ENGLAND, who had been informed that the king of France was following him in order to give him battle, said to his people: "Let us post ourselves here; for we will not go farther, before we have seen our enemies. I have good reason to wait for them on this spot; as I am now upon the lawful inheritance of my lady-mother, which was given her as her marriage-portion; and I am resolved to defend it against my adversary, Philippe de Valois."

On account of his not having more than an eighth part of the forces which the king of France had, his marshals fixed upon the most advantageous situation; and the army went and took possession of it. He then sent his scouts towards Abbeville, to learn if the king of France meant to take the field this Friday; but they returned, and said they saw no appearance of it; upon which, he dismissed his men to their quarters, with orders to be in readiness by times in the morning, and to assemble in the same place.

The king of France remained all Friday in Abbeville, waiting for more troops. He sent his marshals, the lord of St. Venant and lord Charles of Montmorency, out of Abbeville, to examine the country, and get some

From *Sir John Froissart's Chronicles of England, France, Spain and the Adjoining Countries from the Latter Part of the Reign of Edward II to the Coronation of Henry IV*, translated by Thomas Johnes, 12 vols. (London: Longman, Hurst, Rees and Orme, 1806), 2: 156–73; 387–94.

certain intelligence of the English. They returned, about vespers, with information that the English were encamped on the plain.

That night, the king of France entertained at supper, in Abbeville, all the princes and chief lords. There was much conversation relative to war; and the king intreated them, after supper, that they would always remain in friendship with each other; that they would be friends without jealousy, and courteous without pride. The king was still expecting the earl of Savoy, who ought to have been there with a thousand lances, as he had been well paid for them at Troyes in Champaign, three months in advance.

The king of England, as I have mentioned before, encamped this Friday in the plain; for he found the country abounding in provisions; but, if they should have failed, he had plenty in the carriages which attended on him. The army set about furbishing and repairing their armour; and the king gave a supper, that evening, to the earls and barons of his army, where they made good cheer. On their taking leave, the king remained alone, with the lords of his bed-chamber: he retired into his oratory, and, falling on his knees before the altar, prayed to God, that, if he should combat his enemies on the morrow, he might come off with honour. About midnight he went to his bed; and, rising early the next day, he and the prince of Wales heard mass, and communicated. The greater part of his army did the same, confessed, and made proper preparations.

After mass, the king ordered his men to arm themselves, and assemble on the ground he had before fixed on. He had inclosed a large park near a wood, on the rear of his army, in which he placed all his baggage-waggons and horses; and this park had but one entrance: his men at arms and archers remained on foot.

The king afterwards ordered, through his constable and his two marshals, that the army should be divided into three battalions. In the first, he placed the young prince of Wales, and with him the earls of Warwick and Oxford, sir Godfrey de Harcourt, the lord Reginald Cobham, lord Thomas Holland, lord Stafford, lord Mauley, the lord Delaware, sir John Chandos, lord Bartholomew Burgherst, lord Robert Neville, lord Thomas Clifford, the lord Bourchier, the lord Latimer, and many other knights and squires whom I cannot name. There might be, in this first division, about eight hundred men at arms, two thousand archers, and a thousand Welshmen. They advanced in regular order to their ground, each lord under his banner and pennon, and in the centre of his men.

In the second battalion were, the earl of Northampton, the earl of Arundel, the lords Roos, Willoughby, Basset, Saint-albans, sir Lewis Tufton, lord Multon, the lord Lascels, and many others; amounting, in the whole, to about eight hundred men at arms, and twelve hundred archers.

The third battalion was commanded by the king, and was composed of about seven hundred men at arms, and two thousand archers.

The king then mounted a small palfry, having a white wand in his hand, and attended by his two marshals on each side of him: he rode a foot's pace through all the ranks, encouraging and intreating the army, that they would guard his honour and defend his right. He spoke this so sweetly, and with such a cheerful countenance, that all who had been dispirited were directly comforted by seeing and hearing him.

When he had thus visited all the battalions, it was near ten o'clock: he retired to his own division, and ordered them all to eat heartily, and drink a glass after. They eat and drank at their ease; and, having packed up pots, barrels, &c. in the carts, they returned to their battalions, according to the marshals' orders, and seated themselves on the ground, placing their helmets and bows before them, that they might be the fresher when their enemies should arrive.

That same Saturday, the king of France rose betimes, and heard mass in the monastery of St. Peter's in Abbeville, where he was lodged: having ordered his army to do the same, he left that town after sun-rise. When he had marched about two leagues from Abbeville, and was approaching the enemy, he was advised to form his army in order of battle, and to let those on foot march forward, that they might not be trampled on by the horses. The king, upon this, sent off four knights, the lord Moyne of Bastleberg, the lord of Noyers, the lord of Beaujeu, and the lord of Aubigny, who rode so near to the English that they could clearly distinguish their position. The English plainly perceived they were come to reconnoitre them: however, they took no notice of it, but suffered them to return unmolested. When the king of France saw them coming back, he halted his army; and the knights, pushing through the crowds, came near the king, who said to them, 'My-lords, what news?' They looked at each other, without opening their mouths; for neither chose to speak first. At last, the king addressed himself to the lord Moyne, who was attached to the king of Bohemia, and had performed very many gallant deeds, so that he was esteemed one of the most valiant knights in Christendom. The lord Moyne said, 'Sir, I will speak, since it pleases you to order me, but under the correction of my companions. We have advanced far enough to reconnoitre your enemies. Know, then, that they are drawn up in three battalions, and are waiting for you. I would advise, for my part, (submitting, however, to better counsel,) that you halt your army here, and quartered them for the night; for before the rear shall come up, and the army be properly drawn out, it will be very late, your men will be tired and in disorder, whilst they will find your enemies fresh and properly arrayed. On the morrow, you may draw up your army more at your ease, and may reconnoitre at leisure on what part it will be most advantageous to begin the attack; for, be assured, they will wait for you.'

The king commanded that it should be so done: and the two marshals rode, one towards the front, and the other to the rear, crying out, 'Halt banners, in the name of God and St. Denis.' Those that were in the front halted; but those behind said they would not halt, until they were as forward as the front. When the front perceived the rear pressing on, they pushed forward; and neither the king nor the marshals could stop them, but they marched on without any order until they came in sight of their enemies. As soon as the foremost rank saw them, they fell back at once, in great disorder, which alarmed those in the rear, who thought they had been fighting. There was then space and room enough for them to have passed forward, had they been willing so to do: some did so, but others remained shy.

All the roads between Abbeville and Crecy were covered with common people, who, when they were come within three leagues of their enemies, drew their swords, bawling out, 'Kill, kill;' and with them were many great lords that were eager to make shew of their courage. There is no man, unless he had been present, that can imagine, or describe truly, the confusion of that day; especially the bad management and disorder of the French, whose troops were out of number. What I know, and shall relate in this book, I have learnt chiefly from the English, who had well observed the confusion they were in, and from those attached to sir John of Hainault, who was always near the person of the king of France.

The English, who were drawn up in three divisions, and seated on the ground, on seeing their enemies advance, rose undauntedly up, and fell into their ranks. That of the prince was the first to do so, whose archers were formed in the manner of a portcullis, or harrow, and the men at arms in the rear.

The earls of Northampton and Arundel, who commanded the second division, had posted themselves in good order on his wing, to assist and succour the prince, if necessary.

You must know, that these kings, dukes, earls, barons and lords of France, did not advance in any regular order, but one after the other, or any way most pleasing to themselves. As soon as the king of France came in sight of the English, his blood began to boil, and he cried out to his marshals, 'Order the Genoese forward, and begin the battle, in the name of God and St. Denis.'

There were about fifteen thousand Genoese crossbowmen; but they were quite fatigued, having marched on foot that day six leagues, completely armed, and with their cross-bows.

They told the constable, they were not in a fit condition to do any great things that day in battle. The earl of Alençon, hearing this, said, 'This is what one gets by employing such scoundrels, who fall off when there is any need for them.'

During this time, a heavy rain fell, accompanied by thunder and a very terrible eclipse of the sun; and before this rain a great flight of crows hovered in the air over all those battalions, making a loud noise. Shortly afterwards it cleared up, and the sun shone very bright; but the Frenchmen had it in their faces, and the English in their backs.

When the Genoese were somewhat in order, and approached the English, they set up a loud shout, in order to frighten them; but they remained quite still, and did not seem to attend to it. They then set up a second shout, and advanced a little forward; but the English never moved. They hooted a third time, advancing with their cross-bows presented, and began to shoot. The English archers then advanced one step forward, and shot their arrows with such force and quickness, that it seemed as if it snowed.

When the Genoese felt these arrows, which pierced their arms, heads, and through their armour, some of them cut the strings of their cross-bows, others flung them on the ground, and all turned about, and retreated, quite discomfited. The French had a large body of men at arms on horseback, richly dressed, to support the Genoese.

The king of France, seeing them thus fall back, cried out, 'Kill me those scoundrels; for they stop up our road, without any reason.' You would then have seen the above-mentioned men at arms lay about them, killing all they could of these runaways.

The English continued shooting as vigorously and quickly as before: some of their arrows fell among the horsemen, who were sumptuously equipped, and, killing and wounding many, made them caper and fall among the Genoese, so that they were in such confusion they could never rally again. In the English army there were some Cornish and Welshmen on foot, who had armed themselves with large knives: these, advancing through the ranks of the men at arms and archers, who made way for them, came upon the French when they were in this danger, and, falling upon earls, barons, knights and squires, slew many, at which the king of England was afterwards much exasperated.

The valiant king of Bohemia was slain there. He was called Charles of Luxembourg; for he was the son of the gallant king and emperor, Henry of Luxembourg: having heard the order of the battle, he inquired where his son, the lord Charles, was: his attendants answered, that they did not know, but believed he was fighting. The king said to them; 'Gentlemen, you are all my people, my friends and brethren at arms this day: therefore, as I am blind, I request of you to lead me so far into the engagement that I may strike one stroke with my sword.' The knights replied, they would directly lead him forward; and, in order that they might not lose him in the crowd, they fastened all the reins of their horses together, and put the king at their head, that he might gratify his wish, and advanced towards the enemy.

The lord Charles of Bohemia, who already signed his name as king of Germany, and bore the arms, had come in good order to the engagement; but when he perceived that it was likely to turn out against the French, he departed, and I do not well know what road he took.

The king, his father, had rode in among the enemy, and made good use of his sword; for he and his companions had fought most gallantly. They had advanced so far that they were all slain; and on the morrow they were found on the ground, with their horses all tied together.

The earl of Alençon advanced in regular order upon the English, to fight with them; as did the earl of Flanders, in another part. These two lords, with their detachments, coasting, as it were, the archers, came to the prince's battalion, where they fought valiantly for a length of time. The king of France was eager to march to the place where he saw their banners displayed, but there was a hedge of archers before him.

He had that day made a present of a handsome black horse to sir John of Hainault, who had mounted on it a knight of his, called sir John de Fusselles, that bore his banner: which horse ran off with him, and forced his way through the English army, and, when about to return, stumbled and fell into a ditch, and severely wounded him: he would have been dead, if his page had not followed him round the battalions, and found him unable to rise: he had not, however, any other hindrance than from his horse; for the English did not quit the ranks that day to make prisoners. The page alighted, and raised him up; but he did not return the way he came, as he would have found it difficult from the crowd.

This battle, which was fought on the Saturday between la Broyes and Crecy, was very murderous and cruel; and many gallant deeds of arms were performed, that were never known.

Towards evening, many knights and squires of the French had lost their masters: they wandered up and down the plain, attacking the English in small parties: they were soon destroyed; for the English had determined that day to give no quarter, or hear of ransom from any one.

Early in the day, some French, Germans and Savoyards had broken through the archers of the prince's battalion, and had engaged with the men at arms; upon which the second battalion came to his aid, and it was time, for otherwise he would have been hard pressed. The first division, seeing the danger they were in, sent a knight in great haste to the king of England, who was posted upon an eminence, near a windmill. On the knight's arrival, he said, 'Sir, the earl of Warwick, the lord Stafford, the lord Reginald Cobham, and the others who are about your son are vigorously attacked by the French; and they intreat that you would come to their assistance with your battalion, for, if their numbers should increase, they fear he will have too much to do.'

The king replied: 'Is my son dead, unhorsed, or so badly wounded that he cannot support himself?' 'Nothing of the sort, thank God,' re-joined the knight; 'but he is in so hot an engagement, that he has great need of your help.' The king answered, 'Now, sir Thomas, return back to those that sent you, and tell them from me, not to send again for me this day, or expect that I shall come, let what will happen, as long as my son has life; and say, that I command them to let the boy win his spurs; for I am determined, if it please God, that all the glory and honour of this day shall be given to him, and to those into whose care I have intrusted him.'

The knight returned to his lords, and related the king's answer, which mightily encouraged them, and made them repent they had ever sent such a message.

It is a certain fact, that sir Godfrey de Harcourt, who was in the prince's battalion, having been told by some of the English, that they had seen the banner of his brother engaged in the battle against him, was ex-ceedingly anxious to save him; but he was too late, for he was left dead on the field, and so was the earl of Aumarle his nephew.

On the other hand, the earls of Alençon and of Flanders were fighting lustily under their banners, and with their own people; but they could not resist the force of the English, and were there slain, as well as many other knights and squires that were attending on or ac-companying them.

The earl of Blois, nephew to the king of France, and the duke of Lor-raine his brother-in-law, with their troops, made a gallant defence; but they were surrounded by a troop of English and Welsh, and slain in spite of their prowess. The earl of St. Pol and the earl of Auxerre were also killed, as well as many others.

Late after vespers, the king of France had not more about him than sixty men, every one included. Sir John of Hainault, who was of the num-ber, had once remounted the king; for his horse had been killed under him by an arrow: he said to the king, 'Sir, retreat whilst you have an op-portunity, and do not expose yourself so simply: if you have lost this bat-tle, another time you will be the conqueror.' After he had said this, he took the bridle of the king's horse, and led him off by force; for he had before intreated of him to retire.

The king rode on, until he came to the castle of la Broyes, where he found the gates shut, for it was very dark. The king ordered the governor of it to be summoned: he came upon the battlements, and asked who it was that called at such an hour? The king answered, 'Open, open, gover-nor; it is the fortune of France.' The governor, hearing the king's voice, immediately descended, opened the gate, and let down the bridge. The king and his company entered the castle; but he had only with him five barons, sir John of Hainault, the lord Charles of Montmorency, the lord of Beaujeu, the lord of Aubigny, and the lord of Montfort.

The king would not bury himself in such a place as that, but, having taken some refreshments, set out again with his attendants about mid-night, and rode on, under the direction of guides who were well acquainted with the country, until, about daybreak, he came to Amiens, where he halted.

This Saturday the English never quitted their ranks in pursuit of any one, but remained on the field, guarding their position, and defending themselves against all who attacked them. The battle was ended at the hour of vespers.

When, on this Saturday night, the English heard no more hooting or shouting, nor any more crying out to particular lords, or their banners, they looked upon the field as their own, and their enemies as beaten.

They made great fires, and lighted torches because of the obscurity of the night. King Edward then came down from his post, who all that day had not put on his helmet, and, with his whole battalion, advanced to the prince of Wales, whom he embraced in his arms and kissed, and said, 'Sweet son, God give you good perseverance: you are my son, for most loyally have you acquitted yourself this day: you are worthy to be a sovereign.' The prince bowed down very low, and humbled himself, giving all honour to the king his father.

The English, during the night, made frequent thanksgivings to the Lord, for the happy issue of the day, and without rioting; for the king had forbidden all riot or noise.

On the Sunday morning, there was so great a fog that one could scarcely see the distance of half an acre. The king ordered a detachment from the army, under the command of the two marshals, consisting of about five hundred lances and two thousand archers, to make an excursion, and see if there were any bodies of French collected together.

The quota of troops, from Rouen and Beauvais, had, this Sunday morning, left Abbeville, and St. Ricquier in Ponthieu, to join the French army, and were ignorant of the defeat of the preceding evening: they met this detachment, and, thinking they must be French, hastened to join them.

As soon as the English found who they were, they fell upon them; and there was a sharp engagement; but the French soon turned their backs, and fled in great disorder. There were slain in this flight in the open fields, under hedges and bushes, upwards of seven thousand; and had it been clear weather, not one soul would have escaped.

A little time afterwards, this same party fell in with the archbishop of Rouen and the great prior of France, who were also ignorant of the discomfiture of the French; for they had been informed that the king was not to fight before Sunday. Here began a fresh battle; for those two lords were well attended by good men at arms: however, they could not withstand the English, but were almost all slain, with the two chiefs who commanded them; very few escaping.

In the course of the morning, the English found many Frenchmen who had lost their road on the Saturday, and had lain in the open fields, not knowing what was become of the king, or their own leaders. The English put to the sword all they met: and it has been assured to me for fact, that of foot soldiers, sent from the cities, towns and municipalities, there were slain, this Sunday morning, four times as many as in the battle of the Saturday.

This detachment, which had been sent to look after the French, returned as the king was coming from mass, and related to him all that they had seen and met with. After he had been assured by them that there was not any appearance of the French collecting another army, he sent to have the numbers and condition of the dead examined.

He ordered on this business, lord Reginald Cobham, lord Stafford, and three heralds to examine their arms, and two secretaries to write down the names. They took much pains to examine all the dead, and were the whole day in the field of battle, not returning but just as the king was sitting down to supper. They made to him a very circumstantial report of all they had observed, and said, they had found eighty banners, the bodies of eleven princes, twelve hundred knights, and about thirty thousand common men.

The English halted there that day, and on the Monday morning prepared to march off. The king ordered the bodies of the principal knights to be taken from the ground, and carried to the monastery of Montenay, which was hard by, there to be interred in consecrated ground. He had it proclaimed in the neighbourhood, that he should grant a truce for three days, in order that the dead might be buried. He then marched on, passing by Montreuil-sur-mer.

. . . .

Soon after the deliverance of the king of Navarre out of prison, a marvellous and great tribulation befel the kingdom of France, in Beauvoisis, Brie, upon the river Marne, in the Laonnois and in the neighbourhood of Soissons. Some of the inhabitants of the country towns assembled together in Beauvoisis, without any leader: they were not at first more than one hundred men. They said, that the nobles of the kingdom of France, knights and squires, were a disgrace to it, and that it would be a very meritorious act to destroy them all: to which proposition every one assented, as a truth, and added, shame befal him that should be the means of preventing the gentlemen from being wholly destroyed.

They then, without further council, collected themselves in a body, and with no other arms than the slaves shod with iron, which some had, and others with knives, marched to the house of a knight who lived near, and breaking it open, murdered the knight, his lady and all the children, both great and small: they then burnt the house.

After this, their second expedition was to the strong castle of another knight, which they took, and, having tied him to a stake, many of them violated his wife and daughter before his eyes: they then murdered the lady, her daughter and the other children, and last of all the knight himself, with much cruelty. They destroyed and burnt his castle.

They did the like to many castles and handsome houses; and, their numbers increased so much, that they were in a short time upwards of six thousand: wherever they went, they received additions, for all of their rank in life followed them, whilst every one else fled, carrying off with them their ladies, damsels and children ten or twenty leagues distant, where they thought they could place them in security, leaving their houses, with all their riches in them.

These wicked people, without leader and without arms, plundered and burnt all the houses they came to, murdered every gentleman, and violated every lady and damsel they could find. He who committed the most atrocious actions, and such as no human creature would have imagined, was the most applauded, and considered as the greatest man among them. I dare not write the horrible and inconceivable atrocities they committed on the persons of the ladies.

Among other infamous acts, they murdered a knight; and, having fastened him to a spit, roasted him before the eyes of his wife and his children, and, after ten or twelve had violated her, they forced her to eat some of her husband's flesh, and then knocked her brains out.

They had chosen a king among them, who came from Clermont in Beauvoisis: he was elected as the worst of the bad, and they denominated him James Goodman.

These wretches burnt and destroyed in the country of Beauvoisis, and at Corbie, Amiens and Montdidier, upwards of sixty good houses and strong castles. By the acts of such traitors in the country of Brie and thereabout, it behoved every lady, knight and squire, having the means of escape, to fly to Meaux, if they wished to preserve themselves from being insulted, and afterwards murdered. The duchess of Normandy, the duchess of Orleans, and many other ladies had adopted this course to save themselves from violation.

These cursed people thus supported themselves in the countries between Paris, Noyon and Soissons, and in all the territory of Coucy in the county of Valois. In the bishoprics of Noyons, Laon and Soissons, there were upwards of one hundred castles and good houses of knights and squires destroyed.

When the gentlemen of Beauvoisis, Corbie, Vermandois, and of the lands where these wretches were associated, saw to what lengths their madness had extended, they sent for succour to their friends in Flanders, Hainault and Bohemia: from which places numbers soon came, and united themselves with the gentlemen of the country.

They began therefore to kill and destroy these wretches wherever they met them, and hung them up by troops on the nearest trees. The king of Navarre even destroyed in one day, near Clermont in Beauvoisis, upwards of three thousand: but they were by this time so much increased in number, that had they been altogether, they would have amounted to more than one hundred thousand. When they were asked for what reason they acted so wickedly; they replied, they knew not, but they did so because they saw others do it; and they thought that by this means they should destroy all the nobles and gentlemen in the world.

At this period, the duke of Normandy, suspecting the king of Navarre, the provost of merchants and those of his faction, for they were always unanimous in their sentiments, set out from Paris, and went to the bridge at Charenton upon Marne, where he issued a special summons for the attendance of the crown vassals, and sent a defiance to the provost of merchants, and to all those who should support him.

The provost, being fearful he would return in the night-time to Paris (which was then uninclosed), collected as many workmen as possible from all parts, and employed them to make ditches quite round Paris. He also surrounded it by a wall with strong gates. For the space of one year, there were three hundred workmen daily employed; the expence of which was equal to maintaining an army. I must say, that to surround, with a sufficient defence, such a city as Paris, was an act of greater utility than any provost of merchants had ever done before; for otherwise it would have been plundered and destroyed several times by the different factions.

At the time these wicked men were overrunning the country, the earl of Foix and his cousin the captal of Buch were returning from a croisade in Prussia. They were informed on their entering France, of the distress the nobles were in; and they learnt at the city of Chalons, that the duchess of Normandy, the duchess of Orleans, and three hundred other ladies, under the protection of the duke of Orleans, were fled to Meaux on account of these disturbances.

The two knights resolved to go to the assistance of these ladies, and to reinforce them with all their might, notwithstanding the captal was attached to the English; but at that time there was a truce between the two kings. They might have in their company about sixty lances.

They were most cheerfully received, on their arrival at Meaux, by the ladies and damsels; for these Jacks and peasants of Brie had heard what number of ladies, married and unmarried, and young children of quality, were in Meaux: they had united themselves with those of Valois, and were on their road thither.

On the other hand, those of Paris had also been informed of the treasures Meaux contained, and had set out from that place in crowds: having met the others, they amounted together to nine thousand men: their forces were augmenting every step they advanced.

They came to the gates of the town, which the inhabitants opened to them, and allowed them to enter: they did so in such numbers that all the streets were quite filled, as far as the market-place, which is tolerably strong, but it required to be guarded, though the river Marne nearly surrounds it. The noble dames who were lodged there, seeing such multitudes rushing towards them, were exceedingly frightened. On this, the two lords and their company advanced to the gate of the market-place, which they had opened, and marching under the banners of the earl of Foix and duke of Orleans, and the pennon of the captal of Buch, posted themselves in front of this peasantry, who were badly armed.

When these banditti perceived such a troop of gentlemen, so well equipped, sally forth to guard the market-place, the foremost of them began to fall back. The gentlemen then followed them, using their lances and swords. When they felt the weight of their blows, they, through fear, turned about so fast, they fell one over the other. All manner of armed persons then rushed out of the barriers, drove them before them, striking them down like beasts, and clearing the town of them; for they kept neither regularity nor order, slaying so many that they were tired. They flung them in great heaps into the river. In short, they killed upwards of seven thousand. Not one would have escaped, if they had chosen to pursue them further.

On the return of the men at arms, they set fire to the town of Meaux, burnt it; and all the peasants they could find were shut up in it, because they had been of the party of the Jacks. Since this discomfiture which happened to them at Meaux, they never collected again in any great bodies; for the young Enguerrand de Coucy had plenty of gentlemen under his orders, who destroyed them, wherever they could be met with, without mercy.

Bibliography

Allmand, C. T. "Jean Froissart." *History Today* 16 (December 1966): 841–48.
Anderson, G. and W. *The Chronicles of Froissart*. Carbondale, Ill., 1963.
Brereton, Geoffrey. Introduction to *Chronicles*, by Froissart. Translated by Geoffrey Brereton. London, 1968.
Huizinga, Johan. *The Waning of the Middle Ages*. London, 1924.
Paton, William Ker. *Essays in Medieval Literature*. London, 1905.
Shears, F. S. *Froissart*. London, 1930.

CHAPTER 8

Francesco Guicciardini

History of Italy

(1534–40, 1561)

Froissart wrote imaginatively of lives he would like to have led, but Francesco Guicciardini's career in the power politics of sixteenth-century Italy invested the *History of Italy* with an authenticity its author could not have imagined. As a Renaissance diplomat in a family of Florentine politicians, Guicciardini knew the sources, style, and psychology of diplomatic affairs—his exclusive theme—and easily translated his experience into history. Less well known to us than his contemporary, Niccolo Machiavelli, Guicciardini was much the better historian. His significance lies in his recognition that history is better written from original sources than from the sifting and weighing, albeit judiciously, of accounts by previous writers. His family's diplomatic archives and the papal and Florentine archives supplied a rich resource against which memory and legend could be checked as he wrote Italian history from 1490 to 1534.

Guicciardini was born in 1483 to a wealthy, powerful Florentine family closely allied with the wealthier and more powerful Medici family. His education and marriage were arranged for political advancement, and during his fifty-seven years he succeeded to a series of offices, including service as Florentine ambassador to Spain and governor of various Italian cities belonging to the Medici popes. As a lawyer, diplomat, administrator, general, and political adviser, Guicciardini showed a remarkable talent for survival in a period when Florentine and Italian political society was swept by tides of internal faction and external invasion. He died in 1540.

His *History of Italy* interprets these troubles, and though Guicciardini wrote other histories and political commentaries, this last mature work is unquestionably his masterpiece. The disarray began in 1494 with the sudden intervention of the French king, Charles VIII, in the quarrels of various Italian cities. Guicciardini saw that not only could Italian affairs never again regain their insularity but also that the very conception and focus of Italian historical writing must change. Individual histories of city-states—a standard Renaissance format, represented by an early Florentine history by Guicciardini himself, as well as one by Machiavelli—were now impossible. Not the least of his innovations in the *History of Italy* was his vision of provincial history as inextricably bound up with peninsular history and of the peninsula just as tied to Europe.

As a Renaissance historian, Guicciardini made bows to ancient historical writing, such as mentioning omens that betoken human calamity and putting set speeches into the mouths of principal figures in order to sharpen the focus of debate. But his reliance on primary sources and his creation of a broadly Italian historiography were new. As far as causation was concerned, Guicciardini saw *fortuna* as an ultimate determinant in men's affairs, but he reserved his most graphic prose for individual men and especially their weaknesses of character. One still gets no appreciation of large-scale economic forces or any concern with ordinary people, whom Guicciardini despised, but he did understand what a technological innovation like artillery did to the security of old walled cities and, indeed, the old world culture.

These characteristics can be seen in his account of the first invasion by the French in 1494, who got as far as Rome before being turned back. Italian states lay serene in their balance of power, but the death of Lorenzo de Medici precipitated quarreling, the French invasion, and the ignominious fall of the Medici family from power in Guicciardini's own Florence.

I HAVE DECIDED TO WRITE ABOUT the events which have taken place in Italy within living memory since the time when French armies called in by our own princes began to trouble her peace with great upheavals. A very rich theme for its variety and extent, and full of appalling disasters, for Italy has suffered for many years every kind of calamity that may vex wretched mortals either through the just wrath of God or through the impious and wicked actions of their fellow men. From the understanding of these events, so diverse and grave, all men will be able to draw many useful lessons both for themselves and for the public good. It will appear from countless examples how unstable are human affairs—like a sea driven by the winds; how pernicious, nearly always to themselves but invariably to the common people, are the ill-judged actions of rulers when they pursue only vain error or present greed. And forgetting how often fortune changes, and converting to other peoples' harm the power vested

Reprinted by permission of the publisher from [Francesco] Guicciardini, *History of Florence and the History of Italy*, translated by Cecil Grayson, edited and abridged with an introduction by John R. Hale (New York: Twayne Publishers, Inc., 1964), 85–93, 145–54, 160–69. Copyright © 1964 by Washington Square Press, a division of Simon & Schuster, Inc.

in them for the public good, they become through lack of prudence or excess of ambition the authors of fresh upheavals.

The calamities of Italy began (and I say this so that I may make known what was her condition before, and the causes from which so many evils arose), to the greater sorrow and terror of all men, at a time when circumstances seemed universally most propitious and fortunate. It is indisputable that since the Roman Empire, weakened largely by the decay of her ancient customs, began to decline more than a thousand years ago from that greatness to which it had risen with marvelous virtue and good fortune, Italy had never known such prosperity or such a desirable condition as that which it enjoyed in all tranquillity in the year of Our Lord 1490 and the years immediately before and after. For, all at peace and quietness, cultivated no less in the mountainous and sterile places than in the fertile regions and plains, knowing no other rule than that of its own people, Italy was not only rich in population, merchandise and wealth, but she was adorned to the highest degree by the magnificence of many princes, by the splendor of innumerable noble and beautiful cities, by the throne and majesty of religion; full of men most able in the administration of public affairs, and of noble minds learned in every branch of study and versed in every worthy art and skill. Nor did she lack military glory according to the standards of those times; and being so richly endowed, she deservedly enjoyed among all other nations a most brilliant reputation.

Italy was preserved in this happy state, which had been attained through a variety of causes, by a number of circumstances, but among these by common consent no little credit was due to the industry and virtue of Lorenzo de' Medici, a citizen so far above the rank of private citizen in Florence that all the affairs of the Republic were decided by his advice. Florence was at that time powerful by virtue of her geographical position, the intelligence of her people and the readiness of her wealth rather than for the extent of her dominion. Lorenzo had lately allied himself through marriage to Pope Innocent VIII (who listened readily to his counsels); his name was respected throughout Italy and his authority was great in all discussions on matters of common interest. Knowing that it would be very dangerous to himself and to the Florentine Republic if any of the larger states increased their power, he diligently sought to maintain the affairs of Italy in such a balance that they might not favor one side more than another. This would not have been possible without the preservation of peace and without the most careful watch over any disturbance, however small. Ferdinand of Aragon, King of Naples, shared his desire for universal peace—undoubtedly a most prudent and respected prince; though in the past he had often shown ambitious designs contrary to the counsels of peace, and at this time was being egged on by Alfonso, Duke of Calabria, his eldest son, who resented seeing his son-in-law, Giovan

Galeazzo Sforza, Duke of Milan—now over twenty years of age though quite lacking in ability—merely keeping the title of duke and being overborne and crushed by Lodovico Sforza, his uncle. The latter, more than ten years earlier, had taken over the guardianship of the young Duke because of the imprudence and lewd habits of his mother Madonna Bona, and thus little by little had taken into his own hands the fortresses, soldiers, treasury, and all the instruments of power; and he now continued to govern, no longer as guardian or regent, but in everything except the title of Duke of Milan, with all the outward shows and actions of a prince. Nevertheless Ferdinand did not desire any upheaval in Italy, having more regard for present benefits than past ambitions or for his son's indignation, however well-founded. Perhaps because a few years earlier he had experienced, with the gravest danger, the hatred of his barons and his common subjects, and knowing the affection which many of his people still held for the name of the royal house of France, he was afraid that discord in Italy might give the French an opportunity to attack the Kingdom of Naples. Or perhaps he realized that to balance the power of the Venetians, which was then a threat to the whole of Italy, he must remain allied with the other states—particularly Milan and Florence. Lodovico Sforza, though of a restless and ambitious nature, must have shared this view, because the danger from the Venetian senate threatened the rulers of Milan no less than the others and because it was easier for him to maintain the power he had usurped in the tranquillity of peace than in the vicissitudes of war. He always suspected the intentions of Ferdinand and Alfonso of Aragon, but knowing Lorenzo de' Medici's desire for peace and his fear of their power—and believing that because of the difference of attitude and ancient hatred between Ferdinand and the Venetians there was no fear that they might form an alliance—he felt fairly sure that the Aragonese would not find allies to attempt against him what they could not do alone.

Since there was the same will for peace in Ferdinand, Lodovico, and Lorenzo—partly for the same and partly for different reasons—it was easy to maintain an alliance in the name of Ferdinand, King of Naples, Giovan Galeazzo, Duke of Milan, and the Florentine Republic for the mutual defense of their states. This treaty, which was entered into many years before and subsequently interrupted for various reasons, had been renewed in 1480 for twenty-five years with the adherence of nearly all the small states of Italy. Its principal object was to prevent the Venetians from increasing their power, for they were undoubtedly greater than any one of the confederates, but much less so than all of them put together. They kept their own counsel, hoping to increase their power through friction and disunity among others, and stood ready to profit by any event which might open the way for them to the domination of the whole of Italy. It had been clear on more than one occasion that this was what they sought, especially when, on the death of Filippo Maria Visconti, Duke of Milan, they attempted to seize that state under color of defending the freedom of the Milanese; and more recently when in open war they tried to occupy the Duchy of Ferrara. It was easy for the confederation to curb the greed of the Venetian senate, but it did not unite the allies in sincere and faithful friendship, because—full of jealousy and rivalry—they constantly watched one another's movements, mutually thwarting every design whereby any one of them might increase its power or reputation. This did not make peace any less stable, but rather inspired each with a greater promptness to put out any sparks which might be the origin of a new outbreak.

Such was the state of things, such the foundation of the peace of Italy, so arranged and juxtaposed that not only was there no fear of any present disorder but it was difficult to imagine how, by what plots, incidents or forces, such tranquillity might be destroyed. Then, in the month of April 1492 there occurred the death of Lorenzo de' Medici. It was bitter for him, because he was not quite forty-four years of age, and bitter for his republic, which, because of his prudence, reputation and intellect in everything honorable and excellent, flourished marvelously with riches and all those ornaments and advantages with which a long peace is usually accompanied. But it was also a most untimely death for the rest of Italy, both because of the work he constantly did for the common safety and because he was the means by which the disagreements and suspicions that frequently arose between Ferdinand and Lodovico—two princes almost equal in power and ambition—were moderated and held in check.

The death of Lorenzo was followed a few months later by that of the Pope, as day by day things moved toward the coming disaster. The pontiff, though otherwise of no value to the common weal, was at least useful in that—having laid down the arms he had unsuccessfully taken up against Ferdinand at the instigation of many barons of the Kingdom of Naples at the beginning of his tenure—he turned his attention entirely to idle pleasures, and had no longer either any ambitions for himself or his family which might disturb the peace of Italy. Innocent was followed by Rodrigo Borgia of Valencia, one of the royal cities of Spain. A senior cardinal and a leading figure at the court of Rome, he was raised to the papacy, however, by the disagreements between the cardinals Ascanio Sforza and Giuliano di San Piero in Vincoli, and much more by the fact that, setting a new example in that age, he openly bought, partly with money and partly with promises of offices and favors he would bestow, many of the cardinals' votes. These cardinals, despising the teachings of the Gospels, were not ashamed to sell the power to traffic with sacred treasures in God's holy name, in the highest part of the temple. Cardinal Ascanio led many of them into this abominable contract, no less by his own example than by persuasion and pleading. Corrupted by an insatiable appetite for riches, he got for himself as the price of such wickedness the vice-chancellery, the principal office of the Roman court, churches, castles and his own palace in Rome, full of furniture of enormous value. But for all that he did not escape either divine judgment later or the just hatred and contempt of the men of his time, who were full of horror and alarm at an election conducted with such wicked devices, no less so because the character and habits of the man elected were in great part known to many. It is well known that the King of Naples, though in public he hid his grief, told his wife with tears—which he was unaccustomed to shed even at the death of his children—that a pope had been elected who would be fatal to Italy and the whole Christian world: truly a prophecy not unworthy of the wisdom of Ferdinand. For Alexander VI (as the new Pope wished to be called) possessed remarkable sagacity and acumen, excellent counsel, marvelous powers of persuasion and incredible ability and application in all difficult enterprises; but these virtues were far outweighed by his vices: utterly obscene habits, neither sincerity nor shame nor truth nor faith nor religion, insatiable avarice, immoderate ambition, more than barbarous cruelty and a burning desire to advance his many children in any possible way. Some of them—so that to execute his depraved designs a depraved instrument should not be lacking— were in no way less abominable than their father.

Such were the changes brought about in the state of the Church by the death of Innocent VIII. Yet the affairs of Florence had suffered no less a change by the death of Lorenzo de' Medici. Piero, the eldest of his three sons, had succeeded him without meeting any opposition. He was still very young and, both by age and other qualities unfit to carry such a burden; and he was unable to proceed with that moderation by which his father—in internal and foreign affairs, while prudently temporizing with the allied princes—had in his lifetime extended his public and private estate, and at his death left among all men the firm opinion that, principally through his efforts, the peace of Italy had been preserved. For hardly had Piero entered the administration of the Republic than, in direct opposition to his father's advice and without informing the principal citizens whose advice was always sought in grave matters—induced by Virginio Orsino his kinsman (both Piero's mother and his wife were of the Orsini family)—he so closely allied himself with Ferdinand and Alfonso, on whom Virginio was dependent, that Lodovico Sforza had just cause to fear that, whenever the Aragonese wished to attack him, they would have the forces of the Florentine Republic with them by authority of Piero de' Medici. This alliance, the germ and origin of so many evils, though it was at first negotiated and concluded with great secrecy, was almost immediately by obscure conjecture suspected by Lodovico Sforza, a most vigilant prince and of very acute intelligence.

When, according to the age-old custom of all Christendom, ambassadors were to be sent to pay homage to the new Pope as the Vicar of Christ on earth, Lodovico Sforza suggested that all the ambassadors of the allies should enter Rome together, and together present themselves at the public consistory before the Pope, and that one of them should speak for all so that in this way, and with great increase of reputation to all, the whole of Italy should see that there existed between them not merely friendship and alliance, but rather such unity that they seemed as one prince and one state. It was typical of Lodovico to endeavor to appear superior to everyone else in prudence by putting forward ideas no one else had thought of. The value of this plan, he said, was evident, because it had been believed that the late Pope had been encouraged to attack the Kingdom of Naples by the apparent disunity of the allies in having sworn obedience to him at different times and with different orations. Ferdinand made no difficulties about accepting Lodovico's suggestion, and the Florentines approved it on the authority of both, while Piero de' Medici said nothing against it in public council. Privately, however, he disagreed strongly, because as he himself was one of the representatives elected by the Republic and he had planned to make his own train most brilliant with fine and almost regal trappings, he realized that entering Rome and presenting himself before the Pope with the other ambassadors of the allies, he would not be able in such a crowd to display the splendor of his magnificent preparations. He was supported in his youthful vanity by the ambitious counsels of Gentile, bishop of Arezzo, likewise one of the chosen ambassadors. As it was to be his duty, on account of his episcopal office and his having professed those studies which are called the Humanities, to speak in the name of the Florentines, he was disappointed beyond measure to lose in this unexpected and unusual way the opportunity to show off his eloquence on an occasion so honorable and solemn. Therefore Piero, inspired partly by his own frivolity and partly by the ambition of others, and yet unwilling that Lodovico Sforza should learn that he was against his plan, asked the King to suggest that each party should act separately as had been done in the past, and to explain that he had thought it over and now felt that these proceedings could not be carried out together without great confusion. The King was anxious to please him, but not so anxious that he would incur Lodovico's displeasure; and so he complied more in the result than in the manner, for he did not hide the fact that it was only at Piero de' Medici's request that he went back on what he had at first agreed to do. Lodovico was angrier at this sudden change than the importance of the occasion merited in itself, complaining bitterly that as the Pope and the entire Roman court already knew of the first plan and who had put it forward, it was now being withdrawn on purpose to damage his reputation. He was even more displeased when he began to realize, through this small and really unimportant incident, that Piero de' Medici had a secret understanding with Ferdinand. And this became more evident every day from the events which followed.

. . . .

Now not only the preparations made by land and sea, but the heavens and mankind joined in proclaiming the future calamities of Italy. Those who profess to know the future either by science or by divine inspiration affirmed with one voice that greater and more frequent changes were at hand—events stranger and more horrible than had been seen in any part of the world for many centuries. Men were no less terrified by the widespread news that unnatural things in heaven and earth had appeared in various parts of Italy. One night in Puglia three suns stood in an overcast sky with horrible thunder and lightning. In the Arezzo district a vast number of armed men on enormous horses were seen passing through the air day after day with a hideous noise of drums and trumpets. In many places in Italy the sacred statues and images sweated visibly. Everywhere many monsters were born, both human and animal; and many other things outside the order of nature had happened in all kinds of places. All these filled the people of Italy with unspeakable fear, frightened as they were already by the rumors of the power of the French and the ferocity with which (as all the histories related) they had in the past overrun and despoiled the whole of Italy, sacked and put to fire and sword the city of Rome and conquered many provinces in Asia; indeed there was no part of the world that had not at some time felt the force of their arms. Men were only surprised that among so many portents there should not have been seen the comet which the ancients reputed a certain harbinger of the downfall of rulers and states.

The approach of realities daily increased belief in heavenly signs, predictions, prognostications and portents. For Charles, firm in his resolve, now came to Vienne in the Dauphiné. He could not be moved from his decision to invade Italy in person either by the entreaties of all his subjects or by lack of money, which was so scarce that he was only able to provide for his daily needs by pawning for a small sum certain jewels loaned to him by the Duke of Savoy, the Marchioness of Monferrat and other nobles of his court. The money he had earlier collected from the revenues of France, and that which had been given him by Lodovico Sforza, he had spent partly on the navy in which from the start great hopes of victory were placed, and part he had handed out thoughtlessly to a variety of persons before he left Lyons. As at that time princes were not so quick to extort money from their peoples as—riding roughshod over respect for God and men—they were later taught by avarice and excessive greed to do, it was not easy for him to accumulate any more. On so weak a basis was it proposed to mount so vast a war! For he was guided more by rashness and impetuousness than by prudence and good counsel.

Yet as often happens when one begins to carry out new, great and difficult enterprises, although the decision has been made, all the reasons that can be adduced against them come to mind; so when the King was about to leave and in fact his troops were already on their way toward the mountains, a grave murmur of complaint arose throughout the court, some pointing out the difficulties of so large an expedition, others the danger of the faithlessness of the Italians and especially of Lodovico Sforza—recalling the warning that had come from Florence of his treachery (and as it happened, certain moneys which were expected from him were slow in coming). So the expedition was not only boldly opposed by those who had always condemned it (as happens when events seem to confirm one's opinion), but some of those who had been its chief supporters—among them the bishop of St. Malo—began to waver considerably. Finally when this rumor reached the King's ears, it had such an effect throughout the court and in his own mind and created such a disinclination to go any further that he at once ordered his troops to stop. As a result many nobles who were already on their way, hearing the news that it had been decided not to invade Italy, returned to the court. And it is believed that this change of plan would have been easily put into effect if the Cardinal of San Piero in Vincoli—fatal instrument then and before and after of the ills of Italy—had not rekindled with all his authority and vehemence people's flagging enthusiasm and keyed the King up to his original decision. He not only reminded him of the reasons which had inspired him to undertake so glorious an expedition, but showed him with grave arguments what infamy would be his throughout the world from the frivolous changing of so worthy a decision. Why then had he weakened the frontiers of his kingdom by returning the County of Artois? Why to the deep displeasure of nobles and commoners alike had he opened one of the gates of France to the King of Spain by giving him the County of Roussillon? Other kings might give away such things either to free themselves from urgent danger or to achieve some great gain. But what need, what danger had moved him? What reward did he expect, what fruit could result from it if it were not to have bought most dearly a greater humiliation? What accidents had arisen, what difficulties supervened, what dangers appeared since he had made known his intentions to all the world? Had not rather the hope of victory visibly grown? For the foundations on which the enemy had based all their hopes for defense had proved vain. The Aragonese navy, which had shamefully fled into the harbor of Leghorn after its unsuccessful attack on Portovenere, could do nothing further against Genoa, defended by so many troops and by a fleet greater than theirs; and the land army which had been halted in Romagna by the resistance of a small number of French troops did not dare to advance any further. What would they do when the news spread throughout Italy that the King had crossed the mountains with so great an army? What tumults would arise everywhere? What would be the Pope's terror when from his own palace he saw the Colonna troops at the gates of Rome? How terrified Piero de' Medici would be, finding his own family against him and the city faithful to the French and longing to regain the liberty he had oppressed! There was nothing that could hold back the King's advance to the borders of Naples; and when he got there he would find the same tumults and fears and everywhere retreat and rebellion. Was he afraid their money might run out? When they heard the clash of his arms and the terrible roar of his artillery, all the Italians would vie with one another to bring him money. If any resisted, however, the spoils, plunder and wealth of the conquered would support his army. For in Italy, for many years used to the semblance of war rather than to its realities, there was no strength to restrain the fury of the French. What fears, therefore, what confusion, dreams, vain shadows had entered his mind? How had he lost his spirit so soon? Where was the ferocity with which four days earlier he boasted that he could conquer all Italy put together? He should consider that his plans were no longer in his own hands. Things had gone too far, with the handing over of territories, the ambassadors he had heard, sent and expelled, the expenses already laid out, the preparations made, the declarations published everywhere, and his own advance almost as far as the Alps. However dangerous the enterprise, he was obliged to go on with it; for there was now no compromise between glory and infamy, triumph and shame, between being either the greatest king in the world or the most despised. And as his victory and triumph were already prepared and manifest, what ought he to do?

These things, which are the substance of what the cardinal said—although conveyed according to his nature with direct statements and impetuous and fiery gestures rather than ornate words—so moved the King that without listening any longer except to those who urged him to war, he left Vienne the same day accompanied by all the nobles and captains of the Kingdom of France except the Duke of Bourbon in whose hands he left the administration of the realm in his absence, and the admiral and a few others delegated to govern and guard the most important provinces. He crossed into Italy over the pass of Montgenèvre which is much easier than Mont Cenis, and was the pass used by Hannibal the Carthaginian in ancient times though with incredible difficulty. The King entered Asti on September 9, 1494, bringing with him into Italy the seeds of innumerable disasters, terrible events and change in almost everything. His invasion was not only the origin of changes of government, subversion of kingdoms, devastation of the countryside, slaughter of cities, cruel murders, but also of new habits, new customs, new and bloody methods of warfare, diseases unknown until that day; and the instruments of peace and harmony in Italy were thrown into such confusion that they have never since been able to be reconstituted, so that other foreign nations and barbarian armies have been able to devastate and trample wretchedly upon her. To make her unhappy fate worse, so that our humiliation should not be tempered by the qualities of the victor, the man whose coming caused so many ills, though amply endowed with material blessings, lacked practically all virtues of mind and body.

For it is true that Charles from boyhood was physically weak and unhealthy, small in stature, and extremely ugly in appearance except for the brightness and dignity of his eyes. His limbs were so proportioned that he seemed more like a monster than a man. Not only did he lack all knowledge of the arts, but he barely knew how to read and write. He was greedy to rule but quite incapable of it, because allowing himself to be continually influenced by his favorites, he retained neither majesty nor authority with them. Averse from all duties and tasks, he showed little prudence and judgment even in those he did attend to. If anything in him seemed at all praiseworthy, when looked at closely, it appeared further removed from virtue than from vice. He aspired to glory but out of impulse rather than wisdom; he was generous but without discretion or discrimination, often firm in his decisions but more often out of ill-founded obstinacy than true constancy; and what many called kindness in him was more deserving of the name of indifference and weakmindedness.

. . . .

Lodovico Sforza and his wife Beatrice had gone at once to Charles at Asti with the greatest pomp and a most noble company of many highborn and beautiful ladies of the Duchy of Milan, and with them Ercole Duke of Ferrara. There they discussed their affairs and decided the army should move as early as possible. So that this might be done the sooner, Lodovico, who greatly feared their having to spend the winter in the lands of the Duchy if they were caught by the bad weather, again lent money to the King, who was in dire need of it. But he caught a disease which turned out to be smallpox and stayed in Asti about a month, distributing his army in the town and the surrounding country. This consisted (from what I can gather among a great variety of testimony to be the truest estimate) of about 1,600 men-at-arms counting the Swiss who had gone ahead with the Bailli de Dijon to Genoa and the force in Romagna under Aubigny, and in addition to the 200 gentlemen of the royal guard. Of these men-at-arms each had, according to the French usage, two bowmen, so there were six horses under each lancer (which is what their men-at-arms are called). Then there were 6,000 Swiss foot soldiers; 6,000 foot soldiers from his own kingdom—of which half came from Gascony, a province which in the opinion of the French is the best endowed with able infantrymen of any in France. To join up with this army there had been brought to Genoa by sea a great quantity of both siege and field artillery of a kind which had never been seen in Italy.

This pestilential armament—invented many years before in Germany—was first brought into Italy by the Venetians in the war which the Genoese had with them in about 1380. In this the Venetians, beaten on the sea and hard hit by the loss of Chioggia, would have accepted any conditions the victor liked to offer, if sober counsel had not been lacking on such an exceptional occasion. The name of the largest of these weapons was the bombard, which, after the invention had spread all over Italy, was used in sieges. Some were iron, some were bronze, but they were all enormous; so that, because of the size of the machine, the lack of skill of the operators and the unsuitability of the apparatus, they were extremely slow and cumbersome to move. They were set up before towns with the same difficulties, and once set up there was so long an interval between shots that they used up a lot of time with relatively small effect compared with what came after. Hence the defenders of the besieged places had plenty of time to make repairs and fortifications inside. All the same the force of the explosion of the saltpeter with which the gunpowder is made, when it was lit, sent the cannon balls flying through the air with such a terrible noise and astonishing violence that this engine, even before it attained its later perfection, made all the siege instruments used by the ancients with so much fame to Archimedes and the other inventors look ridiculous. But the French made much more manageable pieces and only out of bronze, which they called cannons, and used iron balls where they used to be of stone and incomparably larger and heavier; and they moved them on carts which were drawn not by oxen as was the custom in Italy, but by horses. The men and equipment assigned to this work were so skillful that they could almost always keep up with the rest of the army; and when brought up to the walls they were set up with unbelievable rapidity. With only the briefest interval between shots they fired so rapidly and powerfully that they could do in a few hours what in Italy used to take days. And they employed this diabolical rather than human instrument no less in the field than at sieges, using the same cannon and other smaller pieces—built and transported according to their size with the same skill and speed.

This artillery made Charles' army most formidable to the whole of Italy; and it was formidable besides, not for the number but the caliber of the troops. The men-at-arms were nearly all from among the King's subjects, and not common people but gentlemen, not just taken on or laid off at the wish of the captains; and as the companies were paid not by them but by the King's ministers, they not only had their full numbers but were well set up and well provided with horses and arms—not being unable through poverty to equip themselves—and all competed to serve best from the instinct of honor which noble birth breeds in men's breasts as well as from the hopes they had of rewards for courageous deeds both inside and outside the service, which was arranged so that they could be promoted through various ranks up to captain. The captains had the same incentives, being nearly all barons and lords or at least of very noble birth, and nearly all subjects of the King of France. When they had their full complement of lancers—for according to the custom of the kingdom no one got more than 100 lancers to command—they had no other ambition than to earn their King's praise; so that there did not exist among them either the instability of changing masters out of ambition or greed, or rivalries with other captains for command of more troops.

In the Italian armies everything was just the opposite, for many of the men-at-arms, peasants or common citizens, were subjects of other rulers and entirely dependent on the captains with whom they agreed to serve, and who were responsible for recruiting and paying them, so that neither by nature nor circumstances had they any special incentive to give good service. The captains who were very seldom subjects of those who employed them—and often had very different ambitions and objects—were full of jealousy and hatred for one another; and having no agreed term to their commission and being entirely masters of their companies, they did not keep the number of soldiers they had been paid for; and not satisfied with reasonable conditions they imposed excessive terms on their employers. Unreliable in any service, they often passed into other employment, driven either by ambition or greed or other interests to be not only unreliable but treacherous. Nor was there less difference between the Italian infantry and that of Charles: for the Italians did not fight in firm and orderly squadrons but scattered throughout the field, usually withdrawing to the shelter of banks and ditches. But the Swiss, a most warlike nation, who had revived their ancient fame for ferocity in many brilliant victories and long practice of war, fought in squares arranged with an exact number in each line; and never breaking from this order they faced the enemy like a wall, firm and almost invincible where they could fight in a place large enough to deploy their squadrons. And the French and Gascon infantry fought with the same discipline and method, though not with the same courage.

. . . .

Lorenzo and Giovanni de' Medici came to the King the same day he had left Piacenza. They had fled secretly from their country houses and begged the King to go to Florence, promising much from the friendly disposition of the Florentine people toward the house of France and no less from their hatred for Piero de' Medici. The King's anger against Piero had recently been given fresh stimulus. He had sent an ambassador from Asti to Florence to make all kinds of offers if they granted him free passage and abstained in the future from helping Alfonso, and to threaten them if they persevered in their original intentions. He had also instructed the ambassador, in order to frighten the Florentines, to return if they did not give him a definite answer immediately; and he had been told, as an excuse for delay, that as all the chief citizens in the government had gone to their country houses as the Florentines do during that season, they could not give him a definite answer so quickly. But they would soon send an ambassador themselves to inform the King of their decision.

In the royal council there had never been any question that the better way to proceed with the army was to take the road which leads straight to Naples through Tuscany and the lands of Rome, rather than the one which goes through Romagna and the Marches, across the River Tronto and into the Abruzzi. This was not because they were not confident of beating the Aragonese army which was barely holding its own against Aubigny, but because it seemed unworthy of so great a king and the glory of his arms that—the Pope and the Florentines having declared against him—he should give people cause to think that he was avoiding that road because he was not sure he could subdue them. Besides, it was thought dangerous to fight a war in the Kingdom of Naples leaving a hostile Tuscany and the Papal State in their rear. It was decided to cross the Apennines at Parma, as Lodovico Sforza—who was eager to capture Pisa—had suggested in Asti, rather than by the direct road through Bologna. The vanguard commanded by Gilbert de Montpensier, a Bourbon of the royal family, followed by the King and the rest of the army, went to Pontremoli a town belonging to the Duchy of Milan at the foot of the Apennines on the River Magra which divides the state of Genoa (called Liguria in antiquity) from Tuscany. From Pontremoli Montpensier entered Lunigiana, part of which was under Florentine rule, while some castles belonged to the Genoese and the remainder to the Marchesi Malespini, who each maintained their little states, some under the protection of the Duke of Milan, some of the Florentines and others of the Genoese. There they were met by the Swiss who had been defending Genoa and the artillery that had come by sea to Genoa and then to La Spezia. Moving up to Fivizzano, a castle of the Florentines to which they were led by Gabriello Malaspina, Marchese di Fosdinuovo, their protégé, they took it by storm and sacked it, massacring all the foreign soldiers who were in it as well as many of the civilians. This was unheard of and caused great terror in Italy which had been accustomed for a long time to seeing wars of great splendor, pomp and magnificence—almost like displays, rather than full of danger and bloodshed.

The Florentines put up their main resistance in Sarzana, a small town which they had heavily fortified, though they had not equipped it sufficiently to withstand so powerful an enemy because they had not put in an experienced captain or many soldiers—and these were already full of cowardice at the very news of the approach of the French army. Nevertheless it was not regarded as easy to capture—particularly the fortress; and Sarzanella was even stronger: a well-equipped fort built on the hill above Sarzana. Besides, the army could not remain long in the area because this small and sterile land, shut in between the sea and the mountain, could not support such a multitude. Victuals could only come from places far away and could not arrive in time to meet present needs. Hence it seemed that the King's progress might run into considerable difficulties because, though he could not be prevented from attacking Pisa, leaving behind him the town or the fortress of Sarzana and Sarzanella, or from entering some other part of Florentine territory through the country around Lucca (which had secretly decided to receive him at the instigation of the Duke of Milan), he was unwilling to make such a decision. He thought that if he did not take the first place that offered resistance, all the others would take courage to do likewise. But it was fated that either by good fortune or by order of some other higher power (if, that is, the errors and indiscretions of men deserve such excuses) an immediate solution to this dilemma should appear—for Piero de' Medici had no greater courage or constancy in adversity than he had moderation or prudence in prosperity.

The displeasure which the city of Florence felt from the start at the opposition offered to the King had continued to increase: not so much because the Florentine merchants had been recently banished from the entire Kingdom of France, as from fear of the power of the French, which had grown tremendously since it was heard that their army had begun to cross the Apennines and later, when news came of their cruelty in taking Fivizzano. Everyone openly complained of the rashness of Piero de' Medici, who without any need and trusting in himself and in the advice of ministers reckless and arrogant in time of peace and useless in time of danger—rather than in those citizens who had been his father's friends and who had given him wise counsel—had senselessly provoked the armed might of a King of France, powerful himself and supported by the Duke of Milan, particularly since Piero knew nothing about war. There was Pisa, hostile and not fortified, with few soldiers and munitions, and the rest of Florentine territory likewise ill-prepared for defense against such an attack. As for the Aragonese—for whose sake they were exposed to such dangers—there was no one in sight but the Duke of Calabria, tied up in Romagna with his forces by the opposition of only a small part of the French army. In spite of this their country, abandoned by all, had earned the violent hatred and was certain prey to the man who had earnestly sought not to have to harm them. This feeling which was almost universal in the city, was fanned by many noble citizens who strongly disliked the present government and the fact that one family had usurped the power of the whole Republic. These, working on the fears of those who were already afraid and encouraging those who desired a change of government, had so roused the feelings of the people that it was beginning to be feared that there might be riots in the city. Men were further incensed by the arrogance and immoderate behavior of Piero, who in many ways had abandoned the civilized customs and the gentleness of his forebears. For this he had been disliked almost from boyhood by all the citizens; and it is well known that his father Lorenzo, observing his character, had often complained to his closest friends that his son's imprudence and arrogance would bring about the downfall of his family.

Piero, now terrified of the danger which he had earlier rashly despised and lacking the help promised him by the Pope and Alfonso, who were preoccupied with the loss of Ostia, the siege of Nettuno and their fear of the French fleet, hastily decided to go and seek from his enemies the security which he no longer hoped for from his friends. He thought he was following his father's example, who in 1479 finding himself in grave danger through the war waged on the Florentines by Pope Sixtus and Ferdinand King of Naples went to see Ferdinand in Naples and brought back to Florence peace for his country and security for himself. But it is certainly very dangerous to imitate the example of others, if the same conditions do not apply not only in general but in every particular, if the matter is not managed with equal prudence and if in addition to everything else the same good fortune does not play its part. Leaving Florence with this intention he heard before he reached the King that the cavalry of Paolo Orsino and 300 foot soldiers sent by the Florentines to relieve Sarzana had been routed by some French cavalry which had pushed beyond the Magra. Most of them had been killed or taken prisoner. He awaited the royal safe-conduct at Pietrasanta. The bishop of St. Malo came with other nobles of the court to escort him safely. . . . When Piero was brought before the King and was received with a kindness more apparent than real, he softened his anger a good deal by agreeing to all his demands which were high and excessive: that the fortresses of Pietrasanta, Sarzana and Sarzanella—places which on that side were like keys to the Florentine dominion—and the fortresses of Pisa and Leghorn—which were most vital parts of their state—should be placed in the King's hands; and he gave an agreement in his own writing that he would give them all back as soon as he had conquered the Kingdom of Naples. Piero was to arrange for the

Florentines to lend him 200,000 ducats and the King was to accept them as allies under his protection. The preparation of the documents of these agreements, which were simply promised verbally, was deferred until they were in Florence, through which the King intended to pass. But the handing over of the fortresses was not deferred because Piero immediately had those of Sarzana, Pietrasanta and Sarzanella handed over. And a few days later by his orders the same was done with those of Pisa and Leghorn. The French were astonished that Piero should have agreed so easily to matters of such importance, since the King would doubtless have settled for much less.

I feel I should not omit here Lodovico Sforza's witty reply to Piero de' Medici when he came up with the army the following day. Piero apologized for having missed Lodovico when he went to meet him to do him honor, and said that the reason was that Lodovico had missed his way. Whereupon Lodovico replied promptly: "It is true that one of us missed his way, but perhaps it was you"—as though to rebuke him for not having heeded his advice and so having fallen into such difficulties and dangers. However, later events showed that both of them had missed their way; but the one who did so with the greater misfortune and infamy was the one who from a position of greater eminence professed to be, in his wisdom, the guide of all the others.

Piero's decision not only made Tuscany safe for the King but freed him from all difficulty in Romagna where the Aragonese were already much weakened. It is difficult for one who can barely defend himself against dangers which threaten, to provide against the dangers of others; and while Ferrando was safe in his strong encampment within the moat of Faenza, his enemies returned to the Province of Imola. After they had attacked the castle of Bubano with part of the army—though without success as it was so small that it required but few defenders and the country was so low lying that it was all flooded—they took the castle of Mordano by storm, though it was very strong and well-garrisoned. Such was the force of the artillery, such the ferocity of the French attack that, although many drowned crossing the moats full of water, those within were unable to resist; and such acts of cruelty were committed against them without regard to age or sex that the whole of Romagna was filled with horror. Because of this horrible event Caterina Sforza, despairing of any assistance, came to an agreement with the French to avoid the immediate danger, and promised their army all facilities in the states ruled by her son. Whereupon Ferrando, not trusting the inhabitants of Faenza and considering it dangerous to stay on between Imola an Forli—the more so when he heard of Piero de' Medici's visit to Sarzana—withdrew to the walls of Cesena. He showed such fear that to avoid passing near Forli he led his army by a longer and more difficult route through the hills near Castrocaro, a Florentine castle. A few days later, when he heard of the agreement made by Piero de' Medici whereby the Florentine forces left his army, he set off on the way to Rome. At the same time Don Federigo left the port of Leghorn and retired with his fleet toward Naples, where, as his own affairs were progressing just as badly, Alfonso was beginning to need for his own defense those forces which he had sent so hopefully to attack the states of others. Since his siege of Nettuno had been unsuccessful, he had brought his army back to Terracina; and the French fleet, commanded by the Prince of Salerno and M. de Serenon [Louis de Villeneuve], had appeared off Ostia; but they declared that they had no intention of attacking the states of the Church and they did not put men ashore or show any sign of hostility to the Pope—though a few days before the King had refused to hear Francesco Piccolomini, Cardinal of Siena, whom the Pope had sent to him as legate.

When the news reached Florence of the agreement made by Piero de' Medici—with such loss to their states and such severe and shameful damage to the Republic—violent indignation was felt throughout the city. What enraged the people besides these losses was the fact that Piero had done something his forefathers had never done; he had given away, without the agreement of the citizens or decree of the government, a large part of Florentine territory. For this reason criticism of him was most bitter; everywhere citizens could be heard inciting each other to regain their freedom; those who supported Piero did not dare to oppose this movement either with words or deeds. Though they had no means of defending Pisa and Leghorn and did not think that they could persuade the King not to take over the fortresses, yet in order to distinguish the policy of the Republic from that of Piero—so that at least what belonged to the Republic should not be accepted as belonging to a private person—they at once sent many ambassadors to the King from among those who were dissatisfied with Piero's power. At this Piero, realizing that it was the beginning of a change of government and wishing to see to his own interests before some greater disorder should arise, left the King with the excuse that he was going to attend to the carrying out of the promises he had made. Then Charles also left Sarzana to go to Pisa and Lodovico Sforza returned to Milan, having succeeded, for the payment of a certain sum of money, in getting the investiture of Genoa—which the King had granted a few years earlier to Giovan Galeazzo and his heirs—transferred to himself and his descendants. But he felt annoyed with Charles because he had refused to leave in his care, as he said he had promised, Pietrasanta and Sarzana, which Lodovico claimed had been unjustly taken from the Genoese by the Florentines a very few years before; and he wanted them as a stepping stone in his ambitious greed for Pisa.

When Piero de' Medici returned to Florence, he found the greater part of the magistrates turned against him and his most valuable friends uncertain because he had done everything so imprudently and against their advice. He found the people so turbulent that when he tried the next day, November 9th, to enter the Palazzo della Signoria, the highest office of the Republic, he was prevented by some armed officials guarding the door—the chief of whom was Jacopo de' Nerli, a rich young nobleman. When this was known in the city, the people immediately rose and took up arms. Their agitation was all the greater because Paolo Orsino, with his soldiers recalled by Piero, was approaching. Piero had already gone home and his courage and counsel was failing him when he heard that the Signoria had declared him a rebel. He fled from Florence with all speed followed by Cardinal Giovanni and Giuliano, his brothers on whom the same penalties as rebels were imposed; and they went to Bologna. There Giovanni Bentivoglio, requiring in others that strength of mind which he in his later adversities failed to show, sarcastically rebuked Piero at their first meeting for having, not only to his own detriment but to that of all oppressors of their countries' freedom, abandoned his high position in so cowardly a way and without the loss of a single man. Thus through a young man's temerity the Medici family fell for the time being from that power which they had held continuously in Florence for sixty years virtually as private citizens in name and appearance. It began with Cosimo his great-grandfather, a citizen of rare wisdom and vast wealth and famous on that account throughout Europe; but much more because with splendid liberality and a truly regal spirit, thinking more of the perpetuation of his name than the good of his heirs, he spent more than 400,000 ducats in building monasteries, churches, and other fine buildings not only at home but in many parts of the world. Lorenzo, Cosimo's grandson, a man of great brilliance and excellent counsel, no less generous than his grandfather, and holding more absolute authority in the government of the Republic, though far less rich and enjoying a shorter life, was greatly admired throughout Italy and by many foreign princes. And after his death his reputation became a memory of great renown, for it seemed that with his life the peace and happiness of Italy had come to an end.

Bibliography

Bondanella, Peter. *Francesco Guicciardini*. Boston, 1976.

Ferguson, Wallace K. *The Renaissance in Historical Thought*. Cambridge, 1948.

Gilbert, Felix. *Machiavelli and Guicciardini: Politics and History in Seventeenth Century Florence*. Princeton, 1965.

Hale, John R. Introduction to *History of Italy and History of Florence,* by Guicciardini. Translated by Cecil Grayson. New York, 1964.

Luciani, Vincent. *Francesco Guicciardini and His European Reputation*. New York, 1936.

von Ranke, Leopold. "Guicciardini's Storia d'Italia." In *Leopold von Ranke, The Secret of World History,* edited by Roger Wines. New York, 1981. Essay translated from Ranke's *History of the Latin and Teutonic Nations* (1824).

Ridolfi, Roberto. *The Life of Francesco Guicciardini.* Translated by Cecil Grayson. New York, 1968.

Schevill, Ferdinand. "Introduction: On Florentine Historiography." In *The History of Florence.* New York, 1936.

CHAPTER 9

William Bradford

Of Plymouth Plantation

(c. 1630–1650)

The effect of the sixteenth-century Protestant Reformation on historical writing was ambiguous. On the one hand, it drew the warring sides into the writing of mere polemics as Lutherans and Catholics tried to justify their claims by reference to precepts and practices of the past. Thus the Protestant authors of the voluminous *Magdeburg Centuries* (1539–1546) ransacked church history down to 1300 to show how far Catholicism had diverged from Christ and the Apostles. And the Catholic writers of the *Ecclesiastical Annals* (1588–1607) did likewise, but in defense of the church. On the other hand, such partisan historiography did at least result in the rediscovery and publication of many forgotten historical documents, enhancing the record for later scholars. In any case, the Reformation produced a few histories of lasting value, among them William Bradford's *Of Plymouth Plantation,* which also stands at the beginning of American historiography.

Bradford was born in 1590 in Yorkshire to a family of yeoman farmers. As a teenager, he joined a Separatist congregation that did not recognize the established English Protestant church. When the group emigrated to Holland in 1609 seeking religious freedom, Bradford went with them. He emerged as a leader in the community and figured importantly in the decision to move again in 1620, this time to America under the sponsorship of some English businessmen. He was a signer of the Mayflower Compact in 1620 and was elected governor of Plymouth Colony the next year and thirty times thereafter, so that his personal history became inseparable from the early history of the settlement itself. In his small way, then, Bradford is another historian who had the advantages—and liabilities—of having been an actor in the events he wrote about.

He began writing *Of Plymouth Plantation* about 1630, drawing upon his own memory, the colony's official correspondence, and some rough notes he had made earlier. That was the year in which nearby Massachusetts Bay Colony began to swell as a rival, and Bradford may have wanted to establish the independence and legitimacy of Plymouth, though he was not writing for publication. Book I was finished about 1632, but Bradford probably did not resume writing until 1645. By this time, perhaps, he saw the disintegration of Plymouth's original community and piety and held up its history as a call to virtue. The manuscript was handed down to his descendants after his death in 1657 and was known to later colonial historians. The first part was published in 1841, but the whole was not issued until 1856.

Scholars have read Bradford as an example of Puritan thought, arguing either that his work shows how the Pilgrims were seduced by materialism or, the opposite, how they held to a rigid spiritualism in the face of new realities. Others dismiss his work as history in their enthusiasm for it as literature. More recently, however, readers have realized that *Of Plymouth Plantation* is as much a sophisticated portrayal of Pilgrim piety as it is an example of it, and that it is the best account we have. (See David Levin, "William Bradford," in Everett Emerson, ed., *Major Writers of Early American Literature* [1972].)

What follows is Bradford's account of the Pilgrims' harrowing attempt to cross the North Sea to Holland in 1609, in which the history's recurring theme is sounded: "When man's hope and help wholly failed, the Lord's power and mercy appeared in their recovery." One finds his simple eloquence on every page, but it is nowhere more striking than in Bradford's famous appreciation (as though he were not there, speaking even of himself in the third person) of the Pilgrims' lonely condition on first landing at Cape Cod in 1620 and his evocation of the "starving time" thereafter. Finally, Bradford's account of the summer of 1623, another uneasy time, illustrates his documentary style, which allows readers to draw certain conclusions for themselves and shows him narrating events as they happened to let readers share the suspense of the characters.

Bradford's seventeenth-century English may seem archaic compared to the modern translations of the ancient and medieval writers.

THE NEXT SPRING AFTER, there was another attempt made by some of these and others to get over at another place. And it so fell out that they light of a Dutchman at Hull, having a ship of his own belonging to Zealand. They made agreement with him, and acquainted him with their condition, hoping to find more faithfulness in him than in the former of their own nation; he bade them not fear, for he would do well enough. He was by appointment to take them in between Grimsby and Hull, where was a large common a good way distant from any town. Now against the

Reprinted by permission of Alfred A. Knopf, Inc., from William Bradford, *Of Plymouth Plantation, 1620–1647,* edited by Samuel Eliot Morison (New York: Random House, 1967), 12–15, 61–63, 126–32. Copyright © 1952 by Samuel Eliot Morison; renewed 1980 by Emily M. Beck.

prefixed time, the women and children with the goods were sent to the place in a small bark which they had hired for that end; and the men were to meet them by land. But it so fell out that they were there a day before the ship came, and the sea being rough and the women very sick, prevailed with the seamen to put into a creek hard by where they lay on ground at low water. The next morning the ship came but they were fast and could not stir until about noon. In the meantime, the shipmaster, perceiving how the matter was, sent his boat to be getting the men aboard whom he saw ready, walking about the shore. But after the first boatful was got aboard and she was ready to go for more, the master espied a great company, both horse and foot, with bills and guns and other weapons, for the country was raised to take them. The Dutchman, seeing that, swore his country's oath *sacremente*, and having the wind fair, weighed his anchor, hoisted sails, and away.

But the poor men which were got aboard were in great distress for their wives and children which they saw thus to be taken, and were left destitute of their helps; and themselves also, not having a cloth to shift them with, more than they had on their backs, and some scarce a penny about them, all they had being aboard the bark. It drew tears from their eyes, and anything they had they would have given to have been ashore again; but all in vain, there was no remedy, they must thus sadly part. And afterward endured a fearful storm at sea, being fourteen days or more before they arrived at their port; in seven whereof they neither saw sun, moon nor stars, and were driven near the coast of Norway; the mariners themselves often despairing of life, and once with shrieks and cries gave over all, as if the ship had been foundered in the sea and they sinking without recovery. But when man's hope and help wholly failed, the Lord's power and mercy appeared in their recovery; for the ship rose again and gave the mariners courage again to manage her. And if modesty would suffer me, I might declare with what fervent prayers they cried unto the Lord in this great distress (especially some of them) even without any great distraction. When the water ran into their mouths and ears and the mariners cried out, "We sink, we sink!" they cried (if not with miraculous, yet with a great height or degree of divine faith), "Yet Lord Thou canst save! Yet Lord Thou canst save!" with such other expressions as I will forbear. Upon which the ship did not only recover, but shortly after the violence of the storm began to abate, and the Lord filled their afflicted minds with such comforts as everyone cannot understand, and in the end brought them to their desired haven, where the people came flocking, admiring their deliverance; the storm having been so long and sore, in which much hurt had been done, as the master's friends related unto him in their congratulations.

But to return to the others where we left. The rest of the men that were in greatest danger made shift to escape away before the troop could surprise them, those only staying that best might be assistant unto the women. But pitiful it was to see the heavy case of these poor women in this distress; what weeping and crying on every side, some for their husbands that were carried away in the ship as is before related; others not knowing what should become of them and their little ones; others again melted in tears, seeing their poor little ones hanging about them, crying for fear and quaking with cold. Being thus apprehended, they were hurried from one place to another and from one justice to another, till in the end they knew not what to do with them; for to imprison so many women and innocent children for no other cause (many of them) but that they must go with their husbands, seemed to be unreasonable and all would cry out to them. And to send them home again was as difficult; for they alleged, as the truth was, they had no homes to go to, for they had either sold or otherwise disposed of their houses and livings. To be short, after they had been thus turmoiled a good while and conveyed from one constable to another, they were glad to be rid of them in the end upon any terms, for all were wearied and tired with them. Though in the meantime they (poor souls) endured misery enough; and thus in the end necessity forced a way for them.

But that I be not tedious in these things, I will omit the rest, though I might relate many other notable passages and troubles which they endured and underwent in these their wanderings and travels both at land and sea; but I haste to other things. Yet I may not omit the fruit that came hereby, for by these so public troubles in so many eminent places their cause became famous and occasioned many to look into the same, and their godly carriage and Christian behaviour was such as left a deep impression in the minds of many. And though some few shrunk at these first conflicts and sharp beginnings (as it was no marvel) yet many more came on with fresh courage and greatly animated others. And in the end, notwithstanding all these storms of opposition, they all gat over at length, some at one time and some at another, and some in one place and some in another, and met together again according to their desires, with no small rejoicing.

. . . .

Being thus arrived in a good harbor, and brought safe to land, they fell upon their knees and blessed the God of Heaven who had brought them over the vast and furious ocean, and delivered them from all the perils and miseries thereof, again to set their feet on the firm and stable earth, their proper element. And no marvel if they were thus joyful, seeing wise Seneca was so affected with sailing a few miles on the coast of his own Italy, as he affirmed, that he had rather remain twenty years on his way by land than pass by sea to any place in a short time, so tedious and dreadful was the same unto him.

But here I cannot but stay and make a pause, and stand half amazed at this poor people's present condition; and so I think will the reader, too, when he well considers the same. Being thus passed the vast ocean, and a sea of troubles before in their preparation (as may be remembered by that which went before), they had now no friends to welcome them nor inns to entertain or refresh their weatherbeaten bodies; no houses or much less towns to repair to, to seek for succour. It is recorded in Scripture as a mercy to the Apostle and his shipwrecked company, that the barbarians showed them no small kindness in refreshing them, but these savage barbarians, when they met with them (as after will appear) were readier to fill their sides full of arrows than otherwise. And for the season it was winter, and they that know the winters of that country know them to be sharp and violent, and subject to cruel and fierce storms, dangerous to travel to known places, much more to search an unknown coast. Besides, what could they see but a hideous and desolate wilderness, full of wild beasts and wild men—and what multitudes there might be of them they knew not. Neither could they, as it were, go up to the top of Pisgah to view from this wilderness a more goodly country to feed their hopes; for which way soever they turned their eyes (save upward to the heavens) they could have little solace or content in respect of any outward objects. For summer being done, all things stand upon them with a weatherbeaten face, and the whole country, full of woods and thickets, represented a wild and savage hue. If they looked behind them, there was the mighty ocean which they had passed and was now as a main bar and gulf to separate them from all the civil parts of the world. If it be said they had a ship to succour them, it is true; but what heard they daily from the master and company? But that with speed they should look out a place (with their shallop) where they would be, at some near distance; for the season was such as he would not stir from thence till a safe harbor was discovered by them, where they would be, and he might go without danger; and that victuals consumed apace but he must and would keep sufficient for themselves and their return. Yea, it was muttered by some that if they got not a place in time, they would turn them and their goods ashore and leave them. Let it also be considered what weak hopes of supply and succour they left behind them, that might bear up their minds in this sad condition and trials they were under; and they could not but be very small. It is true, indeed, the affections and love of their brethren at Leyden was cordial and entire towards them, but they had little power to help them or themselves; and how the case stood between them and the merchants at their coming away hath already been declared.

What could now sustain them but the Spirit of God and His grace?

May not and ought not the children of these fathers rightly say: "Our fathers were Englishmen which came over this great ocean, and were ready to perish in this wilderness; but they cried unto the Lord, and He heard their voice and looked on their adversity," etc. "Let them therefore praise the Lord, because He is good: and His mercies endure forever." "Yea, let them which have been redeemed of the Lord, shew how He hath delivered them from the hand of the oppressor. When they wandered in the desert wilderness out of the way, and found no city to dwell in, both hungry and thirsty, their soul was overwhelmed in them. Let them confess before the Lord His lovingkindness and His wonderful works before the sons of men."

. . . .

About the latter end of June came in a ship with Captain Francis West, who had a commission to be Admiral of New England, to restrain interlopers and such fishing ships as came to fish and trade without a license from the Council of New England, for which they should pay a round sum of money. But he could do no good of them, for they were too strong for him, and he found the fishermen to be stubborn fellows. And their owners, upon complaint made to the Parliament, procured an order that fishing should be free. He told the Governor they spoke with a ship at sea, and were aboard her, that was coming for this Plantation, in which were sundry passengers; and they marveled she was not arrived, fearing some miscarriage; for they lost her in a storm that fell shortly after they had been aboard. Which relation filled them full of fear, yet mixed with hope. The master of this ship had some two hogsheads of pease to sell, but seeing their wants, held them at £9 sterling a hogshead, and under £8 he would not take, and yet would have beaver at an under rate. But they told him they had lived so long without, and would do still, rather than give so unreasonably. So they went from hence to Virginia.

About fourteen days after came in this ship, called the *Anne*, whereof Mr. William Peirce was master; and about a week or ten days after came in the pinnace which, in foul weather, they lost at sea, a fine, new vessel of about 44 tun, which the Company had built to stay in the country. They brought about 60 persons for the General, some of them being very useful persons and became good members to the body; and some were the wives and children of such as were here already. And some were so bad as they were fain to be at charge to send them home again the next year. Also, besides these there came a company that did not belong to the General Body but came on their Particular and were to have lands assigned them and be for themselves, yet to be subject to the general government; which caused some difference and disturbance amongst them, as will after appear.

I shall here again take liberty to insert a few things out of such letters as came in this ship, desiring rather to manifest things in their words and apprehensions, than in my own, as much as may be without tediousness.

BELOVED FRIENDS, I kindly salute you all, with trust of your healths and welfare, being right sorry that no supply hath been made to you all this while; for defense whereof, I must refer you to our general letters. Neither indeed have we now sent you many things which we should and would, for want of money. But persons more than enough (though not all we should) for people come flying in upon us, but moneys come creeping in to us. Some few of your old friends are come, as, etc. So they come dropping to you, and by degrees; I hope ere long you shall enjoy them all. And because people press so hard upon us to go, and often such as are none of the fittest, I pray you write earnestly to the Treasurer and direct what persons should be sent. It grieveth me to see so weak a company sent you; and yet had I not been here they had been weaker. You must still call upon the company here to see that honest men be sent you, and threaten to send them back if any other come, etc. We are not any way so much in danger as by corrupt and naughty persons. Such and such came without my consent, but the importunity of their friends got promise of our Treasurer in my absence. Neither is there need we should take any lewd men, for we may have honest men enow, etc.

Your assured friend,
ROBERT CUSHMAN

This following was from the general.

LOVING FRIENDS, We most heartily salute you in all love and hearty affection. Being yet in hope that the same God which hath hitherto preserved you in a marvelous manner doth yet continue your lives and health, to His own praise and all our comforts. Being right sorry that you have not been sent unto all this time, etc. We have in this ship sent such women as were willing and ready to go to their husbands and friends, with their children, etc. We would not have you discontented because we have not sent you more of your old friends, and in special him on whom you most depend. Far be it from us to neglect you or contemn him. But as the intent was at first, so the event at last shall show it, that we will deal fairly, and squarely answer your expectations to the full.

There are also come unto you some honest men to plant upon their own Particulars besides you. A thing which, if we should not give way unto, we should wrong both them and you; them, by putting them on things more inconvenient; and you, for that being honest men they will be a strengthening to the place, and good neighbours unto you. Two things we would advise you of, which we have likewise signified to them here. First, the trade for skins to be retained for the general till the dividend; secondly, that their settling by you be with such distance of place as is neither inconvenient for the lying of your lands, nor hurtful to your speedy and easy assembling together.

We have sent you divers fishermen with salt, etc. Divers other provisions we have sent you, as will appear in your bill of lading, and though we have not sent all we would (because our cash is small) yet it is that we could, etc.

And although it seemeth you have discovered many more rivers and fertile grounds than that where you are; yet seeing by God's providence that place fell to your lot, let it be accounted as your portion, and rather fix your eyes upon that which may be done there than languish in hopes after things elsewhere. If your place be not the best, it is better; you shall be the less envied and encroached upon; and such as are earthly minded will not settle too near your border. If the land afford you bread and the sea yield you fish, rest you a while contented; God will one day afford you better fare. And all men shall know you are neither fugitives nor discontents, but can, if God so order it, take the worst to yourselves with content, and leave the best to your neighbours with cheerfulness.

Let it not be grievous unto you that you have been instruments to break the ice for others who come after with less difficulty; the honour shall be yours to the world's end, etc.

We bear you always in our breasts, and our hearty affection is towards you all, as are the hearts of hundreds, more which never saw your faces; who doubtless pray for your safety as their own, as we ourselves both do and ever shall, that the same God which hath so marvelously preserved you from seas, foes and famine, will still preserve you from all future dangers, and make you honourable amongst men, and glorious in bliss at the last day. And so the Lord be with you all, and send us joyful news from you, and enable us with one shoulder so to accomplish and perfect this work as much glory may come to Him that confoundeth the mighty by the weak, and maketh small things great. To whose greatness be all glory for ever and ever.

This letter was subscribed with thirteen of their names.

These passengers, when they saw their low and poor condition ashore, were much daunted and dismayed, and according to their divers humors were diversely affected. Some wished themselves in England again; others fell a-weeping, fancying their own misery in what they saw now in others; other some pitying the distress they saw their friends had been long in, and still were under. In a word, all were full of sadness. Only some of their old friends rejoiced to see them, and that it was no worse with them, for they could not expect it should be better, and now hoped they should enjoy better days together. And truly it was no marvel they should be thus affected, for they were in a very low condition; many were ragged in apparel and some little better than half naked, though some that were well stored before were well enough in this regard. But for food they were all alike, save some that had got a few pease of the ship that was last here. The best dish they could present their friends with was a lobster or a piece of fish without bread or anything else but a cup of fair spring water. And the long continuance of this diet, and their labours abroad, had something abated the freshness of their former complexion; but God gave them health and strength in a good measure, and showed them by experience the truth of that word, (Deuteronomy viii.3) "That man liveth not by bread only, but by every word that proceedeth out of the mouth of the Lord doth a man live."

When I think how sadly the Scripture speaks of the famine in Jacob's time, when he said to his sons, "Go buy us food, that we may live and not die." (Genesis xlii.2 and xliii.1) that the famine was great or heavy in the land. And yet they had such great herds and store of cattle of sundry kinds, which, besides flesh, must needs produce other food as milk, butter and cheese, etc. And yet it was counted a sore affliction. Theirs here must needs be very great, therefore, who not only wanted the staff of bread but all these things, and had no Egypt to go to. But God fed them out of the sea for the most part, so wonderful is His providence over His in all ages; for His mercy endureth for ever.

I may not here omit how, notwithstand all their great pains and industry, and the great hopes of a large crop, the Lord seemed to blast, and take away the same, and to threaten further and more sore famine unto them. By a great drought which continued from the third week in May, till about the middle of July, without any rain and with great heat for the most part, insomuch as the corn began to wither away though it was set with fish, the moisture whereof helped it much. Yet at length it began to languish sore, and some of the drier grounds were parched like withered hay, part whereof was never recovered. Upon which they set apart a solemn day of humiliation, to seek the Lord by humble and fervent prayer, in this great distress. And He was pleased to give them a gracious and speedy answer, both to their own and the Indians' admiration that lived amongst them. For all the morning, and greatest part of the day, it was clear weather and very hot, and not a cloud or any sign of rain to be seen; yet toward evening it began to overcast, and shortly after to rain with such sweet and gentle showers as gave them cause of rejoicing and blessing God. It came without either wind or thunder or any violence, and by degrees in that abundance as that the earth was thoroughly wet and soaked and therewith. Which did so apparently revive and quicken the decayed corn and other fruits, as was wonderful to see, and made the Indians astonished to behold. And afterwards the Lord sent them such seasonable showers, with interchange of fair warm weather as, through His blessing, caused a fruitful and liberal harvest, to their no small comfort and rejoicing. For which mercy, in time convenient, they also set apart a day of thanksgiving.

On the other hand, the Old Planters were afraid that their corn, when it was ripe, should be imparted to the newcomers, whose provisions which they brought with them they feared would fall short before the year went about, as indeed it did. They came to the Governor and besought him that as it was before agreed that they should set corn for their Particular (and accordingly they had taken extraordinary pains thereabout) that they might freely enjoy the same; and they would not have a bit of the victuals now come, but wait till harvest for their own and let the newcomers enjoy what they had brought; they would have none of it except they could purchase any of it of them by bargain or exchange. Their request was granted them, for it gave both sides good content; for the newcomers were as much afraid that the hungry Planters would have ate up the provisions brought, and they should have fallen into the like condition.

Bibliography

Bradford, E. F. "Conscious Art in Bradford's *History of Plymouth Plantation.*" *New England Quarterly,* 1 (1928): 133–57.

Gay, Peter. *A Loss of Mastery: Puritan Historians in Colonial America.* New York, 1968.

Howard, Alan B. "Art and History in Bradford's *Of Plymouth Plantation.*" *William and Mary Quarterly,* 3d series, 28 (April 1971): 237–66.

Levin, David. "William Bradford, the Value of Puritan Historiography." In *Major Writers of Early American Literature,* edited by Everett Emerson. Madison, Wisc., 1972.

Morison, Samuel Eliot. "Introduction." William Bradford *Of Plymouth Plantation.* New York, 1952.

Murdock, Kenneth. *Literature and Theology in Colonial New England.* Cambridge, Mass., 1949.

Smith, Bradford. *Bradford of Plymouth.* Philadelphia, 1951.

CHAPTER 10

Edward Gibbon

The Decline and Fall of the Roman Empire

(1776–1788)

By the eighteenth century, the historiographical wars of the Reformation had died down, and European historical writing exhibited two new tendencies. One was the work of the *érudits,* or antiquarians, who collected, published, and argued over the minutiae of historical facts, trying to build a canon of source criticism. The other was the writing of the *philosophes,* who believed, with Lord Bolingbroke, that history was merely "philosophy teaching by examples" and who cared less for sound evidence than they did for the preconceived principles—such as the perfectability of man—that led them to search the record for proofs in the first place. An example was Voltaire's *Essay on the Manners and Spirit of the Nations* (1756), a path-breaking but lightly documented study of how climate, government, and religion had affected men and women throughout history. The *érudits* said Voltaire played fast and loose with the facts. The *philosophes* said the antiquarians couldn't see the forest for the trees, and each was alienated from the other.

Edward Gibbon (1737–1794) effected a reconciliation. His *Decline and Fall of the Roman Empire* contemplated history on a vast scale, yet his reading of sources for every culture touched by the Empire was equally vast, and his detailed resolutions of small and large problems showed he was not ungrateful to the antiquarians. Gibbon did not argue a principle of human nature and was not, strictly speaking, a *philosophe.* But his work showed in its systematic explanation of Rome's fall that the two historiographical tendencies could work in harmony.

Gibbon was born in 1737, and though his family was of comfortable means, he was an unhappy and sickly boy who took consolation in extensive reading. He entered Oxford University at the age of sixteen. Two events in his youth seem especially to have shaped his later work. One was his conversion to Catholicism followed within eighteen months by his rejection of the church, which left him with an anti-Christian bias. The other was a visit to Rome which, on a well-remembered day, gave him his subject. "It was at Rome, on the fifteenth of October, 1764," he writes in his *Autobiography* (1796), "as I sat musing amidst the ruins of the Capitol, while the bare-footed friars were singing vespers in the Temple of Jupiter, that the idea of writing the decline and fall of the city first started to my mind." The passing of the Roman temple into the hands of the Christian friars symbolized the decline of one culture and the rise of another.

The *Decline and Fall* was published in six volumes between 1776 and 1788. Its theme is the decay of Roman institutions and virtues from a golden age in the second century to the collapse of the Western Empire in the fifth and the Eastern Empire in the fifteenth. The four excerpts below illustrate aspects of Gibbon's abilities and attitudes. The stately prose of the work's opening befits Gibbon's evocation of Rome at its height. Next is a description of Christian monasticism, followed by an account of the character of Ambrose, fourth-century archbishop of Milan. Gibbon's hostility to Christianity is sometimes heavy handed, sometimes subtle, but his interpretation of St. Ambrose is complex and admiring, suggesting that Gibbon's critique of Christianity was not as sharp as some have thought. Among the "General Observations on the Fall of the Empire in the West," the final selection, is Gibbon's conclusion that Christianity was partly to blame, but even here his language qualifies the charge.

I N THE SECOND CENTURY of the Christian era, the empire of Rome comprehended the fairest part of the earth, and the most civilized portion of mankind. The frontiers of that extensive monarchy were guarded by ancient renown and disciplined valor. The gentle but powerful influence of laws and manners had gradually cemented the union of the provinces. Their peaceful inhabitants enjoyed and abused the advantages of wealth and luxury. The image of a free constitution was preserved with decent reverence: the Roman senate appeared to possess the sovereign authority, and devolved on the emperors all the executive powers of government. During a happy period of more than fourscore years, the public administration was conducted by the virtue and abilities of Nerva, Trajan, Hadrian, and the two Antonines. It is the design of this, and of the two succeeding chapters, to describe the prosperous condition of their empire; and afterwards, from the death of Marcus Antoninus, to deduce the most important circumstances of its decline and fall: a revolution which will

From Edward Gibbon, *The History of the Decline and Fall of the Roman Empire*, 6 vols., with notes by Dean Milman, M. Guizot, and Dr. William Smith (New York: Harper, 1880), 1: 215–21; 3: 681–84, 202–8; 4: 88–99.

ever be remembered, and is still felt by the nations of the earth.

The principal conquests of the Romans were achieved under the republic; and the emperors, for the most part, were satisfied with preserving those dominions which had been acquired by the policy of the senate, the active emulation of the consuls, and the martial enthusiasm of the people. The seven first centuries were filled with a rapid succession of triumphs; but it was reserved for Augustus to relinquish the ambitious design of subduing the whole earth, and to introduce a spirit of moderation into the public councils. Inclined to peace by his temper and situation, it was easy for him to discover that Rome, in her present exalted situation, had much less to hope than to fear from the chance of arms; and that, in the prosecution of remote wars, the undertaking became every day more difficult, the event more doubtful, and the possession more precarious and less beneficial. The experience of Augustus added weight to these salutary reflections, and effectually convinced him that, by the prudent vigor of his counsels, it would be easy to secure every concession which the safety or the dignity of Rome might require from the most formidable barbarians. Instead of exposing his person and his legions to the arrows of the Parthians, he obtained, by an honorable treaty, the restitution of the standards and prisoners which had been taken in the defeat of Crassus.

His generals, in the early part of his reign, attempted the reduction of Æthiopia and Arabia Felix. They marched near a thousand miles to the south of the tropic; but the heat of the climate soon repelled the invaders, and protected the unwarlike natives of those sequestered regions. The northern countries of Europe scarcely deserved the expense and labor of conquest. The forests and morasses of Germany were filled with a hardy race of barbarians, who despised life when it was separated from freedom; and though, on the first attack, they seemed to yield to the weight of the Roman power, they soon, by a signal act of despair, regained their independence, and reminded Augustus of the vicissitude of fortune. On the death of that emperor, his testament was publicly read in the senate. He bequeathed, as a valuable legacy to his successors, the advice of confining the empire within those limits which nature seemed to have placed as its permanent bulwarks and boundaries: on the west the Atlantic Ocean; the Rhine and Danube on the north; the Euphrates on the east; and towards the south the sandy deserts of Arabia and Africa.

Happily for the repose of mankind, the moderate system recommended by the wisdom of Augustus was adopted by the fears and vices of his immediate successors. Engaged in the pursuit of pleasure, or in the exercise of tyranny, the first Cæsars seldom showed themselves to the armies or to the provinces; nor were they disposed to suffer that those triumphs which *their* indolence neglected should be usurped by the conduct and valor of their lieutenants. The military fame of a subject was considered as an insolent invasion of the imperial prerogative; and it became the duty, as well as interest, of every Roman general to guard the frontiers intrusted to his care, without aspiring to conquests which might have proved no less fatal to himself than to the vanquished barbarians.

The only accession which the Roman empire received during the first century of the Christian era was the province of Britain. In this single instance the successors of Cæsar and Augustus were persuaded to follow the example of the former, rather than the precept of the latter. The proximity of its situation to the coast of Gaul seemed to invite their arms; the pleasing, though doubtful, intelligence of a pearl-fishery attracted their avarice; and as Britain was viewed in the light of a distinct and insulated world, the conquest scarcely formed any exception to the general system of continental measures. After a war of about forty years, undertaken by the most stupid, maintained by the most dissolute, and terminated by the most timid of all the emperors, the far greater part of the island submitted to the Roman yoke. The various tribes of Britons possessed valor without conduct, and the love of freedom without the spirit of union. They took up arms with savage fierceness; they laid them down, or turned them against each other, with wild inconstancy; and while they fought singly, they were successively subdued. Neither the fortitude of Caractacus, nor the despair of Boadicea, nor the fanaticism of the Druids, could avert the slavery of their country, or resist the steady progress of the imperial generals, who maintained the national glory, when the throne was disgraced by the weakest or the most vicious of mankind. At the very time when Domitian, confined to his palace, felt the terrors which he inspired, his legions, under the command of the virtuous Agricola, defeated the collected force of the Caledonians at the foot of the Grampian hills; and his fleets, venturing to explore an unknown and dangerous navigation, displayed the Roman arms round every part of the island. The conquest of Britain was considered as already achieved; and it was the design of Agricola to complete and insure his success by the easy reduction of Ireland, for which, in his opinion, one legion and a few auxiliaries were sufficient. The western isle might be improved into a valuable possession, and the Britons would wear their chains with the less reluctance, if the prospect and example of freedom was on every side removed from before their eyes.

But the superior merit of Agricola soon occasioned his removal from the government of Britain; and forever disappointed this rational, though extensive, scheme of conquest. Before his departure the prudent general had provided for security as well as for dominion. He had observed that the island is almost divided into two unequal parts by the opposite gulfs, or, as they are now called, the Friths of Scotland. Across the narrow interval of about forty miles he had drawn a line of military stations, which was afterwards fortified, in the reign of Antoninus Pius, by a turf rampart, erected on foundations of stone. This wall of Antoninus, at a small distance beyond the modern cities of Edinburgh and Glasgow, was fixed as the limit of the Roman province. The native Caledonians preserved, in the northern extremity of the island, their wild independence, for which they were not less indebted to their poverty than to their valor. Their incursions were frequently repelled and chastised, but their country was never subdued. The masters of the fairest and most wealthy climates of the globe turned with contempt from gloomy hills assailed by the winter tempest, from lakes concealed in a blue mist, and from cold and lonely heaths, over which the deer of the forest were chased by a troop of naked barbarians.

Such was the state of the Roman frontiers, and such the maxims of imperial policy, from the death of Augustus to the accession of Trajan.

. . . .

The lives of the primitive monks were consumed in penance and solitude, undisturbed by the various occupations which fill the time and exercise the faculties of reasonable, active, and social beings. Whenever they were permitted to step beyond the precincts of the monastery, two jealous companions were the mutual guards and spies of each other's actions; and, after their return, they were condemned to forget, or at least to suppress, whatever they had seen or heard in the world. Strangers who professed the orthodox faith were hospitably entertained in a separate apartment; but their dangerous conversation was restricted to some chosen elders of approved discretion and fidelity. Except in their presence, the monastic slave might not receive the visits of his friends or kindred; and it was deemed highly meritorious if he afflicted a tender sister or an aged parent by the obstinate refusal of a word or look. The monks themselves passed their lives, without personal attachments, among a crowd which had been formed by accident, and was detained in the same prison by force or prejudice. Recluse fanatics have few ideas or sentiments to communicate; a special license of the abbot regulated the time and duration of their familiar visits; and, at their silent meals, they were enveloped in their cowls, inaccessible, and almost invisible, to each other. Study is the resource of solitude; but education had not prepared and qualified for any liberal studies the mechanics and peasants who filled the monastic communities. They might work; but the vanity of spiritual perfection was tempted to disdain the exercise of manual labor; and the industry must be faint and languid which is not excited by the sense of personal interest.

According to their faith and zeal, they might employ the day, which they passed in their cells, either in vocal or mental prayer; they assembled in the evening, and they were awakened in the night, for the public worship of the monastery. The precise moment was determined by the stars, which are seldom clouded in the serene sky of Egypt; and a rustic horn or trumpet, the signal of devotion, twice interrupted the vast silence of the desert. Even sleep, the last refuge of the unhappy, was rigorously measured; the vacant hours of the monk heavily rolled along, without business or pleasure; and, before the close of each day, he had repeatedly accused the tedious progress of the sun. In this comfortless state, superstition still pursued and tormented her wretched votaries. The repose which they had sought in the cloister was disturbed by tardy repentance, profane doubts, and guilty desires; and, while they considered each natural impulse as an unpardonable sin, they perpetually trembled on the edge of a flaming and bottomless abyss. From the painful struggles of disease and despair, these unhappy victims were sometimes relieved by madness or death; and in the sixth century a hospital was founded at Jerusalem for a small portion of the austere penitents who were deprived of their senses. Their visions, before they attained this extreme and acknowledged term of frenzy, have afforded ample materials of supernatural history. It was their firm persuasion that the air which they breathed was peopled with invisible enemies—with innumerable demons, who watched every occasion, and assumed every form, to terrify, and above all to tempt, their unguarded virtue. The imagination, and even the senses, were deceived by the illusions of distempered fanaticism; and the hermit, whose midnight prayer was oppressed by involuntary slumber, might easily confound the phantoms of horror or delight which had occupied his sleeping and his waking dreams.

The monks were divided into two classes—the *Cœnobites*, who lived under a common and regular discipline; and the *Anchorets*, who indulged their unsocial, independent fanaticism. The most devout or the most ambitious of the spiritual brethren renounced the convent as they had renounced the world. The fervent monasteries of Egypt, Palestine, and Syria were surrounded by a *laura*, a distant circle of solitary cells; and the extravagant penance of the hermits was stimulated by applause and emulation. They sank under the painful weight of crosses and chains; and their emaciated limbs were confined by collars, bracelets, gauntlets, and greaves of massy and rigid iron. All superfluous encumbrance of dress they contemptuously cast away; and some savage saints of both sexes have been admired, whose naked bodies were only covered by their long hair. They aspired to reduce themselves to the rude and miserable state in which the human brute is scarcely distinguished above his kindred animals; and the numerous sect of anchorets derived their name from their humble practice of grazing in the fields of Mesopotamia with the common herd. They often usurped the den of some wild beast which they affected to resemble; they buried themselves in some gloomy cavern which art or nature had scooped out of the rock; and the marble quarries of Thebais are still inscribed with the monuments of their penance. The most perfect hermits are supposed to have passed many days without food, many nights without sleep, and many years without speaking; and glorious was the *man* (I abuse that name) who contrived any cell or seat of a peculiar construction which might expose him, in the most inconvenient posture, to the inclemency of the seasons.

. . . .

Among the ecclesiastics who illustrated the reign of Theodosius, Gregory Nazianzen was distinguished by the talents of an eloquent preacher; the reputation of miraculous gifts added weight and dignity to the monastic virtues of Martin of Tours; but the palm of episcopal vigor and ability was justly claimed by the intrepid Ambrose. He was descended from a noble family of Romans; his father had exercised the important office of Prætorian Præfect of Gaul; and the son, after passing through the studies of a liberal education, attained, in the regular gradation of civil honors, the station of Consular of Liguria, a province which included the imperial residence of Milan. At the age of thirty-four, and before he had received the sacrament of baptism, Ambrose, to his own surprise and to that of the world, was suddenly transformed from a governor to an archbishop. Without the least mixture, as it is said, of art or intrigue, the whole body of the people unanimously saluted him with the episcopal title; the concord and perseverance of their acclamations were ascribed to a preternatural impulse; and the reluctant magistrate was compelled to undertake a spiritual office for which he was not prepared by the habits and occupations of his former life. But the active force of his genius soon qualified him to exercise with zeal and prudence the duties of his ecclesiastical jurisdiction; and while he cheerfully renounced the vain and splendid trappings of temporal greatness, he condescended, for the good of the Church, to direct the conscience of the emperors and to control the administration of the empire. Gratian loved and revered him as a father; and the elaborate treatise on the faith of the Trinity was designed for the instruction of the young prince. After his tragic death, at a time when the Empress Justina trembled for her own safety and for that of her son Valentinian, the Archbishop of Milan was despatched on two different embassies to the Court of Treves. He exercised with equal firmness and dexterity the powers of his spiritual and political characters; and perhaps contributed, by his authority and eloquence, to check the ambition of Maximus and to protect the peace of Italy. Ambrose had devoted his life and his abilities to the service of the Church. Wealth was the object of his contempt; he had renounced his private patrimony; and he sold, without hesitation, the consecrated plate for the redemption of captives. The clergy and people of Milan were attached to their archbishop; and he deserved the esteem, without soliciting the favor or apprehending the displeasure, of his feeble sovereigns.

The government of Italy and of the young emperor naturally devolved to his mother, Justina, a woman of beauty and spirit, but who, in the midst of an orthodox people, had the misfortune of professing the Arian heresy, which she endeavored to instil into the mind of her son. Justina was persuaded that a Roman emperor might claim, in his own dominions, the public exercise of his religion; and she proposed to the archbishop, as a moderate and reasonable concession, that he should resign the use of a single church, either in the city or suburbs of Milan. But the conduct of Ambrose was governed by very different principles. The palaces of the earth might indeed belong to Cæsar, but the churches were the houses of God; and within the limits of his diocese, he himself, as the lawful successor of the apostles, was the only minister of God. The privileges of Christianity, temporal as well as spiritual, were confined to the true believers; and the mind of Ambrose was satisfied that his own theological opinions were the standard of truth and orthodoxy. The archbishop, who refused to hold any conference or negotiation with the instruments of Satan, declared with modest firmness his resolution to die a martyr rather than to yield to the impious sacrilege; and Justina, who resented the refusal as an act of insolence and rebellion, hastily determined to exert the imperial prerogative of her son. As she desired to perform her public devotions on the approaching festival of Easter, Ambrose was ordered to appear before the council. He obeyed the summons with the respect of a faithful subject, but he was followed, without his consent, by an innumerable people; they pressed with impetuous zeal against the gates of the palace; and the affrighted ministers of Valentinian, instead of pronouncing a sentence of exile on the Archbishop of Milan, humbly requested that he would interpose his authority to protect the person of the emperor and to restore the tranquillity of the capital. But the promises which Ambrose received and communicated were soon violated by a perfidious court; and, during six of the most solemn days which Christian piety has set apart for the exercise of religion, the city was agitated by the irregular convulsions of tumult and fanaticism. The officers of the household were directed to prepare, first the Portian, and afterwards the new, *Basilica*, for the immediate reception of the emperor and his mother. The splendid canopy and hangings of the royal seat were arranged in the customary manner; but it was found necessary to defend them, by a strong guard, from the insults of the populace. The Arian ecclesiastics who ventured to show themselves in the streets were exposed to the most imminent danger of their lives; and Ambrose enjoyed the merit and reputation of rescuing his personal enemies from the hands of the enraged multitude.

But while he labored to restrain the effects of their zeal, the pathetic vehemence of his sermons continually inflamed the angry and seditious temper of the people of Milan. The characters of Eve, of the wife of Job, of Jezebel, of Herodias, were indecently applied to the mother of the emperor; and her desire to obtain a Church for the Arians was compared to the most cruel persecutions which Christianity had endured under the reign of paganism. The measures of the court served only to expose the magnitude of the evil. A fine of two hundred pounds of gold was imposed on the corporate body of merchants and manufacturers; an order was signified, in the name of the emperor, to all the officers and inferior servants of the courts of justice that, during the continuance of the public disorders, they should strictly confine themselves to their houses; and the ministers of Valentinian imprudently confessed that the most respectable part of the citizens of Milan was attached to the cause of their archbishop. He was again solicited to restore peace to his country by a timely compliance with the will of his sovereign. The reply of Ambrose was couched in the most humble and respectful terms, which might, however, be interpreted as a serious declaration of civil war. "His life and fortune were in the hands of the emperor; but he would never betray the Church of Christ or degrade the dignity of the episcopal character. In such a cause he was prepared to suffer whatever the malice of the demon could inflict; and he only wished to die in the presence of his faithful flock, and at the foot of the altar; he had not contributed to excite, but it was in the power of God alone to appease the rage of the people; he deprecated the scenes of blood and confusion which were likely to ensue; and it was his fervent prayer that he might not survive to behold the ruin of a flourishing city, and perhaps the desolation of all Italy." The obstinate bigotry of Justina would have endangered the empire of her son if, in this contest with the Church and people of Milan, she could have depended on the active obedience of the troops of the palace. A large body of Goths had marched to occupy the *Basilica*, which was the object of the dispute; and it might be expected from the Arian principles and barbarous manners of these foreign mercenaries that they would not entertain any scruples in the excecution of the most sanguinary orders. They were encountered on the sacred threshold by the archbishop, who, thundering against them a sentence of excommunication, asked them, in the tone of a father and a master, whether it was to invade the house of God that they had implored the hospitable protection of the republic. The suspense of the barbarians allowed some hours for a more effectual negotiation; and the empress was persuaded by the advice of her wisest counsellors to leave the Catholics in possession of all the churches of Milan; and to dissemble, till a more convenient season, her intentions of revenge. The mother of Valentinian could never forgive the triumph of Ambrose; and the royal youth uttered a passionate exclamation that his own servants were ready to betray him into the hands of an insolent priest.

The laws of the empire, some of which were inscribed with the name of Valentinian, still condemned the Arian heresy, and seemed to excuse the resistance of the Catholics. By the influence of Justina, and edict of toleration was promulgated in all the provinces which were subject to the Court of Milan; the free exercise of their religion was granted to those who professed the faith of Rimini; and the emperor declared that all persons who should infringe this sacred and salutary constitution should be capitally punished as the enemies of the public peace. The character and language of the Archbishop of Milan may justify the suspicion that his conduct soon afforded a reasonable ground, or at least a specious pretence, to the Arian ministers, who watched the opportunity of surprising him in some act of disobedience to a law which he strangely represents as a law of blood and tyranny. A sentence of easy and honorable banishment was pronounced, which enjoined Ambrose to depart from Milan without delay, whilst it permitted him to choose the place of his exile and the number of his companions. But the authority of the saints, who have preached and practised the maxims of passive loyalty, appeared to Ambrose of less moment than the extreme and pressing danger of the Church. He boldly refused to obey; and his refusal was supported by the unanimous consent of his faithful people. They guarded by turns the person of their archbishop; the gates of the cathedral and the episcopal palace were strongly secured; and the imperial troops who had formed the blockade were unwilling to risk the attack of that impregnable fortress. The numerous poor who had been relieved by the liberality of Ambrose embraced the fair occasion of signalizing their zeal and gratitude; and as the patience of the multitude might have been exhausted by the length and uniformity of nocturnal vigils, he prudently introduced into the Church of Milan the useful institution of a loud and regular psalmody. While he maintained this arduous contest, he was instructed by a dream to open the earth in a place where the remains of two martyrs, Gervasius and Protasius, had been deposited above three hundred years. Immediately under the pavement of the church two perfect skeletons were found with the heads separated from their bodies, and a plentiful effusion of blood. The holy relics were presented, in solemn pomp, to the veneration of the people; and every circumstance of this fortunate discovery was admirably adapted to promote the designs of Ambrose. The bones of the martyrs, their blood, their garments, were supposed to contain a healing power; and the preternatural influence was communicated to the most distant objects, without losing any part of its original virtue. The extraordinary cure of a blind man, and the reluctant confessions of several demoniacs, appeared to justify the faith and sanctity of Ambrose; and the truth of those miracles is attested by Ambrose himself, by his secretary Paulinus, and by his proselyte the celebrated Augustine, who at that time professed the art of rhetoric in Milan. The reason of the present age may possibly approve the incredulity of Justina and her Arian court, who derided the theatrical representations which were exhibited by the contrivance and at the expense of the archbishop. Their effect, however, on the minds of the people was rapid and irresistible; and the feeble sovereign of Italy found himself unable to contend with the favorite of Heaven. The powers likewise of the earth interposed in the defence of Ambrose. The disinterested advice of Theodosius was the genuine result of piety and friendship; and the mask of religious zeal concealed the hostile and ambitious designs of the tyrant of Gaul.

· ·

GENERAL OBSERVATIONS ON THE FALL OF THE ROMAN EMPIRE IN THE WEST

The Greeks, after their country had been reduced into a province, imputed the triumphs of Rome, not to the merit, but to the FORTUNE, of the republic. The inconstant goddess, who so blindly distributes and resumes her favors, had *now* consented (such was the language of envious flattery) to resign her wings, to descend from her globe, and to fix her firm and immutable throne on the banks of the Tiber. A wiser Greek, who has composed, with a philosophic spirit, the memorable history of his own times, deprived his countrymen of this vain and delusive comfort, by opening to their view the deep foundations of the greatness of Rome. The fidelity of the citizens to each other and to the State was confirmed by the habits of education and the prejudices of religion. Honor, as well as virtue, was the principle of the republic; the ambitious citizens labored to deserve the solemn glories of a triumph; and the ardor of the Roman youth was kindled into active emulation as often as they beheld the domestic images of their ancestors. The temperate struggles of the Patricians and Plebeians had finally established the firm and equal balance of the constitution, which united the freedom of popular assemblies with the authority and wisdom of a senate and the executive powers of a regal magistrate. When the consul displayed the standard of the republic, each citizen bound himself, by the obligation of an oath, to draw his sword in the cause of his country till he had discharged the sacred duty by a military service of ten years. This wise institution continually poured into the field the rising generations of freemen and soldiers; and their numbers were reinforced by the warlike and populous states of Italy, who, after a brave resistance, had yielded to the valor and embraced the alliance of the Romans. The sage historian, who excited the virtue of the younger Scipio and beheld the ruin of Carthage, has accurately described their military system; their levies, arms, exercises, subordination, marches, encampments; and the invincible legion, superior in active strength to the Macedonian phalanx of Philip and Alexander. From these institutions of peace and war Polybius had deduced the spirit and success of a people incapable of fear and impatient of repose. The ambitious design of conquest, which might have been defeated by the seasonable conspiracy of mankind, was attempted and achieved; and the perpetual violation of justice was maintained by the political virtues of prudence and courage. The arms of the republic, sometimes vanquished in battle, always victorious in war, advanced with rapid steps to the Euphrates, the Danube, the Rhine, and the Ocean; and the images of gold, or silver, or brass, that might serve to represent the nations and their kings, were successively broken by the *iron* monarchy of Rome.

The rise of a city, which swelled into an empire, may deserve, as a singular prodigy, the reflection of a philosophic mind. But the decline of Rome was the natural and inevitable effect of immoderate greatness. Prosperity ripened the principle of decay; the causes of destruction multiplied with the extent of conquest; and as soon as time or accident had removed the artificial supports, the stupendous fabric yielded to the pressure of its own weight. The story of its ruin is simple and obvious; and instead of inquiring *why* the Roman empire was destroyed, we should rather be surprised that it had subsisted so long. The victorious legions, who, in distant wars, acquired the vices of strangers and mercenaries, first oppressed the freedom of the republic, and afterwards violated the majesty of the purple. The emperors, anxious for their personal safety and the public peace, were reduced to the base expedient of corrupting the discipline which rendered them alike formidable to their sovereign and to the enemy; the vigor of the military government was relaxed and finally dissolved by the partial institutions of Constantine; and the Roman world was overwhelmed by a deluge of barbarians.

The decay of Rome has been frequently ascribed to the translation of the seat of empire; but this history has already shown that the powers of government were *divided* rather than *removed*. The throne of Constantinople was erected in the East; while the West was still possessed by a series of emperors who held their residence in Italy, and claimed their equal inheritance of the legions and provinces. This dangerous novelty impaired the strength and fomented the vices of a double reign: the instruments of an oppressive and arbitrary system were multiplied; and a vain emulation of luxury, not of merit, was introduced and supported between the degenerate successors of Theodosius. Extreme distress, which unites the virtue of a free people, embitters the factions of a declining monarchy. The hostile favorites of Arcadius and Honorius betrayed the republic to its common enemies; and the Byzantine court beheld with indifference, perhaps with pleasure, the disgrace of Rome, the misfortunes of Italy, and the loss of the West. Under the succeeding reigns the alliance of the two empires was restored; but the aid of the Oriental Romans was tardy, doubtful, and ineffectual; and the national schism of the Greeks and Latins was enlarged by the perpetual difference of language and manners, of interests, and even of religion. Yet the salutary event approved in some measure the judgment of Constantine. During a long period of decay his impregnable city repelled the victorious armies of barbarians, protected the wealth of Asia, and commanded, both in peace and war, the important straits which connect the Euxine and Mediterranean seas. The foundation of Constantinople more essentially contributed to the preservation of the East than to the ruin of the West.

As the happiness of a *future* life is the great object of religion, we may hear without surprise or scandal that the introduction, or at least the abuse, of Christianity, had some influence on the decline and fall of the Roman empire. The clergy successfully preached the doctrines of patience and pusillanimity; the active virtues of society were discouraged; and the last remains of military spirit were buried in the cloister: a large portion of public and private wealth was consecrated to the specious demands of charity and devotion; and the soldiers' pay was lavished on the useless multitudes of both sexes who could only plead the merits of abstinence and chastity. Faith, zeal, curiosity, and the more earthly passions of malice and ambition, kindled the flame of theological discord; the Church, and even the State, were distracted by religious factions, whose conflicts were sometimes bloody and always implacable; the attention of the emperors was diverted from camps to synods; the Roman world was oppressed by a new species of tyranny; and the persecuted sects became the secret enemies of their country. Yet party spirit, however pernicious or absurd, is a principle of union as well as dissension. The bishops, from eighteen hundred pulpits, inculcated the duty of passive obedience to a lawful and orthodox sovereign; their frequent assemblies and perpetual correspondence maintained the communion of distant churches; and the benevolent temper of the Gospel was strengthened, though confined, by the spiritual alliance of the Catholics. The sacred indolence of the monks was devoutly embraced by a servile and effeminate age; but if superstition had not afforded a decent retreat, the same vices would have tempted the unworthy Romans to desert, from baser motives, the standard of the republic. Religious precepts are easily obeyed which indulge and sanctify the natural inclinations of their votaries; but the pure and genuine influence of Christianity may be traced in its beneficial, though imperfect, effects on the barbarian proselytes of the North. If the decline of the Roman empire was hastened by the conversion of Constantine, his victorious religion broke the violence of the fall, and mollified the ferocious temper of the conquerors.

This awful revolution may be usefully applied to the destruction of the present age. It is the duty of a patriot to prefer and promote the exclusive interest and glory of his native country: but a philosopher may be permitted to enlarge his views, and to consider Europe as one great republic, whose various inhabitants have attained almost the same level of politeness and cultivation. The balance of power will continue to fluctuate, and the prosperity of our own or the neighboring kingdoms may be alternately exalted or depressed; but these partial events cannot essentially injure our general state of happiness, the system of arts, and laws, and manners, which so advantageously distinguish, above the rest of mankind, the Europeans and their colonies. The savage nations of the globe are the common enemies of civilized society; and we may inquire, with anxious curiosity, whether Europe is still threatened with a repetition of those calamities which formerly oppressed the arms and institutions of Rome. Perhaps the same reflections will illustrate the fall of that mighty empire, and explain the probable causes of our actual security.

I. The Romans were ignorant of the extent of their danger and the number of their enemies. Beyond the Rhine and Danube the northern countries of Europe and Asia were filled with innumerable tribes of hunters and shepherds, poor, voracious, and turbulent; bold in arms, and impatient to ravish the fruits of industry. The barbarian world was agitated by the rapid impulse of war; and the peace of Gaul or Italy was shaken by the distant revolutions of China. The Huns, who fled before a victorious enemy, directed their march towards the West; and the torrent was swelled by the gradual accession of captives and allies. The flying tribes who yielded to the Huns assumed in *their* turn the spirit of conquest; the endless column of barbarians pressed on the Roman empire with accumulated weight; and, if the foremost were destroyed, the vacant space was instantly replenished by new assailants. Such formidable emigrations no longer issue from the North; and the long repose, which has been imputed to the decrease of population, is the happy consequence of the progress of arts and agriculture. Instead of some rude villages thinly scattered among its woods and morasses, Germany now produces a list of two thousand three hundred walled towns: the Christian kingdoms of Denmark, Sweden, and Poland have been successively established; and the Hanse merchants, with the Teutonic knights, have extended their colonies along the coast of the Baltic as far as the Gulf of Finland. From the Gulf of Finland to the Eastern Ocean, Russia now assumes the form of a powerful and civilized empire. The plough, the loom, and the forge are introduced on the banks of the Volga, the Oby, and the Lena; and the fiercest of the Tartar hordes have been taught to tremble and obey. The reign of independent barbarism is now contracted to a narrow span; and the remnant of Calmucks or Uzbecks, whose forces may be almost numbered, cannot seriously excite the apprehensions of the great republic of Europe. Yet this apparent security should not tempt us to forget that new enemies and unknown dangers may *possibly* arise from some obscure people, scarcely visible in the map of the world. The Arabs or Saracens, who spread their conquest from India to Spain, had languished in poverty and contempt till Mahomet breathed into those savage bodies the soul of enthusiasm.

II. The empire of Rome was firmly established by the singular and perfect coalition of its members. The subject nations, resigning the hope and even the wish of independence, embraced the character of Roman citizens; and the provinces of the West were reluctantly torn by the barbarians from the bosom of their mother country. But this union was purchased by the loss of national freedom and military spirit; and the servile provinces, destitute of life and motion, expected their safety from the mercenary troops and governors who were directed by the orders of a distant court. The happiness of a hundred millions depended on the personal merit of one or two men, perhaps children, whose minds were corrupted by education, luxury, and despotic power. The deepest wounds were inflicted on the empire during the minorities of the sons and grandsons of Theodosius; and, after those incapable princes seemed to attain the age of manhood, they abandoned the Church to the bishops, the State to the eunuchs, and the provinces to the barbarians. Europe is now divided into twelve powerful, though unequal kingdoms, three respectable commonwealths, and a variety of smaller, though independent states: the chances of royal and ministerial talents are multiplied, at least, with the number of its rulers; and a Julian or Semiramis may reign in the North, while Arcadius and Honorius again slumber on the thrones of the South. The abuses of tyranny are restrained by the mutual influence of fear and shame; republics have acquired order and stability; monarchies have imbibed the principles of freedom, or, at least, of moderation; and some sense of honor and justice is introduced into the most defective constitutions by the general manners of the times. In peace, the progress of knowledge and industry is accelerated by the emulation of so many active rivals: in war, the European forces are exercised by temperate and undecisive contests. If a savage conqueror should issue from the deserts of Tartary, he must repeatedly vanquish the robust peasants of Russia, the numerous armies of Germany, the gallant nobles of France, and the intrepid freemen of Britain; who, perhaps, might confederate for their common defence. Should the victorious barbarians carry slavery and desolation as far as the Atlantic Ocean, ten thousand vessels would transport beyond their pursuit the remains of civilized society; and Europe would revive and flourish in the American world, which is already filled with her colonies and institutions.

III. Cold, poverty, and a life of danger and fatigue fortify the strength and courage of barbarians. In every age they have oppressed the polite and peaceful nations of China, India, and Persia, who neglected, and still neglect, to counter-balance these natural powers by the resources of military art. The warlike states of antiquity, Greece, Macedonia, and Rome educated a race of soldiers; exercised their bodies, disciplined their courage, multiplied their forces by regular evolutions, and converted the iron which they possessed into strong and serviceable weapons. But this superiority insensibly declined with their laws and manners: and the feeble policy of Constantine and his successors armed and instructed, for the ruin of the empire, the rude valor of the barbarian mercenaries. The military art has been changed by the invention of gun-powder, which enables man to command the two most powerful agents of nature, air and fire. Mathematics, chemistry, mechanics, architecture, have been applied to the service of war; and the adverse parties oppose to each other the most elaborate modes of attack and of defence. Historians may indignantly observe that the preparations of a siege would found and maintain a flourishing colony; yet we cannot be displeased that the subversion of a city should be a work of cost and difficulty, or that an industrious people should be protected by those arts which survive and supply the decay of military virtue. Cannon and fortifications now form an impregnable barrier against the Tartar horse; and Europe is secure from any future irruption of barbarians; since, before they can conquer, they must cease to be barbarous. Their gradual advances in the science of war would always be accompanied, as we may learn from the example of Russia, with a proportionable improvement in the arts of peace and civil policy; and they themselves must deserve a place among the polished nations whom they subdue.

Should these speculations be found doubtful or fallacious, there still remains a more humble source of comfort and hope. The discoveries of ancient and modern navigators, and the domestic history or tradition of the most enlightened nations, represent the *human savage* naked both in mind and body, and destitute of laws, of arts, of ideas, and almost of language. From this abject condition, perhaps the primitive and universal state of man, he has gradually arisen to command the animals, to fertilize the earth, to traverse the ocean, and to measure the heavens. His progress in the improvement and exercise of his mental and corporeal faculties has been irregular and various; infinitely slow in the beginning, and increasing by degrees with redoubled velocity: ages of laborious ascent have been followed by a moment of rapid downfall; and the several climates of the globe have felt the vicissitudes of light and darkness. Yet the experience of four thousand years should enlarge our hopes and diminish our apprehensions: we cannot determine to what height the human species may aspire in their advances towards perfection; but it may safely be presumed that no people, unless the face of nature is changed, will relapse into their original barbarism. The improvements of society may be viewed under a threefold aspect. 1. The poet or philosopher illustrates his age and country by the efforts of a *single* mind; but these superior powers of reason or fancy are rare and spontaneous productions; and the genius of Homer, or Cicero, or Newton would excite less admiration if they could be created by the will of a prince or the lessons of a preceptor. 2. The benefits of law and policy, of trade and manufactures, of arts and sciences, are more solid and permanent; and *many* individuals may be qualified, by education and discipline, to promote, in their respective stations, the interest of the community. But this general order is the effect of skill and labor; and the complex machinery may be decayed by time or injured by violence. 3. Fortunately for mankind, the more useful, or, at least, more necessary, arts can be performed without superior talents or national subordination; without the powers of *one* or the union of *many*. Each village, each family, each individual, must always possess both ability and inclination to perpetuate the use of fire and of metals; the propagation and service of domestic animals; the methods of hunting and fishing; the rudiments of navigation; the imperfect cultivation of corn or other nutritive grain; and the simple practice of the mechanic trades. Private genius and public industry may be extirpated; but these hardy plants survive the tempest, and strike an everlasting root into the most unfavorable soil. The splendid days of Augustus and Trajan were eclipsed by a cloud of ignorance; and the barbarians subverted the laws and palaces of Rome. But the scythe, the invention or emblem of Saturn, still continued annually to mow the harvests of Italy; and the human feasts of the Læstrigons have never been renewed on the coast of Campania.

Since the first discovery of the arts, war, commerce, and religious zeal have diffused among the savages of the Old and New World these inestimable gifts: they have been successively propagated; they can never be lost. We may therefore acquiesce in the pleasing conclusion that every age of the world has increased and still increases the real wealth, the happiness, the knowledge, and perhaps the virtue, of the human race.

Bibliography

Black, John B. *The Art of History.* New York, 1926.
Braudy, Leo. *Narrative Form in History and Fiction: Hume, Fielding and Gibbon.* Princeton, 1970.
Edward Gibbon and the Decline and Fall of the Roman Empire. Daedalus, 105 (Sum-

mer 1976).Commemorative issue that contains nineteen articles by leading authorities.

Gay, Peter. "Gibbon: A Modern Cynic among Ancient Politicians." In *Style in History.* New York, 1974.

Gibbon, Edward. *Memoirs of My Life,* edited by Georges A. Bonnard. London, 1966.

Low, David M. *Edward Gibbon, 1737–1794.* New York, 1937.

Momigliano, Arnaldo. "Gibbon's Contribution to Historical Method." In *Studies in Historiography.* London, 1966.

Swain, Joseph. *Edward Gibbon the Historian.* New York, 1966.

Trevor-Roper, H. R. "The Idea of the Decline and Fall of the Roman Empire." *The Age of Enlightenment,* edited by W. H. Barber et al. Edinburgh, 1967.

Young, G. M. *Edward Gibbon.* New York, 1932.

CHAPTER 11

Leopold von Ranke

History of the Popes

(1834–1836)

Leopold von Ranke (1795–1886) was the greatest German historian in an era dominated by German historiography. Kaiser Wilhelm I recognized his achievements when Ranke was seventy by granting him hereditary nobility. But his beginnings were not especially auspicious. He was born the son of a small-town lawyer in Thuringia and started his career as a teacher in a secondary school. What brought him to public attention was publication in 1824 of his first book, *History of the Latin and Teutonic Peoples, 1494–1535,* which marked out new directions in the aim of historical writing and in historical method. He was appointed to a professorship at the University of Berlin the next year and received a generous travel grant from the Prussian government two years after that. His research in Vienna and especially Italy enabled him to write more history, and his histories—on the papacy, the Reformation, and English and French political development—brought him more honors and, finally, dominance in his profession. At the age of eighty-five, frail and half blind, Ranke began a *Universal History* of mankind, issuing a volume each year until he died six years later in 1886.

Ranke's innovations, which make him the father of modern historiography, were embodied in the famous phrase from his first book, now almost a cliché: history "as it actually happened"—*"wie es eigentlich gewesen."* Ranke rejected the philosophical history of the eighteenth century, the early nineteenth-century exponent of which was his university colleague, G. W. F. Hegel, and which assumed a certain *a priori* truth and direction in history and a constancy of institutions and human nature. Ranke argued that the origins of all human institutions and values were in the historical process itself, dynamic and changing. Each era and each national culture were therefore unique and could not be comprehended in any abstract definition or principle.

Ranke's approach came to be known as "historicism," and it implied a new historical method.* The French *érudits* had aimed at purifying historical sources, but they had worked to narrow purposes on specialized subjects. Edward Gibbon used their work, but he did not work in archives himself and

---

*See chapter 18 and the note on p.294.

mixed his research with a sometimes credulous reading of ancient commentaries. Ranke exalted original sources as the sole basis for reconstructing the past "as it actually happened." The appendix to his *History of the Latin and Teutonic Peoples* ruthlessly criticized the accounts of earlier historians, like Guicciardini, for relying on mere memoirs in the writing of fifteenth- and sixteenth-century history and getting the story wrong. Modern readers have thought him too critical, for Guicciardini did use some archival sources (see chapter 8), but Ranke's insistence on reading only the reports of people who were there was in keeping with his sense of the uniqueness of the times and the people he studied.

The *History of the Popes,* excerpted below, gave Ranke an international reputation. Though he was a Lutheran, his history left behind the partisan quarrels of the Reformation. Ranke was interested in the church as an historical development, and his account here of Pope Paul IV (Giovanni Pietro Caraffa), who reigned from 1555 to 1559, represents the pontiff not as an anti-Christ, but simply as an Italian prince. Ranke says two passions animated Caraffa's papacy: his desire to expel Spain from Italy and his pursuit of the Counter-reformation within the church. So he offers dramatic accounts of the pope's failed war with Philip II of Spain and Emperor Charles V, as well as Caraffa's relentless attacks on church corruption, even when it involved members of his own family.

Archival sources are the heart of Ranke's narrative. A diplomat's letter allows him to evoke personal character, for example, with a contemporary description of Caraffa sitting "for long hours over the black, thick, fiery wine of Naples" pouring forth "torrents of stormy eloquence." Another source supplies the historian "with much information altogether new" on how the pope isolated his corrupt nephew. Sometimes he introduces a contemporary quotation with the present tense to make the document itself stand out as a living survival from a distant era. (Though some of Ranke's drama lies in his prose footnotes, only a few are reprinted here for illustration.)

Ranke's insistence on the uniqueness of every historical circumstance is suggested in his comment that "there are moments in the history of the world when it would seem that the actions of men are influenced by motives in direct opposition to the principles and ideas that usually govern their lives and conduct." Ranke enjoys the fact that, in his war with Spain, the pope was attacked by devout Catholics and defended by German Protestants.

FREQUENT MENTION HAS ALREADY been made of this pontiff, who is that same Caraffa, the founder of the Theatines, the restorer of the Inquisition, and the speaker who so essentially contributed to the confirmation of the ancient doctrines in the council of Trent. If there were a party whose purpose it was to reinstate Catholicism in all its strictness, not only was it a member, but a founder and chief of that party who now ascended the papal throne. Paul IV had already completed his seventy-ninth year, but his deep-set eyes still retained all the fire of youth: he was extremely tall and thin, walked with rapid steps, and seemed all nerve and muscle. His personal habits were subjected to no rule or order; frequently did he pass the night in study, and sleep in the day—woe then to the servant who should enter the apartment before his bell had rung. In all things it was his custom to follow the impulse of the moment;[1] but this impulse was regulated by a mood of mind formed in the practice of a long life, and become a second nature. He seemed to acknowledge no other duty, no other occupation, than the restoration of the Catholic faith to all its primitive authority. Characters of this description arise from time to time, and are occasionally to be seen even in the present day. Their perceptions of life and the world are gained from a single point of view; the peculiar disposition of their mind is so powerful that all their opinions are tinctured and governed by it; indefatigable speakers, their manner derives a certain freshness from the earnestness of their souls, and the system of thought that, as by a kind of fatality, informs and rules their whole being, is poured forth in a stream inexhaustible. How powerfully do such men act on all around them, when placed in a position wherein their activity is in perfect harmony with their views and sentiments, wherein the power to act is associated with the will! What might men not expect from Paul IV, whose views and opinions had never endured either concession or compromise, but were ever carried out eagerly to their utmost consequences, now that he was raised to the supreme dignity! He was himself amazed at having reached this point—he who had in no manner conciliated a single member of the conclave, and from whom nothing was to be expected but the extreme of severity. He believed that his election had been determined, not by the cardinals, but by God himself, who had chosen him for the accomplishment of his own purposes.

"We do promise and swear," says he in the bull that he published of his accession to the holy see, "to make it our first care that the reform of the universal Church, and of the Roman Court, be at once entered on." The day of his coronation was signalized by the promulgation of edicts respecting monasteries and the religious orders. He sent two monks from

From Leopold von Ranke, *History of the Popes, Their Church and State*, 3 vols., translated by E. Fowler (New York: Colonial Press, 1901), 1: 192–212.

1. "Relatione di M. Bernardo Navagero (che fu poi cardinale) alla Serma. Repca, di Venetia, tornando di Roma Ambasciatore appresso del Pontefice Paolo IV, 1558:" in many Italian libraries, and in the Informationi Politiche in Berlin: "The complexion of this pontiff is adust and choleric; he has incredible gravity and grandeur in all his actions, and seems really born to command."

Monte Cassino into Spain, with command to re-establish the discipline of the convents which had become lax and neglected. He appointed a congregation for the promotion of reforms in general; this consisted of three classes, in each of which were eight cardinals, fifteen prelates, and fifty learned men of differing ranks.

The articles to be discussed by them, in relation to the appointments to clerical offices and collation to benefices, were submitted to the universities. It is manifest that the new pope proceeded with great earnestness in the work of reform. The spiritual tendency which had hitherto affected the lower ranks of the hierarchy only, now seemed to gain possession of the papal throne itself, and promised to assume the exclusive guidance of all affairs during the pontificate of Paul IV.

But now came the question of what part he would take in relation to the general movements of the political world.

The principal direction once given to a government, and which has gradually identified itself with its very existence, is not readily susceptible of change.

A desire to deliver themselves from the heavy preponderance of Spain must ever have been uppermost in the minds of the popes; and at the accession of Paul the moment seemed to have come when his wish appeared to be within the possibility of realization. The war proceeding, as we have seen, from the movements of the Farnesi, was the most unfortunate one ever undertaken by Charles V. He was closely pressed in the Netherlands; Germany had deserted his interests; Italy was no longer faithful to him; he could not rely even on the houses of Este and Gonzaga; he was himself ill, and weary of life. I question whether any pontiff, not immediately attached to the imperial party, could have found strength to withstand the temptations presented by this state of things.

In the case of Paul IV they were more than commonly powerful. Born in the year 1476, he had seen his native Italy in all the unrestrained freedom of her fifteenth century, and his very soul clung to this remembrance. He would sometimes compare the Italy of that period to a well-tuned instrument of four strings—these last being formed by Naples, Milan, Venice, and the States of the Church. He would then utter maledictions on the memory of Alfonso and Louis the Moor: "Lost and unhallowed souls," as he said, "whose discords had disturbed that harmony." That from their time the Spaniard should have become master in the land, was a thought that he could in no way learn to bear. The house of Caraffa, whence he derived his birth, was attached to the French party, and had frequently taken arms against the Castilians and Catalonians. In 1528 they again joined the French; and it was Giovanni Pietro Caraffa who advised Paul III to seize Naples in 1547. To this party spirit came other causes in aid: Caraffa had constantly affirmed that Charles favored the Protestants from jealousy of the Pope, and that "the successes of those heretics were attributable to no other than the Emperor." Charles knew Caraffa well, he once expelled him from the council formed for the administration of affairs in Naples, and would never permit him to hold peaceful possession of his ecclesiastical employments within that kingdom; he had, moreover, made earnest remonstrance against Caraffa's declamations in the consistory. All these things, as may readily be supposed, did but increase the virulence of the Pope's enmity. He detested the Emperor as Neapolitan and as Italian, as Catholic and as pope: there existed in his soul no other passions than that for reform of the Church and his hatred of Charles.

The first act of Paul was to lighten various imports, and to permit the importation of corn. A statue was erected to him for these benefits, and it was not without a certain sense of self-complacency that he viewed this—while in the midst of his splendid court, and surrounded by a glittering body of Neapolitan nobles, proffering him the most obsequious obedience—he received the homage of ambassadors who came crowding from all countries to his presence. But scarcely had he felt himself well-seated on the pontifical chair, than he commenced a series of disputes with the Emperor. That monarch had complained to the cardinals of his party, that a pope so inimical to himself had been chosen; his adherents held suspicious meetings; some of them even carried off certain ships from Civita Vecchia, that had previously been taken from them by the French. The Pope at once breathed fire and flames. Such of his vassals, and the cardinals, as were imperialists, he arrested instantly, confiscating the whole property of those who fled. Nor was this enough. That alliance with France which Paul III never could resolve on completing, was entered into with little hesitation by Paul IV. He declared that the Emperor designed to "finish him by a sort of mental fever," but that he, Paul, was "determined on open fight. With the help of France he would yet free this poor Italy from the tyrannies of Spain, and did not despair of seeing two French princes ruling in Naples and Milan." He would sit for long hours over the black thick fiery wine of Naples, his usual drink (it was of a sort called mangiaguerra, champ-the-war)[2] and pour forth torrents of stormy eloquence, against those schismatics and heretics, those accursed of God, that evil generation of Jews and Moors, that scum of the world, and other titles equally complimentary, bestowed with unsparing liberality on everything Spanish; but he consoled himself with the promise, "thou

---

2. Navagero: "His custom is to eat twice a day, he must be served very delicately; and in the beginning of his pontificate, twenty-five dishes were not sufficient for his table: he drinks much more than he eats; his wine being strong and brisk—it is a black wine, grown in the kingdom of Naples, that they call 'champ-the-war,' and is so thick that one may almost cut it. After his meals he drinks malmsey,

shalt tread upon the lion and adder, the young lion and the dragon shalt thou trample under foot." The time was now come when the Emperor Charles and King Philip should receive the punishment due to their iniquities. He, the Pope, would inflict it, and would free Italy from their grasp. If others would not listen to nor support him, the future world should at least have to tell, how an old Italian, so near to his grave, and who should rather have been employed in preparing for it, had entertained these lofty purposes. We will not enter into the details of the negotiations which he carried on under the influence of these feelings. When the French concluded a truce with Spain,[3] unmindful of an agreement that they had entered into with himself, he sent his nephew, Carlo Caraffa, to France, where the different parties contending for power in that country were gradually gained over to his interests. The Montmorencies and the Guises, the wife of the French King and his mistress, were equally won to aid the pontiff in promoting a new outbreak of hostilities. Paul secured a vigorous Italian ally also in the person of the Duke of Ferrara; nothing less was talked of than completely revolutionizing Italy. Neapolitan and Florentine exiles filled the Curia; their restoration to their homes seemed now approaching; the papal fiscal instituted a legal process against the Emperor Charles and King Philip, in which the excommunication of those princes, and the release of their subjects from their oath of allegiance, was roundly threatened. The Florentines always declared that they held positive evidence of a design to include the house of Medici in the downfall of the Spanish power. Active preparations were everywhere made for war, and the whole character of the century seemed about to suffer change, and become matter of question.

But meanwhile how different a position was this pontificate assuming from that which it had been expected to take up! All purposes of reform were set aside for the struggles of war, and these last entailed consequences of a totally opposite character.

The pontiff, who as cardinal, had most sternly opposed the abuses of nepotism, and had denounced them, even to his own peril, was now seen to abandon himself entirely to this weakness. His nephew, Carlo Caraffa, who had passed his whole life amidst the excesses and license of camps,

---

and this his people call 'washing his teeth.' He used to eat in public like other popes, till his last indisposition, which was considered mortal—once he had lost his appetite. He often spent three hours at table in talk of various matters, according to the occasion, and in the heat of this he sometimes uttered things of secrecy and importance."

3. The account of the incredulity expressed by the Caraffas, when this truce was first named to them, as given by Navagero, is extremely characteristic: "Asking the Pope and Cardinal Caraffa if they had received intelligence of the truce, they looked at each other laughing, as if they would say, as indeed the pontiff openly said to me afterward, that there was but slight hope of that; yet the next day came the news, which so annoyed the Pope and cardinal (though it confronted all Rome), that they could not conceal their rage, and Paul said, "This truce will be the ruin of the world."

was now raised to the rank of cardinal, though Paul himself had often declared of him, that "his arm was dyed in blood to the elbow." Carlo had found means to gain over his superannuated relative; he contrived to be occasionally surprised by him in seeming prayer before the crucifix, and apparently suffering agonies of remorse, but still further was the uncle propitiated by the virulent enmity of his nephew to the Spaniards; this was their true bond of union. Carlo Caraffa had taken military service with the Emperor in Germany, but complained that he had met with neglect only as his reward. A prisoner, from whom he expected a large ransom, had been taken from him, nor had he been suffered to hold possession of a priory belonging to the order of Malta, to which he had been nominated. All these things had awakened his hatred and made him thirst for vengeance. This state of feeling, Paul allowed to stand in the place of all the virtues Carlo wanted; he could find no words eloquent enough to praise him, declaring that the papal seat had never possessed a more efficient servant; he made over to him the greater part, not only of the civil, but even of the ecclesiastical administration, and was perfectly satisfied that he should be regarded as the author of whatever acts of favor were received from the court.

On his other nephews the pontiff would not for some time bestow a glance of kindness; it was not until they had evinced their participation in his anti-Spanish mania, that they were received to his grace. Never could anyone have anticipated what he next did. Declaring that the Colonnas, "those incorrigible rebels against God and the Church," however frequently deprived of their castles, had always managed to regain them, he now resolved that this should be amended; he would give those fortresses to vassals who would know how to hold them. Thereupon he divided the possessions of the house of Colonna among his nephews, making the elder Duke of Palliano and the younger Marquis of Montebello. The cardinals remained silent when he announced these purposes in their assembly; they bent down their heads and fixed their eyes to the earth. The Caraffas now indulged in the most ambitious projects: the daughters of their family should marry into that of the French King, or at least into the ducal house of Ferrara; the sons thought of nothing less than the possession of Sienna. To one who spoke jestingly concerning the jewelled cap of a child of their house, the mother of the nephews replied, "We should rather be talking of crowns than caps."

And indeed everything was now depending on the events of the war which then broke out, but which certainly assumed no very promising aspect even from the commencement.

On that act of the fiscal before alluded to, the Duke of Alva had pressed forward from the Neapolitan territory into the States of the Church. He was accompanied by the Roman vassals, whose confederates also aroused themselves. The papal garrison was driven out of Nettuno, and the troops of the Colonnas recalled. Alva seized Frosinone, Anagni, Tivoli in the mountains, and Ostia on the sea. Rome was thus invested on both sides.

The Pope had first placed his reliance on his Romans, and reviewed them in person. They marched from the Campofiore, three hundred and forty columns armed with harquebuses, two hundred and fifty with pikes. In each rank stood nine men admirably appointed, presenting a most imposing aspect, and commanded by officers who were exclusively of noble birth. These troops passed before the castle of St. Angelo, which saluted them with its artillery, to the piazza of St. Peter, where the pontiff had stationed himself at a window with his nephews, and as each caporion and standard-bearer passed, his holiness bestowed his blessing. All this made a very fair show, but these were not the men by whom the city was to be defended. When the Spaniards had approached near the walls, a false alarm, occasioned by a small body of horse, was sufficient to throw them into such perfect confusion, that not one man was found remaining by his colors. The Pope saw that he must seek elsewhere for effectual aid, and after a time Pietro Strozzi brought him the troops that were serving before Sienna. With these he succeeded in recovering Tivoli and Ostia, thus averting the most imminent danger.

But what a war was this!

There are moments in the history of the world when it would seem that the actions of men are influenced by motives in direct opposition to the principles and ideas that usually govern their lives and conduct.

The Duke of Alva might, in the first instance, have conquered Rome with very little difficulty; but his uncle, Cardinal Giacomo, reminded him of the unhappy end to which all had come who had taken part in the conquest under Bourbon. Alva, being a good Catholic, conducted the war with the utmost discretion; he fought the Pope, but did not cease to pay him reverence; he would fain take the sword from his holiness, but had no desire for the renown of a Roman conqueror. His soldiers complained that they were led against a mere vapor, a mist and smoke that annoyed them, but which they could neither lay hold on nor stifle at its source.

And who were those by whom the Pope was defended against such good Catholics? The most effective among them were Germans, and Protestants to a man! They amused themselves with the saintly images on the highways, they laughed at the mass in the churches, were utterly regardless of the fast days, and did things innumerable, for which, at any other time, the Pope would have punished them with death. I even find that Carlo Caraffa established a very close intimacy with that great Protestant leader, the margrave Albert of Brandenburg.

Contradictions more perfect, a contrast more complete, than that displayed by these circumstances, could be scarcely imagined. On the one side we have the most fervent spirit of Catholicism, which was at least exemplified in the leader (how different were his proceedings from those of the old Bourbon times!); on the other, was that secular tendency of the popedom, by which even Paul IV, however earnestly condemning it, was seized and borne forward. Thus, it came to pass that the followers of his faith were attacking him, while it was by heretics and seceders that he found himself defended! But the first preserved their allegiance, even while opposing his power; the latter displayed their hostility to and contempt for his person even while in arms to protect him.

It was not until the French auxiliaries crossed the Alps that the contest really began; these consisted of ten thousand foot and a less numerous, but very brilliant body of cavalry. Their leader would most willingly have directed his force against Milan, which he believed to be unprepared for defence, but he was unable to resist the impulse by which the Caraffas forced him toward Naples. The latter were fully confident of finding numberless adherents in their own country, they counted on the assistance of the exiles, and hoped for the rising of their party; if not throughout the kingdom, yet certainly in the Abruzzi and round Aquila and Montorio, where their ancestors had always exercised an important influence, both on the paternal and maternal side.

It was manifest that affairs must now arrive at a crisis, in whatever manner this might terminate. The papal power had been too often excited into hostility against the Spanish predominance, not eventually to burst forth without restraint.

The Pope and his nephews were determined that matters should proceed to extremity; not only had Caraffa accepted the aid of the Protestants, he had even made proposals to Solyman I. These were to the effect that the Turkish sovereign should abstain from prosecuting his wars in Hungary, and throw himself with all his force on the two Sicilies.[4] Thus was a pontiff entreating the help of infidels against a Catholic monarch.

In April, 1557, the papal troops crossed the Neapolitan frontier. Holy Thursday was signalized by the conquest and atrocious pillage of Compli, which was full of treasure, in part belonging to the town, but also much was there beside that had been carried thither for safety. This done, Guise also crossed the Tronto, and besieged Civitella.

But he found the kingdom fully prepared to baffle his efforts. Alva knew well that there would be no insurrection among the people, so long

---

4. His confessions in Bromato, "Vita di Paolo IV.," tom. ii. p. 369. Bromato also gives us good information respecting the war; which he takes often word for word—a fact he does not conceal—from a voluminous MS. by Nores, which treats circumstantially of this war, and is to be found in many Italian libraries.

as he should retain the upper hand in the country; he had received a large grant of money from a parliament of the barons. Queen Bona of Poland, of the ancient family of Aragon, and a bitter enemy of the French, who had shortly before arrived in her duchy of Bari, with much treasure, supplied him with half a million of scudi. The ecclesiastical revenues that should have been sent to Rome he poured into his military chest instead, and even seized the gold and silver of the churches, with the bells of the city of Benevento, all which he appropriated to his own purposes. Thus furnished, he proceeded to fortify the towns of the Neapolitan frontier, as also those of the Roman territory that still remained in his hands. His army was composed in the usual manner of Germans, Spaniards, and Italians, but was an extremely formidable one. He also raised Neapolitan centuries under the command of the native nobles. Civitella was bravely defended by Count Santafiore, who had succeeded in rousing the inhabitants to active cooperation, and even to repel an attempt made to take the place by storm.

While the kingdom of Naples thus held firmly to King Philip, and displayed only devotion to his service, the assailants, on the contrary, were weakened by animosities and dissensions. French and Italians, Guise and Montebello, all were in the utmost discord. Guise complained that the Pope did not perform his part in the contract between them, and neglected to send him the promised supplies. When the Duke of Alva appeared with his army in the Abruzzi, toward the middle of May, Guise found it advisable to raise the siege, and retreat across the Tronto; operations were then again transferred to the Roman territories. And now was seen a war in which both sides advanced and then retreated; invested towns only to resign them, made great movements, in short, but on one occasion only did they come to a serious engagement.

Marc Antonio Colonna made demonstrations against Palliano, which had been taken from him by the Pope; seeing which, Giulio Orsino hurried to its relief with provisions and troops; 3,000 Swiss had arrived in Rome under the command of a colonel from Unterwalden. The Pope received them with great delight, decorated their officers with gold chains and knightly titles, and declared that this was a legion of angels sent by God for his behoof. These were the troops that, together with a few companies of Italian cavalry and infantry, marched under the command of Giulio Orsino. They were met by the forces of Marc Antonio Colonna, and once more ensued one of those bold battles in the manner of the Italian wars of 1494–1531, the papal troops against those of the empire, a Colonna opposing an Orsino; the German lanzknechts, under their distinguished leaders, Caspar von Feltz and Hans Walther, stood face to face, as they so often had done, with their ancient antagonists the Swiss. Once again the combatants on either side arrayed themselves for a cause in which neither felt the slightest interest, but for which they none the less fought with determined bravery. Hans Walther at length, "tall and strong," say the Spaniards, "as a giant," threw himself into the midst of a Swiss company. With a pistol in one hand and his naked sword in the other, he rushed upon the standard-bearer, whom he brought down, shooting him in the side, at the same moment that he dealt him a fatal blow on the head. The whole troop fell upon him, but his lanzknechts were already at hand for his support. The Swiss were completely broken and dispersed; their banners, on which had been inscribed in large letters, "Defenders of the faith and of the Holy See," were trampled in the dust, and of the eleven captains that went forth, their commander led two only back to Rome.

While this miniature war was in progress here, the great armies were in action on the frontier of the Netherlands. The battle of St. Quintin ensued, wherein the Spaniards gained a complete victory. In France men even wondered that they did not at once press forward to Paris, which at that moment they might certainly have taken.

Hereupon Henry II writes to Guise, "I hope," he remarks, "that the Pope will do as much for me in my need as I did for him in his straits." So little could Paul now hope from the aid of the French, that it was he on the contrary who was called on to help them. Guise declared, "that no claims would now avail to keep him in Italy," and he instantly hurried with all his forces to the aid of his embarrassed sovereign.

No force remaining that could oppose an obstacle to the imperialists and troops of Colonna, they advanced toward Rome, whose inhabitants once more saw themselves threatened with conquest and plunder. Their condition was all the more desperate from the fact that they had little less to fear from their defenders than from their enemies. During many nights they were compelled to keep lights burning in every window, and through all the streets. A skirmishing party of Spaniards which had reached the gates was frightened back by this demonstration, which was, however, a mere precaution against the papal troops; everyone murmured. The Romans wished their Pope in his grave a thousand times, and demanded that the Spanish army should be admitted by a formal capitulation.

So far did Paul IV permit his affairs to come. It was not until every enterprise had completely failed, till his allies were beaten, his States for the greater part invested by the enemy, and his capital a second time menaced with ruin, that he would bend himself to treat for peace.

This was accorded by the Spaniards in the same spirit by which they had been actuated throughout the war. They restored all such fortresses and cities of the Church as had been taken, and even promised compensation for Palliano, which the Caraffas had lost. Alva came to Rome; with the most profound reverence did he now kiss the foot of his conquered enemy, the sworn adversary of his King and nation. He was heard to say that never had he feared the face of man as he did that of the pontiff.

This peace seemed in every way favorable to the papal interest; it was nevertheless utterly fatal to all the projects hitherto cherished by the popedom. Any further attempt to throw off the Spanish yoke must now be abandoned, and accordingly, none such has ever (in the old sense and manner) been again brought forward. The influence of the Spaniards in Milan and Naples had proved unassailable. Their allies were more than ever powerful. There had been hope among the Caraffas of expelling Duke Cosmo from Florence; but this prince had not only held firm his grasp, but had seized on Sienna likewise, and was now the possessor of an important sovereignty. By the restitution of Placentia, the Farnesi had been gained over to Philip II. Marc Antonio Colonna had made himself a brilliant reputation, and had fully restored the ancient lustre of his family. For the pontiff there was nothing left but to resign himself to this position of affairs. Bitter as was this necessity to Paul IV, he yet felt that he must submit; with what feelings it is not difficult to imagine. Philip II being on some occasion called his friend, "Yes," he replied, "my friend who kept me beleaguered, and who thought to have my soul!" It is true that in the presence of strangers he compared Philip to the prodigal son of the gospel, but in the circle of his intimates he took care to mark his estimation of those pontiffs who had designed to raise the kings of France to the imperial throne, for others he had no praise. His sentiments were what they had always been, but the force of circumstances controlled him. There was nothing more to be hoped for, still less to be undertaken; he dared not even bemoan himself, unless in the closest secrecy.

When once an event is indeed accomplished, it is altogether useless for a man to struggle against its consequences. Even Paul IV felt this, and after a certain time his thoughts took another direction; he experienced a reaction which was of most effective importance, whether as regarded his own administration, or the general transformation brought about in the papal position and system.

Other pontiffs had promoted and favored their nephews from family affection, or mere selfish ambition to raise the house they sprang from; the nepotism of Paul had a totally different origin: his nephews were favored because they assisted his efforts against Spain, and because in this contest he considered them his natural allies; that once over, the utility of the nephews was at an end. It is only by success that a man is maintained in a position of great eminence, more especially if it be not acquired in a manner altogether legitimate. Cardinal Caraffa had undertaken an embassy to King Philip, principally to promote the interests of his own house, for which he desired to receive the compensation promised in lieu of Palliano.

He returned without having accomplished any material purpose, and from that time the Pope became ever colder and colder toward him. The cardinal soon perceived that he could no longer decide, as he had hitherto done, who should or should not be about the person of his uncle; he could no more exclude those who were inimical to himself, and rumors reached the pontiff, by which his unfavorable impressions of former days were revived; a serious illness once seized the cardinal, and on this occasion his uncle paid him a visit unexpectedly, when he found certain persons with him whose reputation was of the worst possible character. "Old people," said Paul, "are mistrustful, and I there saw things that opened a wide field before me." It is obvious that only very slight provocation was needed to arouse the storm within him, and this was presented by an occurrence otherwise of little importance. In the new year's night of 1559, there was a tumult in the streets, during which the young Cardinal Monte, that favorite of Pope Julius before mentioned, drew his sword. This was related to the pontiff the very next morning, and he felt greatly offended with the Cardinal Caraffa for not naming the circumstance to himself. He waited some days, but finding no word said, he then expressed his displeasure. The court, ever delighted with change, caught eagerly at this mark of disgrace. The Florentine ambassador, on whom the Caraffas had inflicted mortifications innumerable, now made his way to the presence, and uttered the most bitter complaints. The Marchese della Valle, one of the pontiff's family, but who had never been allowed access to him, found means to get a note placed in his breviary, in which certain of his nephew's misdeeds were described; "if his holiness should desire further explanations," said this paper, "he has but to sign his name." The Pope gave the required signature, and the promised information did not fail to appear. Thus, well provided with causes for resentment, Paul appeared on the ninth of January at the assembly of the Inquisition. He first spoke of that nocturnal riot, reproved Cardinal Monte with extreme severity, and repeatedly thundered forth "Reform! Reform!" The cardinals, usually so silent, had this time the courage to speak. "Holy father," said Cardinal Pacheco, interrupting the sovereign, "reform must first of all begin among ourselves!" The Pope was silenced; those words struck him to the heart; the half-formed convictions that had been gradually gaining power within him, were at once changed to palpable certainty; he said nothing more of Cardinal Monte's offences, but shut himself up in his apartment, burning with rage, and thinking only of his nephews. Giving immediate directions that no order proceeding from Cardinal Caraffa should be complied with, he sent to demand that minister's papers. Cardinal Vitellozzo Vitelli, who was believed to be in possession of all the Caraffa secrets, was immediately summoned, and compelled to swear that he would disclose all he knew. Camillo Orsino was called from his palace in the

Campagna, for the same purpose. Those of the more austere party, who had long remarked the proceedings of the nephews with disapproval, now made themselves heard. The old Theatine, Don Geremia, who was held to be a saint, passed long hours with his holiness, who was made acquainted with circumstances that he had never suspected, and which equally excited his detestation and horror. He fell into a state of pitiable agitation, could neither eat nor sleep, and passed ten days consumed by fever, resulting from distress of mind. At length he was resolved; and then was seen to occur an event forever memorable, a pope, with self-inflicted violence, tearing asunder the ties that bound him to his kindred. On the twenty-seventh of January a consistory was summoned, wherein the evil lives of his nephews were denounced with passionate emotion by the grieving pontiff, who called God and the world to bear witness that he had never known of these misdoings, but had been constantly deceived by those around him. He deprived the accused of all their offices, and condemned them to banishment, together with their families. The mother of the nephews, seventy years old, bent with age, and sinking beneath her infirmities, entreated for them, throwing herself at the Pope's feet as he entered the palace; but, though she was herself blameless, he passed her by with harsh words. The young Marchesa Montebello arrived in Rome from Naples at this time; she found her palace closed against her, at the inns they refused to receive her, she went from door to door in the rainy night, and could find no shelter, until in a remote quarter, to which no order had been sent, an innkeeper was found who permitted her to take refuge beneath his roof. Cardinal Caraffa vainly offered to constitute himself the Pope's prisoner, and required to have his conduct investigated. Paul commanded the Swiss guard to repel not himself only, but all who, having been in his service, should venture to approach the palace. He made but one exception; this was in favor of the young man, the son of Montorio, whom he loved greatly, and made cardinal in his eighteenth year; this youth he permitted to remain about his person, and take part in his devotional exercises; but he was never allowed to name his banished family, still less to implore their forgiveness; he dared not even hold the slightest intercourse with his father. The misfortunes of his house affected him all the more painfully from this restraint, and the suffering that he was not permitted to express in words, was yet manifest in his face, and legible in his whole person.[5]

---

5. Much valuable information as to these events may be found in Pallavicini, still more in Bromato. In the Berlin "Informationi" there is also, vol. viii., a "Diario d'alcune attioni più notabili nel Pontificato di Paolo IV. l'anno 1558, sino alla sua morte" (beginning from September 10, 1558). This was not known to either of the above writers; it was composed from personal observation, and has supplied me with much information altogether new.

And would it not be supposed that occurrences of this character must react on the mind of the pontiff?

He proceeded as though nothing had happened. Immediately after having pronounced sentence against his kindred with stormy eloquence in the consistory, he betook himself to other business, and while most of the cardinals were paralyzed by fear and astonishment, the pontiff betrayed no emotion. The foreign ambassadors were amazed by this coolness of demeanor. "In the midst of changes so unexpected and so complete," they remarked, "surrounded by ministers and servants all new and strange, he maintains himself steadfastly, unbending and imperturbable; he feels no compassion, and seems not even to retain a remembrance of his ruined house." Henceforth it was to a totally different passion that he surrendered the guidance of his life.

This change was most certainly of the highest importance, and of ever memorable effect. His hatred to the Spaniards, and the hope of becoming the liberator of Italy, had hurried even Paul IV into designs and practices utterly worldly; these had led him to the endowment of his kinsmen with the lands of the Church, and had caused the elevation of a mere soldier to the administration even of ecclesiastical affairs. They had plunged him into deadly feuds and sanguinary hostilities. Events had compelled him to abandon that hope, to suppress that hatred, and then were his eyes gradually opened to the reprehensible conduct of those about him. Against these offenders, after a painful combat with himself, his stern justice prevailed, he shook them off, and from that hour his early plans of reformation were resumed; he began to reign in the manner that had at first been expected from him. And now, with that impetuous energy which he had previously displayed in his enmities, and in the conduct of his wars, he turned to the reform of the State, and above all to that of the Church.

All secular offices, from the highest to the lowest, were transferred to other hands. The existing podestas and governors lost their places, and the manner in which this was effected was occasionally very singular. In Perugia, for example, the newly appointed governor arrived in the night; without waiting for daylight, he caused the anziani to be called together, produced his credentials, and commanded them forthwith to arrest their former governor, who was present. From time immemorial, there had been no pope who governed without nepotism: Paul IV now showed this example. The places hitherto monopolized by his kinsmen were bestowed on Cardinal Carpi, Camillo Orsino who had held so extensive a power under Paul III, and others. Nor were the persons only changed, the whole system and character of the administration were changed also. Important sums were economized, and taxes to a proportional amount were remitted; the pontiff established a chest, of which he only held the key, for the purpose of receiving all complaints that any man should desire to make;

he demanded a daily report from the governor. The public business in general was conducted with great circumspection; nor were any of the old abuses permitted to remain.

Amidst all the commotions prevailing through the early part of his pontificate, Paul IV had never lost sight of his reforming projects; he now resumed them with earnest zeal and undivided attention. A more severe discipline was introduced into the churches: he forbade all begging; even the collection of alms for masses, hitherto made by the clergy, was discontinued; and such pictures as were not, by their subjects, appropriate to the Church, he removed. A medal was struck in his honor, representing Christ driving the money-changers from the temple. All monks who had deserted their monasteries were expelled from the city and States of the Church; the court was enjoined to keep the regular fasts, and all were commanded to solemnize Easter by receiving the Lord's Supper. The cardinals were even compelled to occasional preaching, and Paul himself preached! Many abuses that had been profitable to the Curia he did his best to set aside. Of marriage dispensations, or of the resources they furnished to the treasury, he would not even hear mention. A host of places that, up to his time, had been constantly sold, even those of the clerks of the chamber (chiericati di camera), he would now have disposed of according to merit only. Still more rigidly did he insist on the worth and clerical endowments of all on whom he bestowed the purely ecclesiastical employments. He would no longer endure those compacts by which one man had hitherto been allowed to enjoy the revenues of an office, while he made over its duties to another, by whom, for some mean hire, they were performed, well or ill, as might chance. He had also formed the design of reinstating the bishops in many rights which had been wrongfully withheld from them; and considered it highly culpable that everything should be absorbed by Rome which could in any way be made to yield either profit or influence.

Nor were the reforms of Paul confined to the mere abolition of abuses. Not content with a negative effect only, he proceeded to practical amendments. The services of the Church were performed with increased pomp; it is to him we are indebted for the rich ornaments of the Sixtine chapel, and for the solemn representation of the holy sepulchre. There is an ideal of the modern Catholic service of the altar, full of dignity, devotion, and splendor: this it was that floated before the eyes of Paul, and which he would fain have realized.

He permitted no day to pass over, as he boasts, without the promulgation of some edict tending to restore the Church to its original purity. Many of his decrees present the outlines of those ordinances which were afterward sanctioned by the Council of Trent.

In the course now adopted, Paul displayed, as might have been expected, all that inflexibility of nature peculiar to him.

Above all other institutions, he favored that of the Inquisition, which he had himself re-established. The days appointed for the "segnatura" and the consistory he would often suffer to pass unnoticed; but never did he miss the Thursday, which was that set apart for the congregation of the Inquisition, and when it assembled before him. The powers of this office he desired to see exercised with the utmost rigor. He subjected new classes of offence to its jurisdiction, and conferred on it the barbarous prerogative of applying torture for the detection of accomplices. He permitted no respect of persons; the most distinguished nobles were summoned before this tribunal, and cardinals, such as Morone and Foscherari, were now thrown into prison, because certain doubts had occurred to him as to the soundness of their opinions, although these very men had been formerly appointed to examine the contents, and decide the orthodoxy, of important books—the "Spiritual Exercises" of Loyola, for example. It was Paul IV by whom the festival of St. Domenico was established, in honor of that great inquisitor.

Thus did a rigid austerity and earnest zeal for the restoration of primitive habits become the prevailing tendency of the popedom.

Paul IV seemed almost to have forgotten that he had ever pursued other purposes than those that now occupied him; the memory of past times seemed extinguished; he lived and moved in his reforms and his Inquisition, gave laws, imprisoned, excommunicated, and held *autos-da-fé*; these occupations filled up his life. At length, when laid prostrate by disease, such as would have caused death even to a younger man, he called his cardinals about him, commended his soul to their prayers, and the holy see with the Inquisition, to their earnest care. Once more would he fain have collected his energies: he sought to raise himself, but the disease prevailed; his strength had failed him—he fell back and expired (August 18, A.D. 1559).

In one respect, at least, are these determined and passionate characters more fortunate than men of feebler mould; they are, perhaps, blinded by the force of their feelings—the violence of their prejudices, but they are also steeled by this force; this violence it is that renders them invincible.

The Roman people did not forget what they had suffered under Paul IV so readily as he had done—they could not forgive him the war he had brought on the State; nor, though they abhorred his nephews, did their disgrace suffice to the resentment of the multitude. On his death being made known, large crowds assembled in the capital, and resolved that, as he had not deserved well either of Rome, or of the world, so would they destroy his monuments. Others attacked the buildings of the Inquisition, set fire to them, and roughly handled the servants of the holy office; they even threatened to burn the Dominican convent of Maria alla Minerva. The Colonnas, the Orsini, Cesarini, Massimi, and other nobles whom

Paul had mortally offended, took part in these tumults. The statue that had been erected to this Pope was torn from its pedestal, broken to pieces, and the head, bearing the triple crown, was dragged through the streets.

Bibliography

Engel-Janosi, F. *The Growth of German Historicism.* Baltimore, Md.: 1944.

Gay, Peter, "Ranke: The Respectful Critic." In *Style in History.* New York, 1974.

Geyl, Pieter. *Debates with Historians.* New York, 1958.

Gooch, G. P. *History and Historians of the Nineteenth Century.* London, 1913.

Higham, John, Leonard Krieger, and Felix Gilbert. *History.* Englewood Cliffs, N.J., 1965.

Iggers, Georg. *The German Conception of History, From Herder to the Present.* Middletown, Conn., 1968.

Iggers, Georg and Konrad von Moltke, eds. *Leopold von Ranke, The Theory and Practice of History.* New York, 1973.

Krieger, Leonard. *Ranke: The Meaning of History.* Chicago, 1977.

von Laue, Theodore H. *Leopold von Ranke: The Formative Years.* Princeton, 1950.

White, Hayden. *Metahistory, The Historical Imagination in Nineteenth-Century Europe.* Baltimore, Md.: 1973.

Wines, Roger. ed. *Leopold von Ranke, The Secret of World History, Selected Writings in the Art and Science of History,* New York, 1983.

CHAPTER 12

Thomas Babington Macaulay

The History of England from the Accession of James II

(1849–1861)

The nineteenth century revered Thomas Babington Macaulay (1800–1859) only a little less than Leopold von Ranke, yet a large philosophical gulf separated them. They were aware of each other's work and even met once when Ranke came to London in 1843, but neither knew the other's language, and their "discussion" could not explore their contrasting approaches to history. Ranke was the historicist: "Every period is immediate to God," he wrote, "and its value does not in the least consist in what springs from it, but in its own existence, in its own self." Macaulay, on the other hand, thought the value of an era consisted almost exclusively in what sprang from it, for he was a Whig and wrote Whig history. The past was prologue to the enlightened present and must be judged by it. Thus, his *History of England* evokes not so much England in the seventeenth century as it does the seventeenth-century fight for ideas and institutions like Parliamentary rule, civil liberties, religious toleration, and material progress, which Macaulay hallowed in his own time. Ranke wrote on English history, too, but his seventeenth century is more analytical than judgmental.

Macaulay came from a reformist family. His father, Zachary, was a founder of the "Clapham Sect," a group of Evangelical Christians who made the abolition of slavery their special cause. Thomas was a precocious boy and won honors as an essayist and debater at Cambridge University. Two early essays, "Milton" (1825) and "History" (1828), gave him the subject and method for his later work. His defense of the poet John Milton's antiroyalist politics in the seventeenth century established Macaulay's own sympathy with Parliamentary forces and the whole Whig tradition. And his argument that history should go beyond battles, diplomacy, and politics to embrace whole societies, including the doings of ordinary people, would be reflected in the sheer breadth of his later *History of England*, especially in the famous long third chapter, "England in 1685."

Macaulay was also a long-time member of Parliament, where he was instrumental in the passage of the Reform Bill of 1832. The Reform Bill broadened the membership of Parliament, and to opponents of this Whig idea Macaulay urged "change in order to preserve." That was also the message of his *History of England,* for while he was certainly no radical, Macaulay did expect meaningful gradual changes in politics to match changes in economics and society. His *History,* which covers English society in the volatile years from 1685 to 1702, demonstrated the value of specific changes, especially Parliamentary rule, and the chaos that resulted when a king obstructed them. The first two volumes of his work appeared in 1848, a year of widespread revolution in Europe but not in England, and a year, therefore, that provided an instructive setting for Macaulay's lesson.

The seventeenth century had seen the quarrels between the Stuart kings and Parliament over money, religion, and civil liberties flare into civil war by the 1640s. Charles I was beheaded in 1649, and Oliver Cromwell ruled as a military strongman until 1658. Charles II reestablished Stuart power which held until his death in 1685, but his heir, James II, a Catholic, offered fresh challenges to Whig expectations of Protestantism and a limited, constitutional monarchy. Macaulay picks up the story with the accession of James II and, in a highly colored narrative, describes rebellions by the Duke of Monmouth and the Scottish Earl of Argyle, James's reprisals through the scourges of Lord George Jeffreys and the "Bloody Assizes," the king's pressures on behalf of Catholicism matched by Protestant resistance, and, finally, the arrival of William of Orange from Holland and the flight of James before William's conquering army.

Macaulay was popular and meant to be, for unlike Edward Gibbon, who wrote for men of letters who would appreciate his careful choice of words, Macaulay wrote for anyone who could read. His sense of his readership influenced his style. He is sharply judgmental, given to exaggeration and repetition, rises to a swelling phrase when a more natural one would do and crystallizes human character in brilliant sketches, which often draw meaning from physical attributes. Though his research was extensive, Macaulay often pretends to know more about the interior thoughts of men and masses than he could possibly prove. His fondness for contrasting what happened with what *might* have happened is a clue to his belief that nothing in history is inevitable. Finally, his use of antithesis—contrasting "opposite" events or characteristics—as the organizational principle for single sentences or for whole chapters (as in the antithetical relationship between bad King James and good King William) shows that Macaulay saw history as essentially a series of combats. If Ranke is remembered for his method, Macaulay is remembered for his great skill as a narrator.

These characteristics may be followed in the excerpt below, in which Macaulay treats Lord Jeffreys and the Bloody Assizes, the resistance of the Anglican bishops, William's arrival, and an outbreak of radicalism.

T HE GREAT SEAL was left in Guildford's custody; but a marked indignity was at the same time offered to him. It was determined that another lawyer of more vigour and audacity should be called to assist in the administration. The person selected was Sir George Jeffreys, Chief Justice of the Court of King's Bench. The depravity of this man has passed into a proverb. Both the great English parties have attacked his memory with emulous violence: for the Whigs considered him as their most barbarous enemy; and the Tories found it convenient to throw on him the blame of all the crimes which had sullied their triumph. A diligent and candid enquiry will show that some frightful stories which have been told concerning him are false or exaggerated. Yet the dispassionate historian will be able to make very little deduction from the vast mass of infamy with which the memory of the wicked judge has been loaded.

He was a man of quick and vigorous parts, but constitutionally prone to insolence and to the angry passions. When just emerging from boyhood he had risen into practise at the Old Bailey bar, a bar where advocates have always used a license of tongue unknown in Westminster Hall. Here, during many years his chief business was to examine and cross-examine the most hardened miscreants of a great capital. Daily conflicts with prostitutes and thieves called out and exercised his powers so effectually that he became the most consummate bully ever known in his profession. Tenderness for others and respect for himself were feelings alike unknown to him. He acquired a boundless command of the rhetoric in which the vulgar express hatred and contempt. The profusion of maledictions and vituperative epithets which composed his vocabulary could hardly have been rivalled in the fishmarket or the bear garden. His countenance and his voice must always have been unamiable. But these natural advantages—for such he seems to have thought them—he had improved to such a degree that there were few who, in his paroxysms of rage, could see or hear him without emotion. Impudence and ferocity sate upon his brow. The glare of his eyes had a fascination for the unhappy victim on whom they were fixed. Yet his brow and his eyes were less terrible than the savage lines of his mouth. His yell of fury, as was said by one who had often heard it, sounded like the thunder of the judgment day. These qualifications he carried, while still a young man, from the bar to the bench. He early became Common Serjeant, and then Recorder of London. As a

From James Babington Macaulay, *The History of England from the Accession of James II,* 5 vols. (Philadelphia: Porter and Coates, n.d.), 1: 406–10, 572–79; 2: 341–48, 426–33, 499–504.

judge at the City sessions he exhibited the same propensities which afterwards, in a higher post, gained for him an unenviable immortality. Already might be remarked in him the most odious vice which is incident to human nature, a delight in misery merely as misery. There was a fiendish exultation in the way in which he pronounced sentence on offenders. Their weeping and imploring seemed to titillate him voluptuously; and he loved to scare them into fits by dilating with luxuriant amplification on all the details of what they were to suffer. Thus, when he had an opportunity of ordering an unlucky adventuress to be whipped at the cart's tail, "Hangman," he would exclaim, " I charge you to pay particular attention to this lady! Scourge her soundly, man! Scourge her till the blood runs down! It is Christmas, a cold time for Madam to strip in! See that you warm her shoulders thoroughly!" He was hardly less facetious when he passed judgment on poor Lodowick Muggleton, the drunken tailor who fancied himself a prophet. "Impudent rogue!" roared Jeffreys, "thou shalt have an easy, easy, easy punishment!" One part of this easy punishment was the pillory, in which the wretched fanatic was almost killed with brickbats.

By this time the heart of Jeffreys had been hardened to that temper which tyrants require in their worst implements. He had hitherto looked for professional advancement to the corporation of London. He had therefore professed himself a Roundhead, and had always appeared to be in a higher state of exhilaration when he explained to Popish priests that they were to be cut down alive, and were to see their own bowels burned, than when he passed ordinary sentences of death. But, as soon as he had got all that the city could give, he made haste to sell his forehead of brass and his tongue of venom to the Court. Chiffinch, who was accustomed to act as broker in infamous contracts of more than one kind, lent his aid. He had conducted many amorous and many political intrigues; but he assuredly never rendered a more scandalous service to his masters than when he introduced Jeffreys to Whitehall. The renegade soon found a patron in the obdurate and revengeful James, but was always regarded with scorn and disgust by Charles, whose faults, great as they were, had no affinity with insolence and cruelty. "That man," said the King, "has no learning, no sense, no manners, and more impudence than ten carted streetwalkers." Work was to be done, however, which could be trusted to no man who reverenced law or was sensible of shame; and thus Jeffreys, at an age at which a barrister thinks himself fortunate if he is employed to conduct an important cause, was made Chief Justice of the King's Bench.

His enemies could not deny that he possessed some of the qualities of a great judge. His legal knowledge, indeed, was merely such as he had picked up in practise of no very high kind. But he had one of those happily constituted intellects which, across labyrinths of sophistry, and through masses of immaterial facts, go straight to the true point. Of his intellect, however, he seldom had the full use. Even in civil causes his malevolent and despotic temper perpetually disordered his judgment. To enter his court was to enter the den of a wild beast, which none could tame, and which was as likely to be roused to rage by caresses as by attacks. He frequently poured forth on plaintiffs and defendants, barristers and attorneys, witnesses and jurymen, torrents of frantic abuse, intermixed with oaths and curses. His looks and tones had inspired terror when he was merely a young advocate struggling into practice. Now that he was at the head of the most formidable tribunal in the realm, there were few indeed who did not tremble before him. Even when he was sober, his violence was sufficiently frightful. But in general his reason was overclouded and his evil passions stimulated by the fumes of intoxication. His evenings were ordinarily given to revelry. People who saw him only over his bottle would have supposed him to be a man gross indeed, sottish, and addicted to low company and low merriment, but social and goodhumoured. He was constantly surrounded on such occasions by buffoons selected, for the most part, from among the vilest pettifoggers who practised before him. These men bantered and abused each other for his entertainment. He joined in their ribald talk, sang catches with them, and, when his head grew hot, hugged and kissed them in an ecstasy of drunken fondness. But though wine at first seemed to soften his heart, the effect a few hours later was very different. He often came to the judgment seat, having kept the court waiting long, and yet having but half slept off his debauch, his cheeks on fire, his eyes staring like those of a maniac. When he was in this state, his boon companions of the preceding night, if they were wise, kept out of his way: for the recollection of the familiarity to which he had admitted them inflamed his malignity; and he was sure to take every opportunity of overwhelming them with execration and invective. Not the least odious of his many odious peculiarities was the pleasure which he took in publicly browbeating and mortifying those whom, in his fits of maudlin tenderness, he had encouraged to presume on his favour.

The services which the government had expected from him were performed, not merely without flinching, but eagerly and triumphantly. His first exploit was the judicial murder of Algernon Sidney. What followed was in perfect harmony with this beginning. Respectable Tories lamented the disgrace which the barbarity and indecency of so great a functionary brought upon the administration of justice. But the excesses which filled such men with horror were titles to the esteem of James. Jeffreys, therefore very soon after the death of Charles obtained a seat in the cabinet and a peerage. This last honour was a signal mark of royal approbation. For, since the judicial system of the realm had been remodelled in the thirteenth century, no Chief Justice had been a Lord of Parliament.

At Winchester the Chief Justice first opened his commission. Hampshire had not been the theatre of war; but many of the vanquished rebels had, like their leader, fled thither. Two of them, John Hickes, a Nonconformist divine, and Richard Nelthorpe, a lawyer who had been outlawed for taking part in the Rye House plot, had sought refuge at the house of Alice, widow of John Lisle. John Lisle had sate in the Long Parliament and in the High Court of Justice, had been a commissioner of the Great Seal in the days of the Commonwealth, and had been created a Lord by Cromwell. The titles given by the Protector had not been recognised by any government which had ruled England since the downfall of his house; but they appear to have been often used in conversation even by Royalists. John Lisle's widow was therefore commonly known as the Lady Alice. She was related to many respectable, and to some noble, families; and she was generally esteemed even by the Tory gentlemen of her country. For it was well known to them that she had deeply regretted some violent acts in which her husband had borne a part, that she had shed bitter tears for Charles the First, and that she had protected and relieved many Cavaliers in their distress. The same womanly kindness, which had led her to befriend the Royalists in their time of trouble, would not suffer her to refuse a meal and a hiding place to the wretched men who now entreated her to protect them. She took them into her house, set meat and drink before them, and showed them where they might take rest. The next morning her dwelling was surrounded by soldiers. Strict search was made. Hickes was found concealed in the malthouse, and Nelthorpe in the chimney. If Lady Alice knew her guests to have been concerned in the insurrection, she was undoubtedly guilty of what in strictness was a capital crime. For the law of principal and accessory, as respects high treason, then was, and is to this day, in a state disgraceful to English jurisprudence. In cases of felony, a distinction, founded on justice and reason, is made between the principal and the accessory after the fact. He who conceals from justice one whom he knows to be a murderer is liable to punishment, but not to the punishment of murder. He, on the other hand, who shelters one whom he knows to be a traitor is, according to all our jurists, guilty of high treason. It is unnecessary to point out the absurdity and cruelty of a law which includes under the same definition, and visits with the same penalty, offences lying at the opposite extremes of the scale of guilt. The feeling which makes the most loyal subject shrink from the thought of giving up to a shameful death the rebel who, vanquished, hunted down, and in mortal agony, begs for a morsel of bread and a cup of water, may be a weakness; but it is surely a weakness very nearly allied to virtue, a weakness which, constituted as human beings are, we can hardly eradicate from the mind without eradicating many noble and benevolent sentiments. A wise and good ruler may not think it right to sanction this weakness; but he will generally connive at it, or punish it very tenderly. In no case will he treat it as a crime of the blackest dye. Whether Flora Macdonald was justified in concealing the attainted heir of the Stuarts, whether a brave soldier of our time was justified in assisting the escape of Lavalette, are questions on which casuists may differ: but to class such actions with the crimes of Guy Faux and Fieschi is an outrage to humanity and common sense. Such, however, is the classification of our law. It is evident that nothing but a lenient administration could make such a state of the law endurable. And it is just to say that, during many generations, no English government, save one, has treated with rigour persons guilty merely of harbouring defeated and flying insurgents. To women especially has been granted, by a kind of tacit prescription, the right of indulging, in the midst of havoc and vengeance, that compassion which is the most endearing of all their charms. Since the beginning of the great civil war, numerous rebels, some of them far more important than Hickes or Nelthorpe, have been protected from the severity of victorious governments by female adroitness and generosity. But no English ruler who has been thus baffled, the savage and implacable James alone excepted, has had the barbarity even to think of putting a lady to a cruel and shameful death for so venial and amiable a transgression.

Odious as the law was, it was strained for the purpose of destroying Alice Lisle. She could not, according to the doctrine laid down by the highest authority, be convicted till after the conviction of the rebels whom she had harboured. She was, however, set to the bar before either Hickes or Nelthorpe had been tried. It was no easy matter in such a case to obtain a verdict for the crown. The witnesses prevaricated. The jury, consisting of the principal gentlemen of Hampshire, shrank from the thought of sending a fellow creature to the stake for conduct which seemed deserving rather of praise than of blame. Jeffreys was beside himself with fury. This was the first case of treason on the circuit; and there seemed to be a strong probability that his prey would escape him. He stormed, cursed, and swore in language which no wellbred man would have used at a race or a cockfight. One witness named Dunne, partly from concern for Lady Alice, and partly from fright at the threats and maledictions of the Chief Justice, entirely lost his head, and at last stood silent. "Oh how hard the truth is," said Jeffreys, "to come out of a lying Presbyterian knave." The witness, after a pause of some minutes, stammered a few unmeaning words. "Was there ever," exclaimed the judge, with an oath, "was there ever such a villain on the face of the earth? Dost thou believe that there is a God? Dost thou believe in hell fire? Of all the witnesses that I ever met with I never saw thy fellow." Still the poor man, scared out of his senses, remained mute; and again Jeffreys burst forth. "I hope, gentlemen of the jury, that you take notice of the horrible carriage of this fellow. How can one help abhorring both these men and their religion? A Turk is a saint to such a fellow as this. A Pagan would be ashamed of such villany. Oh blessed Jesus! What a generation of vipers do we live among!" "I cannot tell what to say, my Lord," faltered Dunne. The judge again broke forth into a volley of oaths. "Was there ever," he cried, "such an impudent rascal? Hold the candle to him that we may see his brazen face. You, gentlemen, that are of counsel for the crown, see that an information for perjury be preferred against this fellow." After the witnesses had been thus handled, the Lady Alice was called on for her defence. She began by saying, what may possibly have been true, that though she knew Hickes to be in trouble when she took him in, she did not know or suspect that he had been concerned in the rebellion. He was a divine, a man of peace. It had, therefore, never occurred to her that he could have borne arms against the government; and she had supposed that he wished to conceal himself because warrants were out against him for field preaching. The Chief Justice began to storm. "But I will tell you. There is not one of those lying, snivelling, canting Presbyterians but, one way or another, had a hand in the rebellion. Presbytery has all manner of villany in it. Nothing but Presbytery could have made Dunne such a rogue. Show me a Presbyterian; and I'll show thee a lying knave." He summed up in the same style, declaimed during an hour against Whigs and Dissenters, and reminded the jury that the prisoner's husband had borne a part in the death of Charles the First, a fact which had not been proved by any testimony, and which, if it had been proved, would have been utterly irrelevant to the issue. The jury retired, and remained long in consultation. The judge grew impatient. He could not conceive, he said, how, in so plain a case, they should even have left the box. He sent a messenger to tell them that, if they did not instantly return, he would adjourn the court and lock them up all night. Thus put to the torture, they came, but came to say that they doubted whether the charge had been made out. Jeffreys expostulated with them vehemently, and, after another consultation, they gave a reluctant verdict of Guilty.

On the following morning sentence was pronounced. Jeffreys gave directions that Alice Lisle should be burned alive that very afternoon. This excess of barbarity moved the pity and indignation even of the class which was most devoted to the crown. The clergy of Winchester Cathedral remonstrated with the Chief Justice, who, brutal as he was, was not mad enough to risk a quarrel on such a subject with a body so much respected by the Tory party. He consented to put off the execution five days. During that time the friends of the prisoner besought James to be merciful. Ladies of high rank interceded for her. Feversham, whose recent victory had increased his influence at court, and who, it is said, had been bribed to take the compassionate side, spoke in her favour. Clarendon, the King's brother in law, pleaded her cause. But all was vain. The utmost that could be obtained was that her sentence should be commuted from burning to beheading. She was put to death on a scaffold in the marketplace of Winchester, and underwent her fate with serene courage.

In Hampshire Alice Lisle was the only victim: but, on the day following her execution, Jeffreys reached Dorchester, the principal town of the county in which Monmouth had landed; and the judicial massacre began. The court was hung, by order of the Chief Justice, with scarlet; and this innovation seemed to the multitude to indicate a bloody purpose. It was also rumoured that, when the clergyman who preached the assize sermon enforced the duty of mercy, the ferocious mouth of the Judge was distorted by an ominous grin. These things made men augur ill of what was to follow.

More than three hundred prisoners were to be tried. The work seemed heavy; but Jeffreys had a contrivance for making it light. He let it be understood that the only chance of obtaining pardon or respite was to plead guilty. Twenty-nine persons, who put themselves on their country and were convicted, were ordered to be tied up without delay. The remaining prisoners pleaded guilty by scores. Two hundred and ninety-two received sentence of death. The whole number hanged in Dorsetshire amounted to seventy-four.

From Dorchester Jeffreys proceeded to Exeter. The civil war had barely grazed the frontier of Devonshire. Here, therefore, comparatively few persons were capitally punished. Somersetshire, the chief seat of the rebellion, had been reserved for the last and the most fearful vengeance. In this county two hundred and thirty-three prisoners were in a few days hanged, drawn, and quartered. At every spot where two roads met, on every marketplace, on the green of every large village which had furnished Monmouth with soldiers, ironed corpses clattering in the wind, or heads and quarters stuck on poles, poisoned the air, and made the traveller sick with horror. In many parishes the peasantry could not assemble in the house of God without seeing the ghastly face of a neighbour grinning at them over the porch. The Chief Justice was all himself. His spirits rose higher and higher as the work went on. He laughed, shouted, joked, and swore in such a way that many thought him drunk from morning to night. But in him it was not easy to distinguish the madness produced by evil passions from the madness produced by brandy. A prisoner affirmed that the witnesses who appeared against him were not entitled to credit. One of them, he said, was a Papist, and another a prostitute. "Thou impudent rebel," exclaimed the Judge, "to reflect on the King's evidence! I see thee, villain, I see thee already with the halter round thy neck." Another produced testimony that he was a good Protestant. "Protestant!" said Jeffreys; "you mean Presbyterian. I'll hold you a wager of it. I can smell a Presbyterian forty miles." One wretched man moved the pity even of bitter Tories. "My Lord," they said, "this poor creature is on the parish." "Do not trouble yourselves," said the Judge, "I will ease the parish of the burden." It was not only against the prisoners that his fury broke forth. Gentlemen and noblemen of high consideration and stainless loyalty, who ventured to bring to his notice any extenuating circumstances, were almost sure to receive what he called, in the coarse dialect which he had learned in the pothouses of Whitechapel, a lick with the rough side of his tongue. Lord Stawell, a Tory peer, who could not conceal his horror at the remorseless manner in which his poor neighbours were butchered, was punished by having a corpse suspended in chains at his park gate. In such spectacles originated many tales of terror, which were long told over the cider by the Christmas fires of the farmers of Somersetshire. Within the last forty years, peasants, in some districts, well knew the accursed spots, and passed them unwillingly after sunset.

Jeffreys boasted that he had hanged more traitors than all his predecessors together since the Conquest. It is certain that the number of persons whom he put to death in one month, and in one shire, very much exceeded the number of all the political offenders who have been put to death in our island since the Revolution. The rebellions of 1715 and 1745 were of longer duration, of wider extent, and of more formidable aspect than that which was put down at Sedgemoor. It has not been generally thought that, either after the rebellion of 1715, or after the rebellion of 1745, the House of Hanover erred on the side of clemency. Yet all the executions of 1715 and 1745 added together will appear to have been few indeed when compared with those which disgraced the Bloody Assizes. The number of the rebels whom Jeffreys hanged on this circuit was three hundred and twenty.

Such havoc must have excited disgust even if the sufferers had been generally odious. But they were, for the most part, men of blameless life, and of high religious profession. They were regarded by themselves, and by a large proportion of their neighbours, not as wrongdoers, but as martyrs who sealed with blood the truth of the Protestant religion. Very few of the convicts professed any repentance for what they had done. Many, animated by the old Puritan spirit, met death, not merely with fortitude, but with exultation. It was in vain that the ministers of the Established Church lectured them on the guilt of rebellion and on the importance of priestly absolution. The claim of the King to unbounded authority in things temporal, and the claim of the clergy to the spiritual power of binding and loosing, moved the bitter scorn of the intrepid sectaries. Some of them composed hymns in the dungeon, and chaunted them on the fatal sledge. Christ, they sang while they were undressing for the butchery, would soon come to rescue Zion and to make war on Babylon, would set up his standard, would blow his trumpet, and would requite his foes tenfold for all the evil which had been inflicted on his servants. The dying words of these men were noted down: their farewell letters were kept as treasures; and, in this way, with the help of some invention and exaggeration, was formed a copious supplement to the Marian martyrology.

. . . .

The trial then commenced, a trial which, even when cooly perused after the lapse of more than a century and a half, has all the interest of a drama. The advocates contended on both sides with far more than professional keenness and vehemence; the audience listened with as much anxiety as if the fate of every one of them was to be decided by the verdict; and the turns of fortune were so sudden and amazing that the multitude repeatedly passed in a single minute from anxiety to exultation, and back again from exultation to still deeper anxiety.

The information charged the Bishops with having written or published, in the county of Middlesex, a false, malicious, and seditious libel. The Attorney and Solicitor first tried to prove the writing. For this purpose several persons were called to speak to the hands of the Bishops. But the witnesses were so unwilling that hardly a single plain answer could be extracted from any of them. Pemberton, Pollexfen, and Levinz contended that there was no evidence to go to the jury. Two of the Judges, Holloway and Powell, declared themselves of the same opinion; and the hopes of the spectators rose high. All at once the crown lawyers announced their intention to take another line. Powis, with shame and reluctance which he could not dissemble, put into the witness box Blathwayt, a Clerk of the Privy Council, who had been present when the King interrogated the Bishops. Blathwayt swore that he had heard them own their signatures. His testimony was decisive. "Why," said Judge Holloway to the Attorney, "when you had such evidence, did you not produce it at first, without all this waste of time?" It soon appeared why the counsel for the crown had been unwilling, without absolute necessity, to resort to this mode of proof. Pemberton stopped Blathwayt, subjected him to a searching cross-examination, and insisted upon having all that had passed between the King and the defendants fully related. "That is a pretty thing indeed," cried Williams. "Do you think," said Powis, "that you are at liberty to ask our witnesses any impertinent question that comes into your heads?" The advocates of the Bishops were not men to be so put down. "He is sworn," said Pollexfen, "to tell the truth and the whole truth; and an answer we must and will have." The witness shuffled, equivocated, pretended to misunderstand the questions, implored the protection of the Court. But he was in hands from which it was not easy to escape. At length the Attorney again interposed. "If," he said, "you persist in asking such a question, tell us, at least, what use you mean to make of it." Pemberton, who, through the whole trial, did his duty manfully and ably, replied without hesitation: "My Lords, I will answer Mr. Attorney. I will deal plainly with the Court. If the Bishops owned this paper under a promise from His Majesty that their confession should not be used against them, I hope that no unfair advantage will be taken of them." "You put on His Majesty what I dare hardly name," said Williams. "Since you will be so pressing, I demand, for the King, that the question may be recorded." "What do you mean, Mr. Solicitor?" said Sawyer, interposing. "I know what I mean," said the apostate: "I desire that the question may be recorded in court." "Record what you will. I am not afraid of you, Mr. Solicitor," said Pemberton. Then came a loud and fierce altercation, which Wright could with difficulty quiet. In other circumstances, he would probably have ordered the question to be recorded, and Pemberton to be committed. But on this great day the unjust Judge was overawed. He often cast a side glance towards the thick rows of Earls and Barons by whom he was watched, and before whom, in the next Parliament, he might stand at the bar. He looked, a bystander said, as if all the peers present had halters in their pockets. At length Blathwayt was forced to give a full account of what had passed. It appeared that the King had entered into no express covenant with the Bishops. But it appeared also that the Bishops might not unreasonably think that there was an implied engagement. Indeed from the unwillingness of the crown lawyers to put the Clerk of the Council into the witness box, and from the vehemence with which they objected to Pemberton's cross-examination, it is plain that they were themselves of this opinion.

However, the handwriting was now proved. But a new and serious objection was raised. It was not sufficient to prove that the Bishops had written the alleged libel. It was necessary to prove also that they had written it in the county of Middlesex. And not only was it out of the power of the Attorney and Solicitor to prove this; but it was in the power of the defendants to prove the contrary. For it so happened that Sancroft had never once left the palace at Lambeth from the time when the Order in Council appeared till after the petition was in the King's hands. The whole case for the prosecution had therefore completely broken down; and the audience, with great glee, expected a speedy acquittal.

The crown lawyers then changed their ground again, abandoned altogether the charge of writing a libel, and undertook to prove that the Bishops had published a libel in the county of Middlesex. The difficulties were great. The delivery of the petition to the King was undoubtedly, in the eye of the law, a publication. But how was this delivery to be proved? No person had been present at the audience in the royal closet except the King and the defendants. The King could not well be sworn. It was therefore only by the admissions of the defendants that the fact of publication could be established. Blathwayt was again examined, but in vain. He well remembered, he said, that the Bishops owned their hands; but he did not remember that they owned the paper which lay on the table of the Privy Council to be the same paper which they had delivered to the King, or that they were even interrogated on that point. Several other official men who had been in attendance on the Council were called, and among them Samuel Pepys, Secretary of the Admiralty, but none of them could remember that anything was said about the delivery. It was to no purpose that Williams put leading questions till the counsel on the other side declared that such twisting, such wiredrawing, was never seen in a court of justice, and till Wright himself was forced to admit that the Solicitor's mode of examination was contrary to all rule. As witness after witness answered in the negative, roars of laughter and shouts of triumph, which the Judges did not even attempt to silence, shook the hall.

It seemed that at length this hard fight had been won. The case for the crown was closed. Had the counsel for the Bishops remained silent, an acquittal was certain; for nothing which the most corrupt and shameless Judge could venture to call legal evidence of publication had been given. The Chief Justice was beginning to charge the jury, and would undoubtedly have directed them to acquit the defendants; but Finch, too anxious to be perfectly discreet, interfered, and begged to be heard. "If you will be heard," said Wright, "you shall be heard; but you do not understand your own interests." The other counsel for the defence made Finch sit down, and begged the Chief Justice to proceed. He was about to do so, when a messenger came to the Solicitor General with news that Lord Sunderland could prove the publication, and would come down to the court immediately. Wright maliciously told the counsel for the defence that they had only themselves to thank for the turn which things had taken. The countenances of the great multitude fell. Finch was, during some hours, the most unpopular man in the country. Why could he not sit still as his betters, Sawyer, Pemberton, and Pollexfen, had done? His love of meddling, his ambition to make a fine speech, had ruined everything.

Meanwhile the Lord President was brought in a sedan chair through the hall. Not a hat moved as he passed; and many voices cried out "Popish dog." He came into court pale and trembling, with eyes fixed on the ground, and gave his evidence in a faltering voice. He swore that the Bishops had informed him of their intention to present a petition to the King, and that they had been admitted into the royal closet for that purpose. This circumstance, coupled with the circumstance that, after they left the closet, there was in the King's hands a petition signed by them, was such proof as might reasonably satisfy a jury of the fact of the publication.

Publication in Middlesex was then proved. But was the paper thus published a false, malicious, and seditious libel? Hitherto the matter in dispute had been whether a fact which every body well knew to be true could be proved according to technical rules of evidence; but now the contest became one of deeper interest. It was necessary to inquire into the limits of prerogative and liberty, into the right of the King to dispense with statutes, into the right of the subject to petition for the redress of grievances. During three hours the counsel for the petitioners argued with great force in defence of the fundamental principles of the constitution, and proved from the Journals of the House of Commons that the Bishops had affirmed no more than the truth when they represented to the King that the dispensing power which he claimed had been repeatedly declared illegal by Parliament. Somers rose last. He spoke little more than five minutes: but every word was full of weighty matter; and when he sate down his reputation as an orator and a constitutional lawyer was established. He went through the expressions which were used in the information to describe the offence imputed to the Bishops, and showed that every word, whether adjective or substantive, was altogether inappropriate. The offence imputed was a false, a malicious, a seditious libel. False the paper was not; for every fact which it set forth had been shown from the journals of Parliament to be true. Malicious the paper was not; for the defendants had not sought an occasion of strife, but had been placed by the government in such a situation that they must either oppose themselves to the royal will, or violate the most sacred obligations of conscience and honour. Seditious the paper was not; for it had not been scattered by the writers among the rabble, but delivered privately into the hands of the King alone; and a libel it was not, but a decent petition such as, by the laws of England, nay by the laws of imperial Rome, by the laws of all civilized states, a subject who thinks himself aggrieved may with propriety present to the sovereign.

The Attorney replied shortly and feebly. The Solicitor spoke at great length and with great acrimony, and was often interrupted by the clamours and hisses of the audience. He went so far as to lay it down that no subject or body of subjects, except the Houses of Parliament, had a right to petition the King. The galleries were furious; and the Chief Justice himself stood aghast at the effrontery of this venal turncoat.

At length Wright proceeded to sum up the evidence. His language showed that the awe in which he stood of the government was tempered by the awe with which the audience, so numerous, so splendid, and so strongly excited, had impressed him. He said that he would give no opinion on the question of the dispensing power; that it was not necessary for him to do so; that he could not agree with much of the Solicitor's speech; that it was the right of the subject to petition; but that the particular petition before the Court was improperly worded, and was, in the contemplation of law, a libel. Allibone was of the same mind, but, in giving his opinion, showed such gross ignorance of law and history as brought on him the contempt of all who heard him. Holloway evaded the question of the dispensing power, but said that the petition seemed to him to be such as subjects who think themselves aggrieved are entitled to present, and therefore no libel. Powell took a bolder course. He avowed that, in his judgment, the Declaration of Indulgence was a nullity, and that the dispensing power, as lately exercised, was utterly inconsistent with all law. If these encroachments of prerogative were allowed, there was an end of Parliaments. The whole legislative authority would be in the King. "That issue, gentlemen," he said, "I leave to God and to your consciences."

It was dark before the jury retired to consider of their verdict. The night was a night of intense anxiety. Some letters are extant which were dispatched during that period of suspense, and which have therefore an interest of a peculiar kind. "It is very late," wrote the Papal Nuncio, "and the decision is not yet known. The judges and the culprits have gone to their own homes. The jury remain together. Tomorrow we shall learn the event of this great struggle."

The solicitor for the Bishops sate up all night with a body of servants on the stairs leading to the room where the jury was consulting. It was absolutely necessary to watch the officers who watched the doors; for those officers were supposed to be in the interest of the crown, and might, if not carefully observed, have furnished a courtly juryman with food, which would have enabled him to starve out the other eleven. Strict guard was therefore kept. Not even a candle to light a pipe was permitted to enter. Some basins of water for washing were suffered to pass at about four in the morning. The jurymen, raging with thirst, soon lapped up the whole. Great numbers of people walked the neighbouring streets till dawn. Every hour a messenger came from Whitehall to know what was passing. Voices, high in altercation, were repeatedly heard within the room: but nothing certain was known.

At first nine were for acquitting and three for convicting. Two of the minority soon gave way: but Arnold was obstinate. Thomas Austin, a country gentleman of great estate, who had paid close attention to the evidence and speeches, and had taken full notes, wished to argue the question. Arnold declined. He was not used, he doggedly said, to reasoning and debating. His conscience was not satisfied; and he should not acquit the Bishops. "If you come to that," said Austin, "look at me. I am the largest and strongest of the twelve; and before I find such a petition as this a libel, here I will stay till I am no bigger than a tobacco pipe." It was six in the morning before Arnold yielded. It was soon known that the jury were agreed: but what the verdict would be was still a secret.

At ten the Court again met. The crowd was greater than ever. The jury appeared in the box; and there was a breathless stillness.

Sir Samuel Astry spoke. "Do you find the defendants, or any of them, guilty of the misdemeanor whereof they are impeached, or not guilty?" Sir Roger Langley answered, "Not Guilty." As the words were uttered, Halifax sprang up and waved his hat. At that signal, benches and galleries raised a shout. In a moment ten thousand persons, who crowded the great hall, replied with a still louder shout, which made the old oaken roof crack; and in another moment the innumerable throng without set up a third huzza, which was heard at Temple Bar. The boats which covered the Thames gave an answering cheer. A peal of gunpowder was heard on the water, and another, and another; and so in a few moments, the glad tidings went flying past the Savoy and the Friars to London Bridge, and to the forest of masts below. As the news spread, streets and squares, market-places and coffeehouses, broke forth into acclamations. Yet were the acclamations less strange than the weeping. For the feelings of men had been wound up to such a point that at length the stern English nature, so little used to outward signs of emotion, gave way, and thousands sobbed aloud for very joy. Meanwhile, from the outskirts of the multitude, horsemen were spurring off to bear along all the great roads intelligence of the victory of our Church and nation. Yet not even that astounding explosion could awe the bitter and intrepid spirit of the Solicitor. Striving to make himself heard above the din, he called on the Judges to commit those who had violated, by clamour, the dignity of a court of justice. One of the rejoicing populace was seized. But the tribunal felt that it would be absurd to punish a single individual for an offence common to hundreds of thousands, and dismissed him with a gentle reprimand.

. . . .

On the sixteenth of October, according to the English reckoning, was held a solemn sitting of the States of Holland. The Prince came to bid them farewell. He thanked them for the kindness with which they had watched over him when he was left an orphan child, for the confidence which they had reposed in him during his administration, and for the assistance which they had granted to him at this momentous crisis. He entreated them to believe that he had always meant and endeavoured to promote the interest of his country. He was now quitting them, perhaps never to return. If he should fall in defence of the reformed religion and of the independence of Europe, he commended his beloved wife to their care. The Grand Pensionary answered in a faltering voice; and in all that grave senate there was none who could refrain from shedding tears. But the iron stoicism of William never gave way; and he stood among his weeping friends calm and austere as if he had been about to leave them only for a short visit to his hunting grounds at Loo.

The deputies of the principal towns accompanied him to his yacht. Even the representatives of Amsterdam, so long the chief seat of opposition to his administration, joined in paying him this compliment. Public prayers were offered for him on that day in all the churches of the Hague.

In the evening he arrived at Helvoetsluys and went on board of a frigate called the Brill. His flag was immediately hoisted. It displayed the arms of Nassau quartered with those of England. The motto, embroidered in letters three feet long, was happily chosen. The House of Orange had long used the elliptical device, "I will maintain." The ellipsis was now filled up with words of high import, "The liberties of England and the Protestant religion."

The Prince had not been many hours on board when the wind became fair. On the nineteenth the armament put out to sea, and traversed, before a strong breeze, about half the distance between the Dutch and English coasts. Then the wind changed, blew hard from the west and swelled into a violent tempest. The ships, scattered and in great distress, regained the shore of Holland as they best might. The Brill reached Helvoetsluys on the twenty-first. The Prince's fellow passengers had observed with admiration that neither peril nor mortification had for one moment disturbed his composure. He now, though suffering from sea sickness, refused to go on shore: for he conceived that, by remaining on board, he should in the most effectual manner notify to Europe that the late misfortune had only delayed for a very short time the execution of his purpose. In two or three days the fleet reassembled. One vessel only had been cast away. Not a single soldier or sailor was missing. Some horses had perished: but this loss the Prince with great expedition repaired; and, before the London Gazette had spread the news of his mishap, he was again ready to sail.

His Declaration preceded him only by a few hours. On the first of November it began to be mentioned in mysterious whispers by the politicians of London, was passed secretly from man to man, and was slipped into the boxes of the post office. One of the agents was arrested, and the packets of which he was in charge were carried to Whitehall. The King read, and was greatly troubled. His first impulse was to hide the paper from all human eyes. He threw into the fire every copy which had been brought to him, except one; and that one he would scarcely trust out of his own hands.

The paragraph in the manifesto which disturbed him most was that in which it was said that some of the Peers, Spiritual and Temporal, had invited the Prince of Orange to invade England. Halifax, Clarendon, and Nottingham were then in London. They were immediately summoned to the palace and interrogated. Halifax, though conscious of innocence, refused at first to make any answer. "Your Majesty asks me," said he "whether I have committed high treason. If I am suspected, let me be brought before my peers. And how can Your Majesty place any dependence on the answer of a culprit whose life is at stake? Even if I had invited His Highness over, I should without scruple plead Not Guilty." The King declared that he did not at all consider Halifax as a culprit, and that he had asked the question as one gentleman asks another who has been calumniated whether there be the least foundation for the calumny. "In that case," said Halifax, "I have no objection to aver, as a gentleman speaking to a gentleman, on my honour, which is as sacred as my oath, that I have not invited the Prince of Orange over." Clarendon and Nottingham said the same. The King was still more anxious to ascertain the temper of the Prelates. If they were hostile to him, his throne was indeed in danger. But it could not be. There was something monstrous in the supposition that any Bishop of the Church of England could rebel against his Sovereign. Compton was called into the royal closet, and was asked whether he believed that there was the slightest ground for the Prince's assertion. The Bishop was in a strait; for he was himself one of the seven who had signed the invitation; and his conscience, not a very enlightened conscience, would not suffer him, it seems, to utter a direct falsehood. "Sir," he said, "I am quite confident that there is not one of my brethren who is not as guiltless as myself in this matter." The equivocation was ingenious: but whether the difference between the sin of such an equivocation and the sin of a lie be worth any expense of ingenuity may perhaps be doubted. The King was satisfied. "I fully acquit you all," he said. "But I think it necessary that you should publicly contradict the slanderous charge brought against you in the Prince's Declaration." The Bishop very naturally begged that he might be allowed to read the paper which he was required to contradict: but the King would not suffer him to look at it.

On the following day appeared a proclamation threatening with the severest punishment all who should circulate, or who should even dare to read William's manifesto. The Primate and the few Spiritual Peers who happened to be then in London had orders to wait upon the King. Preston was in attendance with the Prince's Declaration in his hand. "My Lords," said James, "listen to this passage. It concerns you." Preston then read the sentence in which the Spiritual Peers were mentioned. The King proceeded: "I do not believe one word of this: I am satisfied of your innocence: but I think it fit to let you know of what you are accused."

The Primate, with many dutiful expressions, protested that the King did him no more than justice. "I was born in Your Majesty's allegiance. I have repeatedly confirmed that allegiance by my oath. I can have but one King at one time. I have not invited the Prince over; and I do not believe that a single one of my brethren has done so." "I am sure I have not," said Crewe of Durham. "Nor I," said Cartwright of Chester. Crewe and Cartwright might well be believed; for both had sat in the Ecclesiastical Commission. When Compton's turn came, he parried the question with an adroitness which a Jesuit might have envied. "I gave Your Majesty my answer yesterday."

James repeated again and again that he fully acquitted them all. Nevertheless it would, in his judgment, be for his service and for their own honour that they should publicly vindicate themselves. He therefore required them to draw up a paper setting forth their abhorrence of the Prince's design. They remained silent: their silence was supposed to imply consent; and they were suffered to withdraw.

Meanwhile the fleet of William was on the German Ocean. It was on the evening of Thursday the first of November that he put to sea the second time. The wind blew fresh from the east. The armament, during twelve hours, held a course towards the northwest. The light vessels sent out by the English Admiral for the purpose of obtaining intelligence brought back news which confirmed the prevailing opinion that the enemy would try to land in Yorkshire. All at once, on a signal from the Prince's ship, the whole fleet tacked, and made sail for the British Channel. The same breeze which favoured the voyage of the invaders, prevented Dartmouth from coming out of the Thames. His ships were forced to strike yards and topmasts; and two of his frigates, which had gained the open sea, were shattered by the violence of the weather and driven back into the river.

The Dutch fleet ran fast before the gale, and reached the Straits at about ten in the morning of Saturday, the third of November. William himself, in the Brill, led the way. More than six hundred vessels, with canvas spread to a favourable wind, followed in his train. The transports were in the centre. The men of war, more than fifty in number, formed an outer rampart. Herbert, with the title of Lieutenant Admiral General, commanded the whole fleet. His post was in the rear, and many English sailors, inflamed against Popery, and attracted by high pay, served under him. It was not without great difficulty that the Prince had prevailed on some Dutch officers of high reputation to submit to the authority of a stranger. But the arrangement was eminently judicious. There was, in the King's fleet, much discontent and an ardent zeal for the Protestant faith. But within the memory of old mariners the Dutch and English navies had thrice, with heroic spirit and various fortune, contended for the empire of the sea. Our sailors had not forgotten the broom with which Tromp had threatened to sweep the Channel, or the fire which De Ruyter had lighted in the dockyards of the Medway. Had the rival nations been once more brought face to face on the element of which both claimed the sovereignty, all their thoughts might have given place to mutual animosity. A bloody and obstinate battle might have been fought. Defeat would have been fatal to William's enterprise. Even victory would have deranged all his deeply meditated schemes of policy. He therefore wisely determined that the pursuers, if they overtook him, should be hailed in their own mother tongue, and adjured, by an admiral under whom they had served, and whom they esteemed, not to fight against old messmates for Popish tyranny. Such an appeal might possibly avert a conflict. If a conflict took place, one English commander would be opposed to another; nor would the pride of the islanders be wounded by learning that Dartmouth had been compelled to strike to Herbert.

Happily William's precautions were not necessary. Soon after midday he passed the Straits. His fleet spread to within a league of Dover on the north and of Calais on the south. The men of war on the extreme right and left saluted both fortresses at once. The troops appeared under arms on the decks. The flourish of trumpets, the clash of cymbals, and the rolling of drums were distinctly heard at once on the English and French shores. An innumerable company of gazers blackened the white beach of Kent. Another mighty multitude covered the coast of Picardy. Rapin de Thoyras, who, driven by persecution from his country, had taken service in the Dutch army, and not went with the Prince to England, described the spectacle, many years later as the most magnificent and affecting that was ever seen by human eyes. At sunset the armament was off Beachy Head. Then the lights were kindled. The sea was in a blaze for many miles. But the eyes of all the steersmen were directed throughout the night to three huge lanterns which flamed on the stern of the Brill.

Meanwhile a courier had been riding post from Dover Castle to Whitehall with news that the Dutch had passed the Straits and were steering westward. It was necessary to make an immediate change in all the military arrangements. Messengers were despatched in every direction. Officers were roused from their beds at dead of night. At three on Sunday morning there was a great muster by torchlight in Hyde Park. The King had sent several regiments northward in the expectation that William would land in Yorkshire. Expresses were despatched to recall them. All the forces except those which were necessary to keep the peace of the capital were ordered to move to the West. Salisbury was appointed as the place of rendezvous; but, as it was thought possible that Portsmouth might be the first point of attack, three battalions of guards and a strong body of cavalry set out for that fortress. In a few hours it was known that Portsmouth was safe; and these troops then received orders to change their route and to hasten to Salisbury.

When Sunday the fourth of November dawned, the cliffs of the Isle of Wight were full in view of the Dutch armament. That day was the anniversary both of William's birth and of his marriage. Sail was slackened during part of the morning; and divine service was performed on board of the ships. In the afternoon and through the night the fleet held on its course. Torbay was the place where the Prince intended to land. But the morning of Monday the fifth of November was hazy. The pilot of the Brill could not discern the sea marks, and carried the fleet too far to the west. The danger was great. To return in the face of the wind was impossible. Plymouth was the next port. But at Plymouth a garrison had been posted under the command of the Earl of Bath. The landing might be opposed: and a check might produce serious consequences. There could be little doubt, moreover, that by this time the royal fleet had got out of the Thames and was hastening full sail down the Channel. Russell saw the whole extent of the peril, and exclaimed to Burnet, "You may go to prayers, Doctor. All is over." At that moment the wind changed: a soft breeze sprang up from the south: the mist dispersed: the sun shone forth; and, under the mild light of an autumnal noon, the fleet turned back, passed round the lofty cape of Berry Head, and rode safe in the harbour of Torbay.

. . . .

Never, within the memory of man, had there been so near an approach to entire concord among all intelligent Englishmen as at this conjuncture; and never had concord been more needed. All those evil passions which it is the office of government to restrain, and which the best governments restrain but imperfectly, were on a sudden emancipated from control; avarice, licentiousness, revenge, the hatred of sect to sect, the hatred of nation to nation. On such occasions it will ever be found that the human vermin, which, neglected by ministers of state, and ministers of religion, barbarous in the midst of civilisation, heathen in the midst of Christianity, burrows, among all physical and all moral pollution, in the cellars and garrets of great cities, will at once rise into a terrible importance. So it was now in London. When the night, the longest night, as it chanced, of the year approached, forth came from every den of vice, from the bear garden at Hockley, and from the labyrinth of tippling houses and brothels in the Friars, thousands of housebreakers and highwaymen, cutpurses and ringdroppers. With these were mingled thousands of idle apprentices, who wished merely for the excitement of a riot. Even men of peaceable and honest habits were impelled by religious animosity to join the lawless part of the population. For the cry of No Popery, a cry which has more than once endangered the existence of London, was the signal for outrage and rapine. First the rabble fell on the Roman Catholic places of worship. The buildings were demolished. Benches, pulpits, confessionals, breviaries were heaped up and set on fire. A great mountain of books and furniture blazed on the site of the convent at Clerkenwell. Another pile was kindled before the ruins of the Franciscan house in Lincoln's Inn Fields. The chapel in Lime Street, the chapel in Bucklersbury, were pulled down. The pictures, images, and crucifixes were carried along the streets in triumph, amidst lighted tapers torn from the altars. The procession bristled thick with swords and staves, and on the point of every sword and of every staff was an orange. The King's printing house, whence had issued, during the preceding three years, innumerable tracts in defence of Papal supremacy, image worship, and monastic vows, was—to use a coarse metaphor which then, for the first time, came into fashion—completely gutted. The vast stock of paper, much of which was still unpolluted by types, furnished an immense bonfire. From monasteries, temples, and public offices, the fury of the multitude turned to private dwellings. Several houses were pillaged and destroyed: but the smallness of the booty disappointed the plunderers: and soon a rumour was spread that the most valuable effects of the Papists had been placed under the care of the foreign Ambassadors. To the savage and ignorant populace the law of nations and the risk of bringing on their country the just vengeance of all Europe were as nothing. The houses of the Ambassadors were besieged. A great crowd assembled before Barillon's door in St. James's Square. He, however, fared better than might have been expected. For, though the government which he represented was held in abhorrence, his liberal housekeeping and exact payments had made him personally popular. Moreover he had taken the precaution of asking for a guard of soldiers; and, as several men of rank, who lived near him had done the same, a considerable force was collected in the square. The rioters, therefore, when they were assured that no arms or priests were concealed under his roof, left him unmolested. The Venetian Envoy was protected by a detachment of troops: but the mansions occupied by the ministers of the Elector Palatine and of the Grand Duke of Tuscany were destroyed. One precious box the Tuscan minister was able to save from the marauders. It contained nine volumes of memoirs, written in the hand of James himself. These volumes reached France in safety, and, after the lapse of more than a century, perished there in the havoc of a revolution far more terrible than that from which they had escaped. But some fragments still remain, and though grievously mutilated, and imbedded in masses of childish fiction, well deserve to be attentively studied.

The rich plate of the Chapel Royal had been deposited at Wild House, near Lincoln's Inn Fields, the residence of the Spanish ambassador Ronquillo. Ronquillo, conscious that he and his court had not deserved ill of the English nation, had thought it unnecessary to ask for soldiers: but the mob was not in a mood to make nice distinctions. The name of Spain had long been associated in the public mind with the Inquisition and the Armada, with the cruelties of Mary and the plots against Elizabeth. Ronquillo had also made himself many enemies among the common people by availing himself of his privilege to avoid the necessity of paying his debts. His house was therefore sacked without mercy; and a noble library, which he had collected, perished in the flames. His only comfort was that the host in his chapel was rescued from the same fate.

The morning of the twelfth of December rose on a ghastly sight. The capital in many places presented the aspect of a city taken by storm. The Lords met at Whitehall, and exerted themselves to restore tranquillity. The trainbands were ordered under arms. A body of cavalry was kept in readiness to disperse tumultuous assemblages. Such atonement as was at that moment possible was made for the gross insults which had been offered to foreign governments. A reward was promised for the discovery of the property taken from Wild House; and Ronquillo, who had not a bed or an ounce of plate left, was splendidly lodged in the deserted palace of the Kings of England. A sumptuous table was kept for him; and the yeomen of the guard were ordered to wait in his antechamber with the same observance which they were in the habit of paying to the Sovereign. These marks of respect soothed even the punctilious pride of the Spanish court, and averted all danger of a rupture.

In spite, however, of the well meant efforts of the provisional government, the agitation grew hourly more formidable. It was heightened by an event which, even at this distance of time, can hardly be related without a feeling of vindictive pleasure. A scrivener who lived at Wapping, and whose trade was to furnish the seafaring men there with money at high interest, had some time before lent a sum on bottomry. The debtor applied to equity for relief against his own bond; and the case came before Jeffreys. The counsel for the borrower having little else to say, said that the lender was a Trimmer. The Chancellor instantly fired. "A Trimmer! where is he? Let me see him. I have heard of that kind of monster. What is it made like?" The unfortunate creditor was forced to stand forth. The Chancellor glared fiercely on him, stormed at him, and sent him away half dead with fright. "While I live," the poor man said, as he tottered out of the court, "I shall never forget that terrible countenance." And now the day of retribution had arrived. The Trimmer was walking through Wapping, when he saw a well-known face looking out of the window of an alehouse. He could not be deceived. The eyebrows, indeed, had been shaved away. The dress was that of a common sailor from Newcastle, and was black with coal dust: but there was no mistaking the savage eye and mouth of Jeffreys. The alarm was given. In a moment the house was surrounded by hundreds of people shaking bludgeons and bellowing curses. The fugitive's life was saved by a company of the trainbands; and he was carried before the Lord Mayor. The Mayor was a simple man who had passed his whole life in obscurity, and was bewildered by finding himself an important actor in a mighty revolution. The events of the last twenty-four hours, and the perilous state of the city which was under his charge, had disordered his mind and his body. When the great man, at whose frown, a few days before, the whole kingdom had trembled, was dragged into the justice room begrimed with ashes, half dead with fright, and followed by a raging multitude, the agitation of the unfortunate Mayor rose to the height. He fell into fits, and was carried to his bed, whence he never rose. Meanwhile the throng without was constantly becoming more numerous and more savage. Jeffreys begged to be sent to prison. An order to that effect was procured from the Lords who were sitting at Whitehall; and he was conveyed in a carriage to the Tower. Two regiments of militia were drawn out to escort him, and found the duty a difficult one. It was repeatedly necessary for them to form, as if for the purpose of repelling a charge of cavalry, and to present a forest of pikes to the mob. The thousand who were disappointed of their revenge pursued the coach, with howls of rage, to the gate of the Tower, brandishing cudgels, and holding up halters full in the prisoner's view. The wretched man meantime was in convulsions of terror. He wrung his hands: he looked wildly out, sometimes at one window, sometimes at the other, and was heard even above the tumult, crying "Keep them off, gentlemen! For God's sake keep them off!" At length having suffered far more than the bitterness of death, he was safely lodged in the fortress where some of his most illustrious victims had passed their last days, and where his own life was destined to close in unspeakable ignominy and horror.

Bibliography

Clive, John. "Macaulay, History and the Historians." *History Today,* 9 (December 1959): 830–36.
Clive, John. *Macaulay: The Shaping of the Historian.* New York, 1973.
Cruikshank, Margaret. *Thomas Babington Macaulay.* Boston, 1978.
Firth, Charles. *A Commentary on Macaulay's History of England.* London, 1938.
Gay, Peter. "Macaulay: Intellectual Voluptuary." In *Style in History.* New York, 1974.
Geyl, Pieter. *Debates with Historians.* New York, 1958.
Gooch, G. P. *History and Historians of the Nineteenth Century.* London, 1913.
Schuyler, Robert L. "Macaulay and His History—A Hundred Years After." *Political Science Quarterly, 63* (June 1948): 161–93.
Trevelyan, George O. *The Life and Letters of Lord Macaulay.* Oxford, 1961.
Yoder, Edwin. "Macaulay Revisited." *South Atlantic Quarterly, 63* (Autumn 1964): 542–51.

CHAPTER 13

Jules Michelet

History of the French Revolution
(1847–1853)

As Macaulay was England's most eminent national historian, so Jules Miche-let (1798–1874), his contemporary, would gradually emerge as the most re-vered historian in France. Though they drew inspiration from different sources, Michelet reads like an extreme version of Macaulay. Both judged the past from a modern vantage point: the blessings of nineteenth-century liberalism for Macaulay and, for Michelet, the French Revolution of 1789. Both broadened history to include the lives of ordinary people, but Michelet went beyond Macaulay to create "the People" as a character, moved by a common will, admitting no variation, and knowable by the historian with confi-dence. Individual characters are hated or praised, but Michelet portrays them as receiving inspiration from the common will rather than giving it. Fi-nally, Michelet moves beyond Macaulay's detached superiority as a judge and becomes consciously and personally involved with events and princi-pals. "So forty years have passed by," he wrote in an epilogue to his *History of the French Revolution.* "I have lost myself in this work. . . . For it I have given the world a miss, and history to me has become life."

Michelet did not start out with these ideas. He was born in 1798 to a poor Parisian family. His father had a printing shop in a church that had been secular-ized in the Revolution, but censorship under Napoleon ruined him. Michelet's father was a fervent republican and brought his son up on eyewitness stories of the Revolution; but, though Michelet would use them in his own later writing, they made little impression on him at the time. His abilities won him an education and, thereafter, teaching positions in institutions of increasing prestige, culminating in his appointment to the Collège de France in 1838. His initial philosophy of his-tory, as developed in the opening volumes of *History of France* (1833–1867), resembled Ranke's historicism, with an emphasis on the legitimacy of characters whose behavior was appropriate to their time. He also stressed other peculiari-ties, like geography, as creators of unique historical cultures.

Then, in the 1840s, Michelet went through a political transformation that called for a new subject and a new approach. The constitutional monarchy of Louis Phillipe—the so-called July Monarchy of 1830—was coming under increasing pressure from French liberals and radicals, and Michelet joined the agitation for a republic. His inspiration was the original Revolution of 1789, which emerged in his university lectures and in his polemic, *The People* (1846), as the event toward which French history had aimed and whose spirit the nation could now, after decades of reaction, recapture. Michelet had brought his *History of France* as far as the fifteenth century, but in 1847, very much a historian *engage*, he jumped forward to bring out the first of seven volumes on the Revolution. His enthusiasm eventually turned to bitterness, however, as he saw the Revolution of 1848 produce the Second Republic and then the Republic collapse in 1852 in the coup of Napoleon III and the Second Empire. Dismissed from his university post, Michelet finished his *French Revolution* in 1853.

Michelet's faults are easy to name. His creation of "the People" is a romantic construct that ignores crosscurrents of opinion and the complicated dynamics of how things happen. His justification of outrageous events like the Terror (even when he outwardly deplores them) according to an end-justifies-the-means argument is, to use Pieter Geyl's words, "positively repulsive." And Michelet's abandonment of historicism sometimes reduces his *French Revolution* to a mere tract for the times.

Yet his contributions to historical study are just as real. Michelet's writing reestablished two ideas of Giambattista Vico, a forgotten but very "modern" eighteenth-century philosopher: first, that true understanding *is* historical and depends on seeing things come into being rather than assuming that institutions and ideas are fixed and immutable; and, second, that men and women can know their history with confidence because, unlike nature, history is made by other men and women. No doubt this thought led to Michelet's overconfident sense of "the People's" mind, but it also led him to urge a study of all things made by people as the sources for history, including myths and legends as well as traditional documents.

Another contribution, of course, was Michelet's extensive use of documents—more than any French predecessor—in reconstructing French history. His position as director of the Archives Nationales from 1831 to 1852 gave him broad access to the survivals of the past. And, finally, his prose style, for all its romantic excesses, gives the reader a compelling sense of participation in the dramatic events another historian would have been content only to describe.

Michelet's faults and virtues are discernible in his chapter on the fall of the Bastille.

VERSAILLES, WITH AN ORGANISED GOVERNMENT, a king, ministers, a general, and an army, was all hesitation, doubt, uncertainty, and in a state of the most complete moral anarchy.

Paris, all commotion, destitute of every legal authority, and in the utmost confusion, attained, on the 14th of July, what is morally the highest degree of order,—unanimity of feeling.

On the 13th, Paris thought only of defending itself; on the 14th, it attacked.

On the evening of the 13th, some doubt still existed, but none remained in the morning. The evening had been stormy, agitated by a whirlwind of ungovernable frenzy. The morning was still and serene,—an awful calm.

With daylight, one idea dawned upon Paris, and all were illumined with the same ray of hope. A light broke upon every mind, and the same voice thrilled through every heart: "Go! and thou shalt take the Bastille!" That was impossible, unreasonable, preposterous. And yet everybody believed it. And the thing was done.

The Bastille, though an old fortress, was nevertheless impregnable, unless besieged for several days and with an abundance of artillery. The people had, in that crisis, neither the time nor the means to make a regular siege. Had they done so, the Bastille had no cause for fear, having enough provisions to wait for succour so near at hand, and an immense supply of ammunition. Its walls, ten feet thick at the top of the towers, and thirty or forty at the base, might long laugh at cannon-balls; and its batteries firing down upon Paris, could, in the meantime, demolish the whole of the Marais and the Faubourg Saint-Antoine. Its towers, pierced with windows and loop-holes, protected by double and triple gratings, enabled the garrison, in full security, to make a dreadful carnage of its assailants.

The attack on the Bastille was by no means reasonable. It was an act of faith.

Nobody proposed; but all believed, and all acted. Along the streets, the quays, the bridges, and the boulevards, the crowd shouted to the crowd: "To the Bastille! The Bastille!" And the tolling of the tocsin thundered in every ear: *"à la Bastille!"*

Nobody, I repeat, gave the impulse. The orators of the Palais Royal passed the time in drawing up a list of proscription, in condemning the queen to death, as well as Madame de Polignac, Artois, Flesselles the provost, and others. The names of the conquerors of the Bastille do not include one of these makers of motions. The Palais Royal was not the starting-point, neither was it to the Palais Royal that the conquerors brought back the spoils and prisoners.

Still less had the electors, assembled in the Hôtel-de-Ville, the idea of the attack. On the contrary, in order to prevent it, as well as the carnage

From J. Michelet, *Historical View of the French Revolution*, translated by C. Cocks (London: H. G. Bohn, 1848), 142–60.

which the Bastille could so easily make, they went so far as to promise the governor, that if he withdrew his cannon he should not be attacked. The electors did not behave treacherously, though they were accused of having done so; but they had no faith.

Who had? They who had also the devotion and the strength to accomplish their faith. Who? Why, the people,—everybody.

Old men who have had the happiness and the misery to see all that has happened in this unprecedented half century, in which ages seem to be crowded together, declare, that the grand and national achievements of the Republic and the Empire, had nevertheless a partial non-unanimous character, but that the 14th of July alone was the day of the whole people. Then let that grand day remain ever one of the eternal *fêtes* of the human race, not only as having been the first of deliverance, but as having been superlatively the day of concord!

What had happened during that short night, on which nobody slept, for every uncertainty and difference of opinion to disappear with the shades of darkness, and all to have the same thoughts in the morning?

What took place at the Palais Royal and the Hôtel-de-Ville is well known; but what would be far more important to know, is, what took place on the domestic hearth of the people.

For there indeed, as we may sufficiently divine by what followed, there every heart summoned the past to its day of judgment, and every one, before a blow was struck, pronounced its irrevocable condemnation. History returned that night a long history of sufferings to the avenging instinct of the people. The souls of fathers who, for so many ages, had suffered and died in silence, descended into their sons, and spoke.

O brave men, you who till then had been so patient, so pacific, who, on that day, were to inflict the heavy blow of Providence, did not the sight of your families, whose only resource is in you, daunt your hearts? Far from it: gazing once more at your slumbering children, those children for whom that day was to create a destiny, your expanding minds embraced the free generations arising from their cradle, and felt at that moment the whole battle of the future!

The future and the past both gave the same reply; both cried Advance! And what is beyond all time,—beyond the future and the past,—immutable right said the same. The immortal sentiment of the Just imparted a temper of adamant to the fluttering heart of man; it said to him: "Go in peace; what matters? Whatever may happen, I am with thee, in death or victory!"

And yet what was the Bastille to them? The lower orders seldom or never entered it. Justice spoke to them, and, a voice that speaks still louder to the heart, the voice of humanity and mercy; that still small voice which seems so weak but that overthrows towers, had, for ten years, been shaking the very foundations of the doomed Bastille.

Let the truth be told; if anyone had the glory of causing its downfall, it was that intrepid woman who wrought so long for the deliverance of Latude against all the powers in the world. Royalty refused, and the nation forced it to pardon; that woman, or that hero, was crowned in a public solemnity. To crown her who had, so to speak, forced open the state prisons, was already branding them with infamy, devoting them to public execration, and demolishing them in the hearts and desires of men. That woman had shaken the Bastille to its foundations.

From that day, the people of the town and the faubourg, who, in that much-frequented quarter, were ever passing and repassing in its shadow, never failed to curse it. And well did it deserve their hatred. There were many other prisons, but this one was the abode of capricious arbitrariness, wanton despotism, and ecclesiastical and bureaucratic inquisition. The court, so devoid of religion in that age, had made the Bastille a dungeon for free minds,—the prison of thought. Less crowded during the reign of Louis XVI, it had become more cruel; the prisoners were deprived of their walk: more rigorous, and no less unjust: we blush for France, to be obliged to say that the crime of one of the prisoners was to have given a useful secret to our navy! They were afraid lest he should tell it elsewhere.

The Bastille was known and detested by the whole world. Bastille and tyranny were, in every language, synonymous terms. Every nation, at the news of its destruction, believed it had recovered its liberty.

In Russia, that empire of mystery and silence,—that monstrous Bastille between Europe and Asia, scarcely had the news arrived when you might have seen men of every nation shouting and weeping for joy in the open streets; they rushed into each other's arms to tell the news: "Who can help weeping for joy? *The Bastille is taken.*"

On the very morning of that great day, the people had as yet no arms.

The powder they had taken from the arsenal the night before, and put in the Hôtel-de-Ville, was slowly distributed to them, during the night, by only three men. The distribution having ceased for a moment, about two o'clock, the desperate crowd hammered down the doors of the magazine, every blow striking fire on the nails.

No guns!—It was necessary to go and take them, to carry them off from the Invalides; that was very hazardous. The *Hotel des Invalides* is, it is true, an open mansion; but Sombreuil, the governor, a brave old soldier, had received a strong detachment of artillery and some cannon, without counting those he had already. Should those cannon be brought to act, the crowd might be taken in the flank, and easily dispersed by the regiments that Besenval had at the military school.

Would those foreign regiments have refused to act? In spite of what

Besenval says to the contrary, there is reason to doubt it. What is much plainer, is, that being left without orders, he was himself full of hesitation, and appeared paralysed in mind. At five o'clock that same morning, he had received a strange visit;—a man rushed in; his countenance was livid, his eyes flashed fire, his language was impetuous and brief, and his manner audacious. The old coxcomb, who was the most frivolous officer of the *ancien régime*, but brave and collected, gazed at the man, and was struck with admiration. "Baron," said the man, "I come to advise you to make no resistance; the barriers will be burnt to-day; I am sure of it, but cannot prevent it; neither can you—do not try."

Besenval was not afraid; but he had, nevertheless, felt the shock, and suffered its moral effect. "There was something eloquent in that man," says he, "that struck me; I ought to have had him arrested, and yet I did not." It was the *ancien régime* and the Revolution meeting face to face, and the latter left the former lost in astonishment.

Before nine o'clock thirty thousand men were in front of the Invalides; the Attorney General of the City was at their head: the committee of the electors had not dared to refuse him. Among them were seen a few companies of the French Guards, who had escaped from their barracks, the Clerks of the Basoche, in their old red dresses, and the Curate of Saint-Etienne-du-Mont, who, being named president of the Assembly formed in his church, did not decline the perilous office of heading this armed multitude.

Old Sombreuil acted very adroitly. He showed himself at the gate, said it was true he had guns, but that they had been intrusted to him as a deposit, and that his honour, as a soldier and a gentleman, did not allow him to be a traitor.

This unexpected argument stopped the crowd at once; a proof of the admirable candour of the people in that early age of the Revolution. Sombreuil added, that he had sent a courier to Versailles, and was expecting the answer; backing all this with numerous protestations of attachment and friendship for the Hôtel-de-Ville and the city in general.

The majority was willing to wait. Luckily, there was one man present who was less scrupulous, and prevented the crowd from being so easily mystified.

"There is no time to be lost," said he, "and whose arms are these but the nation's?" Then they leaped into the trenches, and the Hôtel was invaded; twenty-eight thousand muskets were found in the cellars, and carried off, together with twenty pieces of cannon.

All this between nine and eleven o'clock; but, let us hasten to the Bastille.

The governor, De Launey, had been under arms ever since two o'clock in the morning of the 13th; no precaution had been neglected;

besides his cannon on the towers, he had others from the arsenal, which he placed in the court, and loaded with grape-shot. He caused six cart-loads of paving-stones, cannon-balls, and old iron, to be carried to the tops of the towers, in order to crush his assailants. In the bottom loop-holes he had placed twelve large rampart guns, each of which carried a pound and a half of bullets. He kept below his trustiest soldiers, thirty-two Swiss, who had no scruple in firing upon Frenchmen. His eighty-two Invalids were mostly distributed in different posts, far from the gates, upon the towers. He had evacuated the outer buildings which covered the foot of the fortress.

On the 13th, nothing save curses bestowed on the Bastille by passers by.

On the 14th, about midnight, seven shots were fired at the sentinels upon the towers.—Alarm!—The governor ascends with staff, remains half-an-hour, listening to the distant murmuring of the town; finding all quiet he descends.

The next morning many people were about, and, from time to time, young men (from the Palais Royal, or others) were calling out that they must give them arms. They pay no attention to them. They hear and introduce the pacific deputation of the Hôtel-de-Ville, which, about ten o'clock, intreats the governor to withdraw his cannon, promising that if he does not fire, he shall not be attacked. He, willingly, accepts, having no orders to fire, and highly delighted, obliges the envoys to breakfast with him.

As they were leaving, a man arrives who speaks in a very different tone.

A violent, bold man, unacquainted with human respect, fearless and pitiless, knowing neither obstacle nor delay, and bearing in his breast the passionate genius of the Revolution—he came to summon the Bastille.

Terror accompanied him. The Bastille was afraid; the governor, without knowing why, was troubled and stammered.

That man was Thuriot, a monster of ferocity, one of the race of Danton. We meet with him twice, in the beginning and at the end. And twice his words are deadly; he destroys the Bastille, and he kills Robespierre.

He was not to pass the bridge; the governor would not allow it; and yet he passed. From the first court, he marches to a second; another refusal; but he passes on, and crosses the second ditch by the draw-bridge. Behold him now in front of the enormous iron gate by which the third court was shut. This seemed a monstrous well rather than a court, its eight towers united together, forming its inside walls. Those frightful gigantic towers did not look towards the court, nor had they a single window. At their feet, in their shadow, was the prisoners' only walk. Lost at the bottom of the pit, and overwhelmed by those enormous masses, he could contemplate only the stern nudity of the walls. On one side only, had been placed a clock, between two figures of captives in chains, as if to fetter time itself, and make the slow succession of hours still more burdensome.

There were the loaded cannon, the garrison, and the staff. Thuriot was daunted by nothing. "Sir," said he to the governor, "I summon you, in the name of the people, in the name of honour, and of our native land, to withdraw your cannon, and surrender the Bastille."—Then, turning towards the garrison, he repeated the same words.

If M. De Launey had been a true soldier, he would not thus have introduced the envoy into the heart of the citadel; still less would he have let him address the garrison. But, it is very necessary to remark, that the officers of the Bastille were mostly officers by favour of the lieutenant of police; even those who had never seen service, wore the cross of Saint Louis. All of them, from the governor down to the scullions, had bought their places, and turned them to the best advantage. The governor found means to add every year to his salary of sixty thousand francs, (£2400), a sum quite as large by his rapine. He supplied his establishment at the prisoners' expense; he had reduced their supply of firewood, and made a profit on their wine, and their miserable furniture. What was most infamous and barbarous, was, that he let out to a gardener the little garden of the Bastille, over a bastion; and, for that miserable profit, he had deprived the prisoners of that walk, as well as of that on the towers; that is to say, of air and light.

That greedy, sordid soul had moreover good reason to be dispirited; he felt he was known; Linguet's terrible memoirs had rendered De Launey infamous throughout Europe. The Bastille was hated; but the governor was personally detested. The furious imprecations of the people, which he heard, he appropriated to himself; and he was full of anxiety and fear.

Thuriot's words acted differently on the Swiss and the French. The Swiss did not understand them; their captain, M. de Flue, was resolved to hold out. But the Staff and the Invalids were much shaken; those old soldiers, in habitual communication with the people of the faubourg, had no desire to fire upon them. Thus the garrison was divided; what will these two parties do? If they cannot agree, will they fire upon each other?

The dispirited governor said, in an apologetical tone, what had just been agreed with the town. He swore, and made the garrison swear, that if they were not attacked they would not begin.

Thuriot did not stop there. He desired to ascend to the top of the towers, to see whether the cannon were really withdrawn. De Launey, who had been all this time repenting of having allowed him already to penetrate so far, refused; but, being pressed by his officers, he ascended with Thuriot.

The cannon were drawn back and masked, but still pointed. The view from that height of a hundred and forty feet was immense and startling; the streets and openings full of people, and all the garden of the arsenal crowded with armed men. But, on the other side, a black mass was advancing. It was the faubourg Saint Antoine.

The governor turned pale. He grasped Thuriot by the arm: "What have you done? You abuse your privilege as an envoy! You have betrayed me!"

They were both standing on the brink, and De Launey had a sentinel on the tower. Everybody in the Bastille was bound by oath to the governor; in his fortress, he was king and the law. He was still able to avenge himself.

But, on the contrary, it was Thuriot who made him afraid: "Sir," said he, "one word more, and I swear to you that one of us two shall be hurled headlong into the moat!"

At the same moment, the sentinel approached, as frightened as the governor, and, addressing Thuriot: "Pray, Sir," said he, "show yourself; there is no time to lose; they are marching forward. Not seeing you, they will attack us." He leaned over through the battlements; and the people seeing him alive, and standing boldly upon the tower, uttered deafening shouts of joy and approbation.

Thuriot descended with the governor, again crossed through the court, and addressing the garrison once more: "I am going to give my report," said he; "I hope the people will not refuse to furnish a citizen guard to keep the Bastille with you."

The people expected to enter the Bastille as soon as Thuriot came forth. When they saw him depart, to make his report to the Hôtel-de-Ville, they took him for a traitor, and threatened him. Their impatience was growing into fury. The crowd seized on three Invalids, and wanted to tear them to pieces. They also seized on a young lady whom they believed to be the governor's daughter, and some wanted to burn her, if he refused to surrender. Others dragged her from them.

What will become of us, said they, if the Bastille be not taken before night? The burly Santerre, a brewer, whom the faubourg had elected its commander, proposed to burn the place by throwing into it poppy and spikenard oil that they had seized the night before, and which they could fire with phosphorus. He was sending to fetch the engines.

A blacksmith, an old soldier, without wasting time in idle talk, sets bravely to work. He marches forward, hatchet in hand, leaps upon the roof of a small guard-house, near the first drawbridge, and, under a shower of bullets, coolly plies his hatchet, cuts away, and loosens the chains; down falls the bridge. The crowd rush over it, and enter the court.

The firing began at once from the towers and from the loopholes below. The assailants fell in crowds, and did no harm to the garrison. Of all the shots they fired that day, two took effect: only one of the besieged was killed.

The committee of electors, who saw the wounded already arriving at the Hôtel-de-Ville, and deplored the shedding of blood, would have wished to stop it. There was now but one way of doing so, which was to summon the Bastille, in the name of the city, to surrender, and to allow the citizen-guard to enter. The provost hesitated for a long time; Fauchet insisted; and other electors entreated him. They went as deputies; but in the fire and smoke, they were not even seen; neither the Bastille nor the people ceased firing. The deputies were in the greatest danger. A second deputation, headed by the city proctor, with a drum and a flag of truce, was perceived from the fortress. The soldiers who were upon the towers hoisted a white flag, and reversed their arms. The people ceased firing, followed the deputation, and entered the court. There, they were welcomed by a furious discharge, which brought down several men by the side of the deputies. Very probably the Swiss who were below with De Launey, paid no attention to the signs made by the Invalids.

The rage of the people was inexpressible. Ever since the morning, it had been said that the governor had enticed the crowd into the court to fire upon them; they believed themselves twice deceived, and resolved to perish, or to be revenged on the traitors. To those who were calling them back, they exclaimed in a transport of frenzy: "Our bodies at least shall serve to fill the moats!" And on they rushed obstinately and nothing daunted, amid a shower of bullets and against those murderous towers, as if, by dying in heaps, they could at length overthrow them.

But then, numbers of generous men, who had hitherto taken no part in the action, beheld, with increased indignation, such an unequal struggle, which was actual assassination. They wanted to lend their assistance. It was no longer possible to hold back the French Guards; they all sided with the people. They repaired to the commandants nominated by the town, and obliged them to surrender their five cannons. Two columns were formed, one of workmen and citizens, the other of French Guards. The former took for its chief a young man, of heroic stature and strength, named Hullin, a clockmaker of Geneva, but now a servant, being gamekeeper to the Marquis de Conflans; his Hungarian costume as a *chasseur* was doubtless taken for a uniform; and thus did the livery of servitude guide the people to the combat of liberty. The leader of the other column was Élie, an officer of fortune belonging to the Queen's regiment, who, changing his private dress for his brilliant uniform, showed himself bravely a conspicuous object to both friends and foes.

Among his soldiers, was one admirable for his valour, youth, and candour, Marceau, one of the glories of France, who remained satisfied with fighting, and claimed no share in the honour of the victory.

Things were not very far advanced when they arrived. Three cart-loads of straw had been pushed forward and set on fire, and the barracks and kitchens had been burnt down. They knew not what else to do. The despair of the people was vented upon the Hôtel-de-Ville. They blamed the provost and the electors, and urged them, in threatening language, to issue formal orders for the siege of the Bastille. But they could never in-duce them to give those orders.

Several strange singular means were proposed to the electors for tak-ing the fortress. A carpenter advised the erection of a Roman catapult, in wood-work, to hurl stones against the walls. The commanders of the town said it was necessary to attack in a regular way, and open a trench. During this long and useless debate, a letter at that moment intercepted, was brought in and read; it was from Besenval to de Launey, commanding him to hold out to the last extremity.

To appreciate the value of time at that momentous crisis, and under-stand the dread felt at any delay, we must know that there were false alarms every instant. It was supposed that the court, informed at two o'clock of the attack on the Bastille, which had begun at noon, would take that opportunity of pouring down its Swiss and German troops upon Paris. Again, would those at the Military School pass the day in inaction? That was unlikely. What Besenval says about the little reliance he could place on his troops seems like an excuse. The Swiss showed themselves very firm at the Bastille, as appeared from the carnage; the German dra-goons had, on the 12th, fired several times, and killed some of the French Guards; the latter had killed several dragoons; a spirit of mutual hatred ensured fidelity.

In the faubourg Saint Honoré, the paving-stones were dug up, the attack being expected every moment; La Villette was in the same state, and a regiment really came and occupied it, but too late.

Every appearance of dilatoriness appeared treason. The provost's shuffling conduct caused him to be suspected, as well as the electors. The exasperated crowd perceived it was losing time with them. An old man exclaimed: "Friends, why do we remain with these traitors? Let us rather hasten to the Bastille!" They all vanished. The electors, thunderstruck, found themselves alone. One of them goes out, but returns with a livid, spectral countenance: "You have not two minutes to live," says he, "if you remain here. La Grève is filled by a furious crowd. Here they are coming." They did not, however, attempt to fly; and that saved their lives.

All the fury of the people was now concentrated on the provost. The envoys of the different districts came successively to accuse him of treachery to his face. A part of the electors, finding themselves compromised with the people, by his imprudence and falsehood, turned round and accused him. Others, the good old Dussaulx (the translator of Juvenal), and the intrepid Fauchet endeavoured to defend him, innocent or guilty, and to save him from death. Being forced by the people to remove from their bureau into the grand hall of Saint Jean, they surrounded him, and Fauchet sat down by his side. The terrors of death were impressed on his countenance. "I saw him," says Dussaulx, "chewing his last mouthful of bread; it stuck in his teeth, and he kept it in his mouth two hours before he could swallow it." Surrounded with papers, letters, and people who came to speak to him on business, and amid shouts of death, he strove hard to reply with affability. The crowds of the Palais Royal and from the district of Saint Roch, being the most inveterate, Fauchet hastened to them to pray for pardon. The district body was assembled in the church of Saint Roch; twice did Fauchet ascend the pulpit, praying, weeping, and uttering the fervent language which his noble heart dictated in that hour of need; his robe, torn to tatters by the bullets of the Bastille, was eloquent also; it prayed for the people, for the honour of that great day, and that the cradle of liberty might be left pure and undefiled.

The provost and the electors remained in the hall of Saint Jean, between life and death, guns being levelled at them several times. All those who were present, says Dussaulx, were like savages; sometimes they would listen and look on in silence; sometimes a terrible murmur, like distant thunder, arose from the crowd. Many spoke and shouted; but the greater number seemed astounded by the novelty of the sight. The uproar, the exclamations, the news, the alarms, the intercepted letters, the discoveries, true or false, so many secrets revealed, so many men brought before the tribunal, perplexed the mind and reason. One of the electors exclaimed: "Is not doomsday come?" So dizzy, so confounded was the crowd, that they had forgotten everything, even the provost and the Bastille.

It was half-past five when a shout arose from La Grève. An immense noise, like the growling of distant thunder, resounds nearer and nearer, rushing on with the rapidity and roaring of a tempest. The Bastille is taken.

That hall already so full is at once invaded by a thousand men, and ten thousand pushing behind. The wood-work cracks, the benches are thrown down, and the barrier driven upon the bureau, the bureau upon the president.

All were armed in a fantastical manner; some almost naked, others dressed in every colour. One man was borne aloft upon their shoulders and crowned with laurel; it was Élie, with all the spoils and prisoners around him. At the head, amid all that din, which would have drowned a clap of thunder, advanced a young man full of meditation and religion; he carried suspended and pierced with his bayonet a vile, a thrice-accursed object,—the regulations of the Bastille.

The keys too were carried,—those monstrous, vile, ignoble keys, worn out by centuries and the sufferings of men. Chance or Providence directed that they should be intrusted to a man who knew them but too well,—a former prisoner. The National Assembly placed them in its Archives; the old machine of tyrants thus lying beside the laws that had destroyed them. We still keep possession of those keys, in the iron safe of the Archives of France. Oh! would that the same iron-chest might contain the keys of all the Bastilles in the world!

Correctly speaking, the Bastille was not taken; it surrendered. Troubled by a bad conscience it went mad, and lost all presence of mind.

Some wanted to surrender; others went on firing, especially the Swiss, who, for five hours, pointed out, aimed at, and brought down whomsoever they pleased, without any danger or even the chance of being hurt in return. They killed eighty-three men and wounded eighty-eight. Twenty of the slain were poor fathers of families, who left wives and children to die of hunger.

Shame for such cowardly warfare, and the horror of shedding French blood, which but little affected the Swiss, at length caused the Invalids to drop their arms. At four o'clock the subaltern officers begged and prayed De Launey to put an end to this massacre. He knew what he deserved; obliged to die one way or other, he had, for a moment, the horribly ferocious idea of blowing up the citadel: he would have destroyed one-third of Paris. His hundred and thirty-five barrels of gunpowder would have blown the Bastille into the air, and shattered or buried the whole faubourg, all the Marais, and the whole of the quartier of the Arsenal. He seized a match from a cannon. Two subaltern officers prevented the crime; they crossed their bayonets, and barred his passage to the magazines. He then made a show of killing himself, and seized a knife, which they snatched from him.

He had lost his senses and could give no orders. When the French Guards had ranged their cannon and fired (according to some), the captain of the Swiss saw plainly that it was necessary to come to terms; he wrote and passed a note, in which he asked to be allowed to go forth with the honours of war. Refused. Next, that his life should be spared. Hullin and Élie promised it. The difficulty was to perform their promise. To prevent a revenge accumulating for ages, and now incensed by so many murders perpetrated by the Bastille, was beyond the power of man. An authority of an hour's existence, that had but just come from La Grève, and was known only to the two small bands of the vanguard, was not adequate to keep in order the hundred thousand men behind.

The crowd was enraged, blind, drunk with the very sense of their danger. And yet they killed but one man in the fortress. They spared their enemies the Swiss, whom their smockfrocks caused to pass for servants or prisoners; but they ill-treated and wounded their friends the Invalids. They wished to have annihilated the Bastille; they pelted and broke to pieces the two captives of the dial; they ran up to the top of the towers to spurn the cannon; several attacked the stones, and tore their hands in dragging them away. They hastened to the dungeons to deliver the prisoners: two had become mad. One, frightened by the noise, wanted to defend himself, and was quite astonished when those who had battered down his door threw themselves into his arms and bathed him with their tears. Another, whose beard reached to his waist, inquired about the health of Louis XV, believing him to be still reigning. To those who asked him his name, he replied that he was called the Major of Immensity.

The conquerors were not yet at the end of their labours: in the Rue Saint Antoine they had to fight a battle of a different kind. On approaching La Grève, they came successfully on crowds of men, who, having been unable to take any part in the fight, wanted at all events to do something, were it merely to massacre the prisoners. One was killed at the Rue des Tournelles, and another on the quay. Women, with dishevelled hair, came rushing forward, and recognizing their husbands among the slain, left them to fly upon their assassins; one of them, foaming at the mouth, ran about asking everybody for a knife.

De Launey was conducted and supported in that extreme danger by two men of extraordinary courage and strength, Hullin, and another. The latter went with him as far as the Petit Antoine, but was there torn from his side by the rush of the crowd. Hullin held fast. To lead his man from that spot to La Grève, which is so near, was more than the twelve labours of Hercules. No longer knowing how to act, and perceiving that they knew De Launey only by his being alone without a hat, he conceived the heroic idea of putting his own upon his head; and, from that moment, he received the blows intended for the governor. At length, he passed the Arcade Saint Jean; if he could but get him on the flight of steps, and push him towards the stairs, all was over. The crowd saw that very plainly, and accordingly made a desperate onset. The Herculean strength hitherto displayed by Hullin no longer served him here. Stifled by the pressure of the crowd around him, as in the crushing fold of an enormous boa, he lost his footing, was hurled to and fro, and thrown upon the pavement. Twice he regained his feet. The second time he beheld aloft the head of De Launey at the end of a pike.

Another scene was passing in the hall of Saint Jean. The prisoners were there, in great danger of death. The people were especially inveterate towards three Invalids, whom they supposed to have been the cannoneers of the Bastille. One was wounded; De la Salle, the commandant, by in-credible efforts, and proclaiming loudly his title of commandant, at last managed to save him; whilst he was leading him out, the two others were dragged out and hung up to the lamp at the corner of the Vannerie, facing the Hôtel-de-Ville.

All this great commotion, which seemed to have caused Flesselles to be forgotten, was nevertheless what caused his destruction. His implaca-ble accusers of the Palais Royal, few in number, but discontented to see the crowd occupied with any other business, kept close to the bureau, menacing him, and summoning him to follow them. At length he yielded: whether the long expectation of death appeared to him worse than death itself, or that he hoped to escape in the universal pre-occupation about the great event of the day. "Well! gentlemen," said he, "let us go to the Palais Royal." He had not reached the quay before a young man shot him through the head with a pistol bullet.

The dense multitude crowding the hall did not wish for bloodshed; according to an eye-witness, they were stupefied on beholding it. They stared gaping at that strange, prodigious, grotesque, and maddening spec-tacle. Arms of the middle ages and of every age were mingled together; centuries had come back again. Élie, standing on a table, with a helmet on his brow, and a sword hacked in three places, in his hand, seemed a Ro-man warrior. He was entirely surrounded by prisoners, and pleading for them. The French Guards demanded the pardon of the prisoners as their reward.

At that moment, a man, followed by his wife, was brought or rather carried in; it was the Prince de Montbarrey, an ancient minister, arrested at the barrier. The lady fainted; her husband was thrown upon the bu-reau, held down by the arms of twelve men, and bent double. The poor man, in that strange posture, explained that he had not been minister for a long time, and that his son had taken a prominent part in the revolution of his province. De la Salle, the commandant, spoke for him, and exposed himself to great danger. Meanwhile, the people relented a little, and for a moment let go their hold. De la Salle, a very powerful man, caught him up, and carried him off. This trial of strength pleased the people, and was received with applause.

At the same moment, the brave and excellent Élie found means to put an end at once to every intention of trial or condemnation. He perceived the children of the Bastille, and began to shout: "Pardon! for the children, pardon!"

Then you might have seen sunburnt faces and hands blackened with gunpowder, washed with big tears, falling like heavy drops of rain after a shower. Justice and vengeance were thought of no longer. The tribunal was broken up; for Élie had conquered the conquerors of the Bastille.

They made the prisoners swear fidelity to the nation, and led them away; the Invalids marched off in peace to their Hôtel; the French Guards took charge of the Swiss, placed them in safety within their ranks, conducting them to their own barracks, and gave them lodging and food.

What was most admirable, the widows showed themselves equally magnanimous. Though needy, and burdened with children, they were unwilling to receive alone a small sum allotted to them; they shared it with the widow of a poor Invalid who had prevented the Bastille from being blown up, but was killed by mistake. The wife of the besieged was thus adopted, as it were, by those of the besiegers.

Bibliography

Atherton, John. "Michelet: Three Conceptions of Historical Becoming." *Studies in Romanticism,* 4 (Summer 1965): 220–39.

Barzun, Jacques. "Romantic Historiography as a Political Force in France." *Journal of the History of Ideas,* 2 (June 1941): 318–29.

Geyl, Pieter. *Debates with Historians.* New York, 1958.

Haac, Oscar A. *Jules Michelet.* Boston, Mass., 1982.

Kaplan, Edward K. *Michelet's Poetic Vision: A Romantic Philosophy of Nature.* Amherst, Mass., 1977.

Kippur, Stephen A. *Jules Michelet: A Study of Mind and Sensibility.* New York, 1980.

Manuel, Frank. *The Prophets of Paris.* New York, 1962.

White, Hayden. *Metahistory, The Historical Imagination in Nineteenth-Century Europe.* Baltimore, Md., 1973.

CHAPTER 14

Karl Marx

The Eighteenth Brumaire of Louis Bonaparte

(1852)

The 1840s, which were years of political passion for Michelet and which re-kindled in him the spirit of the French Revolution, were years of ferment for another thinker, one whose influence would far outreach Michelet's. The figure is, of course, Karl Marx (1818–1883), whose philosophy would reject the Revolution of 1789 as a model for the future and place it simply as a stage in a much larger vision of world historical development.

Marx was born in Trier in the kingdom of Prussia. His father was a prosperous lawyer who, in 1817, the year before Karl was born, changed his religion from Judaism to Christianity in the face of laws that would have forced him otherwise to give up his profession. As a student, Marx took up successively law, literature, art, and, finally, philosophy. He received a doctorate in 1841 following studies in Bonn and Berlin, where he came under the influence of G. W. F. Hegel, whose works eventually inspired his own philosophy of "historical materialism." Marx's career as a journalist, philosopher, and revolutionary spanned more than four decades, and his influence extends deep into our own time. Yet, much of his writing was unpublished while he was alive, and what he did publish was not widely read. A philosopher of revolution, he was not the center of a personality cult like Mazzini or Kossuth, charismatic leaders in Italy and Hungary; his personal relationships were few, including chiefly his wife, Jenny, their children, and, of course, his life-long friend and collaborator, Friedrich Engels. The public took little notice when he died in 1883, a London exile of some thirty years, who, in the midst of Europe's mid-nineteenth century revolutions and reactions, had been expelled from one country after another.

Marx's world view, historical materialism, loses its real complexity in any attempt to reduce it to a capsule description. Readers should examine for themselves *The German Ideology* (1846, 1932) or *A Critique of Political Economy* (1859), his own fullest elaborations. Marx's basic point was that history is a process of development governed by knowable laws. Hegel had taught that the cosmos progressed towards perfection by means of a dialectic of forces, Ideas in conflict with each other that, in a series of cataclysms, produced higher and higher forms. The unifying thread that ran through this movement was the universal Spirit, which could not be known except by supersensible intuition. Earthly events could be read, however, as manifestations of the cosmic process. Thus, the conflict of nations as embodiments of cultures or unifying Ideas was a reflection of the larger dialectic.

Marx was a Hegelian, but he rejected the notion of an extra-historical Spirit on the grounds that it was empirically unprovable and therefore arbitrary. Instead, the dynamic force in history lay in the material world itself, not outside it, especially in the history of social relationships. Human history began with the primary need for survival, which was met by an increasingly complex set of social and work relationships to provide food and shelter. The practice of division of labor led to an increase in productivity but also to the emergence of classes, in which one's status depended upon one's relationship to the means of production. Some people controlled the labor and lives of others. Marx used the Hegelian concept of tension (dialectic) to explain that history involved a succession of struggles between classes necessarily locked in conflict. Recent centuries had seen the feudal class give way to the rising bourgeoisie, and recent decades exhibited class war between the bourgeoisie and the new industrial proletariat—the final conflict, which the latter must win and beyond which lay social harmony. In the meantime, to understand the politics, the institutions, and the values of a current or historical society, one had first to note how far its production relationships had developed, for everything in life depended upon a person's relationship to the means of production.

Since he believed historical development could be verified by observation of the events themselves, Marx devoted much of his journalistic writing to recent history. The *Eighteenth Brumaire of Louis Bonaparte* (1852), excerpted here, is a standard example. Louis Bonaparte was the nephew of the Emperor Napoleon, and his *coup d'état* in France in 1851 was the unexpected result of the Revolution of 1848. The Revolution in February 1848 was succeeded by the bloody Paris uprising of the "June Days," and in the aftermath, Louis Bonaparte emerged, it seemed from nowhere, to be elected president of France by a huge popular vote. Two years later, legally unable to run for reelection, Bonaparte effected a *coup d'état* and, a year after that, proclaimed himself Emperor Napoleon III.

How did the resurgence of "Bonapartism" fit the concept of class struggle? Whom did the new Napoleon represent?

The following four excerpts embody Marx's answer. In the first Marx establishes his world view and places the Revolution of 1848 in the context of that world view. Next, he describes an immediate body of support for a possible *coup,* the "Society of 10 December," a band of Paris vagabands whom

Marx contrasts with the "real" workers of France. Then he takes up the *coup* itself—Napoleon's "Eighteenth Brumaire," which imitates Napoleon I's *coup* in the revolutionary month of Brumaire. Finally, Marx goes back to analyze the deeper class support for Bonapartism, the growth of bureaucracy, the "state machine" independent of ideology (this discussion is omitted below), and the larger French peasantry.

Observe Marx's language and tone throughout. He is now satirical, now caught up in the imagery of the circus and the theatre to underscore the superficiality of the men he describes, and in the end soberly analytical in a series of dense paragraphs.

H EGEL REMARKS SOMEWHERE that all facts and personages of great importance in world history occur, as it were, twice. He forgot to add: the first time as tragedy, the second as farce. Caussidière for Danton, Louis Blanc for Robespierre, the *Montagne* of 1848 to 1851 for the *Montagne* of 1793 to 1795, the Nephew for the Uncle. And the same caricature occurs in the circumstances attending the second edition of the eighteenth Brumaire!

Men make their own history, but they do not make it just as they please; they do not make it under circumstances chosen by themselves, but under circumstances directly encountered, given and transmitted from the past. The tradition of all the dead generations weighs like a nightmare on the brain of the living. And just when they seem engaged in revolutionizing themselves and things, in creating something that has never yet existed, precisely in such periods of revolutionary crisis they anxiously conjure up the spirits of the past to their service and borrow from them names, battle cries and costumes in order to present the new scene of world history in this time-honoured disguise and this borrowed language. Thus Luther donned the mask of the Apostle Paul, the Revolution of 1789 to 1814 draped itself alternately as the Roman republic and the Roman empire, and the Revolution of 1848 knew nothing better to do than to parody, now 1789, now the revolutionary tradition of 1793 to 1795. In like manner a beginner who has learnt a new language always translates it back into his mother tongue, but he has assimilated the spirit of the new language and can freely express himself in it only when he finds his way in it without recalling the old and forgets his native tongue in the use of the new.

Reprinted by permission of the publisher from Karl Marx, *The Eighteenth Brumaire of Louis Bonaparte* (New York: International Publishers, 1963), 15–26, 75–78, 111–17, 123–29. Copyright © 1963 by International Publishers Co., Inc., New York.

Consideration of this conjuring up of the dead of world history re-veals at once a salient difference. Camille Desmoulins, Danton, Robes-pierre, Saint-Just, Napoleon, the heroes as well as the parties and the masses of the old French Revolution, performed the task of their time in Roman costume and with Roman phrases, the task of unchaining and set-ting up modern *bourgeois* society. The first ones knocked the feudal basis to pieces and mowed off the feudal heads which had grown on it. The other created inside France the conditions under which alone free compe-tition could be developed, parcelled landed property exploited, and the unchained industrial productive power of the nation employed; and be-yond the French borders he everywhere swept the feudal institutions away, so far as was necessary to furnish bourgeois society in France with a suitable up-to-date environment on the European Continent. The new social formation once established, the antediluvian Colossi disappeared and with them resurrected Romanity—the Brutuses, Gracchi, Publicolas, the tribunes, the senators, and Caesar himself. Bourgeois society in its so-ber reality had begotten its true interpreters and mouthpieces in the Says, Cousins, Royer-Collards, Benjamin Constants and Guizots; its real mili-tary leaders sat behind the office desks, and the hog-headed Louis XVIII was its political chief. Wholly absorbed in the production of wealth and in peaceful competitive struggle, it no longer comprehended that ghosts from the days of Rome had watched over its cradle. But unheroic as bour-geois society is, it nevertheless took heroism, sacrifice, terror, civil war and battles of peoples to bring it into being. And in the classically austere traditions of the Roman republic its gladiators found the ideals and the art forms, the self-deceptions that they needed in order to conceal from them-selves the bourgeois limitations of the content of their struggles and to keep their enthusiasm on the high plane of the great historical tragedy. Similarly, at another stage of development, a century earlier, Cromwell and the English people had borrowed speech, passions and illusions from the Old Testament for their bourgeois revolution. When the real aim had been achieved, when the bourgeois transformation of English society had been accomplished, Locke supplanted Habakkuk.

Thus the awakening of the dead in those revolutions served the pur-pose of glorifying the new struggles, not of parodying the old; of magnify-ing the given task in imagination, not of fleeing from its solution in reality; of finding once more the spirit of revolution, not of making its ghost walk about again.

From 1848 to 1851 only the ghost of the old revolution walked about, from Marrast, the *républicain en gants jaunes*, who disguised himself as the old Bailly, down to the adventurer, who hides his commonplace repulsive features under the iron death mask of Napoleon. An entire people, which had imagined that by means of a revolution it had imparted to itself an accelerated power of motion, suddenly finds itself set back into a defunct epoch and, in order that no doubt as to the relapse may be possible, the old dates arise again, the old chronology, the old names, the old edicts, which had long become a subject of antiquarian erudition, and the old minions of the law, who had seemed long decayed. The nation feels like that mad Englishman in Bedlam who fancies that he lives in the times of the ancient Pharaohs and daily bemoans the hard labour that he must perform in the Ethiopian mines as a gold digger, immured in this subterranean prison, a dimly burning lamp fastened to his head, the overseer of the slaves behind him with a long whip, and at the exits a confused welter of barbarian mercenaries, who understand neither the forced labourers in the mines nor one another, since they speak no common language. "And all this is expected of me," sighs the mad Englishman, "of me, a freeborn Briton, in order to make gold for the old Pharaohs." "In order to pay the debts of the Bonaparte family," sighs the French nation. The Englishman, so long as he was in his right mind, could not get rid of the fixed idea of making gold. The French, so long as they were engaged in revolution, could not get rid of the memory of Napoleon, as the election of December 10 proved. They hankered to return from the perils of revolution to the fleshpots of Egypt, and December 2, 1851 was the answer. They have not only a caricature of the old Napoleon, they have the old Napoleon himself, caricatured as he must appear in the middle of the nineteenth century.

The social revolution of the nineteenth century cannot draw its poetry from the past, but only from the future. It cannot begin with itself before it has stripped off all superstition in regard to the past. Earlier revolutions required recollections of past world history in order to drug themselves concerning their own content. In order to arrive at its own content, the revolution of the nineteenth century must let the dead bury their dead. There the phrase went beyond the content; here the content goes beyond the phrase.

The February Revolution was a surprise attack, a *taking* of the old society *unawares*, and the people proclaimed this unexpected *stroke* as a deed of world importance, ushering in a new epoch. On December 2 the February Revolution is conjured away by a cardsharper's trick, and what seems overthrown is no longer the monarchy but the liberal concessions that were wrung from it by centuries of struggle. Instead of *society* having conquered a new content for itself, it seems that the *state* only returned to its oldest form, to the shamelessly simple domination of the sabre and the cowl. This is the answer to the *coup de main* of February 1848, given by the *coup de tête* of December 1851. Easy come, easy go. Meanwhile the interval of time has not passed by unused. During the years 1848 to 1851 French society has made up, and that by an abbreviated because revolutionary method, for the studies and experiences which, in a regular, so to speak, textbook course of development would have had to precede the February Revolution, if it was to be more than a ruffling of the surface. Society now seems to have fallen back behind its point of departure; it has in truth first to create for itself the revolutionary point of departure, the situation, the relations, the conditions under which alone modern revolution becomes serious.

Bourgeois revolutions, like those of the eighteenth century, storm swiftly from success to success; their dramatic effects outdo each other; men and things seem set in sparkling brilliants; ecstasy is the everyday spirit; but they are short-lived; soon they have attained their zenith, and a long crapulent depression lays hold of society before it learns soberly to assimilate the results of its storm-and-stress period. On the other hand, proletarian revolutions, like those of the nineteenth century, criticize themselves constantly, interrupt themselves continually in their own course, come back to the apparently accomplished in order to begin it afresh, deride with unmerciful thoroughness the inadequacies, weaknesses and paltrinesses of their first attempts, seem to throw down their adversary only in order that he may draw new strength from the earth and rise again, more gigantic, before them, recoil ever and anon from the indefinite prodigiousness of their own aims, until a situation has been created which makes all turning back impossible, and the conditions themselves cry out:

> Hic Rhodus, hic salta!
> Here is the rose, here dance!

For the rest, every fairly competent observer, even if he had not followed the course of French developments step by step, must have had a presentiment that an unheard-of fiasco was in store for the revolution. It was enough to hear the self-complacent howl of victory with which Messieurs the Democrats congratulated each other on the expected gracious consequences of the second Sunday in May 1852. In their minds the second Sunday in May 1852 had become a fixed idea, a dogma, like the day on which Christ should reappear and the millennium begin, in the minds of the Chiliasts. As ever, weakness had taken refuge in a belief in miracles, fancied the enemy overcome when he was only conjured away in imagination, and it lost all understanding of the present in a passive glorification of the future that was in store for it and of the deeds it had in petto but which it merely did not want to carry out as yet. Those heroes who seek to disprove their demonstrated incapacity by mutually offering each other their sympathy and getting together in a crowd had tied up their bundles, collected their laurel wreaths in advance and were just then engaged in discounting on the exchange market the republics in partibus for which they had already providently organized the government personnel with all the calm of their unassuming disposition. December 2 struck them like a thunderbolt from a clear sky, and the peoples that in periods of pusillanimous depression gladly let their inward apprehension be drowned by the loudest bawlers will perchance have convinced themselves that the times are past when the cackle of geese could save the Capitol.

The Constitution, the National Assembly, the dynastic parties, the blue and the red republicans, the heroes of Africa, the thunder from the platform, the sheet lightning of the daily press, the entire literature, the political names and the intellectual reputations, the civil law and the penal code, the *liberté, égalité, fraternité* and the second Sunday in May 1852—all has vanished like a phantasmagoria before the spell of a man whom even his enemies do not make out to be a sorcerer. Universal suffrage seems to have survived only for a moment, in order that with its own hand it may make its last will and testament before the eyes of all the world and declare in the name of the people itself: All that exists deserves to perish.

It is not enough to say, as the French do, that their nation was taken unawares. A nation and a woman are not forgiven the unguarded hour in which the first adventurer that came along could violate them. The riddle is not solved by such turns of speech, but merely formulated differently. It remains to be explained how a nation of thirty-six millions can be surprised and delivered unresisting into captivity by three *chevaliers d'industrie*.

Let us recapitulate in general outline the phases that the French Revolution went through from February 24, 1848, to December 1851.

Three main periods are unmistakable: *the February period;* May 4, 1848, to May 28, 1849: *the period of the constitution of the republic, or of the Constituent National Assembly;* May 28, 1849, to December 2, 1851: *the period of the constitutional republic or of the Legislative National Assembly.*

The *first period,* from February 24, or the overthrow of Louis Philippe, to May 4, 1848, the meeting of the Constituent Assembly, the *February period* proper, may be described as the *prologue* to the revolution. Its character was officially expressed in the fact that the government improvised by it itself declared that it was *provisional* and, like the government, everything that was mooted, attempted or enunciated during this period proclaimed itself to be only *provisional.* Nothing and nobody ventured to lay claim to the right of existence and of real action. All the elements that had prepared or determined the revolution, the dynastic opposition, the republican bourgeoisie, the democratic-republican petty bourgeoisie and the social-democratic workers, provisionally found their place in the February *government.*

It could not be otherwise. The February days originally intended an electoral reform, by which the circle of the politically privileged among the possessing class itself was to be widened and the exclusive domination of the aristocracy of finance overthrown. When it came to the actual conflict, however, when the people mounted the barricades, the National Guard maintained a passive attitude, the army offered no serious resistance and the monarchy ran away, the republic appeared to be a matter of course. Every party construed it in its own way. Having secured it arms in hand, the proletariat impressed its stamp upon it and proclaimed it to be a *social republic*. There was thus indicated the general content of the modern revolution, a content which was in most singular contradiction to everything that, with the material available, with the degree of education attained by the masses, under the given circumstances and relations, could be immediately realized in practice. On the other hand, the claims of all the remaining elements that had collaborated in the February Revolution were recognized by the lion's share that they obtained in the government. In no period do we, therefore, find a more confused mixture of high-flown phrases and actual uncertainty and clumsiness, of more enthusiastic striving for innovation and more deeply-rooted domination of the old routine, of more apparent harmony of the whole of society and more profound estrangement of its elements. While the Paris proletariat still revelled in the vision of the wide prospects that had opened before it and indulged in seriously-meant discussions on social problems, the old powers of society had grouped themselves, assembled, reflected and found unexpected support in the mass of the nation, the peasants and petty bourgeois, who all at once stormed onto the political stage, after the barriers of the July Monarchy had fallen.

The *second period*, from May 4, 1848, to the end of May 1849, is the period of the *constitution*, the *foundation, of the bourgeois republic*. Directly after the February days not only had the dynastic opposition been surprised by the republicans and the republicans by the Socialists, but all France by Paris. The National Assembly, which met on May 4, 1848, had emerged from the national elections and represented the nation. It was a living protest against the pretensions of the February days and was to reduce the results of the revolution to the bourgeois scale. In vain the Paris proletariat, which immediately grasped the character of this National Assembly, attempted on May 15, a few days after it met, forcibly to negate its existence, to dissolve it, to disintegrate again into its constituent parts the organic form in which the proletariat was threatened by the reacting spirit of the nation. As is known, May 15 had no other result save that of removing Blanqui and his comrades, that is, the real leaders of the proletarian party, from the public stage for the entire duration of the cycle we are considering.

The *bourgeois monarchy* of Louis Philippe can be followed only by a *bourgeois republic*, that is to say, whereas a limited section of the bourgeoisie ruled in the name of the king, the whole of the bourgeoisie will now rule in the name of the people. The demands of the Paris proletariat are utopian nonsense, to which an end must be put. To this declaration of the Constituent National Assembly the Paris proletariat replied with the *June Insurrection*, the most colossal event in the history of European civil wars. The bourgeois republic triumphed. On its side stood the aristocracy of finance, the industrial bourgeoisie, the middle class, the petty bourgeois, the army, the *lumpenproletariat* organized as the Mobile Guard, the intellectual lights, the clergy and the rural population. On the side of the Paris proletariat stood none but itself. More than three thousand insurgents were butchered after the victory, and fifteen thousand were transported without trial. With this defeat the proletariat passes into the *background* of the revolutionary stage. It attempts to press forward again on every occasion, as soon as the movement appears to make a fresh start, but with ever decreased expenditure of strength and always slighter results. As soon as one of the social strata situated above it gets into revolutionary ferment, the proletariat enters into an alliance with it and so shares all the defeats that the different parties suffer, one after another. But these subsequent blows become the weaker, the greater the surface of society over which they are distributed. The more important leaders of the proletariat in the Assembly and in the press successively fall victims to the courts, and ever more equivocal figures come to head it. In part it throws itself into *doctrinaire experiments, exchange banks and workers' associations, hence into a movement in which it renounces the revolutionizing of the old world by means of the latter's own great, combined resources, and seeks, rather, to achieve its salvation behind society's back, in private fashion, within its limited conditions of existence, and hence necessarily suffers shipwreck.* It seems to be unable either to rediscover revolutionary greatness in itself or to win new energy from the connections newly entered into, until *all classes* with which it contended in June themselves lie prostrate beside it. But at least it succumbs with the honours of the great, world-historic struggle; not only France, but all Europe trembles at the June earthquake, while the ensuing defeats of the upper classes are so cheaply bought that they require bare-faced exaggeration by the victorious party to be able to pass for events at all, and become the more ignominious the further the defeated party is removed from the proletarian party.

The defeat of the June insurgents, to be sure, had now prepared, had levelled the ground on which the bourgeois republic could be founded and built up, but it had shown at the same time that in Europe the questions at issue are other than that of "republic or monarchy." It had revealed that here *bourgeois republic* signifies the unlimited despotism of one class over other classes. It had proved that in countries with an old civilization, with a developed formation of classes, with modern conditions of production and with an intellectual consciousness in which all traditional ideas have been dissolved by the work of centuries, *the republic signifies in general only the political form of revolution of bourgeois society* and not its *conservative form of life*, as, for example, in the United States of North America, where, though classes already exist, they have not yet become fixed, but continually change and interchange their elements in constant flux, where the modern means of production, instead of coinciding with a stagnant surplus population, rather compensate for the relative deficiency of heads and hands, and where, finally, the feverish, youthful movement of material production, which has to make a new world its own, has left neither time nor opportunity for abolishing the old spirit world.

During the June days all classes and parties had united in the *party of Order* against the proletarian class as the *party of Anarchy*, of Socialism, of Communism. They had "saved" society from *"the enemies of society."* They had given out the watchwords of the old society, *"property, family, religion, order,"* to their army as passwords and had proclaimed to the counter-revolutionary crusaders: "In this sign thou shalt conquer!" From that moment, as soon as one of the numerous parties which had gathered under this sign against the June insurgents seeks to hold the revolutionary battlefield in its own class interest, it goes down before the cry: "Property, family, religion, order." Society is saved just as often as the circle of its rulers contracts, as a more exclusive interest is maintained against a wider one. Every demand of the simplest bourgeois financial reform, of the most ordinary liberalism, of the most formal republicanism, of the most shallow democracy, is simultaneously castigated as an "attempt on society" and stigmatized as "Socialism." And, finally, the high priests of "the religion and order" themselves are driven with kicks from their Pythian tripods, hauled out of their beds in the darkness of night, put in prison-vans, thrown into dungeons or sent into exile; their temple is razed to the ground, their mouths are sealed, their pens broken, their law torn to pieces in the name of religion, of property, of the family, of order. Bourgeois fanatics for order are shot down on their balconies by mobs of drunken soldiers, their domestic sanctuaries profaned, their houses bombarded for amusement—in the name of property, of the family, of religion and of order. Finally, the scum of bourgeois society forms the *holy phalanx of order* and the hero Crapulinski installs himself in the Tuileries as the *"saviour of society."*

. . . .

[H]e was constantly accompanied by persons affiliated with the *Society of December 10*. This society dates from the year 1849. On the pretext of founding a benevolent society, the *lumpenproletariat* of Paris had been organized into secret sections, each section being led by Bonapartist agents, with a Bonapartist general at the head of the whole. Alongside decayed *roués* with dubious means of subsistence and of dubious origin, alongside ruined and adventurous offshoots of the bourgeoisie were vagabonds, discharged soldiers, discharged jailbirds, escaped galley slaves, swindlers, mountebanks, *lazzaroni*, pickpockets, tricksters, gamblers, *maquereaus*, brothel keepers, porters, *literati*, organ-grinders, ragpickers, knife grinders, tinkers, beggars—in short, the whole indefinite, disintegrated mass, thrown hither and thither, which the French term *la bohème*; from this kindred element Bonaparte formed the core of the Society of December 10. A "benevolent society"—in so far as, like Bonaparte, all its members felt the need of benefiting themselves at the expense of the labouring nation. This Bonaparte, who constitutes himself *chief of the lumpenproletariat*, who here alone rediscovers in mass form the interests which he personally pursues, who recognizes in this scum, offal, refuse of all classes the only class upon which he can base himself unconditionally, is the real Bonaparte, the Bonaparte *sans phrase*. An old crafty *roué*, he conceives the historical life of the nations and their performances of state as comedy in the most vulgar sense, as a masquerade where the grand costumes, words and postures merely serve to mask the pettiest knavery. Thus on his expedition to Strasbourg, where a trained Swiss vulture had played the part of the Napoleonic eagle. For his irruption into Boulogne he puts some London lackeys into French uniforms. They represent the army. In his Society of December 10, he assembles ten thousand rascally fellows, who are to play the part of the people, as Nick Bottom that of the lion. At a moment when the bourgeoisie itself played the most complete comedy, but in the most serious manner in the world, without infringing any of the pedantic conditions of French dramatic etiquette, and was itself half deceived, half convinced of the solemnity of its own performance of state, the adventurer, who took the comedy as plain comedy, was bound to win. Only when he has eliminated his solemn opponent, when he himself now takes his imperial role seriously and under the Napoleonic mask imagines he is the real Napoleon, does he become the victim of his own conception of the world, the serious buffoon who no longer takes world history for a comedy but his comedy for world history. What the national *ateliers* were for the socialist workers, what the *Gardes mobiles* were for the bourgeois republicans, the Society of December 10 was for Bonaparte, the party fighting force peculiar to him. On his journeys the detachments of this society packing the railways had to improvise a public for him, stage public enthusiasm, roar *vive l'Empereur*, insult and thrash republicans, of course, under the protection of the police. On his return journeys to Paris they had to form the advance guard, forestall counter-demonstrations or disperse them. The Society of December 10 belonged to him, it was *his* work, his very own idea. Whatever else he appropriates is put into his hands by the force of circumstances; whatever else he does, the circumstances do for him or he is content to copy from the deeds of others. But Bonaparte with official phrases about order, religion, family and property in public, before the citizens, and with the secret society of the Schufterles and Spiegelbergs, the society of disorder, prostitution and theft, behind him—that is Bonaparte himself as original author, and the history of the Society of December 10 is his own history.

Now it had happened by way of exception that people's representatives belonging to the party of Order came under the cudgels of the Decembrists. Still more. Yon, the Police Commissioner assigned to the National Assembly and charged with watching over its safety, acting on the deposition of a certain Alais, advised the Permanent Commission that a section of the Decembrists had decided to assassinate General Changarnier and Dupin, the President of the National Assembly, and had already designated the individuals who were to perpetrate the deed. One comprehends the terror of M. Dupin. A parliamentary enquiry into the Society of December 10, that is, the profanation of the Bonapartist secret world, seemed inevitable. Just before the meeting of the National Assembly Bonaparte providently disbanded his society, naturally only on paper, for in a detailed memoir at the end of 1851 Police Prefect Carlier still sought in vain to move him to really break up the Decembrists.

The Society of December 10 was to remain the private army of Bonaparte until he succeeded in transforming the public army into a Society of December 10. Bonaparte made the first attempt at this shortly after the adjournment of the National Assembly, and precisely with the money just wrested from it. As a fatalist, he lives in the conviction that there are certain higher powers which man, and the soldier in particular, cannot withstand. Among these powers he counts, first and foremost, cigars and champagne, cold poultry and garlic sausage. Accordingly, to begin with, he treats officers and non-commissioned officers in his Elysée apartments to cigars and champagne, to cold poultry and garlic sausage. On October 3 he repeats this manoeuvre with the mass of the troops at the St. Maur review, and on October 10 the same manoeuvre on a still larger scale at the Satory army parade. The Uncle remembered the campaigns of Alexander in Asia, the Nephew the triumphal marches of Bacchus in the same land. Alexander was a demigod, to be sure, but Bacchus was a god and moreover the tutelary deity of the Society of December 10.

. . . .

If ever an event has, well in advance of its coming, cast its shadow before, it was Bonaparte's *coup d'état*. As early as January 29, 1849, barely a month after his election, he had made a proposal about it to Changarnier. In the summer of 1849 his own Prime Minister, Odilon Barrot, had covertly denounced the policy of *coups d'état*; in the winter of 1850 Thiers had openly done so. In May 1851, Persigny had sought once more to win Changarnier for the *coup*; the *Messager de l'Assemblée* had published an account of these negotiations. During every parliamentary storm, the Bonapartist journals threatened a *coup d'état*, and the nearer the crisis drew, the louder grew their tone. In the orgies that Bonaparte kept up every night with men and women of the "swell mob," as soon as the hour of midnight approached and copious potations had loosened tongues and fired imaginations, the *coup d'état* was fixed for the following morning. Swords were drawn, glasses clinked, the Representatives were thrown out of the window, the imperial mantle fell upon Bonaparte's shoulders, until the following morning banished the spook once more and astonished Paris learned, from vestals of little reticence and from indiscreet paladins, of the danger it had once again escaped. During the months of September and October rumours of a *coup d'état* followed fast one after the other. Simultaneously, the shadow took on colour, like a variegated daguerreotype. Look up the September and October copies of the organs of the European daily press and you will find, word for word, intimations like the following: "Paris is full of rumours of a *coup d'état*. The capital is to be filled with troops during the night, and the next morning is to bring decrees which will dissolve the National Assembly, declare the Department of the Seine in a state of siege, restore universal suffrage and appeal to the people. Bonaparte is said to be seeking ministers for the execution of these illegal decrees." The letters that bring these tidings always end with the fateful word *"postponed."* The *coup d'état* was ever the fixed idea of Bonaparte. With this idea he had again set foot on French soil. He was so obsessed by it that he continually betrayed it and blurted it out. He was so weak that, just as continually, he gave it up again. The shadow of the *coup d'état* had become so familiar to the Parisians as a spectre that they were not willing to believe in it when it finally appeared in the flesh. What allowed the *coup d'état* to succeed was, therefore, neither the reticent reserve of the chief of the Society of December 10 nor the fact that the National Assembly was caught unawares. If it succeeded, it succeeded despite *his* indiscretion and with *its* foreknowledge, a necessary, inevitable result of antecedent developments.

On October 10 Bonaparte, announced to his ministers his decision to restore universal suffrage; on the sixteenth they handed in their resignations; on the twenty-sixth Paris learned of the formation of the Thorigny ministry. Police Prefect Carlier was simultaneously replaced by Maupas;

the head of the First Military Division, Magnan, concentrated the most reliable regiments in the capital. On November 4, the National Assembly resumed its sittings. It had nothing better to do than to recapitulate in a short, succinct form the course it had gone through and to prove that it was buried only after it had died.

The first post that it forfeited in the struggle with the executive power was the ministry. It had solemnly to admit this loss by accepting at full value the Thorigny ministry, a mere shadow cabinet. The Permanent Commission had received M. Giraud with laughter when he presented himself in the name of the new ministers. Such a weak ministry for such strong measures as the restoration of universal suffrage! Yet the precise object was to get nothing through *in* parliament, but everything *against* parliament.

On the very first day of its re-opening, the National Assembly received the message from Bonaparte in which he demanded the restoration of universal suffrage and the abolition of the law of May 31, 1850. The same day his ministers introduced a decree to this effect. The National Assembly at once rejected the ministry's motion of urgency and rejected the law itself on November 13 by three hundred and fifty-five votes to three hundred and forty-eight. Thus, it tore up its mandate once more; it once more confirmed the fact that it had transformed itself from the freely elected representatives of the people into the usurpatory parliament of a class; it acknowledged once more that it had itself cut in two the muscles which connected the parliamentary head with the body of the nation.

If by its motion to restore universal suffrage the executive power appealed from the National Assembly to the people, the legislative power appealed by its Quaestors' Bill from the people to the army. This Quaestors' Bill was to establish its right of directly requisitioning troops, of forming a parliamentary army. While it thus designated the army as the arbitrator between itself and the people, between itself and Bonaparte, while it recognized the army as the decisive state power, it had to confirm, on the other hand, the fact that it had long given up its claim to dominate this power. By debating its right to requisition troops, instead of requisitioning them at once, it betrayed its doubts about its own powers. By rejecting the Quaestors' Bill, it made public confession of its impotence. This bill was defeated, its proponents lacking 108 votes of a majority. The *Montagne* thus decided the issue. It found itself in the position of Buridan's ass, not, indeed, between two bundles of hay with the problem of deciding which was the more attractive, but between two showers of blows with the problem of deciding which was the harder. On the one hand, there was the fear of Changarnier; on the other, the fear of Bonaparte. It must be confessed that the position was no heroic one.

On November 18, an amendment was moved to the law on municipal elections introduced by the party of Order, to the effect that instead of three years', one year's domicile should suffice for municipal electors. The amendment was lost by a single vote, but this one vote immediately proved to be a mistake. By splitting up into its hostile factions, the party of Order had long ago forfeited its independent parliamentary majority. It showed now that there was no longer any majority at all in parliament. The National Assembly had become *incapable of transacting business.* Its atomic constituents were no longer held together by any force of cohesion; it had drawn its last breath; it was dead.

Finally, a few days before the catastrophe, the extraparliamentary mass of the bourgeoisie was solemnly to confirm once more its breach with the bourgeoisie in parliament. Thiers, as a parliamentary hero infected more than the rest with the incurable disease of parliamentary cretinism, had, after the death of parliament, hatched out, together with the Council of State, a new parliamentary intrigue, a Responsibility Law by which the President was to be firmly held within the limits of the Constitution. Just as, on laying the foundation stone of the new market halls in Paris on September 15, Bonaparte, like a second Masaniello, had enchanted the *dames des halles,* the fishwives—to be sure, one fishwife outweighed seventeen burgraves in real power; just as after the introduction of the Quaestors' Bill he enraptured the lieutenants he regaled in the Elysée, so now, on November 25, he swept off their feet the industrial bourgeoisie, which had gathered at the circus to receive at his hands prize medals for the London Industrial Exhibition. I shall give the significant portion of his speech as reported in the *Journal des Débats:*

> With such unhoped-for successes, I am justified in reiterating how great the French republic would be if it were permitted to pursue its real interests and reform its institutions, instead of being constantly disturbed by demagogues, on the one hand, and by monarchist hallucinations, on the other. (Loud, stormy and repeated applause from every part of the amphitheatre.) The monarchist hallucinations hinder all progress and all important branches of industry. In place of progress nothing but struggle. One sees men who were formerly the most zealous supporters of the royal authority and prerogative become partisans of a Convention merely in order to weaken the authority that has sprung from universal suffrage. (Loud and repeated applause.) We see men who have suffered most from the Revolution, and have deplored it most, provoke a new one, and merely in order to fetter the nation's will. . . . I promise you tranquillity for the future, etc., etc. (Bravo, bravo, a storm of bravos).

Thus the industrial bourgeoisie applauds with servile bravos the *coup d'état* of December 2, the annihilation of parliament, the downfall of its own rule, the dictatorship of Bonaparte. The thunder of applause on November 25 had its answer in the thunder of cannon on December 4, and it was on the house of Monsieur Sallandrouze, who had clapped most, that they clapped most of the bombs.

Cromwell, when he dissolved the Long Parliament, went alone into its midst, drew out his watch in order that it should not continue to exist a minute after the time limit fixed by him, and drove out each one of the members of parliament with hilariously humourous taunts. Napoleon, smaller than his prototype, at least betook himself on the eighteenth Brumaire to the legislative body and read out to it, though in a faltering voice, its sentence of death. The second Bonaparte, who, moreover, found himself in possession of an executive power very different from that of Cromwell or Napoleon, sought his model not in the annals of world history, but in the annals of the Society of December 10, in the annals of the criminal courts. He robs the Bank of France of twenty-five million francs, buys General Magnan with a million, the soldiers with fifteen francs apiece and liquor, comes together with his accomplices secretly like a thief in the night, has the houses of the most dangerous parliamentary leaders broken into and Cavaignac, Lamoricière, Le Flô, Changarnier, Charras, Thiers, Baze, etc., dragged from their beds and put in prison, the chief squares of Paris and the parliamentary building occupied by troops, and cheap-Jack placards posted early in the morning on all the walls, proclaiming the dissolution of the National Assembly and the Council of State, the restoration of universal suffrage and the placing of the Seine Department in a state of siege. In like manner, he inserted a little later in the Moniteur a false document which asserted that influential parliamentarians had grouped themselves round him and formed a state consulta.

The rump parliament, assembled in the mairie building of the tenth arrondissement and consisting mainly of Legitimists and Orleanists, votes the deposition of Bonaparte amid repeated cries of "Long live the Republic," unavailingly harangues the gaping crowds before the building and is finally led off in the custody of African sharpshooters, first to the d'Orsay barracks, and later packed into prison vans and transported to the prisons of Mazas, Ham and Vincennes. Thus ended the party of Order, the Legislative Assembly and the February Revolution. Before hastening to close, let us briefly summarize the latter's history:

I. *First period.* From February 24 to May 4, 1848. February period. Prologue. Universal brotherhood swindle.

II. *Second period.* Period of constituting the republic and of the Constituent National Assembly.

1. May 4 to June 25, 1848. Struggle of all classes against the proletariat. Defeat of the proletariat in the June days.

2. June 25 to December 10, 1848. Dictatorship of the pure bourgeois republicans. Drafting of the Constitution. Proclamation of a state of siege in Paris. The bourgeois dictatorship set aside on December 10 by the election of Bonaparte as President.

3. December 20, 1848 to May 28, 1849. Struggle of the Constituent

Assembly with Bonaparte and with the party of Order in alliance with him. Passing of the Constituent Assembly. Fall of the republican bourgeoisie.

III. *Third period.* Period of the *constitutional republic* and of the *Legislative National Assembly.*

1. May 28, 1849 to June 13, 1849. Struggle of the petty bourgeoisie with the bourgeoisie and with Bonaparte. Defeat of the petty-bourgeois democracy.

2. June 13, 1849 to May 31, 1850. Parliamentary dictatorship of the party of Order. It completes its rule by abolishing universal suffrage, but loses the parliamentary ministry.

3. May 31, 1850 to December 2, 1851. Struggle between the parliamentary bourgeoisie and Bonaparte.

(a) May 31, 1850 to January 12, 1851. Parliament loses the supreme command of the army.

(b) January 12 to April 11, 1851. It is worsted in its attempts to regain the administrative power. The party of Order loses its independent parliamentary majority. Its coalition with the republicans and the *Montagne.*

(c) April 11, 1851 to October 9, 1851. Attempts at revision, fusion, prorogation. The party of Order decomposes into its separate constituents. The breach between the bourgeois parliament and press and the mass of the bourgeoisie becomes definite.

(d) October 9 to December 2, 1851. Open breach between parliament and the executive power. Parliament performs its dying act and succumbs, left in the lurch by its own class, by the army and by all the remaining classes. Passing of the parliamentary regime and of bourgeois rule. Victory of Bonaparte. Parody of restoration of empire.

. . . .

And yet the state power is not suspended in midair. Bonaparte represents a class, and the most numerous class of French society at that, the *small-holding [Parzellen] peasants.*

Just as the Bourbons were the dynasty of big landed property and just as the Orleans were the dynasty of money, so the Bonapartes are the dynasty of the peasants, that is, the mass of the French people. Not the Bonaparte who submitted to the bourgeois parliament, but the Bonaparte who dispersed the bourgeois parliament is the chosen of the peasantry. For three years the towns had succeeded in falsifying the meaning of the election of December 10 and in cheating the peasants out of the restoration of the empire. The election of December 10, 1848, has been consummated only by the *coup d'état* of December 2, 1851.

The small-holding peasants form a vast mass, the members of which live in similar conditions but without entering into manifold relations with one another. Their mode of production isolates them from one another instead of bringing them into mutual intercourse. The isolation is increased by France's bad means of communication and by the poverty of the peasants. Their field of production, the small holding, admits of no division of labour in its cultivation, no application of science and, therefore, no diversity of development, no variety of talent, no wealth of social relationships. Each individual peasant family is almost self-sufficient; it itself directly produces the major part of its consumption and thus acquires its means of life more through exchange with nature than in intercourse with society. A small holding, a peasant and his family; alongside them another small holding, another peasant and another family. A few score of these make up a village, and a few score of villages make up a Department. In this way, the great mass of the French nation is formed by simple addition of homologous magnitudes, much as potatoes in a sack form a sack of potatoes. In so far as millions of families live under economic conditions of existence that separate their mode of life, their interests and their culture from those of the other classes, and put them in hostile opposition to the latter, they form a class. In so far as there is merely a local interconnection among these small-holding peasants, and the identity of their interests begets no community, no national bond and no political organization among them, they do not form a class. They are consequently incapable of enforcing their class interest in their own name, whether through a parliament or through a convention. They cannot represent themselves, they must be represented. Their representative must at the same time appear as their master, as an authority over them, as an unlimited governmental power that protects them against the other classes and sends them rain and sunshine from above. The political influence of the small-holding peasants, therefore, finds its final expression in the executive power subordinating society to itself.

Historical tradition gave rise to the belief of the French peasants in the miracle that a man named Napoleon would bring all the glory back to them. And an individual turned up who gives himself out as the man because he bears the name of Napoleon, in consequence of the *Code Napoléon*, which lays down that *la recherche de la paternité est interdite*. After a vagabondage of twenty years and after a series of grotesque adventures, the legend finds fulfilment and the man becomes Emperor of the French. The fixed idea of the Nephew was realized, because it coincided with the fixed idea of the most numerous class of the French people.

But, it may be objected, what about the peasant risings in half of France, the raids on the peasants by the army, the mass incarceration and transportation of peasants?

Since Louis XIV, France has experienced no similar persecution of the peasants "on account of demagogic practices."

But let there be no misunderstanding. The Bonaparte dynasty represents not the revolutionary, but the conservative peasant; not the peasant that strikes out beyond the condition of his social existence, the small holding, but rather the peasant who wants to consolidate this holding, not the country folk who, linked up with the towns, want to overthrow the old order through their own energies, but on the contrary those who, in stupified seclusion within this old order, want to see themselves and their small holdings saved and favoured by the ghost of the empire. It represents not the enlightenment, but the superstition of the peasant; not his judgment, but his prejudice; not his future, but his past; not his modern Cevennes, but his modern Vendée.

The three years' rigorous rule of the parliamentary republic had freed a part of the French peasants from the Napoleonic illusion and had revolutionized them, even if only superficially; but the bourgeoisie violently repressed them, as often as they set themselves in motion. Under the parliamentary republic the modern and the traditional consciousness of the French peasant contended for mastery. This progress took the form of an incessant struggle between the schoolmasters and the priests. The bourgeoisie struck down the schoolmasters. For the first time the peasants made efforts to behave independently in the face of the activity of the government. This was shown in the continual conflict between the *maires* and the prefects. The bourgeoisie deposed the *maires*. Finally, during the period of the parliamentary republic, the peasants of different localities rose against their own offspring, the army. The bourgeoisie punished them with states of siege and punitive expeditions. And this same bourgeoisie now cries out about the stupidity of the masses, the vile multitude, that has betrayed it to Bonaparte. It has itself forcibly strengthened the empire sentiments [*Imperialismus*] of the peasant class, it conserved the conditions that form the birthplace of this peasant religion. The bourgeoisie, to be sure, is bound to fear the stupidity of the masses as long as they remain conservative, and the insight of the masses as soon as they become revolutionary.

In the risings after the *coup d'état*, a part of the French peasants protested, arms in hand, against their own vote of December 10, 1848. The school they had gone through since 1848 had sharpened their wits. But they had made themselves over to the underworld of history; history held them to their word, and the majority was still so prejudiced that in precisely the reddest Departments the peasant population voted openly for Bonaparte. In its view, the National Assembly had hindered his progress. He had now merely broken the fetters that the towns had imposed on the will of the countryside. In some parts the peasants even entertained the grotesque notion of a convention side by side with Napoleon.

After the first revolution had transformed the peasants from semi-villeins into freeholders, Napoleon confirmed and regulated the conditions on which they could exploit undisturbed the soil of France which had only just fallen to their lot and slake their youthful passion for property. But what is now causing the ruin of the French peasant is his small holding itself, the division of the land, the form of property which Napoleon consolidated in France. It is precisely the material conditions which made the feudal peasant a small-holding peasant and Napoleon an emperor. Two generations have sufficed to produce the inevitable result: progressive deterioration of agriculture, progressive indebtedness of the agriculturist. The "Napoleonic" form of property, which at the beginning of the nineteenth century was the condition for the liberation and enrichment of the French country folk, has developed in the course of this century into the law of their enslavement and pauperization. And precisely this law is the first of the *"idées napoléoniennes"* which the second Bonaparte has to uphold. If he still shares with the peasants the illusion that the cause of their ruin is to be sought, not in this small-holding property itself, but outside it, in the influence of secondary circumstances, his experiments will burst like soap bubbles when they come in contact with the relations of production.

The economic development of small-holding property has radically changed the relation of the peasants to the other classes of society. Under Napoleon, the fragmentation of the land in the countryside supplemented free competition and the beginning of big industry in the towns. The peasant class was the ubiquitous protest against the landed aristocracy which had just been overthrown. The roots that small-holding property struck in French soil deprived feudalism of all nutriment. Its landmarks formed the natural fortifications of the bourgeoisie against any surprise attack on the part of its old overlords. But in the course of the nineteenth century the feudal lords were replaced by urban usurers; the feudal obligation that went with the land was replaced by the mortgage; aristocratic landed property was replaced by bourgeois capital. The small holding of the peasant is now only the pretext that allows the capitalist to draw profits, interest and rent from the soil, while leaving it to the tiller of the soil himself to see how he can extract his wages. The mortgage debt burdening the soil of France imposes on the French peasantry payment of an amount of interest equal to the annual interest on the entire British national debt. Small-holding property, in this enslavement by capital to which its development inevitably pushes forward, has transformed the mass of the French nation into troglodytes. Sixteen million peasants (including women and children) dwell in hovels, a large number of which have but one opening, others only two and the most favoured only three. And windows are to a house what the five senses are to the head. The bourgeois order, which at the beginning of the century set the state to stand guard over the newly arisen small holding and manured it with laurels, has become a vampire that sucks out its blood and brains and throws it into the alchemistic cauldron of capital. The *Code Napoléon* is now nothing but a *codex* of distraints, forced sales and compulsory auctions. To the four million (including children, etc.) officially recognized paupers, vagabonds, criminals and prostitutes in France must be added five million who hover on the margin of existence and either have their haunts in the countryside itself or, with their rags and their children, continually desert the countryside for the towns and the towns for the countryside. The interests of the peasants, therefore, are no longer, as under Napoleon, in accord with, but in opposition to the interests of the bourgeoisie, to capital. Hence the peasants find their natural ally and leader in the *urban proletariat*, whose task is the overthrow of the bourgeois order. But *strong and unlimited government*—and this is the second *"idée napoléonienne,"* which the second Napoleon has to carry out—is called upon to defend this "material" order by force. This *"ordre matériel"* also serves as the catchword in all of Bonaparte's proclamations against the rebellious peasants.

Besides the mortgage which capital imposes on it, the small holding is burdened by *taxes*. Taxes are the source of life for the bureaucracy, the army, the priests and the court, in short, for the whole apparatus of the executive power. Strong government and heavy taxes are identical. By its very nature, small-holding property forms a suitable basis for an all-powerful and innumerable bureaucracy. It creates a uniform level of relationships and persons over the whole surface of the land. Hence it also permits of uniform action from a supreme centre on all points of this uniform mass. It annihilates the aristocratic intermediate grades between the mass of the people and the state power. On all sides, therefore, it calls forth the direct interference of this state power and the interposition of its immediate organs. Finally, it produces an unemployed surplus population for which there is no place either on the land or in the towns, and which accordingly reaches out for state offices as a sort of respectable alms, and provokes the creation of state posts. By the new markets which he opened at the point of the bayonet, by the plundering of the Continent, Napoleon repaid the compulsory taxes with interest. These taxes were a spur to the industry of the peasant, whereas now they rob his industry of its last resources and complete his inability to resist pauperism. And an enormous bureaucracy, well-galloned and well-fed, is the *"idée napoléonienne"* which is most congenial of all to the second Bonaparte.

Bibliography

Barzun, Jacques. *Darwin, Marx, and Wagner.* Boston, Mass., 1941.

Berlin, Isaiah. *Karl Marx, His Life and Environment.* 3d ed. Oxford, 1963.

Bober, M. M. *Karl Marx's Interpretation of History.* 2d ed. New York, 1948.

Clive, John. "Why Read the Great 19th-Century Historians?" *American Scholar,* 48 (Winter 1979): 37–48.

Hyman, Stanley Edgar. *The Tangled Bank, Darwin, Marx, Frazer and Freud as Imaginative Writers.* New York, 1962.

Krieger, Leonard. "Marx and Engels as Historians." *Journal of the History of Ideas,* 14 (June 1953): 381–403.

McLellan, David E. *Karl Marx, His Life and Thought.* New York, 1973.

Mazlish, Bruce. "Marx." In *The Riddle of History, The Great Speculators from Vico to Freud.* New York, 1966.

Mazlish, Bruce. "The Tragic Farce of Marx, Hegel, and Engels: A Note." *History and Theory,* 11, 335–37.

Riquelme, John Paul. "The Eighteenth Brumaire of Karl Marx as Symbolic Action." *History and Theory,* 19, 58–72.

White, Hayden. *Metahistory, The Historical Imagination in Nineteenth-Century Europe.* Baltimore, Md., 1973.

CHAPTER 15

Francis Parkman

LaSalle and the Discovery of the Great West

(1869, revised 1879)

Francis Parkman (1821–1893) was as significant a nineteenth-century figure as Ranke, Macaulay, Michelet, or Marx, though not because he
brought new insight to politics, economics, or historical method. The
value of his multivolume *France and England in North America,* of which
the book about Ferdinand La Salle excerpted here is a part, lies in
Parkman's force as a romantic narrator and creator of character and also
in his desire to provide New England with a sense of its past well beyond
the Puritan parochialism of William Bradford and Cotton Mather.
Nineteenth-century America had historians to celebrate democracy, like
George Bancroft, and it would have its "scientists," like Frederick Jackson Turner (see chapter 16), but Parkman's appreciation of the past as
romantic epic was unmatched.

Parkman was born to Boston's aristocracy, the "Brahmin" caste in Oliver Wendell Holmes' phrase, descended from the great colonial families. He
made no small contribution to their distinctive intellectual culture, and the
scheme of his life seems typical: Harvard College (1844), the right clubs, a
European grand tour (1843–1844), a proper marriage, and life-long residence on Boston's Beacon Hill.

Yet, there were differences. Parkman had a more than literary fascination with the wilderness and extended himself, sometimes beyond reason, to
experience it firsthand. Boyhood rambles in the forest near his grandparents'
home led to long college vacations in the White Mountains of New Hampshire
and finally to his famous excursion by covered wagon to the far west in 1846.
His account of the trip, *The Oregon Trail* (1849), became Parkman's most
famous book. Later he would visit the sites around which key actions of his
history were played out so that his prose could evoke the sense he had of
primeval nature as an active force in men's lives. When he relied upon others'
accounts, especially for developing characters in or out of harmony with nature, he preferred contemporary, firsthand observation. The fruit of these im-

pulses is the ground-level sense of fresh discovery that animates Parkman's "history of the American forest."

Parkman was different, too, in having to overcome a severe nervous disorder and limited eyesight in order to write anything at all. Some critics suggest that his appreciation of the lonely, failed heroism of figures like La Salle was a remembrance of his own struggle. Still, if one finds brooding Byronic men in Parkman's work, their presence comes only partly from the historian's unique psychology. For Parkman was a Romantic, and, as David Levin has pointed out, his *France and England in North America* contains many traits common to romantic literature. One expects passionate personalities, then, but also figures, like Montcalm and Wolfe in their famous battle on the Plains of Abraham (1759), who represent whole civilizations. And often the world is construed in contrasts larger than these: nature versus artifice, energy versus torpor, liberty versus absolutism.

Unlike Ranke, Macaulay, Michelet, and Marx, Parkman never wrote a manifesto on how history should be construed. His philosophy of history is, nonetheless, implicit in every page he wrote, and, again, his *writing,* his expansive powers as a narrator, is what earns him a place among the others.

The excerpts describe two expeditions of the great French explorer, Robert Cavelier de La Salle, who came to New France in 1666 and, after extensive travels along the rivers and lakes of North America, was killed in a mutiny in 1687. In the first section, Parkman tells the story of La Salle's voyage by ship and canoe on the Great Lakes in 1679; in the other, La Salle travels down the Mississippi River in 1681–1682 to claim an empire for King Louis XIV. Parkman's La Salle is defeated by circumstances both outside of and within himself—especially his ambition. Here nature emerges as a powerful force to compromise his effort. Staying close to eyewitness sources, Parkman nonetheless imaginatively orders the sequence of events to produce the psychological mood of irony and foreboding that is the hallmark of his *La Salle and the Discovery of the Great West.* Compare the following paragraphs from one of his sources, Louis Hennepin, *A Description of Louisiana,* translated by John G. Shea (New York, 1880, pp. 108f), with the paragraph of narration Parkman derives from it on page 239, beginning with the words "The parting was not auspicious." This comparison is suggested by Richard C. Vitzthum, whose work is cited in the bibliography.

We set out the next day, September 19th, with 14 persons in four canoes, I directing the smallest, loaded with five hundred pounds. With a carpenter just arrived from France, who did not know how to avoid the waves during rough weather, I had every difficulty to manage this little craft. These four bark canoes were loaded with a forge and all its appurtenances, carpenter's, joiner's and pit sawyer's tools, arms and merchandise.

We took our course southerly towards the mainland four good leagues distant from the island of the Poutouatamis. In the middle of the traverse and amid the most beautiful calm in the world, a storm arose which endangered our lives, and which made us fear for the bark, and more for ourselves. We completed this great passage amid the darkness of night, calling to one another so as not to part company. The water often entered our canoes, and the impetuous wind lasted four days with a fury like the greatest tempest of ocean. We nevertheless reached the shore in a little sandy bay, and stayed five days, waiting for the lake to grow calm. During this stay, the Indian hunter who accompanied us, was killed while hunting only a single porcupine which served to season our squashes and the Indian corn that we had.

On the 25th, we continued our route all day, and part of the night favored by the moon, along the western shore of Lake Dauphin, but the wind coming up a little too strong, we were forced to land on a bare rock, on which we endured the rain and snow for two days, sheltered by our blankets, and near a little fire which we fed with wood that waves drove ashore.

What comes from the source and in what order? What comes from Parkman's imagination or latter-day observation?

THE "GRIFFIN" HAD LAIN MOORED by the shore, so near that Hennepin could preach on Sundays from the deck to the men encamped along the bank. She was now forced up against the current with tow-ropes and sails, till she reached the calm entrance of Lake Erie. On the seventh of August, the voyagers, thirty-four in all, embarked, sang *Te Deum*, and fired their cannon. A fresh breeze sprang up; and with swelling canvas the "Griffin" ploughed the virgin waves of Lake Erie, where sail was never seen before. For three days they held their course over these unknown waters, and on the fourth turned northward into the strait of Detroit. Here, on the right hand and on the left, lay verdant prairies, dotted with groves and bordered with lofty forests. They saw walnut, chestnut, and wild plum trees, and oaks festooned with grape-vines; herds of deer, and flocks of swan and wild turkeys. The bulwarks of the "Griffin" were plentifully hung with game which the men killed on shore, and among the rest with a number of bears, much commended by Hennepin for their want of ferocity and the excellence of their flesh. "Those," he says, "who will one day have the happiness to possess this fertile and pleasant strait, will be very much obliged to those who have shown them the way." They crossed Lake St. Clair, and still sailed northward against the current, till now, sparkling in the sun, Lake Huron spread before them like a sea.

For a time, they bore on prosperously. Then the wind died to a calm, then freshened to a gale, then rose to a furious tempest; and the vessel

From Francis Parkman, *The Discovery of the Great West* (Boston, Mass.: Little, Brown, and Co., 1874), 139–50, 271–83.

tossed wildly among the short, steep, perilous waves of the raging lake. Even La Salle called on his followers to commend themselves to Heaven. All fell to their prayers but the godless pilot, who was loud in complaint against his commander for having brought him, after the honor he had won on the ocean, to drown at last ignominiously in fresh water. The rest clamored to the saints. St. Anthony of Padua was promised a chapel to be built in his honor, if he would but save them from their jeopardy; while in the same breath La Salle and the friars declared him patron of their great enterprise. The saint heard their prayers. The obedient winds were tamed; and the "Griffin" plunged on her way through foaming surges that still grew calmer as she advanced. Now the sun shone forth on woody islands, Bois Blanc and Mackinaw and the distant Manitoulins,—on the forest wastes of Michigan and the vast blue bosom of the angry lake; and now her port was won, and she found her rest behind the point of St. Ignace of Michillimackinac, floating in that tranquil cove where crystal waters cover but cannot hide the pebbly depths beneath. Before her rose the house and chapel of the Jesuits, enclosed with palisades; on the right, the Huron village, with its bark cabins and its fence of tall pickets; on the left, the square compact houses of the French traders; and, not far off, the clustered wigwams of an Ottawa village. Here was a centre of the Jesuit missions, and a centre of the Indian trade; and here, under the shadow of the cross, was much sharp practice in the service of Mammon. Keen traders, with or without a license; and lawless *coureurs de bois*, whom a few years of forest life had weaned from civilization, made St. Ignace their resort; and here there were many of them when the "Griffin" came. They and their employers hated and feared La Salle, who, sustained as he was by the Governor, might set at nought the prohibition of the king, debarring him from traffic with these tribes. Yet, while plotting against him, they took pains to allay his distrust by a show of welcome.

The "Griffin" fired her cannon, and the Indians yelped in wonder and amazement. The adventurers landed in state, and marched, under arms, to the bark chapel of the Ottawa village, where they heard mass. La Salle knelt before the altar, in a mantle of scarlet, bordered with gold. Soldiers, sailors, and artisans knelt around him,—black Jesuits, gray Recollets, swarthy *voyageurs*, and painted savages; a devout but motley concourse.

As they left the chapel, the Ottawa chiefs came to bid them welcome, and the Hurons saluted them with a volley of musketry. They saw the "Griffin" at her anchorage, surrounded by more than a hundred bark canoes, like a Triton among minnows. Yet it was with more wonder than good-will that the Indians of the mission gazed on the floating fort, for so they called the vessel. A deep jealousy of La Salle's designs had been infused into them. His own followers, too, had been tampered with. In the autumn before, it may be remembered, he had sent fifteen men up the lakes, to trade for him, with orders to go thence to the Illinois, and make preparation against his coming. Early in the summer, Tonty had been despatched in a canoe, from Niagara, to look after them. It was high time. Most of the men had been seduced from their duty, and had disobeyed their orders, squandered the goods intrusted to them, or used them in trading on their own account. La Salle found four of them at Michilli-mackinac. These he arrested, and sent Tonty to the Falls of Ste. Marie, where two others were captured, with their plunder. The rest were in the woods, and it was useless to pursue them.

Early in September, long before Tonty had returned from Ste. Marie, La Salle set sail again, and, passing westward into Lake Michigan, cast anchor near one of the islands at the entrance of Green Bay. Here, for once, he found a friend in the person of a Pottawattamie chief, who had been so wrought upon the politic kindness of Frontenac, that he declared himself ready to die for the children of Onontio. Here, too, he found sev-eral of his advanced party, who had remained faithful, and collected a large store of furs. It would have been better had they proved false, like the rest. La Salle, who asked counsel of no man, resolved, in spite of his fol-lowers, to send back the "Griffin," laden with these furs, and others col-lected on the way, to satisfy his creditors. She fired a parting shot, and, on the eighteenth of September, spread her sails for Niagara, in charge of the pilot, who had orders to return with her to the Illinois as soon as he had discharged his cargo. La Salle, with the fourteen men who remained, in four canoes, deeply laden with a forge, tools, merchandise, and arms, put out from the island and resumed his voyage.

The parting was not auspicious. The lake, glassy and calm in the after-noon, was convulsed at night with a sudden storm, when the canoes were midway between the island and the main shore. It was with much ado that they could keep together, the men shouting to each other through the darkness. Hennepin, who was in the smallest canoe, with a heavy load, and a carpenter for a companion, who was awkward at the paddle, found himself in jeopardy which demanded all his nerve. The voyagers thought themselves happy when they gained at last the shelter of a little sandy cove, where they dragged up their canoes, and made their cheerless bivouac in the drenched and dripping forest. Here they spent five days, living on pumpkins and Indian corn, the gift of their Pottawattamie friends, and on a Canada porcupine, brought in by La Salle's Mohegan hunter. The gale raged meanwhile with a relentless fury. They trembled when they thought of the "Griffin." When at length the tempest lulled, they re-embarked, and steered southward, along the shore of Wisconsin; but again the storm fell upon them, and drove them, for safety, to a bare, rocky islet. Here they made a fire of driftwood, crouched around it, drew their blankets over their heads, and in this miserable plight, pelted with sleet and rain, remained for two days.

At length they were afloat again; but their prosperity was brief. On the twenty-eighth, a fierce squall drove them to a point of rocks, covered with bushes, where they consumed the little that remained of their provisions. On the first of October, they paddled about thirty miles, without food, when they came to a village of Pottawattamies, who ran down to the shore to help them to land; but La Salle, fearing that some of his men would steal the merchandise and desert to the Indians, insisted on going three leagues farther, to the great indignation of his followers. The lake, swept by an easterly gale, was rolling its waves against the beach, like the ocean in a storm. In the attempt to land, La Salle's canoe was nearly swamped. He and his three canoe-men leaped into the water, and, in spite of the surf, which nearly drowned them, dragged their vessel ashore, with all its load. He then went to the rescue of Hennepin, who, with his awkward companion, was in woful need of succor. Father Gabriel, with his sixty-four years, was no match for the surf and the violent undertow. Hennepin, finding himself safe, waded to his relief and carried him ashore on his sturdy shoulders; while the old friar, though drenched to the skin, laughed gayly under his cowl, as his brother missionary staggered with him up the beach.

When all were safe ashore, La Salle, who distrusted the Indians they had passed, took post on a hill, and ordered his followers to prepare their guns for action. Nevertheless, as they were starving, an effort must be risked to gain a supply of food; and he sent three men back to the village to purchase it. Well armed, but faint with toil and famine, they made their way through the stormy forest, bearing a pipe of peace; but on arriving saw that the scared inhabitants had fled. They found, however, a stock of corn, of which they took a portion, leaving goods in exchange, and then set out on their return.

Meanwhile, about twenty of the warriors, armed with bows and arrows, approached the camp of the French, to reconnoitre. La Salle went to meet them, with some of his men, opened a parley with them, and kept them seated at the foot of the hill till his three messengers returned, when, on seeing the peace-pipe, the warriors set up a cry of joy. In the morning, they brought more corn to the camp, with a supply of fresh venison, not a little cheering to the exhausted Frenchmen, who, in dread of treachery, had stood under arms all night.

This was no journey of pleasure. The lake was ruffled with almost ceaseless storms; clouds big with rain above; a turmoil of gray and gloomy waves beneath. Every night the canoes must be shouldered through the breakers and dragged up the steep banks, which, as they neared the site of Milwaukee, became almost insurmountable. The men paddled all day, with no other food than a handful of Indian corn. They were spent with toil, sick with the haws and wild berries which they ravenously devoured, and dejected at the prospect before them. Father Gabriel's good spirits began to fail. He fainted several times, from famine and fatigue, but was revived by a certain "confection of Hyacinth," administered by Hennepin, who had a small box of this precious specific.

At length they descried, at a distance, on the stormy shore, two or three eagles among a busy congregation of crows or turkey-buzzards. They paddled in all haste to the spot. The feasters took flight; and the starved travellers found the mangled body of a deer, lately killed by the wolves. This good luck proved the inauguration of plenty. As they approached the head of the lake, game grew abundant; and, with the aid of the Mohegan, there was no lack of bear's meat and venison. They found wild grapes, too, in the woods, and gathered them by cutting down the trees to which the vines clung.

While thus employed, they were startled by a sight often so fearful in the waste and the wilderness, the print of a human foot. It was clear that Indians were not far off. A strict watch was kept, not, as it proved, without cause; for that night, while the sentry thought of little but screening himself and his gun from the floods of rain, a party of Outagamies crept under the bank, where they lurked for some time before he discovered them. Being challenged, they came forward, professing great friendship, and pretending to have mistaken the French for Iroquois. In the morning, however, there was an outcry from La Salle's servant, who declared that the visitors had stolen his coat from under the inverted canoe where he had placed it; while some of the carpenters also complained of being robbed. La Salle well knew that if the theft were left unpunished, worse would come of it. First, he posted his men at the woody point of a peninsula, whose sandy neck was interposed between them and the main forest. Then he went forth, pistol in hand, met a young Outagami, seized him, and led him prisoner to his camp. This done, he again set out, and soon found an Outagami chief,—for the wigwams were not far distant,—to whom he told what he had done, adding that unless the stolen goods were restored, the prisoner should be killed. The Indians were in perplexity, for they had cut the coat to pieces and divided it. In this dilemma, they resolved, being strong in numbers, to rescue their comrade by force. Accordingly, they came down to the edge of the forest, or posted themselves behind fallen trees on the banks, while La Salle's men in their stronghold braced their nerves for the fight. Here three Flemish friars, with their rosaries, and eleven Frenchmen, with their guns, confronted a hundred and twenty screeching Outagamies. Hennepin, who had seen service, and who had always an exhortation at his tongue's end, busied himself to inspire the rest with a courage equal to his own. Neither party, however, had an appetite for the fray. A parley ensued: full compensation was made for the stolen goods, and the aggrieved Frenchmen were farther propitiated with a gift of beaver-skins.

Their late enemies, now become friends, spent the next day in dances, feasts, and speeches. They entreated La Salle not to advance further, since the Illinois, through whose country he must pass, would be sure to kill him; for, added these friendly counsellors, they hated the French because they had been instigating the Iroquois to invade their country. Here was a new subject of anxiety. La Salle thought that he saw in it another device of his busy and unscrupulous enemies, intriguing among the Illinois for his destruction.

He pushed on, however, circling around the southern shore of Lake Michigan, till he reached the mouth of the St. Joseph, called by him the Miamis. Here Tonty was to have rejoined him, with twenty men, making his way from Michillimackinac, along the eastern shore of the lake: but the rendezvous was a solitude; Tonty was nowhere to be seen. It was the first of November. Winter was at hand, and the streams would soon be frozen. The men clamored to go forward, urging that they should starve if they could not reach the villages of the Illinois before the tribe scattered for the winter hunt. La Salle was inexorable. If they should all desert, he said, he, with his Mohegan hunter and the three friars, would still remain and wait for Tonty. The men grumbled, but obeyed; and, to divert their thoughts, he set them at building a fort of timber, on a rising ground at the mouth of the river.

They had spent twenty days at this task, and their work was well advanced, when at length Tonty appeared. He brought with him only half of his men. Provisions had failed; and the rest of his party had been left thirty leagues behind, to sustain themselves by hunting. La Salle told him to return and hasten them forward. He set out with two men. A violent north wind arose. He tried to run his canoe ashore through the breakers. The two men could not manage their vessel, and he with his one hand could not help them. She swamped, rolling over in the surf. Guns, baggage, and provisions were lost; and the three voyagers returned to the Miamis, subsisting on acorns by the way. Happily, the men left behind, excepting two deserters, succeeded, a few days after, in rejoining the party.

Thus was one heavy load lifted from the heart of La Salle. But where was the "Griffin"? Time enough, and more than enough, had passed for her voyage to Niagara and back again. He scanned the dreary horizon with an anxious eye. No returning sail gladdened the watery solitude, and a dark foreboding gathered on his heart. Yet farther delay was impossible. He sent back two men to Michillimackinac to meet her, if she still existed, and pilot her to his new fort of the Miamis, and then prepared to ascend the river, whose weedy edges were already glassed with thin flakes of ice.

. . . .

The season was far advanced. On the bare limbs of the forest hung a few withered remnants of its gay autumnal livery; and the smoke crept upward through the sullen November air from the squalid wigwams of La Salle's Abenaki and Mohegan allies. These, his new friends, were savages, whose midnight yells had startled the border hamlets of New England; who had danced around Puritan scalps, and whom Puritan imaginations painted as incarnate fiends. La Salle chose eighteen of them, "all well inured to war," as his companion Membré writes, and added them to the twenty-three Frenchmen who composed his party. They insisted on taking their women with them, to cook for them, and do other camp work. These were ten in number, besides three children; and thus the expedition included fifty-four persons, of whom some were useless, and others a burden.

On the twenty-first of December, Tonty and Membré set out from Fort Miamis with some of the party in six canoes, and crossed to the little river Chicago. La Salle, with the rest of the men, joined them a few days later. It was the dead of winter, and the streams were frozen. They made sledges, placed on them the canoes, the baggage, and a disabled Frenchman; crossed from the Chicago to the northern branch of the Illinois, and filed in a long procession down its frozen course. They reached the site of the great Illinois village, found it tenantless, and continued their journey, still dragging their canoes, till at length they reached open water below Lake Peoria.

La Salle had abandoned, for the time, his original plan of building a vessel for the navigation of the Mississippi. Bitter experience had taught him the difficulty of the attempt, and he resolved to trust to his canoes alone. They embarked again, floating prosperously down between the leafless forests that flanked the tranquil river; till, on the sixth of February, they issued forth on the majestic bosom of the Mississippi. Here, for the time, their progress was stopped; for the river was full of floating ice. La Salle's Indians, too, had lagged behind; but, within a week, all had arrived, the navigation was once more free, and they resumed their course. Towards evening, they saw on their right the mouth of a great river; and the clear current was invaded by the headlong torrent of the Missouri, opaque with mud. They built their campfires in the neighboring forest; and, at daylight, embarking anew on the dark and mighty stream, drifted swiftly down towards unknown destinies. They passed a deserted town of the Tamaroas; saw, three days after, the mouth of the Ohio; and, gliding by the wastes of bordering swamp, landed, on the twenty-fourth of February, near the Third Chickasaw Bluffs. They encamped, and the hunters went out for game. All returned, excepting

Pierre Prudhomme; and, as the others had seen fresh tracks of Indians, La Salle feared that he was killed. While some of his followers built a small stockade fort on a high bluff by the river, others ranged the woods in pursuit of the missing hunter. After six days of ceaseless and fruitless search, they met two Chickasaw Indians in the forest; and, through them, La Salle sent presents and peace-messages to that warlike people, whose villages were a few days' journey distant. Several days later, Prudhomme was found, and brought in to the camp, half dead. He had lost his way while hunting; and, to console him for his woes, La Salle christened the newly built fort with his name and left him, with a few others, in charge of it.

Again they embarked; and, with every stage of their adventurous progress, the mystery of this vast New World was more and more unveiled. More and more they entered the realms of spring. The hazy sunlight, the warm and drowsy air, the tender foliage, the opening flowers, betokened the reviving life of Nature. For several days more they followed the writhings of the great river, on its tortuous course through wastes of swamp and cane-brake, till on the thirteenth of March they found themselves wrapped in a thick fog. Neither shore was visible; but they heard on the right the booming of an Indian drum, and the shrill outcries of the war-dance. La Salle at once crossed to the opposite side, where, in less than an hour, his men threw up a rude fort of felled trees. Meanwhile, the fog cleared; and, from the farther bank, the astonished Indians saw the strange visitors at their work. Some of the French advanced to the edge of the water, and beckoned them to come over. Several of them approached, in a wooden canoe, to within the distance of a gun-shot. La Salle displayed the calumet, and sent a Frenchman to meet them. He was well received; and the friendly mood of the Indians being now apparent, the whole party crossed the river.

On landing, they found themselves at a town of the Kappa band of the Arkansas, a people dwelling near the mouth of the river which bears their name. The inhabitants flocked about them with eager signs of welcome; built huts for them, brought them firewood, gave them corn, beans, and dried fruits, and feasted them without respite for three days. "They are a lively, civil, generous people," says Membré, "very different from the cold and taciturn Indians of the North." They showed, indeed, some slight traces of a tendency towards civilization; for domestic fowls and tame geese were wandering among their rude cabins of bark.

La Salle and Tonty at the head of their followers marched to the open area in the midst of the village. Here, to the admiration of the gazing crowd of warriors, women, and children, a cross was raised bearing the arms of France. Membré, in canonicals, sang a hymn; the men shouted *Vive le Roi*; and La Salle, in the king's name, took formal possession of the country. The friar, not, he flatters himself, without success, labored to expound by signs the mysteries of the faith; while La Salle, by methods equally satisfactory, drew from the chief an acknowledgment of fealty to Louis XIV.

After touching at several other towns of this people, the voyagers resumed their course, guided by two of the Arkansas; passed the sites, since become historic, of Vicksburg and Grand Gulf; and, about three hundred miles below the Arkansas, stopped by the edge of a swamp on the western side of the river. Here, as their two guides told them, was the path to the great town of the Taensas. Tonty and Membré were sent to visit it. They and their men shouldered their birch canoe through the swamp, and launched it on a lake which had once formed a portion of the channel of the river. In two hours they reached the town, and Tonty gazed at it with astonishment. He had seen nothing like it in America; large square dwellings, built of sun-baked mud mixed with straw, arched over with a dome-shaped roof of canes, and placed in regular order around an open area. Two of them were larger and better than the rest. One was the lodge of the chief; the other was the temple, or house of the Sun. They entered the former, and found a single room, forty feet square, where, in the dim light, for there was no opening but the door, the chief sat awaiting them on a sort of bedstead, three of his wives at his side, while sixty old men, wrapped in white cloaks woven of mulberry-bark, formed his divan. When he spoke, his wives howled to do him honor; and the assembled councillors listened with the reverence due to a potentate for whom, at his death, a hundred victims were to be sacrificed. He received the visitors graciously, and joyfully accepted the gifts which Tonty laid before him. This interview over, the Frenchmen repaired to the temple, wherein were kept the bones of the departed chiefs. In construction it was much like the royal dwelling. Over it were rude wooden figures, representing three eagles turned towards the east. A strong mud wall surrounded it, planted with stakes, on which were stuck the skulls of enemies sacrificed to the Sun; while before the door was a block of wood, on which lay a large shell surrounded with the braided hair of the victims. The interior was rude as a barn, dimly lighted from the doorway, and full of smoke. There was a structure in the middle which Membré thinks was a kind of altar; and before it burned a perpetual fire, fed with three logs laid end to end, and watched by two old men devoted to this sacred office. There was a mysterious recess, too, which the strangers were forbidden to explore, but which, as Tonty was told, contained the riches of the nation, consisting of pearls from the Gulf, and trinkets obtained, probably through other tribes, from the Spaniards and other Europeans.

The chief condescended to visit La Salle at his camp; a favor which he would by no means have granted, had the visitors been Indians. A master of ceremonies, and six attendants, preceded him, to clear the path and prepare the place of meeting. When all was ready, he was seen advancing, clothed in a white robe, and preceeded by two men bearing white fans; while a third displayed a disk of burnished copper, doubtless to represent the Sun, his ancestor; or, as others will have it, his elder brother. His aspect was marvellously grave, and he and La Salle met with gestures of ceremonious courtesy. The interview was very friendly; and the chief returned well pleased with the gifts which his entertainer bestowed on him, and which, indeed, had been the principal motive of his visit.

On the next morning, as they descended the river, they saw a wooden canoe full of Indians; and Tonty gave chase. He had nearly overtaken it, when more than a hundred men appeared suddenly on the shore, with bows bent to defend their countrymen. La Salle called out to Tonty to withdraw. He obeyed; and the whole party encamped on the opposite bank. Tonty offered to cross the river with a peace-pipe, and set out accordingly with a small party of men. When he landed, the Indians made signs of friendship by joining their hands,—a proceeding by which Tonty, having but one hand, was somewhat embarrassed; but he directed his men to respond in his stead. La Salle and Membré now joined him, and went with the Indians to their village, three leagues distant. Here they spent the night. "The Sieur de la Salle," writes Membré, "whose very air, engaging manners, tact, and address attract love and respect alike, produced such an effect on the hearts of these people, that they did not know how to treat us well enough."

The Indians of this village were the Natchez; and their chief was brother of the great chief, or Sun, of the whole nation. His town was several leagues, distant, near the site of the city of Natchez; and thither the French repaired to visit him. They saw what they had already seen among the Taensas,—a religious and political despotism, a privileged caste descended from the Sun, a temple, and a sacred fire. La Salle planted a large cross, with the arms of France attached, in the midst of the town; while the inhabitants looked on with a satisfaction which they would hardly have displayed, had they understood the meaning of the act.

The French next visited the Coroas, at their village, two leagues below; and here they found a reception no less auspicious. On the thirty-first of March, as they approached Red River, they passed in the fog a town of the Oumas; and, three days later, discovered a party of fishermen, in wooden canoes, among the canes along the margin of the water. They fled at sight of the Frenchmen. La Salle sent men to reconnoitre, who, as they struggled through the marsh, were greeted with a shower of arrows; while, from the neighboring village of the Quinipissas, invisible behind the cane-brake, they heard the sound of an Indian drum, and the whoops of the mustering warriors. La Salle, anxious to keep the peace with all the tribes along the river, recalled his men, and pursued his voyage. A few leagues below, they saw a cluster of Indian lodges on the left bank, apparently void of inhabitants. They landed, and found three of them filled with corpses. It was a village of the Tangibao, sacked by their enemies only a few days before.

And now they neared their journey's end. On the sixth of April, the river divided itself into three broad channels. La Salle followed that of the west, and D'Autray that of the east; while Tonty took the middle passage. As he drifted down the turbid current, between the low and marshy shores, the brackish water changed to brine, and the breeze grew fresh with the salt breath of the sea. Then the broad bosom of the great Gulf opened on his sight, tossing its restless billows, limitless, voiceless, lonely, as when born of chaos, without a sail, without a sign of life.

La Salle, in a canoe, coasted the marshy borders of the sea; and then the reunited parties assembled on a spot of dry ground, a short distance above the mouth of the river. Here a column was made ready, bearing the arms of France, and inscribed with the words,—

LOUIS LE GRAND, ROY DE FRANCE ET DE NAVARRE,
RÈGNE LE NEUVIÈME AVRIL, 1682.

The Frenchmen were mustered under arms; and, while the New-England Indians and their squaws stood gazing in wondering silence, they chanted the *Te Deum*, the *Exaudiat*, and the *Domine salvum fac Regem*. Then, amid volleys of musketry and shouts of *Vive le Roi*, La Salle planted the column in its place, and, standing near it, proclaimed in a loud voice,—

"In the name of the most high, mighty, invincible, and victorious Prince, Louis the Great, by the grace of God King of France and of Navarre, Fourteenth of that name, I, this ninth day of April, one thousand six hundred and eighty-two, in virtue of the commission of his Majesty, which I hold in my hand, and which may be seen by all whom it may concern, have taken, and do now take, in the name of his Majesty and of his successors to the crown, possession of this country of Louisiana, the seas, harbors, ports, bays, adjacent straits, and all the nations, peoples, provinces, cities, towns, villages, mines, minerals, fisheries, streams, and rivers, within the extent of the said Louisiana, from the mouth of the great river St. Louis, otherwise called the Ohio, . . . as also along the River Colbert, or Mississippi, and the rivers which discharge themselves therein, from its source beyond the country of the Nadouessious . . . as far as its mouth at the sea, or Gulf of Mexico, and also to the mouth of the River of Palms, upon the assurance we have had from the natives of these countries, that we are the first Europeans who have descended or ascended the said River Colbert; hereby protesting against all who may hereafter undertake to invade any or all of these aforesaid countries, peoples, or lands, to the prejudice of the rights of his Majesty, acquired by the consent of the nations dwelling herein. Of which, and of all else that is needful, I hereby take to witness those who hear me, and demand an act of the notary here present."

Shouts of *Vive le Roi* and volleys of musketry responded to his words. Then a cross was planted beside the column, and a leaden plate buried near it, bearing the arms of France, with a Latin inscription, *Ludovicus Magnus regnat*. The weather-beaten voyagers joined their voices in the grand hymn of the *Vexilla Regis*:—

> The banners of Heaven's King advance,
> The mystery of the Cross shines forth;

and renewed shouts of *Vive le Roi* closed the ceremony.

On that day, the realm of France received on parchment a stupendous accession. The fertile plains of Texas; the vast basin of the Mississippi, from its frozen northern springs to the sultry borders of the Gulf; from the woody ridges of the Alleghanies to the bare peaks of the Rocky Mountains,—a region of savannahs and forests, sun-cracked deserts, and grassy prairies, watered by a thousand rivers, ranged by a thousand war-like tribes, passed beneath the sceptre of the Sultan of Versailles; and all by virtue of a feeble human voice, inaudible at half a mile.

Bibliography

Doughty, Howard. *Francis Parkman.* New York, 1962.

Jennings, Francis P. "A Vanishing Indian: Francis Parkman Versus His Sources." *Pennsylvania Magazine of History and Biography,* 87 July 1963): 306–23.

Levin, David. *History as Romantic Art: Bancroft, Prescott, Motley, and Parkman.* Stanford, Calif., 1959.

Pease, Otis A. *Parkman's History: The Historian as Literary Artist.* Hamden, Conn., 1968.

Parkman, Francis. *The Parkman Reader,* edited by Samuel Eliot Morison. Boston, Mass., 1955.

Taylor, William R. "Francis Parkman." In *Pastmasters, Some Essays on American Historians,* edited by Marcus Cunliffe and Robin W. Winks. New York, 1969.

Vitzthum, Richard C. *The American Compromise: Theme and Method in the Histories of Bancroft, Parkman, and Adams.* Norman, Okla., 1974.

Wade, Mason. *Francis Parkman: Heroic Historian.* New York, 1962.

CHAPTER 16

Frederick Jackson Turner

"The Significance of the Frontier in American History"

(1893)

For sheer impact on American historiography, Frederick Jackson Turner stands alone. And considering that his influence rests almost exclusively upon the brief essay reprinted here—Turner was not a prolific writer—the commanding position of his "frontier thesis" is the more remarkable.

Turner argued that the presence of a constantly advancing frontier shaped American culture and made it different from the European world. America, unlike any other society, went through "perennial rebirth" as each generation in the westward movement had to face anew the sparse conditions of frontier life and be reduced from civilization to primitive life in nature. Everyone knew American life was fluid and democratic, but why? Some, like Herbert Baxter Adams, Turner's teacher, argued that democracy was an inheritance from America's Old World, Anglo-Saxon past. Turner said American democracy was American, the necessary response to the demands of raw nature. There is an echo of Francis Parkman here, of course, though Turner saw that civilization must eventually triumph over nature. More importantly, Turner was part of a new generation of graduate-school-educated, professional historians. His German methodology made him think he could demonstrate the force of nature more scientifically than the Romantics could. .

Turner was born in 1861 in Portage, Wisconsin, and grew up close to the frontier. In an autobiographical reminiscence, he once measured the influence of a western upbringing upon his later thinking:

> I have poled down the Wisconsin [river] in a dugout with Indian guides . . . through virgin forests of balsam firs, seeing deer in the river,—antlered beauties who watched us come down with curious eyes and then broke for the tall timber,—hearing the squaws in their village on the high bank talk their low treble to the bass of our Indian polesmen,—feeling that I belonged to it all. I have seen a lynched man hanging from a tree when I came home from school in Portage, have played around old fort Winnebago at its outskirts, have seen the red shirted Irish raftsmen *take* the town when they tied up and came ashore. . . . [T]he frontier in that sense, you see, was real to me, and when I

studied history I did not keep my personal experience in a water tight compartment away from my studies.

Yet there was another influence on Turner's thinking that was, if anything, more powerful: Darwinism, or, more broadly, naturalism. Turner was educated at the University of Wisconsin (B.A., 1884; M.A., 1888) and at the Johns Hopkins University (Ph.D., 1890), where he read Herbert Spencer and Charles Darwin, the twin pillars of nineteenth-century naturalism. Their doctrines concerning evolution were well established in the United States by the 1880s, and one is not surprised to see Turner working with the ideas of heredity and environmental pressures in his famous essay or to find it littered with Darwinian language. Thus, he observes "the differentiation of simple colonial governments into complex organs" and says civilization is fed by river "arteries" that make for "the steady growth of a complex nervous system."

Apart from the essay itself, Turner's influence spread through his teaching, first at the University of Wisconsin and later at Harvard. Scientific history is what he taught. A photograph survives from 1894 of Turner's Wisconsin seminar: sixteen men and women in a narrow book-lined room. The photographer has posed them in the act of research, handing books and pointing out things to each other, writing, and reading. Turner himself sits at the edge of the frame staring fixedly off camera, his hand resting on a table piled with books and papers. The room is a laboratory, a place where the past could be isolated and where a group of researchers could cooperate to discover how it works once and for all.

Among his students were the twentieth-century professionals who would soon replace the gentlemen amateurs of the nineteenth century, and their new sense of scientific discipline transformed American historical writing. Turner's own style suggested the direction, for much of his prose exhibits a plodding patience as he documents the stages of the frontier movement. Blocks of fine-print footnotes give assurance that he has seen and understood the interrelation of original manuscripts, statistics, and current authorities. A note on page 204 of the original cites eighteen separate sources for a statement about the location of the frontier line in 1850. Scientific history could be awfully dull.

Yet Turner's conversion to science was incomplete, and his essay is not without literary interest. He is capable of evoking the force of nature with an old-fashioned romantic urgency, as in the lines on page 252 beginning with the words "The wilderness masters the colonist." And if most of the essay finds Turner working amongst his sources at ground level, so to speak, he argues his main point—that American history is a microcosm of the whole world's transit from savagery to civilization—metaphorically and at considerable height. "The United States lies like a huge page in the history of society," he says on page 256. "Line by line as we read this continental page from west to east we find the record of social evolution." The metaphor extends over several lines as Turner "reads" the most primitive society on the most recent frontier and lets his eye move down the page to the now most civilized area of the urban east. At the end he sees that his page is really a palimpsest, a parchment written on several times, with the earlier writing only partly erased. Any settlement in America, he is saying, continues to show evidence of every stage through which it has passed. Then, too, on page 257, the paragraph that follows the command, "Stand at Cumberland Gap and watch the process of civilization marching single file," offers not just a review of frontier types as they pass, but strikingly invites the reader to join in the historian's own omniscience.

I N A RECENT BULLETIN of the Superintendent of the Census for 1890 appear these significant words: "Up to and including 1880 the country had a frontier of settlement, but at present the unsettled area has been so broken into by isolated bodies of settlement that there can hardly be said to be a frontier line. In the discussion of its extent, its westward movement, etc., it can not, therefore, any longer have a place in the census reports." This brief official statement marks the closing of a great historic movement. Up to our own day American history has been in a large degree the history of the colonization of the Great West. The existence of an area of free land, its continuous recession, and the advance of American settlement westward, explain American development.

Behind institutions, behind constitutional forms and modifications, lie the vital forces that call these organs into life and shape them to meet changing conditions. The peculiarity of American institutions is the fact that they have been compelled to adapt themselves to the changes of an expanding people—to the changes involved in crossing a continent, in winning a wilderness, and in developing at each area of this progress out of the primitive economic and political conditions of the frontier into the complexity of city life. Said Calhoun in 1817, "We are great, and rapidly—I was about to say fearfully—growing!" So saying, he touched the distinguishing feature of American life. All peoples show development; the germ theory of politics has been sufficiently emphasized. In the case of most nations, however, the development has occurred in a limited area; and if the nation has expanded, it has met other growing peoples whom it has conquered. But in the case of the United States we have a different phenomenon. Limiting our attention to the Atlantic coast, we have the familiar phenomenon of the evolution of institutions in a limited area,

From *The Miscellaneous Documents of the Senate of the United States for the Second Session of the Fifty-third Congress, 1893–94*, Vol. 4: *Annual Report of the American Historical Association* (Washington, D.C.: U.S. Government Printing Office, 1895), 199–227.

such as the rise of representative government; the differentiation of simple colonial governments into complex organs; the progress from primitive industrial society, without division of labor, up to manufacturing civilization. But we have in addition to this a recurrence of the process of evolution in each western area reached in the process of expansion. Thus American development has exhibited not merely advance along a single line, but a return to primitive conditions on a continually advancing frontier line, and a new development for that area. American social development has been continually beginning over again on the frontier. This perennial rebirth, this fluidity of American life, this expansion westward with its new opportunities, its continuous touch with the simplicity of primitive society, furnish the forces dominating American character. The true point of view in the history of this nation is not the Atlantic coast, it is the great West. Even the slavery struggle, which is made so exclusive an object of attention by writers like Prof. von Holst, occupies its important place in American history because of its relation to westward expansion.

In this advance, the frontier is the outer edge of the wave—the meeting point between savagery and civilization. Much has been written about the frontier from the point of view of border warfare and the chase, but as a field for the serious study of the economist and the historian it has been neglected.

The American frontier is sharply distinguished from the European frontier—a fortified boundary line running through dense populations. The most significant thing about the American frontier is, that it lies at the hither edge of free land. In the census reports it is treated as the margin of that settlement which has a density of two or more to the square mile. The term is an elastic one, and for our purposes does not need sharp definition. We shall consider the whole frontier belt, including the Indian country and the outer margin of the "settled area" of the census reports. This paper will make no attempt to treat the subject exhaustively; its aim is simply to call attention to the frontier as a fertile field for investigation, and to suggest some of the problems which arise in connection with it.

In the settlement of America we have to observe how European life entered the continent, and how America modified and developed that life and reacted on Europe. Our early history is the study of European germs developing in an American environment. Too exclusive attention has been paid by institutional students to the Germanic origins, too little to the American factors. The frontier is the line of most rapid and effective Americanization. The wilderness masters the colonist. It finds him a European in dress, industries, tools, modes of travel, and thought. It takes him from the railroad car and puts him in the birch canoe. It strips off the garments of civilization and arrays him in the hunting shirt and the moccasin. It puts him in the log cabin of the Cherokee and Iroquois and runs an Indian palisade around him. Before long he has gone to planting Indian corn and plowing with a sharp stick; he shouts the war cry and takes the scalp in orthodox Indian fashion. In short, at the frontier the environment is at first too strong for the man. He must accept the conditions which it furnishes, or perish, and so he fits himself into the Indian clearings and follows the Indian trails. Little by little he transforms the wilderness, but the outcome is not the old Europe, not simply the development of Germanic germs, any more than the first phenomenon was a case of reversion to the Germanic mark. The fact is, that here is a new product that is American. At first, the frontier was the Atlantic coast. It was the frontier of Europe in a very real sense. Moving westward, the frontier became more and more American. As successive terminal moraines result from successive glaciations, so each frontier leaves its traces behind it, and when it becomes a settled area the region still partakes of the frontier characteristics. Thus the advance of the frontier has meant a steady movement away from the influence of Europe, a steady growth of independence on American lines. And to study this advance, the men who grew up under these conditions, and the political, economic, and social results of it, is to study the really American part of our history.

STAGES OF FRONTIER ADVANCE.

In the course of the seventeenth century the frontier was advanced up the Atlantic river courses, just beyond the "fall line," and the tidewater region became the settled area. In the first half of the eighteenth century another advance occurred. Traders followed the Delaware and Shawnese Indians to the Ohio as early as the end of the first quarter of the century. Gov. Spotswood, of Virginia, made an expedition in 1714 across the Blue Ridge. The end of the first quarter of the century saw the advance of the Scotch-Irish and the Palatine Germans up the Shenandoah Valley into the western part of Virginia, and along the Piedmont region of the Carolinas. The Germans in New York pushed the frontier of settlement up the Mohawk to German Flats. In Pennsylvania the town of Bedford indicates the line of settlement. Settlements had begun on New River, a branch of the Kanawha, and on the sources of the Yadkin and French Broad. The King attempted to arrest the advance by his proclamation of 1763, forbidding settlements beyond the sources of the rivers flowing into the Atlantic; but in vain. In the period of the Revolution the frontier crossed the Alleghanies into Kentucky and Tennessee, and the upper waters of the Ohio were settled. When the first census was taken in 1790, the continuous settled area was bounded by a line which ran near the coast of Maine, and included New England except a portion of Vermont and New Hampshire, New York along the Hudson and up the Mohawk about Schenectady, eastern and southern Pennsylvania, Virginia well across the

Shenandoah Valley, and the Carolinas and eastern Georgia. Beyond this region of continuous settlement were the small settled areas of Kentucky and Tennessee, and the Ohio, with the mountains intervening between them and the Atlantic area, thus giving a new and important character to the frontier. The isolation of the region increased its peculiarly American tendencies, and the need of transportation facilities to connect it with the East called out important schemes of internal improvement, which will be noted farther on. The "West," as a self-conscious section, began to evolve.

From decade to decade distinct advances of the frontier occurred. By the census of 1820 the settled area included Ohio, southern Indiana and Illinois, southeastern Missouri, and about one-half of Louisiana. This settled area had surrounded Indian areas, and the management of these tribes became an object of political concern. The frontier region of the time lay along the Great Lakes, where Astor's American Fur Company operated in the Indian trade, and beyond the Mississippi, where Indian traders extended their activity even to the Rocky Mountains; Florida also furnished frontier conditions. The Mississippi River region was the scene of typical frontier settlements.

The rising steam navigation on western waters, the opening of the Erie Canal, and the westward extension of cotton culture added five frontier states to the Union in this period. Grund, writing in 1836, declares: "It appears then that the universal disposition of Americans to emigrate to the western wilderness, in order to enlarge their dominion over inanimate nature, is the actual result of an expansive power which is inherent in them, and which by continually agitating all classes of society is constantly throwing a large portion of the whole population on the extreme confines of the State, in order to gain space for its development. Hardly is a new State or Territory formed before the same principle manifests itself again and gives rise to a further emigration; and so is it destined to go on until a physical barrier must finally obstruct its progress."

In the middle of this century the line indicated by the present eastern boundary of Indian Territory, Nebraska, and Kansas marked the frontier of the Indian country. Minnesota and Wisconsin still exhibited frontier conditions, but the distinctive frontier of the period is found in California, where the gold discoveries had sent a sudden tide of adventurous miners, and in Oregon, and the settlements in Utah. As the frontier has leaped over the Alleghanies, so now it skipped the Great Plains and the Rocky Mountains; and in the same way that the advance of the frontiersmen beyond the Alleghanies had caused the rise of important questions of transportation and internal improvement, so now the settlers beyond the Rocky Mountains needed means of communication with the East, and in the furnishing of these arose the settlement of the Great Plains and the development of still another kind of frontier life. Railroads, fostered by land grants, sent an increasing tide of immigrants into the far West. The United States Army fought a series of Indian wars in Minnesota, Dakota, and the Indian Territory.

By 1880 the settled area had been pushed into northern Michigan, Wisconsin, and Minnesota, along Dakota rivers, and in the Black Hills region, and was ascending the rivers of Kansas and Nebraska. The development of mines in Colorado had drawn isolated frontier settlements into that region, and Montana and Idaho were receiving settlers. The frontier was found in these mining camps and the ranches of the Great Plains. The superintendent of the census for 1890 reports, as previously stated, that the settlements of the West lie so scattered over the region that there can no longer be said to be a frontier line.

In these successive frontiers we find natural boundary lines which have served to mark and to affect the characteristics of the frontiers, namely: The "fall line"; the Alleghany Mountains; the Mississippi; the Missouri, where its direction approximates north and south; the line of the arid lands, approximately the ninety-ninth meridian; and the Rocky Mountains. The fall line marked the frontier of the seventeenth century; the Alleghanies that of the eighteenth; the Mississippi that of the first quarter of the nineteenth; the Missouri that of the middle of this century (omitting the California movement); and the belt of the Rocky Mountains and the arid tract, the present frontier. Each was won by a series of Indian wars.

THE FRONTIER FURNISHES A FIELD FOR COMPARATIVE
STUDY OF SOCIAL DEVELOPMENT.

At the Atlantic frontier one can study the germs of processes repeated at each successive frontier. We have the complex European life sharply precipitated by the wilderness into the simplicity of primitive conditions. The first frontier had to meet its Indian question, its question of the disposition of the public domain, of the means of intercourse with older settlements, of the extension of political organization, of religious and educational activity. And the settlement of these and similar questions for one frontier served as a guide for the next. The American student needs not to go to the "prim little townships of Sleswick" for illustrations of the law of continuity and development. For example, he may study the origin of our land policies in the colonial land policy; he may see how the system grew by adapting the statutes to the customs of the successive frontiers. He may see how the mining experience in the lead regions of Wisconsin, Illinois, and Iowa was applied to the mining laws of the Rockies, and how our Indian policy has been a series of experimentations on successive frontiers. Each tier of new States has found in the older ones material for its constitutions. Each frontier has made similar contributions to American character, as will be discussed farther on.

But with all these similarities there are essential differences, due to the place element and the time element. It is evident that the farming frontier of the Mississippi Valley presents different conditions from the mining frontier of the Rocky Mountains. The frontier reached by the Pacific Railroad, surveyed into rectangles, guarded by the United States Army, and recruited by the daily immigrant ship, moves forward at a swifter pace and in a different way than the frontier reached by the birch canoe or the pack horse. The geologist traces patiently the shores of ancient seas, maps their areas, and compares the older and the newer. It would be a work worth the historian's labors to mark these various frontiers and in detail compare one with another. Not only would there result a more adequate conception of American development and characteristics, but invaluable additions would be made to the history of society.

Loria, the Italian economist, has urged the study of colonial life as an aid in understanding the stages of European development, affirming that colonial settlement is for economic science what the mountain is for geology, bringing to light primitive stratifications. "America," he says, "has the key to the historical enigma which Europe has sought for centuries in vain, and the land which has no history reveals luminously the course of universal history." There is much truth in this. The United States lies like a huge page in the history of society. Line by line as we read this continental page from west to east we find the record of social evolution. It begins with the Indian and the hunter; it goes on to tell of the disintegration of savagery by the entrance of the trader, the pathfinder of civilization; we read the annals of the pastoral stage in ranch life; the exploitation of the soil by the raising of unrotated crops of corn and wheat in sparsely settled farming communities; the intensive culture of the denser farm settlement; and finally the manufacturing organization with city and factory system. This page is familiar to the student of census statistics, but how little of it has been used by our historians. Particularly in eastern States this page is a palimpsest. What is now a manufacturing State was in an earlier decade an area of intensive farming. Earlier yet it had been a wheat area, and still earlier the "range" had attracted the cattleherder. Thus Wisconsin, now developing manufacture, is a State with varied agricultural interests. But earlier it was given over to almost exclusive grain-raising, like North Dakota at the present time.

Each of these areas has had an influence in our economic and political history; the evolution of each into a higher stage has worked political transformations. But what constitutional historian has made any adequate attempt to interpret political facts by the light of these social areas and changes?

The Atlantic frontier was compounded of fisherman, fur-trader, miner, cattle-raiser, and farmer. Excepting the fisherman, each type of industry was on the march toward the West impelled by an irresistible attraction. Each passed in successive waves across the continent. Stand at Cumberland Gap and watch the procession of civilization, marching single file—the buffalo following the trail to the salt springs, the Indian, the fur-trader and hunter, the cattle-raiser, the pioneer farmer—and the frontier has passed by. Stand at South Pass in the Rockies a century later and see the same procession with wider intervals between. The unequal rate of advance compels us to distinguish the frontier into the trader's frontier, the rancher's frontier, or the miner's frontier, and the farmer's frontier. When the mines and the cow pens were still near the fall line the traders' pack trains were tinkling across the Alleghanies, and the French on the Great Lakes were fortifying their posts, alarmed by the British trader's birch canoe. When the trappers scaled the Rockies, the farmer was still near the mouth of the Missouri.

THE INDIAN TRADER'S FRONTIER.

Why was it that the Indian trader passed so rapidly across the continent? What effects followed from the trader's frontier? The trade was coeval with American discovery. The Norsemen, Vespuccius, Verrazani, Hudson, John Smith, all trafficked for furs. The Plymouth pilgrims settled in Indian cornfields, and their first return cargo was of beaver and lumber. The records of the various New England colonies show how steadily exploration was carried into the wilderness by this trade. What is true for New England is, as would be expected, even plainer for the rest of the colonies. All along the coast from Maine to Georgia the Indian trade opened up the river courses. Steadily the trader passed westward, utilizing the older lines of French trade. The Ohio, the Great Lakes, the Mississippi, the Missouri, and the Platte, the lines of western advance, were ascended by traders. They found the passes in the Rocky Mountains and guided Lewis and Clarke, Fremont, and Bidwell. The explanation of the rapidity of this advance is connected with the effects of the trader on the Indian. The trading post left the unarmed tribes at the mercy of those that had purchased fire-arms—a truth which the Iroquois Indians wrote in blood, and so the remote and unvisited tribes gave eager welcome to the trader. "The savages," wrote La Salle, "take better care of us French than of their own children; from us only can they get guns and goods." This accounts for the trader's power and the rapidity of his advance. Thus the disintegrating forces of civilization entered the wilderness. Every river valley and Indian trail became a fissure in Indian society, and so that society became honeycombed. Long before the pioneer farmer appeared on the scene, primitive Indian life had passed away. The farmers met Indians armed with guns. The trading frontier, while steadily undermining Indian power by making the tribes ultimately dependent on the whites, yet, through its sale of guns, gave to the Indians increased power of resistance to the farming frontier. French colonization was dominated by its trading frontier; English colonization by its farming frontier. There was an antagonism between the two frontiers as between the two nations. Said Duquesne to the Iroquois, "Are you ignorant of the difference between the king of England and the king of France? Go see the forts that our king has established and you will see that you can still hunt under their very walls. They have been placed for your advantage in places which you frequent. The English, on the contrary, are no sooner in possession of a place than the game is driven away. The forest falls before them as they advance, and the soil is laid bare so that you can scarce find the wherewithal to erect a shelter for the night."

And yet, in spite of this opposition of the interests of the trader and the farmer, the Indian trade pioneered the way for civilization. The buffalo trail became the Indian trail, and this because the trader's "trace;" the trails widened into roads, and the roads into turnpikes, and these in turn were transformed into railroads. The same origin can be shown for the railroads of the South, the far West, and the Dominion of Canada. The trading posts reached by these trails were on the sites of Indian villages which had been placed in positions suggested by nature; and these trading posts, situated so as to command the water systems of the country, have grown into such cities as Albany, Pittsburg, Detroit, Chicago, St. Louis, Council Bluffs, and Kansas City. Thus civilization in America has followed the arteries made by geology, pouring an ever richer tide through them, until at last the slender paths of aboriginal intercourse have been broadened and interwoven into the complex mazes of modern commercial lines; the wilderness has been interpenetrated by lines of civilization growing ever more numerous. It is like the steady growth of a complex nervous system for the originally simple, inert continent. If one would understand why we are to-day one nation, rather than a collection of isolated states, he must study this economic and social consolidation of the country. In this progress from savage conditions lie topics for the evolutionist.

The effect of the Indian frontier as a consolidating agent in our history is important. From the close of the seventeenth century various intercolonial congresses have been called to treat with Indians and establish common measures of defense. Particularism was strongest in colonies with no Indian frontier. This frontier stretched along the western border like a cord of union. The Indian was a common danger, demanding united action. Most celebrated of these conferences was the Albany congress of 1754, called to treat with the Six Nations, and to consider plans of union. Even a cursory reading of the plan proposed by the congress reveals the importance of the frontier. The powers of the general council and the officers were, chiefly, the determination of peace and war with the Indians, the regulation of Indian trade, the purchase of Indian lands, and the creation and government of new settlements as a security against the Indians. It is evident that the unifying tendencies of the Revolutionary period were facilitated by the previous cooperation in the regulation of the frontier. In this connection may be mentioned the importance of the frontier, from that day to this, as a military training school, keeping alive the power of resistance to aggression, and developing the stalwart and rugged qualities of the frontiersman.

THE RANCHER'S FRONTIER.

It would not be possible in the limits of this paper to trace the other frontiers across the continent. Travelers of the eighteenth century found the "cowpens" among the canebrakes and peavine pastures of the South, and the "cow drivers" took their droves to Charleston, Philadelphia, and New York. Travelers at the close of the War of 1812 met droves of more than a thousand cattle and swine from the interior of Ohio going to Pennsylvania to fatten for the Philadelphia market. The ranges of the Great Plains, with ranch and cowboy and nomadic life, are things of yesterday and of to-day. The experience of the Carolina cowpens guided the ranchers of Texas. One element favoring the rapid extension of the rancher's frontier is the fact that in a remote country lacking transportation facilities the product must be in small bulk, or must be able to transport itself, and the cattle raiser could easily drive his product to market. The effect of these great ranches on the subsequent agrarian history of the localities in which they existed should be studied.

THE FARMER'S FRONTIER.

The maps of the census reports show an uneven advance of the farmer's frontier, with tongues of settlement pushed forward and with indentations of wilderness. In part this is due to Indian resistance, in part to the location of river valleys and passes, in part to the unequal force of the centers of frontier attraction. Among the important centers of attraction may be mentioned the following: fertile and favorably situated soils, salt springs, mines, and army posts.

ARMY POSTS.

The frontier army post, serving to protect the settlers from the Indians, has also acted as a wedge to open the Indian country, and has been a nucleus for settlement. In this connection mention should also be made of the Government military and exploring expeditions in determining the lines of settlement. But all the more important expeditions were greatly indebted to the earliest pathmakers, the Indian guides, the traders and trappers, and the French voyageurs, who were inevitable parts of governmental expeditions from the days of Lewis and Clarke. Each expedition was an epitome of the previous factors in western advance.

SALT SPRINGS.

In an interesting monograph, Victor Hehn has traced the effect of salt upon early European development, and has pointed out how it affected the lines of settlement and the form of administration. A similar study might be made for the salt springs of the United States. The early settlers were tied to the coast by the need of salt, without which they could not preserve their meats or live in comfort. Writing in 1752, Bishop Spangenburg says of a colony for which he was seeking lands in North Carolina, "They will require salt & other necessaries which they can neither manufacture nor raise. Either they must go to Charleston, which is 300 miles distant . . . Or else they must go to Boling's Point in Virginia on a branch of the James & is also 300 miles from here . . . Or else they must go down the Roanoke—I know not how many miles—where salt is brought up from the Cape Fear." This may serve as a typical illustration. An annual pilgrimage to the coast for salt thus became essential. Taking flocks or furs and ginseng root, the early settlers sent their pack trains after seeding time each year to the coast. This proved to be an important educational influence, since it was almost the only way in which the pioneer learned what was going on in the East. But when discovery was made of the salt springs of the Kanawha, and the Holston, and Kentucky, and central New York, the West began to be freed from dependence on the coast. It was in part the effect of finding these salt springs that enabled settlement to cross the mountains.

From the time the mountains rose between the pioneer and the seaboard, a new order of Americanism arose. The West and the East began to get out of touch of each other. The settlements from the sea to the mountains kept connection with the rear and had a certain solidarity. But the overmountain men grew more and more independent. The East took a narrow view of American advance, and nearly lost these men. Kentucky and Tennessee history bears abundant witness to the truth of this statement. The East began to try to hedge and limit westward expansion. Though Webster could declare that there were no Alleghanies in his politics, yet in politics in general they were a very solid factor.

LAND.

The exploitation of the beasts took hunter and trader to the west, the exploitation of the grasses took the rancher west, and the exploitation of the virgin soil of the river valleys and prairies attracted the farmer. Good soils have been the most continuous attraction to the farmer's frontier. The land hunger of the Virginians drew them down the rivers into Carolina, in early colonial days; the search for soils took the Massachusetts men to Pennsylvania and to New York. As the eastern lands were taken up migration flowed across them to the west. Daniel Boone, the great backwoodsman, who combined the occupations of hunter, trader, cattle-raiser farmer, and surveyor—learning, probably from the traders, of the fertility of the lands on the upper Yadkin, where the traders were wont to rest as they took their way to the Indians, left his Pennsylvania home with his father, and passed down the Great Valley road to that stream. Learning from a trader whose posts were on the Red River in Kentucky of its game and rich pastures, he pioneered the way for the farmers to that region. Thence he passed to the frontier of Missouri, where his settlement was long a landmark on the frontier. Here again he helped to open the way for civilization, finding salt licks, and trails, and land. His son was among the earliest trappers in the passes of the Rocky Mountains, and his party are said to have been the first to camp on the present site of Denver. His grandson, Col. A. J. Boone, of Colorado, was a power among the Indians of the Rocky Mountains, and was appointed an agent by the Government. Kit Carson's mother was a Boone. Thus this family epitomizes the backwoodsman's advance across the continent.

The farmer's advance came in a distinct series of waves. In Peck's New Guide to the West, published in Boston in 1837, occurs this suggestive passage:

> Generally, in all the western settlements, three classes, like the waves of the ocean, have rolled one after the other. First comes the pioneer, who depends for the subsistence of his family chiefly upon the natural growth of vegetation, called the "range," and the proceeds of hunting. His implements of agriculture are rude, chiefly of his own make, and his efforts directed mainly to a crop of corn and a "truck patch." The last is a rude garden for growing cabbage, beans, corn for roasting ears, cucumbers, and potatoes. A log cabin, and, occasionally, a stable and corn-crib, and a field of a dozen acres, the timber girdled or "deadened," and fenced, are enough for his occupancy. It is quite immaterial whether he ever becomes the owner of the soil. He is the occupant for the time being, pays no rent, and feels as independent as the "lord of the manor." With a horse, cow, and one or two breeders of swine, he strikes into the woods with his family, and becomes the founder of a new county, or perhaps state. He builds his cabin, gathers around him a few other families of similar tastes and habits, and occupies till the range is somewhat subdued, and hunting a little precarious, or, which is more frequently the case, till the neighbors crowd around, roads, bridges, and fields annoy him, and he lacks elbow room. The preemption law enables him to dispose of his cabin and cornfield to the next class of emigrants; and, to employ his own figures, he "breaks for the high timber," "clears out for the New Purchase," or migrates to Arkansas or Texas, to work the same process over.

The next class of emigrants purchase the lands, add field to field, clear out the roads, throw rough bridges over the streams, put up hewn log houses with glass windows and brick or stone chimneys, occasionally plant orchards, build mills, schoolhouses, court-houses, etc., and exhibit the picture and forms of plain, frugal, civilized life.

Another wave rolls on. The men of capital and enterprise come. The settler is ready to sell out and take the advantage of the rise in property, push farther into the interior and become, himself, a man of capital and enterprise in turn. The small village rises to a spacious town or city; substantial edifices of brick, extensive fields, orchards, gardens, colleges, and churches are seen. Broadcloths, silks, leghorns, crapes, and all the refinements, luxuries, elegancies, frivolities, and fashions are in vogue. Thus wave after wave is rolling westward; the real Eldorado is still farther on.

A portion of the two first classes remain stationary amidst the general movement, improve their habits and condition, and rise in the scale of society.

The writer has traveled much amongst the first class, the real pioneers. He has lived many years in connection with the second grade; and now the third wave is sweeping over large districts of Indiana, Illinois, and Missouri. Migration has become almost a habit in the West. Hundreds of men can be found, not over 50 years of age, who have settled for the fourth, fifth, or sixth time on a new spot. To sell out and remove only a few hundred miles makes up a portion of the variety of backwoods life and manners.

Omitting those of the pioneer farmers who move from the love of adventure, the advance of the more steady farmer is easy to understand. Obviously the immigrant was attracted by the cheap lands of the frontier, and even the native farmer felt their influence strongly. Year by year the farmers who lived on soil whose returns were diminished by unrotated crops were offered the virgin soil of the frontier at nominal prices. Their growing families demanded more lands, and these were dear. The competition of the unexhausted, cheap, and easily tilled prairie lands compelled the farmer either to go west and continue the exhaustion of the soil on a new frontier, or to adopt intensive culture. Thus the census of 1890 shows, in the Northwest, many counties in which there is an absolute or a relative decrease of population. These States have been sending farmers to advance the frontier on the plains, and have themselves begun to turn to intensive farming and to manufacture. A decade before this, Ohio had shown the same transition stage. Thus the demand for land and the love of wilderness freedom drew the frontier ever onward.

Having now roughly outlined the various kinds of frontiers, and their modes of advance, chiefly from the point of view of the frontier itself, we may next inquire what were the influences on the East and on the Old World. A rapid enumeration of some of the more noteworthy effects is all that I have time for.

COMPOSITE NATIONALITY.

First, we note that the frontier promoted the formation of a composite nationality for the American people. The coast was preponderantly English, but the later tides of continental immigration flowed across to the free lands. This was the case from the early colonial days. The Scotch Irish and the Palatine Germans, or "Pennsylvania Dutch," furnished the dominant element in the stock of the colonial frontier. With these peoples were also the freed indented servants, or redemptioners, who at the expiration of their time of service passed to the frontier. Governor Spottswood of Virginia writes in 1717, "The inhabitants of our frontiers are composed generally of such as have been transported hither as servants, and, being out of their time, settle themselves where land is to be taken up and that will produce the necessarys of life with little labour." Very generally these redemptioners were of non-English stock. In the crucible of the frontier the immigrants were Americanized, liberated, and fused into a mixed race, English in neither nationality or characteristics. The process has gone on from the early days to our own. Burke and other writers in the middle of the eighteenth century believed that Pennsylvania was "threatened with the danger of being wholly foreign in language, manners, and perhaps even inclinations." The German and Scotch-Irish elements in the frontier of the South were only less great. In the middle of the present century the German element in Wisconsin was already so considerable that leading publicists looked to the creation of a German state out of the commonwealth by concentrating their colonization. Such examples teach us to beware of misinterpreting the fact that there is a common English speech in America into a belief that the stock is also English.

INDUSTRIAL INDEPENDENCE.

In another way the advance of the frontier decreased our dependence on England. The coast, particularly of the South, lacked diversified industries, and was dependent on England for the bulk of its supplies. In the South there was even a dependence on the Northern colonies for articles of food. Governor Glenn, of South Carolina, writes in the middle of the eighteenth century: "Our trade with New York and Philadelphia was of this sort, draining us of all the little money and bills we could gather from other places for their bread, flour, beer, hams, bacon, and other things of their produce, all which, except beer, our new townships begin to supply us with, which are settled with very industrious and thriving Germans. This no doubt diminishes the number of shipping and the appearance of our trade, but it is far from being a detriment to us." Before long the frontier created a demand for merchants. As it retreated from the coast it became less and less possible for England to bring her supplies directly to the consumer's wharfs, and carry away staple crops, and staple crops began to give way to diversified agriculture for a time. The effect of this phase of the frontier action upon the northern section is perceived when we realize how the advance of the frontier aroused seaboard cities like Boston, New York, and Baltimore, to engage in rivalry for what Washington called "the extensive and valuable trade of a rising empire."

EFFECTS ON NATIONAL LEGISLATION.

The legislation which most developed the powers of the National Government, and played the largest part in its activity, was conditioned on the frontier. Writers have discussed the subjects of tariff, land, and internal improvement, as subsidiary to the slavery question. But when American history comes to be rightly viewed it will be seen that the slavery question is an incident. In the period from the end of the first half of the present century to the close of the civil war slavery rose to primary, but far from exclusive, importance. But this does not justify Dr. von Holst (to take an example) in treating our constitutional history in its formative period down to 1828 in a single volume, giving six volumes chiefly to the history of slavery from 1828 to 1861, under the title "Constitutional History of the United States." The growth of nationalism and the evolution of American political institutions were dependent on the advance of the frontier. Even so recent a writer as Rhodes, in his History of the United States since the compromise of 1850, has treated the legislation called out by the western advance as incidental to the slavery struggle.

This is a wrong perspective. The pioneer needed the goods of the coast, and so the grand series of internal improvement and railroad legislation began, with potent nationalizing effects. Over internal improvements occurred great debates, in which grave constitutional questions were discussed. Sectional groupings appear in the votes, profoundly significant for the historian. Loose construction increased as the nation marched westward. But the West was not content with bringing the farm to the factory. Under the lead of Clay—"Harry of the West"—protective tariffs were passed, with the cry of bringing the factory to the farm. The disposition of the public lands was a third important subject of national legislation influenced by the frontier.

THE PUBLIC DOMAIN.

The public domain has been a force of profound importance in the nationalization and development of the Government. The effects of the struggle of the landed and the landless States, and of the ordinance of 1787, need no discussion. Administratively the frontier called out some of the highest and most vitalizing activities of the General Government. The purchase of Louisiana was perhaps the constitutional turning point in the history of the

Republic, inasmuch as it afforded both a new area for national legislation and the occasion of the downfall of the policy of strict construction. But the purchase of Louisiana was called out by frontier needs and demands. As frontier States accrued to the Union the national power grew. In a speech on the dedication of the Calhoun monument Mr. Lamar explained: "In 1789 the States were the creators of the Federal Government; in 1861 the Federal Government was the creator of a large majority of the States."

When we consider the public domain from the point of view of the sale and disposal of the public lands we are again brought face to face with the frontier. The policy of the United States in dealing with its lands is in sharp contrast with the European system of scientific administration. Efforts to make this domain a source of revenue, and to withhold it from emigrants in order that settlement might be compact, were in vain. The jealousy and the fears of the East were powerless in the face of the demands of the frontiersmen. John Quincy Adams was obliged to confess: "My own system of administration, which was to make the national domain the inexhaustible fund for progressive and unceasing internal improvement, has failed." The reason is obvious; a system of administration was not what the West demanded; it wanted land. Adams states the situation as follows: "The slaveholders of the South have bought the cooperation of the western country by the bribe of the western lands, abandoning to the new Western States their own proportion of the public property and aiding them in the design of grasping all the lands into their own hands. Thomas H. Benton was the author of this system, which he brought forward as a substitute for the American system of Mr. Clay, and to supplant him as the leading statesman of the West. Mr. Clay, by his tariff compromise with Mr. Calhoun, abandoned his own American system. At the same time he brought forward a plan for distributing among all the States of the Union the proceeds of the sales of the public lands. His bill for that purpose passed both Houses of Congress, but was vetoed by President Jackson, who, in his annual message of December, 1832, formally recommended that all public lands should be gratuitously given away to individual adventurers and to the States in which the lands are situated.

"No subject," said Henry Clay, "which has presented itself to the present, or perhaps any preceding, Congress, is of greater magnitude than that of the public lands." When we consider the far-reaching effects of the Government's land policy upon political, economic, and social aspects of American life, we are disposed to agree with him. But this legislation was framed under frontier influences, and under the lead of Western statesmen like Benton and Jackson. Said Senator Scott of Indiana in 1841: "I consider the preemption law merely declaratory of the custom or common law of the settlers."

NATIONAL TENDENCIES OF THE FRONTIER.

It is safe to say that the legislation with regard to land, tariff, and internal improvements—the American system of the nationalizing Whig party—was conditioned on frontier ideas and needs. But it was not merely in legislative action that the frontier worked against the sectionalism of the coast. The economic and social characteristics of the frontier worked against sectionalism. The men of the frontier had closer resemblances to the Middle region than to either of the other sections. Pennsylvania had been the seed-plot of frontier emigration, and, although she passed on her settlers along the Great Valley into the west of Virginia and the Carolinas, yet the industrial society of these Southern frontiersmen was always more like that of the Middle region than like that of the tide-water portion of the South, which later came to spread its industrial type throughout the South.

The Middle region, entered by New York harbor, was an open door to all Europe. The tide-water part of the South represented typical Englishmen, modified by a warm climate and servile labor, and living in baronial fashion on great plantations; New England stood for a special English movement—Puritanism. The Middle region was less English than the other sections. It had a wide mixture of nationalities, a varied society, the mixed town and county system of local government, a varied economic life, many religious sects. In short, it was a region mediating between New England and the South, and the East and the West. It represented that composite nationality which the contemporary United States exhibits, that juxtaposition of non-English groups, occupying a valley or a little settlement, and presenting reflections of the map of Europe in their variety. It was democratic and nonsectional, if not national; "easy, tolerant, and contented"; rooted strongly in material prosperity. It was typical of the modern United States. It was least sectional, not only because it lay between North and South, but also because with no barriers to shut out its frontiers from its settled region, and with a system of connecting waterways, the Middle region mediated between East and West as well as between North and South. Thus it became the typically American region. Even the New Englander, who was shut out from the frontier by the Middle region, tarrying in New York or Pennsylvania on his westward march, lost the acuteness of his sectionalism on the way.

The spread of cotton culture into the interior of the South finally broke down the contrast between the "tide-water" region and the rest of the State, and based Southern interests on slavery. Before this process revealed its results the western portion of the South, which was akin to Pennsylvania in stock, society, and industry, showed tendencies to fall away from the faith of the fathers into internal improvement legislation and nationalism. In the Virginia convention of 1829–30, called to revise the constitution, Mr. Leigh, of Chesterfield, one of the tidewater counties, declared:

> One of the main causes of discontent which led to this convention, that which had the strongest influence in overcoming our veneration for the work of our fathers, which taught us to contemn the sentiments of Henry and Mason and Pendleton, which weaned us from our reverence for the constituted authorities of the State, was an overweening passion for internal improvement. I say this with perfect knowledge, for it has been avowed to me by gentlemen from the West over and over again. And let me tell the gentleman from Albemarle (Mr. Gordon) that it has been another principal object of those who set this ball of revolution in motion, to overturn the doctrine of State rights, of which Virginia has been the very pillar, and to remove the barrier she has interposed to the interference of the Federal Government in that same work of internal improvement, by so reorganizing the legislature that Virginia, too, may be hitched to the Federal car.

It was this nationalizing tendency of the West that transformed the democracy of Jefferson into the national republicanism of Monroe and the democracy of Andrew Jackson. The West of the war of 1812, the West of Clay, and Benton, and Harrison, and Andrew Jackson, shut off by the Middle States and the mountains from the coast sections, had a solidarity of its own with national tendencies. On the tide of the Father of Waters, North and South met and mingled into a nation. Interstate migration went steadily on—a process of cross-fertilization of ideas and institutions. The fierce struggle of the sections over slavery on the western frontier does not diminish the truth of this statement; it proves the truth of it. Slavery was a sectional trait that would not down, but in the West it could not remain sectional. It was the greatest of frontiersmen who declared: "I believe this Government can not endure permanently half slave and half free. It will become all of one thing or all of the other." Nothing works for nationalism like intercourse within the nation. Mobility of population is death to localism, and the western frontier worked irresistibly in unsettling population. The effects reached back from the frontier and affected profoundly the Atlantic coast and even the Old World.

GROWTH OF DEMOCRACY.

But the most important effect of the frontier has been in the promotion of democracy here and in Europe. As has been indicated, the frontier is productive of individualism. Complex society is precipitated by the wilderness into a kind of primitive organization based on the family. The tendency is anti-social. It produces antipathy to control, and particularly to any direct control. The tax-gatherer is viewed as a representative of oppression. Prof. Osgood, in an able article, has pointed out that the frontier conditions prevalent in the colonies are important factors in the explanation of the American Revolution, where individual liberty was sometimes confused with absence of all effective government. The same conditions aid in explaining the difficulty of instituting a strong government in the period of the confederacy. The frontier individualism has from the beginning promoted democracy.

The frontier States that came into the Union in the first quarter of a century of its existence came in with democratic suffrage provisions, and had reactive effects of the highest importance upon the older States whose peoples were being attracted there. An extension of the franchise became essential. It was *western* New York that forced an extension of suffrage in the constitutional convention of that State in 1821; and it was *western* Virginia that compelled the tide-water region to put a more liberal suffrage provision in the constitution framed in 1830, and to give to the frontier region a more nearly proportionate representation with the tide-water aristocracy. The rise of democracy as an effective force in the nation came in with western preponderance under Jackson and William Henry Harrison, and it meant the triumph of the frontier—with all of its good and with all of its evil elements. An interesting illustration of the tone of frontier democracy in 1830 comes from the same debates in the Virginia convention already referred to. A representative from western Virginia declared:

> But, sir, it is not the increase of population in the West which this gentleman ought to fear. It is the energy which the mountain breeze and western habits impart to those emigrants. They are regenerated, politically I mean, sir. They soon become *working politicians*; and the difference, sir, between a *talking* and a *working* politician is immense. The Old Dominion has long been celebrated for producing great orators; the ablest metaphysicians in policy; men that can split hairs in all abstruse questions of political economy. But at home, or when they return from Congress, they have negroes to fan them asleep. But a Pennsylvania, a New York, an Ohio, or a western Virginia statesman, though far inferior in logic, metaphysics, and rhetoric to an old Virginia statesman, has this advantage, that when he returns home he takes off his coat and takes hold of the plow. This gives him bone and muscle, sir, and preserves his republican principles pure and uncontaminated.

So long as free land exists, the opportunity for a competency exists, and economic power secures political power. But the democracy born of free land, strong in selfishness and individualism, intolerant of administrative experience and education, and pressing individual liberty beyond its proper bounds, has its dangers as well as it benefits. Individualism in America has allowed a laxity in regard to governmental affairs which has rendered possible the spoils system and all the manifest evils that follow from the lack of a highly developed civic spirit. In this connection may be noted also the influence of frontier conditions in permitting lax business honor, inflated paper currency and wild-cat banking. The colonial and revolutionary frontier was the region whence emanated many of the worst forms of an evil currency. The West in the war of 1812 repeated the phenomenon on the frontier of that day, while the speculation and wild-cat banking of the period of the crisis of 1837 occurred on the new frontier belt of the next tier of States. Thus each one of the periods of lax financial integrity coincides with periods when a new set of frontier communities had arisen, and coincides in area with these successive frontiers, for the most part. The recent Populist agitation is a case in point. Many a State that now declines any connection with the tenets of the Populists, itself adhered to such ideas in an earlier stage of the development of the State. A primitive society can hardly be expected to show the intelligent appreciation of the complexity of business interests in a developed society. The continued recurrence of these areas of paper money agitation is another evidence that the frontier can be isolated and studied as a factor in American history of the highest importance.

ATTEMPTS TO CHECK AND REGULATE THE FRONTIER.

The East has always feared the result of an unregulated advance of the frontier, and has tried to check and guide it. The English authorities would have checked settlement at the headwaters of the Atlantic tributaries and allowed the "savages to enjoy their deserts in quiet lest the peltry trade should decrease." This called out Burke's splendid protest:

> If you stopped your grants, what would be the consequence? The people would occupy without grants. They have already so occupied in many places. You can not station garrisons in every part of these deserts. If you drive the people from one place, they will carry on their annual tillage and remove with their flocks and herds to another. Many of the people in the back settlements are already little attached to particular situations. Already they have topped the Appalachian mountains. From thence they behold before them an immense plain, one vast, rich, level meadow: a square of five hundred miles. Over this they would wander without a possibility of restraint; they would change their manners with their habits of life; would soon forget a government by which they were disowned; would become hordes of English Tartars; and, pouring down upon your unfortified frontiers a fierce and irresistible cavalry, become masters of your governors and your counselers, your collectors and comptrollers, and of all the slaves that adhered to them. Such would, and in no long time must, be the effect of attempting to forbid as a crime and to suppress as an evil the command and blessing of Providence, "Increase and multiply." Such would be the happy result of an endeavor to keep as a lair of wild beasts that earth which God, by an express charter, has given to the children of men.

But the English Government was not alone in its desire to limit the advance of the frontier and guide its destinies. Tidewater Virginia and

South Carolina gerrymandered those colonies to insure the dominance of the coast in their legislatures. Washington desired to settle a State at a time in the Northwest; Jefferson would reserve from settlement the territory of his Louisiana purchase north of the thirty-second parallel, in order to offer it to the Indians in exchange for their settlements east of the Mississippi. "When we shall be full on this side," he writes, "we may lay off a range of States on the western bank from the head to the mouth, and so range after range, advancing compactly as we multiply." Madison went so far as to argue to the French minister that the United States had no interest in seeing population extend itself on the right bank of the Mississippi, but should rather fear it. When the Oregon question was under debate, in 1824, Smyth, of Virginia, would draw an unchangeable line for the limits of the United States at the outer limit of two tiers of States beyond the Mississippi, complaining that the seaboard States were being drained of the flower of their population by the bringing too much land into market. Even Thomas Benton, the man of widest views of the destiny of the West, at this stage of his career declared that along the ridge of the Rocky mountains "the western limits of the Republic should be drawn, and the statue of the fabled god Terminus should be raised upon its highest peak, never to be thrown down." But the attempts to limit the boundaries, to restrict land sales and settlement, and to deprive the West of its share of political power were all in vain. Steadily the frontier of settlement advanced and carried with it individualism, democracy, and nationalism, and powerfully affected the East and the Old World.

MISSIONARY ACTIVITY.

The most effective efforts of the East to regulate the frontier came through its educational and religious activity, exerted by interstate migration and by organized societies. Speaking in 1835, Dr. Lyman Beecher declared: "It is equally plain that the religious and political destiny of our nation is to be decided in the West," and he pointed out that the population of the West "is assembled from all the States of the Union and from all the nations of Europe, and is rushing in like the waters of the flood, demanding for its moral preservation the immediate and universal action of those institutions which discipline the mind and arm the conscience and the heart. And so various are the opinions and habits, and so recent and imperfect is the acquaintance, and so sparse are the settlements of the West, that no homogeneous public sentiment can be formed to legislate immediately into being the requisite institutions. And yet they are all needed immediately in their utmost perfection and power. A nation is being 'born in a day.' . . . But what will become of the West if her prosperity rushes up to such a majesty of power, while those great institutions linger which are necessary to form the mind and the conscience and the heart of that vast world. It must not be permitted. . . . Let no man at the East quiet himself and dream of liberty, whatever may become of the West. . . . Her destiny is our destiny."

With the appeal to the conscience of New England, he adds appeals to her fears lest other religious sects anticipate her own. The New England preacher and school-teacher left their mark on the West. The dread of Western emancipation from New England's political and economic control was paralleled by her fears lest the West cut loose from her religion. Commenting in 1850 on reports that settlement was rapidly extending northward in Wisconsin, the editor of the Home Missionary writes: "We scarcely know whether to rejoice or mourn over this extension of our settlements. While we sympathize in whatever tends to increase the physical resources and prosperity of our country, we can not forget that with all these dispersions into remote and still remoter corners of the land the supply of the means of grace is becoming relatively less and less." Acting in accordance with such ideas, home missions were established and Western colleges were erected. As seaboard cities like Philadelphia, New York, and Baltimore strove for the mastery of Western trade, so the various denominations strove for the possession of the West. Thus an intellectual stream from New England sources fertilized the West. Other sections sent their missionaries; but the real struggle was between sects. The contest for power and the expansive tendency furnished to the various sects by the existence of a moving frontier must have had important results on the character of religious organization in the United States. The multiplication of rival churches in the little frontier towns had deep and lasting social effects. The religious aspects of the frontier make a chapter in our history which needs study.

INTELLECTUAL TRAITS.

From the conditions of frontier life came intellectual traits of profound importance. The works of travelers along each frontier from colonial days onward describe certain common traits, and these traits have, while softening down, still persisted as survivals in the place of their origin, even when a higher social organization succeeded. The result is that to the frontier the American intellect owes its striking characteristics. That coarseness and strength combined with acuteness and inquisitiveness; that practical, inventive turn of mind, quick to find expedients; that masterful grasp of material things, lacking in the artistic but powerful to effect great ends; that restless, nervous energy; that dominant individualism, working for good and for evil, and withal that buoyancy and exuberance which comes with freedom—these are traits of the frontier, or traits called out elsewhere because of the existence of the frontier. Since the days when the fleet of Columbus sailed into the waters of the New World,

America has been another name for opportunity, and the people of the United States have taken their tone from the incessant expansion which has not only been open but has even been forced upon them. He would be a rash prophet who should assert that the expansive character of American life has now entirely ceased. Movement has been its dominant fact, and, unless this training has no effect upon a people, the American energy will continually demand a wider field for its exercise. But never again will such gifts of free land offer themselves. For a moment, at the frontier, the bonds of custom are broken and unrestraint is triumphant. There is not *tabula rasa*. The stubborn American environment is there with its imperious summons to accept its conditions; the inherited ways of doing things are also there; and yet, in spite of environment, and in spite of custom, each frontier did indeed furnish a new field of opportunity, a gate of escape from the bondage of the past; and freshness, and confidence, and scorn of older society, impatience of its restraints and its ideas, and indifference to its lessons, have accompanied the frontier. What the Mediterranean Sea was to the Greeks, breaking the bond of custom, offering new experiences, calling out new institutions and activities, that, and more, the ever retreating frontier has been to the United States directly, and to the nations of Europe more remotely. And now, four centuries from the discovery of America, at the end of a hundred years of life under the Constitution, the frontier has gone, and with its going has closed the first period of American history.

Bibliography

Benson, Lee. *Turner and Beard: American Historical Writing Reconsidered.* Glencoe, Ill., 1960.

Billington, Ray Allen. *Frederick Jackson Turner, Historian, Scholar, Teacher.* New York, 1973.

Higham, John; Leonard Krieger; and Felix Gilbert. *History.* Princeton, N.J., 1965.

Hofstadter, Richard. *The Progressive Historians: Turner, Parrington, Beard.* New York, 1968.

Jacobs, Wilbur, ed. *Frederick Jackson Turner's Legacy.* San Marino, Calif., 1965.

Jacobs, Wilbur R., "Turner's Methodology: Multiple Working Hypotheses or Ruling Theory." *Journal of American History,* 54 (March 1968): 853–63.

Lamar, Howard R. "Frederick Jackson Turner." In *Pastmasters: Some Essays on American Historians,* edited by Marcus Cunliffe and Robin W. Winks. New York, 1969.

Taylor, George R. ed. *The Turner Thesis Concerning the Role of the Frontier in American History,* rev. ed. Boston, 1956.

Turner, Frederick Jackson. *Frontier and Section, Selected Essays of Frederick Jackson Turner,* edited by Ray Allen Billington. Englewood Cliffs, N.J., 1961.

CHAPTER 17

Charles and Mary Beard
The Rise of American Civilization
(1927)

As the nineteenth century turned into the twentieth, Turner's students and others, thinking they stood in the tradition of Leopold von Ranke,[1] established the monograph as a standard form for "scientific" history: a book-length research report composed in a style dull and flat enough to convince reader and writer that the author was uninvolved in the work except as recorder of objective reality. Less and less did such books consciously pursue a larger hypothesis, not even Turner's, in American history.

Not the least of Charles Beard's significance is that his monograph, *An Economic Interpretation of the Constitution* (1913), broke through this pattern—and even the dullness of his own prose—to report a finding that challenged Americans' most basic assumptions about politics and behavior. The evidence he collected appeared to show that the Founding Fathers of 1787 created a frame of government to serve their own personal and class interests as much as the welfare of the broader commonwealth. They owned government securities, the book's famous fifth chapter argued, whose value would be enhanced by provisions of the Constitution they wrote. Beard's argument was a sensation in the intellectual community at a time (the Progressive Era) when "muckraking" journalists were writing in the press about the sordid corruption of contemporary public life. Beard's book on the Constitution was no best seller, but he wrote more, his reputation grew, and in 1927 he and his wife, Mary,[2] published their massive, two-volume *Rise of American Civilization,* which *was* a best seller and cast all of American history in an economic mold.

Beard was born in Knightstown, Indiana, in 1874 and was educated at DePauw, Oxford, and Columbia universities, completing his Ph.D. at Columbia in 1904. His career as a dissenter and reformer fit his family's history of bucking the mainstream. His grandfather ran a "station" on the underground railroad in antebellum North Carolina, and his father came north when the Civil War broke out and was, among other things, an admirer of Robert G. Ingersoll, the famous atheist. Beard himself was much influenced by the attack on the inhumanities of industrialization in John Ruskin's *Unto This Last* (1862), which he read at Oxford, where he also promoted projects for workingmen's improvement. He taught history and politics at Columbia from 1905 to 1917, but resigned in protest over the university's dismissal of colleagues who opposed United States entry into the First World War. His *Economic Interpretation of the Constitution* was hugely controversial, but Beard rose to the top of his profession nonetheless, assuming the presidency of the American Historical Association in 1933. Meanwhile, the Beards' *Rise of American Civilization* became the conventional wisdom on the content and direction of American history. Its dominance continued even after Beard tarnished his reputation with intemperate and selectively documented attacks on President Franklin Roosevelt and American entry into the Second World War, a subject to which he devoted six books from 1934 to 1948, the year he died.

Richard Hofstadter remembered that, as a young man in the 1930s, reading *The Rise of American Civilization* was like a revelation. Yet when he reread it in the 1960s, he found it hard to recapture the sense of its first freshness, so much had the economic interpretation been absorbed into mid-twentieth-century perceptions or supplemented by other approaches. The Beards argued that the chief motivation in American history was economic interest, and if movements like abolitionism in the 1830s and 1840s, for example, could not be explained that way, they were probably not important anyway. The Beards repeated the central thesis of the book on the Constitution in their section on the Revolution, but the most arresting chapter was the one on the Civil War, "The Second American Revolution." To the military aspects and constitutional arguments, which had occupied the largest place in Civil War writing to that time, the Beards gave only a spare few paragraphs. Their main argument was that, in mildly Marxist terms, the Civil War resulted in the overthrow of the southern "feudal" landed aristocracy by the new northern capitalist class in a way that matched other countries' bourgeois revolutions. The Beards did not project the future as an inevitable uprising of the working class or a "dictatorship of the proletariat," however, and in their expectation of a "collectivist democracy" *The Rise of American Civilization* has a decidedly optimistic tone.

In this excerpt from "The Second American Revolution" perhaps the most striking element is the Beards' style. Grand, sweeping, florid, and sententious, their writing reaches back to the nineteenth century, to the time before the coldly analytical style of Charles Beard's *Economic Interpretation of the Constitution*. If it seems ironic that a modern materialist interpretation of history should be cast in an old-fashioned mode, the Beards' olympian all-seeing pose does at least seem appropriate to their assumption that history has not only content but discernible direction as well. And if the direction is discernible, the authors have to see it with confidence, even sweeping confidence, because the scale of the study is too large for the elaborate proofs of a "scientific" monograph.

Large forces and whole classes of people are the real subjects of the Beards' chapter, as they are, grammatically, the subjects of sentence after sentence. Individuals discover here and there the real direction beneath the superficial features of the Civil War, and they frequently comment on it in quoted lines, but they are rarely more active than that. The character of even so major a force as Abraham Lincoln is evoked merely as a function of the mesh of men and circumstances that surrounded him rather than as a personality that transcended his times.

A few years after *The Rise of American Civilization* was published, Charles Beard became interested in theoretical questions about historical knowledge. In his presidential address to the American Historical Association in 1933, "Written History as an Act of Faith," he backed off from history as all-knowing science and recognized that what historians wrote was relative to the time in which they wrote it. Yet he held to the idea that history had direction and said, as he had in the last chapter of *Rise,* that however imperfectly it could be projected, history was moving toward collectivist democracy. The presidential address is worth reading with the excerpt from *Rise* and is listed in this chapter's bibliography.

Notes

1. George Iggers, "The Image of Ranke in American and German Historical Thought," *History and Theory* 2 (1962): 17–40, has shown that Americans wholly misunderstood Ranke, who would hardly have approved what they did in his name. See chapter 11 on Ranke himself and the explanatory note on page 294 for later developments and uses of Ranke's "historicism."
2. Mary Ritter Beard (1876–1958), in addition to collaborating on several books with her husband, became an established social critic in her own right. Educated at DePauw and Columbia (Ph.D., 1897), she wrote extensively on labor, sociology, and women's affairs. Her most remembered book is *Women as a Force in History* (1946), a milestone in the rediscovery of women's history.

IN THE SPRING OF 1861 the full force of the irrepressible conflict burst upon the hesitant and bewildered nation and for four long years the clash of arms filled the land with its brazen clangor. For four long years the anguish, the calamities, and the shocks of the struggle absorbed the energies of the multitudes, blared in the headlines of the newspapers, and loomed

Reprinted by permission of the publisher from Charles A. Beard and Mary R. Beard, *The Rise of American Civilization*, 2 vols in 1 (New York: Macmillan, 1927), II, 52–54, 59–66, 94–98, 105–15. Copyright © 1927 by Macmillan Publishing Co.; renewed 1955 by Mary A. Beard.

impressively in the minds of the men and women who lived and suffered in that age.

Naturally, therefore, all who wrote of the conflict used the terms of war. In its records, the government of the United States, officially referred to the contest as the War of the Rebellion, thus by implication setting the stigma of treason on those who served under the Stars and Bars. Repudiating this brand and taking for his shield the righteousness of legitimacy, one of the leading southern statesmen, Alexander H. Stephens, in his great history of the conflict, called it the War between the States. This, too, no less than the title chosen by the federal government, is open to objections; apart from the large assumptions involved, it is not strictly accurate for, in the border states, the armed struggle was a guerrilla war and in Virginia the domestic strife ended in the separation of several counties, under the ægis of a new state constitution, as West Virginia. More recently a distinguished historian, Edward Channing, entitled a volume dealing with the period The War for Southern Independence—a characterization which, though fairly precise, suffers a little perhaps from abstraction.

As a matter of fact all these symbols are misleading in that they overemphasize the element of military force in the grand dénouement. War there was unquestionably, immense, wide-sweeping, indubitable, as Carlyle would say. For years the agony of it hung like a pall over the land. And yet with strange swiftness the cloud was lifted and blown away. Merciful grass spread its green mantle over the cruel scars and the gleaming red splotches sank into the hospitable earth.

It was then that the economist and lawyer, looking more calmly on the scene, discovered that the armed conflict had been only one phase of the cataclysm, a transitory phase; that at bottom the so-called Civil War, or the War between the States, in the light of Roman analogy, was a social war, ending in the unquestioned establishment of a new power in the government, making vast changes in the arrangement of classes, in the accumulation and distribution of wealth, in the course of industrial development, and in the Constitution inherited from the Fathers. Merely by the accidents of climate, soil, and geography was it a sectional struggle. If the planting interest had been scattered evenly throughout the industrial region, had there been a horizontal rather than a perpendicular cleavage, the irrepressible conflict would have been resolved by other methods and accompanied by other logical defense mechanisms.

In any event neither accident or rhetoric should be allowed to obscure the intrinsic character of that struggle. If the operations by which the middle classes of England broke the power of the king and the aristocracy are to be known collectively as the Puritan Revolution, if the series of acts by which the bourgeois and peasants of France overthrew the king, nobility, and clergy is to be called the French Revolution, then accuracy compels us to characterize by the same term the social cataclysm in which the capitalists, laborers, and farmers of the North and West drove from power in the national government the planting aristocracy of the South. Viewed under the light of universal history, the fighting was a fleeting incident; the social revolution was the essential, portentous outcome.

To be sure the battles and campaigns of the epoch are significant to the military strategist; the tragedy and heroism of the contest furnish inspiration to patriots and romance to the makers of epics. But the core of the vortex lay elsewhere. It was in the flowing substance of things limned by statistical reports of finance, commerce, capital, industry, railways, and agriculture, by provisions of constitutional law, and by the pages of statute books—prosaic muniments which show that the so-called civil war was in reality a Second American Revolution and in a strict sense, the First.

The physical combat that punctuated the conflict merely hastened the inevitable. As was remarked at the time, the South was fighting against the census returns—census returns that told of accumulating industrial capital, multiplying captains of industry, expanding railway systems, widening acres tilled by free farmers. Once the planting and the commercial states, as the Fathers with faithful accuracy described them, had been evenly balanced; by 1860 the balance was gone.

. . . .

From the early days of November, 1860, to March 4, 1861, while planters prepared for the worst, the government at Washington drifted, helpless in the conflicting currents. According to the terms of the Constitution, Lincoln could not be inaugurated until the day lawfully appointed, and so for four critical months the Democratic party, which had been split wide by the campaign and defeated at the polls, continued to hold the reins of power. Its titular leader, President James Buchanan, had no popular mandate to deal with the question of secession. Nor had he any overmastering will of his own in the premises. Obviously bewildered by the stirring events taking place about him, he exclaimed in one breath that the southern states had no right to withdraw from the Union and in the next that he had no power to compel them to retain their allegiance. His Cabinet crumbled away, his host of advisers wrangled among themselves, and inaction seemed to him the better part of valor—at least it could be defended on the ground that nothing should be done to embarrass the incoming President.

On every side were heard the buzzing voices of politicians attempting to forecast the future, effect compromises, soothe angry passions. The Congress which assembled in December had no mandate from the election of the preceding month; the House had been chosen two years earlier and the Senate piecemeal over a period of six years. Congressmen were as perplexed as the President. To the public generally it seemed as if the solid earth were dissolving.

Southern residents of the capital were rapidly closing their houses and leaving for "their own country," most of them with confidence in coming events. Henry Watterson of Kentucky, who was on the ground, tells of a southern belle who drove away waving the Palmetto flag defiantly as her carriage rolled toward the blue hills of Virginia. She was a type of her class.

"She truly believed secession a constitutional right, slavery a divine institution. To her the mudsills of the North, as she dubbed them, were an inferior people. Cotton was king and she preferred a monarchy to a republic. If there should be any war at all, which was unlikely, it would be short-lived. Washington would become quickly the seat of the Confederate government. . . . All Europe would welcome the New Aristocracy of the South into the firmament of nations."

During the winter preceding Lincoln's inauguration the whole Washington scene was dismal beyond description. In an imperial system when Cæsar rides in state to the capitol, with unclouded brow and firm-set jaw, he spreads around him, no matter how great the perturbation of his inner spirit, an atmosphere of authority, stability, decision, and prescience. In the swirling democracy of Washington there was no Cæsar, though Sumner and Seward at least felt competent to steer the ship of state away from the rocks. Instead of Augustan assurance, confusion, difference of opinion, and uncertainty as to the outcome prevailed among the victorious Republicans. When it rained or snowed the unpaved streets of the uncouth city swam in mud; when they were dry the wintry winds swept clouds of dust up and down the thoroughfares—a physical condition that typified the mental atmosphere. The air was thick with gossip and opinion.

Amid the babel of tongues, presumably speaking for the North, only three clear notes were discernible: far to the left declaimed the professors of a simple doctrine—let the seceding states depart in peace; far to the right shouted the professors of immediate and unconditional coercion, with Sumner and Chase in the lead; in the middle were the conciliators and opportunists led by Seward, the former fireeating promoter of the irrepressible conflict. In the autobiography of Charles Francis Adams these anxious saviors of their country are represented as rushing to and fro in eager haste to be doing something. Charles Sumner, who did not take the Adams view of the dilemma, was "a crazy man, orating, gesticulating, rolling out deep periods in theatrical whispered tones—repeating himself and doing everything but reason." William H. Seward was always running in and out of the Senate, "the small, thin, shallow man, with the pale, wrinkled, strongly marked face—plain and imperturbable—the thick, guttural voice and the everlasting cigar," the Wellington of the picture, at Waterloo, praying in vain for night or Bluecher. In the White House, poor distraught Buchanan, he of "the wry neck and dubious eye," was wringing his hands, proclaiming the Union indissoluble, and himself unable to prevent it from dissolving. Meanwhile the unknown and unfathomable Lincoln "was perambulating the country, kissing little girls, and growing whiskers."

In that milling tumult, not one statesman foresaw the immediate future or read correctly the handwriting on the wall. Those oldest in experience and most learned in the arts and sciences of the schools turned out to be no wiser than the rough men of the frontier who stumbled and blundered along in the dim light of their conscience and understanding. All were caught up and whirled in a blast too powerful for their wills, too swift for their mental operations.

Even the safe inauguration of Lincoln and the straigtforward words of his first address made no immediate change in the situation. The new President took a positive stand on the nature of the Union: it was perpetual and no state could lawfully withdraw from it. He was equally firm in declaring that he would enforce the Constitution and the statutes against states that sought to violate or defy the law but his tone was conciliatory and he closed with a simple and moving appeal to sentiments of union, peace, and friendship.

Still these were merely spoken words which left the affairs of state exactly as they stood, great events continuing to wait on action, on the movement of federal authorities, on some overt physical stroke, on some outward manifestation of will and decision. Though on both sides hotheads clamored for bloodshed, all hesitated to make the fateful thrust that was to draw it. Day after day passed with the ship of state rolling erratically in the trough. April came and the warm spring sun seemed to beckon the nation to the pursuits of peace; dark clouds on the horizon looked dim and far away. In the White House, plagued by the horde of office-seekers hungry for jobs and by advisers swollen with infallibility, Lincoln wrestled with the multiplicity of minor questions permitting of decision.

Beyond all dispute Lincoln's problems in those tense days were stupendous. He spoke for a minority. He was no dictator standing for a triumphant majority and commissioned to carry out its appointed task. On the contrary he was aware, as southern planters were aware, that the North was torn by factions and he had no way of discovering how the bulk of his own party wanted him to act in the crisis. He knew that the anti-slavery sentiment in the country, though strong, was limited in its appeal; that, except in the hearts of the abolitionists, it was timid; that the Quakers who professed it were in general against emancipation by war.

Moreover abolitionists were divided on secession. Henry Ward Beecher, when informed that the southern states were withdrawing from the Union, burst forth: "I do not care if they do." Horace Greeley wrote in the Tribune: "If the cotton states shall decide that they can do better out of the Union than in it, we insist on letting them go in peace. The right to secede may be a revolutionary one but it exists nevertheless." It required events to drive that editor into the ranks of the coercionists.

Few, indeed, were the prophetic opponents of slavery who welcomed the test of battle and believed that the great solution of force foretold by John Quincy Adams was at hand. To no one except the fanatic was the issue simple. A wide belt of slave states had not seceded: a single utterance or act by Lincoln savoring of a war on slavery could have sent them all into the arms of the Confederacy. Nor could Lincoln count with certainty on undivided economic support above the Potomac. Ardently as they desired the preservation of the great customs union, northern business interests did not want war, save in the last bitter extremity. With respect to this problem Greeley estimated that southern debtors owed at least $200,000,000 to creditors in New York City alone, drawing from his figures the conclusion that a resort to arms meant general ruin in commercial circles. Unless human experience was as naught, the watchword of the solemn hour was Caution.

For good reasons, therefore, all practical men, including Jefferson Davis on the one side and Abraham Lincoln on the other, feverishly sought some middle ground of compromise. Speaking for eastern finance, Thurlow Weed, an Albany journalist and politician, who had done valiant work in carrying New York for the Republicans, proposed that the Missouri Compromise line be extended by common consent to the Pacific. Though this offer called for a partial surrender, Davis, warning his followers that a war would be terrible, expressed a willingness to accept the adjustment. But Lincoln stood rigid as a rock against it, pointing to his own pledges and to those of his party—promises to drive slavery from the territories. Eastern business men might bargain over the matter but the western farmers had decided that national lands must be dedicated to freedom and the President could not ignore their resolve. In Congress, Senator Crittenden of Kentucky proposed a compromise similar to that offered by Weed but Lincoln's followers could not be induced to support it.

On this point the fate of the nation seemed to turn. Lincoln was prepared to give any reasonable guarantee to the slave owners against interference with their peculiar institution as it stood. As evidence of his sincerity, he wrote to Alexander H. Stephens of Georgia, assuring the planters that the Republican administration would not "directly or indirectly interfere with their slaves or with them about their slaves;" that "the South would be in no more danger in this respect than it was in the days of Washington."

Not only that; Lincoln and his Republican brethren, offering proof of their readiness to seal the covenant forever, supported and carried through Congress an amendment to the Constitution declaring that for all the future the federal government should be denied the power to abolish or interfere with slavery in any state. On March 4, 1861, the resolution was sent forth to the states for their ratification, with Lincoln's approval, and three states had actually ratified it when the outbreak of physical combat stopped the operation. By the irony of fate, not the deliberate choice of men, the Thirteenth Amendment to the Constitution, when it finally came, was to abolish slavery in the United States, not to fasten it upon the continent to the end of time.

Why was the fatal blow that substituted armed might for negotiation ever struck? According to all outward and visible signs the opposing sections might have stood indefinitely in the posture of expectancy. Why did any one seek to break the spell? In whose brain, in the final analysis, was made the decision which directed the hand to light the powder train and blow up the wall of doubt that divided peace from war? No unanimous verdict on that point has yet been rendered by a court of last resort; one more question of war guilt remains unsolved.

It has been said that Lincoln, by deciding to send relief to Fort Sumter in the harbor of Charleston, splashed blood on his own head. The answer to such a thesis is that the relief sent to the beleaguered fort consisted mainly of provisions for a starving garrison and offered no direct menace to the Confederacy. It has been alleged that the inner leaders of the Confederacy, feeling the ground slipping from under them, thought bloodshed necessary to consolidate their forces and bring the hesitant states into their fold. The answer commonly made to this argument is that President Davis, in his final instructions to General Beauregard, commanding the Confederates at Charleston, spoke merely in general terms about the reduction of Sumter and advised action only if certain conditions of evacuation were rejected.

As a matter of fact, Major Anderson, in charge of Union forces, offered a compromise which should have been sent to Davis for review but Beauregard's aides, spurred on by an ardent secessionist from Virginia, made the decision on their own account in favor of audacity and at 4:30 on the morning of April 12, started the conflagration by firing on Fort Sumter. This bombardment and the surrender of the fort had just the effect foreseen by the extremists: the South, by striking the first blow and hauling down the Stars and Stripes, kindled the quivering opinion of the

North and a devouring flame. Lincoln's call for volunteers and answer of force by force pushed Virginia, North Carolina, Tennessee, and Arkansas into the Confederacy. The die was cast.

. . . .

All the passions of the war inevitably got into politics, giving intensity to emotions naturally bitter enough. The confederate administration, although it was not shaken from center to circumference by a presidential election in the midst of the conflict, was continually disturbed by dissenters. On every hand, doubters, and critics assailed the policies of the Richmond government, making the days of President Davis heavy with jarring discords and heedless abuse. Indeed recent historians, such as Frank L. Owsley and A. B. Moore, are inclined to attribute the final collapse of the Confederacy not so much to a failure of material goods as to a lack of support from state authorities, to evasions of the draft, and to discouragement among the masses; above and beyond everything, to the growing conviction among the southern farmers of the uplands that the confederate government was a slave owners' agency of power given to class favoritism, that the conflict was "a rich man's war and a poor man's fight," all the more poignantly evident when the draft laws exempted first the owners of at least twenty and then fifteen Negroes from military service on the ground of supervisory requirements.

No less trying perplexities vexed Lincoln to the day of his death. Constantly was he reminded that he was the leader of a minority. Democrats of all schools and Whigs of the old line who wanted to preserve the Constitution and maintain "business as usual" could not forget their partisan interests even when they cordially supported the Union. And many of them were aggressively hostile to the administration. Stephen A. Douglas did indeed pledge his allegiance to Lincoln at the opening of the war but death soon laid that masterful leader low, leaving no Democrat of equal power to succeed him as a unifying force.

Never for an instant was Lincoln allowed to forget politics, either by his followers or by his opponents. At the outset, he was simply besieged by office-seekers. "I seem like one sitting in a palace, assigning apartments to importunate applicants while the structure is on fire and likely soon to perish in ashes," he said in his direct way a short time after his inauguration; and until the last shadows fell, job hunters asking for places in the administration and in the army tormented his waking hours. Nearly every action, civil or military, had to be taken with reference to politics. Frémont was given a high position in the army, not for his talents, but to satisfy the radical Republicans who had once voted for him. Battles were fought and blood was shed with relation to election returns. And so the story ran. No matter what he did,

Lincoln came under the censure of editors who had no respect for the bounds of propriety. On one occasion, a New York paper went so far as to inquire: "Mr. Lincoln, has he or has he not an interest in the profits of public contracts?" and then without giving any evidence, answered its own query in the affirmative. Members of his Cabinet esteemed him lightly and thought themselves far wiser than he; one of them, Chase, Secretary of the Treasury, thought it not unworthy of his honor to carry on a lively backstairs campaign to wrest the presidency from Lincoln in 1864.

Attacked on all sides, Lincoln held true to his central idea of saving the Union and when the end of his first term arrived the Republicans decided that they would not "swap horses while crossing a stream." Taking the name Union Party as their title, they renominated Lincoln for President and selected as his associate a southern man, a Unionist from Tennessee, Andrew Johnson. Having to meet this call for an endorsement of the administration, northern Democrats, in their platform, denounced the war as a failure, advocated an immediate peace, and favored a restoration of the federal system—with slavery as before. Choosing as their candidate, General McClellan, who was in their eyes "a military hero," they tried to carry the country by means of drum and trumpet, expedients that had so often brought victory in the past. The appeal and the array of strength were ominous, especially as McClellan took the sting out of his platform by saying that he could not look his soldiers in the face and pronounce the war a failure.

But the answer of the people at the polls was decisive. The Republicans, besides reelecting Lincoln, returned enough Senators and Representatives to force Congress to adopt the [Thirteenth] Amendment abolishing slavery forever within the jurisdiction of the United States. The war was to go on, therefore, until peace could be won by the sword. Thus the voters vindicated the great mystic in the White House, disclosing as if by some subtle instinct the fateful mission of their generation.

At this distant day it is difficult to discern the man Lincoln through the clouds of myth that surrounded him or to imagine what his status in history would have been had the war ended in defeat or had he lived through the reconstruction scandals and the malodorous frauds of the gilded age. If we look at him through the letters and diaries of the men associated with his administration in the early days of the war, we certainly see a person far removed from the picture of the neat bourgeois which Ida Tarbell has drawn. Taking as authoritative the testimony of men like Sumner, Chase, Seward, and Charles Francis Adams, Lincoln displayed a lack of sensibilities, an uncouthness of manner, and a coarse jocularity that were shocking to persons of taste two or three generations removed from the soil. He told tales none too elegant for chaste ears. "An ignorant Western boor," sniffed a hostile New York editor.

His pictures reveal him as a tall, lanky, homely, awkward countryman.

And yet the severest of his critics was arrested by something impelling about the personality of Lincoln—something transcending the roughness of the frontier. In his face during repose, in his glance, in his messages and decisions, lay proof that he "knew the sadness of things," as the Japanese would say. It was his nature to temper official words and deeds with moderation. He was in very fact President of the United States in a tragic hour, measuring up in full length to his Augustan authority and responsibility. When the more cultured Seward proposed to act with churlish rudeness in foreign relations, Lincoln softened his caustic notes by words of wisdom. While men like Adams who could boast of education and refinement were cocksure that they could avoid war and save the Union, Lincoln was the soul of modesty. If politicians besieged him with their personal bickerings, he tried to draw them to high ground by fixing their attention on the main challenge of the moment. He never heedlessly turned a deaf ear to the plea of mercy. When he addressed the country through a message to Congress, wrote a letter to a mother who had given her sons to the supreme sacrifice, or made a speech dedicating a battlefield, he emphasized great issues, offered wise counsel, revealed the "deathless music" of his spirit. In all things, however, he was practical, watching the strategy of the war with the eyes of a hawk and giving advice at every crucial point.

Notwithstanding the elusive phases of his character, Lincoln was an astute politician rather than an idealist or a doctrinaire. He was made the "Emancipator" by circumstances and expediency rather than by his own initiative. When it became necessary to traffic in petty jobs to get votes with which to carry the Thirteenth Amendment abolishing slavery, he made use of the tools of the trade. He never invited the purist's doom by flying in the face of organized society but he had the good sense to grasp the inexorable by the forelock. With a resignation that seemed to betray a belief in the philosophy of history cherished by Bishop Bossuet, he wrote in the spring of 1864: "I claim not to have controlled events but confess plainly that events have controlled me. Now at the end of three years' struggle, the nation's condition is not what either party or any man devised or expected. God alone can claim it. Whither it is tending seems plain." It was fate that gave Lincoln the martyr's crown and the good fortune of being justified by events. He steered the ship of state with the gale, not against it, and it was one of the ironies of historic destiny that he was assassinated, on April 14, 1865, as the spokesman of the triumphant cause for which Wendell Phillips and William Lloyd Garrison had defied mobs and courted the fate of Lovejoy.

. . . .

While the planting class was being trampled in the dust—stripped of its wealth and political power—the capitalist class was marching onward in seven league boots. Under the feverish stimulus of war the timid army marshaled by Webster in support of the Constitution and Whig policies had been turned into a confident host, augmented in numbers by the thousands and tens of thousands who during the conflict made profits out of war contracts and out of the rising prices of manufactured goods. At last the economic structure of machine industry towered high above agriculture—a grim monument to the fallen captain, King Cotton. Moreover, the bonds and notes of the federal government, issued in its extremity, furnished the substance for still larger business enterprise. And the beneficent government, which had carefully avoided laying drastic imposts upon profits during the war, soon afterward crowned its generosity to capitalists by abolishing the moderate tax on incomes and shifting the entire fiscal burden to goods consumed by the masses.

To measurable accumulations were added legal gains of high economic value. All that two generations of Federalists and Whigs had tried to get was won within four short years, and more besides. The tariff, which the planters had beaten down in 1857, was restored and raised to the highest point yet attained. A national banking system was established to take the place of the institution abolished in 1811 by Jeffersonian Democracy and the second institution destroyed by Jacksonian Democracy in 1836. At the same time the policy of lavish grants from the federal treasury to aid internal improvements so necessary to commerce was revived in the form of imperial gifts to railway corporations; it was in the year of emancipation that the construction of the Pacific railway, opening the overland route to the trade of the Orient, was authorized by the Congress of the United States. With similar decisiveness, the federal land question which had long vexed eastern manufacturers was duly met; the Homestead Act of 1862, innumerable grants to railways, and allotments to the states in aid of agricultural colleges provided for the disposal of the public domain. As a counter stroke, the danger of higher wages, threatened by the movement of labor to the land, was partially averted by the Immigration Act of 1864—an extraordinary law which gave federal authorization to the importation of working people under terms of contract analogous to the indentured servitude of colonial times.

While all these positive advantages were being won by capitalists in the halls of Congress, steps were taken to restrain the state legislatures which had long been the seats of agrarian unrest. By the Fourteenth Amendment, proclaiming that no state should deprive any person of life, liberty or property without due process of law, the Supreme Court at Washington was granted constitutional power to strike down any act of any state or local government menacing to "sound" business policies. Finally the crowning result of the sacrifice, the salvation of the Union, with which so many lofty sentiments were justly associated, assured to industry an immense national market surrounded by a tariff wall bidding defiance to the competition of Europe.

Since this view of the so-called "Civil War" or "War between the States" will appear novel to many, it seems desirable to reinforce it by some illustrative details. First of all a word may be said on the methods employed by the federal government in financing the war—methods which served to increase the amount of fluid capital in private hands. As we have noted, the profitable principle was adopted that the generation which directed the war should not bear the main burden of paying for it. At the very start, the Secretary of the Treasury took the position that there should be no extraordinary taxes except to meet the interest on the new loans and redeem a small part of the debt annually; so the first year of the war saw loans amounting to nearly half a billion dollars and no material increase in taxation. Later this easy-going philosophy was modified; taxes were increased in all directions; and an income tax running as high as ten percent on incomes above five thousand dollars was imposed; but at the close of the conflict it was found that in the operation the government had floated loans to the amount of $2,621,000,000 and collected from various sources taxes totaling only the sum of $667,000,000.

Although the bonds issued from time to time varied greatly in their stipulations, according to the prospects of ultimate success which seemed to lie before the Union cause, their provisions were seldom ungenerous to the money lenders. Often the rate of interest ran to seven per cent, occasionally slightly higher. In some cases certain depreciated Greenbacks were received in exchange for bonds payable, interest and principal, in gold, thus giving the holder two or three times the rate of annual return nominally written in the contract. As always, necessity was the mother of policy: the exigencies of the federal government were great; the risks incurred by money-lenders were serious though time proved their faith well justified; and in its distress the federal treasury had to deal gently with its creditors. If the Union had been dissolved their losses would have been overwhelming; as things turned out, their earnings were immense.

Industry as well as finance had its reward in the Second American Revolution. The armed conflict, the withdrawal of southern members of Congress, and the demand for revenue enabled the advocates of the high protective tariff to push through measure after measure and to fasten their system upon the nation so tightly that it was not even shaken for nearly half a century. Until the eve of the war the doctrine of free trade, or rather of tariff for revenue only, had been steadily gaining under southern leadership; suddenly this process was completely reversed. When secession came, the cotton planters, long the bulwark of low duties or no duties, passed from the picture; an enormous economic power exercised against protection was shattered.

Relieved of heavy pressure from this quarter, the protectionists, now firmly in the saddle, were able to frame tariff bills primarily designed to afford advantages to industries. Even after the federal government had been at war for many months and the treasury was on the brink of bankruptcy, customs schedules were still drawn up mainly with reference to protection rather than revenue. At no time was the issue lost to sight as Congress ground out act after act with mechanical regularity. In the operation the general average of tariff rates was raised from about nineteen per cent as fixed by the measure of 1857 to forty-seven per cent in the law of 1864. Futhermore when it was found that other internal taxes bore heavily upon manufacturers, "proper reparation" was made in the form of higher and countervailing tariff duties. The demands of the war gave excellent justification for the inevitable. There were protests from some agricultural districts—echoes of former days—but there were no longer any powerful southern planters to direct the low-tariff hosts and turn the engines of the federal government against the spokesmen of machine industries.

That other great requirement of business enterprise—the national banking system—was also scrutinized by the politicians during the storm of the war. As as matter of prosaic fact, in those dark and trying days, the statesmen of sound money found a chance to return to the policies which had been so ruthlessly discarded by Jacksonian Democracy. When the Republicans came to power in 1861, local banks, either managed or chartered by states, possessed the field, having in circulation seven thousand kinds of paper notes, to say nothing of more than five thousand varieties of counterfeit and fraudulent issues.

Viewed in any light, the confusion was unendurable to Secretary Chase, long a foe of all agrarian devices, especially of easy money; and soon after his installation in the Treasury Department he took up the problem of ending the financial chaos. In the first year of his service, he recommended to Congress the establishment of a new national banking system; and, when he was defeated on the merits of his case, he made full use of the opportunity presented by the necessity of selling war bonds, wringing from Congress at last the national banking act of 1863. By express terms, this law authorized the formation of local banking associations under federal authority and empowered them to emit notes on the basis of United States bonds up to ninety per cent of the par value. In other words, a local bank could buy federal securities, receive interest from the government on its holdings, and then issue on the strength of those securities paper bills to be lent to borrowers at the current discount.

Having driven this wedge into the system of local currency and hav-

ing attracted the support of powerful banks by favorable terms, the party
of sound money completed its program in 1865 by carrying through Congress an act which imposed a tax of ten percent on all state bank notes,
absolutely wiping them out by a single stroke. In this fashion sweeping
designs, which neither Clay nor Webster had been able to accomplish by
oratory in days of peace, Republican leaders effected by arrangement during the pressing time of war. When southern statesmen returned to the
Union after the curtain was rung down on the battlefield, they found the
national banking system intrenched in the financial structure of the
nation.

But capital, no matter how enormous or carefully buttressed by tariffs
and sound finance, was helpless without an adequate labor supply—a
plain economic truth well known to the industrial members of the Republican party. Their forerunners, the Federalists, had understood that;
Hamilton, in his Report on Manufacturers in 1791, had spoken about the
necessity of drawing upon Europe in addition to native sources for labor
to operate the machinery set in motion by tariffs. His Whig successors
often emphasized the point.

Continuing the refrain, the Republicans, known temporarily as the
Union party, declared in their platform of 1864 that "foreign immigration, which in the past has added so much to the wealth, the development
of resources, and the increase of power to this nation—the asylum of the
oppressed of all nations—should be fostered and encouraged by a liberal
and just policy." Responding to the new demand that every year Congress incorporated the policy in law by creating a bureau of immigration
and, as pointed out, authorizing a modified form of indentured labor
which permitted the importation of workers bound for a term of service.
Though the latter feature of the law was soon repealed, the corresponding
practice was long continued, eastern capitalists bringing in laborers from
Europe under contract and western railway builders drawing upon the
inexhaustible supplies of the Orient.

To the cry of survivors from the Know-Nothing faction that the old
Anglo-Saxon stock was being diluted and submerged, the champions of
free immigration answered that America was the asylum of the oppressed.
So it was—and incidentally the coming of the oppressed augmented the
earnings of stockholders and land speculators tremendously. Thus light
and shadow continued to play down the ages.

While winning its essential economic demands in the federal sphere,
the party of industrial progress and sound money devoted fine calculation
to another great desideratum—the restoration and extension of federal
judicial supremacy over the local legislature which had been so trouble-
some since the age of Daniel Shays. Restoration was heartily desired because the original limitations imposed by the Constitution on the power

of the state to issue money and impair contracts had been practically destroyed by adroit federal judges imbued with the spirit of Jacksonian Democracy. An extension of federal control was perhaps more heartily desired because, for nationalists of the Federalist and Whig tradition, those limitations had been pitifully inadequate even when applied strictly by Chief Justice Marshall—inadequate to meet the requirements of individuals and corporations that wanted to carry on their business in their own way, immune from legislative interference.

In all this there was nothing esoteric. Among conservative adepts in federal jurisprudence the need for more efficient judicial protection has been keenly felt for some time; and when the problem of defining the rights of Negroes came before Congress in the form of a constitutional amendment, experts in such mysteries took advantage of the occasion to enlarge the sphere of national control over the states, by including among the safeguards devised for Negroes a broad provision for the rights of all "persons," natural and artificial, individual and corporate.

Their project was embodied in the second part of the Fourteenth Amendment in the form of a short sentence intended by the man who penned it to make a revolution in the federal Constitution. The sentence reads: "No state shall make or enforce any law which shall abridge the privileges or immunities of citizens of the United States; nor shall any state deprive any person of life, liberty, or property without due process of law, or deny to any person within its jurisdiction the equal protection of the laws."

Just how this provision got into the draft of the Fourteenth Amendment was not generally known at the time of its adoption but in after years the method was fully revealed by participants in the process. By the end of the century an authentic record, open to all, made the operation as plain as day. According to the evidence now available, there were two factions in the congressional committee which framed the Amendment—one bent on establishing the rights of Negroes; the other determined to take in the whole range of national economy. Among the latter was a shrewd member of the House of Representatives, John A. Bingham, a prominent Republican and a successful railroad lawyer from Ohio familiar with the possibilities of jurisprudence; it was he who wrote the mysterious sentence containing the "due process" clause in the form in which it now stands; it was he who finally forced it upon the committee by persistent efforts.

In a speech delivered in Congress a few years later, Bingham explained his purpose in writing it. He had read, he said, in the case of Barron *versus* the Mayor and Council of Baltimore, how the city had taken private property for public use, as alleged without compensation, and how Chief Justice Marshall had been compelled to hold that there was no redress in the Supreme Court of the United States—no redress simply because the first ten Amendments to the Constitution were limitations on Congress, not on the states. Deeming this hiatus a grave legal defect in the work of the Fathers, Bingham designed "word for word and syllable for syllable" the cabalistic clause of the Fourteenth Amendment in order, he asserted, that "the poorest man in his hovel . . . may be as secure in his person and property as the prince in his palace or the king upon his throne." Hence the provision was to apply not merely to former slaves struggling for civil rights but to all persons, rich and poor, individuals and corporations, under the national flag.

Long afterward Roscoe Conkling, the eminent corporation lawyer of New York, a colleague of Bingham on the congressional committee, confirmed this view. While arguing a tax case for a railway company before the Supreme Court in 1882, he declared that the protection of freedmen was by no means the sole purpose of the Fourteenth Amendment. "At the time the Fourteenth Amendment was ratified," he said, "individuals and joint stock companies were appealing for congressional and administrative protection against invidious and discriminating state and local taxes. . . . That complaints of oppression in respect of property and other rights made by citizens of northern states who took up residence in the South were rife in and out of Congress, none of us can forget. . . . Those who devised the Fourteenth Amendment wrought in grave sincerity. . . . They planted in the Constitution a monumental truth to stand four square to whatever wind might blow. That truth is but the golden rule, so entrenched as to curb the many who would do to the few as they would not have the few do to them."

In this spirit, Republican lawmakers restored to the Constitution the protection for property which Jacksonian judges had whittled away and made it more sweeping in its scope by forbidding states, in blanket terms, to deprive any person of life, liberty, or property without due process of law. By a few words skillfully chosen every act of every state and local government which touched adversely the rights of persons and property was made subject to review and liable to annulment by the Supreme Court at Washington, appointed by the President and Senate for life and far removed from local feelings and prejudices.

Although the country at large did not grasp the full meaning of the Fourteenth Amendment while its adoption was pending, some far-sighted editors and politicians realized at the time that it implied a fundamental revolution in the Constitution, at least as interpreted by Chief Justice Taney. Ohio and New Jersey Democrats, reckoning that it would make the Supreme Court at Washington the final arbiter in all controversies over the powers of local governments, waged war on it, carrying the fight into the state legislatures and forcing the repeal of resolutions approving the Amendment even after they had been duly sealed. As a matter of course all the southern states were still more fiercely opposed to the Amendment but they were compelled to ratify it under federal military authority as the price of restoration to the Union. Thus the triumphant Republican minority, in possession of the federal government and the military power, under the sanction of constitutional forms, subdued the states for all time to the unlimited jurisdiction of the federal Supreme Court.

While business enterprise received its share of the advantages accruing from the Second American Revolution, other elements in the combination of power effected in 1860—namely the free farmers of the West and the radical reformers of the East—also had their rewards. On the outbreak of the war, their old opponents on the land question were no longer in a position to dictate. The planters of the South were out of the political lists and northern mill owners, who had feared that free farms would lure away wage-workers, were shown the possibilities of a counterpoise in the promotion of alien immigration. If some were unconvinced by such reasoning, they could at least see that the agrarian element in the Republican party was too strong to be thwarted by the business wing. So eventually in 1862 the hard contest over the public domain came to an end with the passage of the Homestead Act which provided for the free distribution of land in lots of one hundred and sixty acres each to men and women of strong arms and willing hearts, prepared to till the soil. In this action, the appealing slogan, "Vote yourself a farm," was realized and before the ink of Lincoln's signature was dry the rush to the free land commenced.

To northern farmers who had no thought of going to the frontier, the war likewise brought marked advantages. Especially did the Mississippi Valley, former home of agrarian discontent and Jacksonian Democracy, reap immense gains in inflated prices paid for farm produce, in spite of the mounting cost of manufactured goods. At one time wheat rose to more than two dollars and a half a bushel and other commodities followed its flight. From overflowing coffers debt-burdened tillers of the soil who had once raged against the money-power now discharged their obligations in Greenback "legal tenders" received for the fruits of their labor. The more fortunate farmers collected large returns from rising land values, accumulated capital, and became stockholders in local railway and banking enterprises. For many years a prosperous farming class, tasting the sweets of profit, could look upon the new course of politics and pronounce it good. There was discontent, no doubt, and a reaction against industrialism was bound to come but the political union of 1860, though strained, was never successfully broken.

Bibliography

Beale, Howard K., ed. *Charles A. Beard. An Appraisal.* Lexington, Ky., 1954.

Beard, Charles A. "Written History as an Art of Faith." *American Historical Review,* 39 (January 1934): 219–29.

Benson, Lee. *Turner and Beard: American Historical Writing Reconsidered.* Glencoe, Ill., 1960.

Borning, Bernard C. *The Political and Social Thought of Charles A. Beard.* Seattle, Wash., 1962.

Higham, John. Leonard Krieger, and Felix Gilbert. *History.* Princeton, N.J., 1965.

Hofstadter, Richard. *The Progressive Historians: Turner, Beard and Parrington.* New York, 1968.

McDonald, Forrest. "Charles A. Beard." In *Pastmasters: Some Essays on American Historians,* edited by Marcus Cunliffe and Robin W. Winks. New York, 1969.

Nore, Ellen. *Charles A. Beard: An Intellectual Biography.* Carbondale, Ill., 1983.

Strout, Cushing. *The Pragmatic Revolt in American History: Carl Becker and Charles Beard.* New Haven, Conn., 1959.

CHAPTER 18

Lucien Febvre
"The Silhouette of a Civilization"
(1925)

For many scholars, twentieth-century historical writing came down to two choices, both of them inherited from the nineteenth century. One was historicism, which stressed the unique, unrepeatable, and incomparable in history; the other was history conceived as a social science, which argued for uniformities and even laws of human experience across the years and centuries. Historicism[1] was an outgrowth of Leopold von Ranke's thinking (see Chapter 11) and social science history, sometimes called nomological (oriented around laws), owed much to the influence of Auguste Comte (1798–1857), the French sociologist who assumed human experience could be understood in the same way as the phenomena of chemistry or physics.

The essay reprinted here represents the historicist view, but its author, Lucien Febvre (1878–1956), was such a commanding figure in mid-twentieth-century historiography that merely calling him an historicist badly understates the range of his thinking and influence. Indeed, as Georg Iggers has pointed out, by seeking the middle ground between extremes, Febvre and his "Annalist school" found a way out of the dichotomy. For while, on one hand, he and his colleagues were trained in the Rankean historicist tradition and Febvre spent a lifetime attacking anachronism as the cardinal sin of historical writing, on the other hand, his own works discovered patterns within discrete eras and recognized long-term continuities like geography and mental states as shaping influences. In the end, however, what Febvre wrote himself was less important than what he encouraged others to write and how. His editorship of the *Annales d' histoire economique et sociale*[2] placed him in a position to change the direction of French historiography for generations to come.

Febvre was born to a cultured family in Nancy, capital of Lorraine. He was educated partly in his father's library, where he found and began a lifelong admiration for the histories of Jules Michelet (see chapter 13), and partly in lycées that prepared him for advanced studies at the Ećole Normale Supérieur. He completed his doctoral dissertation in 1911, pointing the way, in his study of sixteenth-century Franche-Comté, to a new history that analyzed the economic, social, and geographical "structures" that underlay a given historical culture and made it unique. Febvre was influenced in his multidisciplinary approach by Henri Berr, whose *Revue de Synthése* (1900 ff.) was a colloquium among scholars in various social fields. By 1929, when Febvre and the great medievalist, Marc Bloch, founded the *Annales,* the Annalist school would move others further in the cooperative direction and attempt to establish history as the field that presided over all the others.

Febvre taught at the universities of Dijon and Strasbourg and in 1933 accepted the chair in history of the Collége de France. He was conscious that Jules Michelet had once held that post and that, like Michelet, who had used geography and folklore to broaden the scope of history, he, too, must encourage an expanded definition of history. By that time he had already written *A Geographical Introduction to History* (1922) and a psychological study of Martin Luther (1929). In 1942 he published his greatest work, *The Problem of Unbelief in the 16th Century,* which, from a radically historicist point of view, showed that the twentieth-century characterization of the French satirist François Rabelais as an atheist was anachronistic. The intellectual and psychological mode of addressing the idea of God in the sixteenth century simply did not admit the possibility of atheism, which was a modern concept.

Febvre died in 1956, leaving generations of students with memories of his conversations, his long "letters of guidance," and the sense that, as his colleague Fernand Braudel put it, he had been their intellectual "banker."

Braudel, one of the most famous Annalists after Febvre, continued his mentor's study of the semipermanent structures, like geography, which, if they did not determine, at least limited the range of possibilities in economic and social life. Yet Braudel's sense of the very long persistence of such structures implicitly challenged the historicist insistence on the uniqueness of historical cultures. Another Annalist, Emmanuel LeRoy Ladurie, seemed in the 1960s to define history as statistics or data that could be "quantified" to reveal the underlying structures of an era, leaving out altogether the historicists concerned with the experience of unique people as well as their circumstances. But his *Carnival at Romains* (1979) and *Montaillou, the Promised Land of Error* (1975) saw him allow the voices of people to speak once again.

Notes

1. The development and definition of "historicism" is a two-hundred-year old tangle. It began with Leopold von Ranke (chapter 11), whose own experience and reading of Giambattista Vico, the eighteenth-century humanist, taught him to emphasize development and individuality in human history in contrast to the Enlightenment's belief in human nature as fixed and stable in all places at all times. Society was genetic, events were unique, and, said Ranke, the sole guide to understanding them was a sympathetic reading of the documents—carefully verified for authenticity—a given society produced.

These ideas were developed by Wilhelm Dilthey (1894, 1910), Friedrich Meinecke (1936), Benedetto Croce (1893, 1917), and R. G. Collingwood (1946) among others, who, if they disagreed with each other on some points, believed nonetheless that history concerned development and individuality and stressed the historian's imaginative understanding of documents. Collingwood, in *The Idea of History* (1946), contended that one must try to recreate in one's own mind the thoughts of whoever produced a letter or diary. And if Ranke had rebelled against the eighteenth century's sense of stability in human nature, these later historicists defended *their* ideas against nineteenth-century positivism, the idea that events in both natural and social sciences could be known and externally studied by an observer and that patterns and laws could be derived from such observation. Positivism aimed at abolishing the historicist distinction between nomothetic, or "law oriented" studies, and idiographic, or "individual oriented" studies.

In America, confusion as to the meaning of historicism arose when scholars stressed only the source criticism of Ranke and read too much into Ranke's famous dictum that history could be written *"wie es eigentlich gewesen"* ("as it actually happened"). Americans, like Charles Beard, for example, forgot Ranke's stress on the unique and the historian's intuitive understanding of documents and rejected him and his "historicism" as though he were a positivist, which, of course, neither he nor the later historicists were. Beard's own sense that an historian's ideas must be understood as relative to the time and circumstance in which they arise is an obvious extension of the basic tenets of real historicism, though he seemed unaware of it.

More confusion came from Karl Popper, whose *Poverty of Historicism* (1957) rejected the concept as though it meant "determinist." Popper championed the unique and unpredictable in history—in other words, historicism.

See the following key articles: Dwight E. Lee and Robert N. Beck, "The Meaning of Historicism," *American Historical Review,* 19 (April 1954): 568–77; Calvin G. Rand, "Two Meanings of Historicism in the Writings of Dilthey, Troeltsch, and Meinecke," *Journal of the History of Ideas,* 25 (October–December 1964): 503–18; Georg G. Iggers, "The Image of Ranke in American and German Historical Thought," *History and Theory,* 2 (1962): 17–40. Some classic works very much worth reading are Wilhelm Dilthey, *Pattern and Meaning in History,* edited and introduced by H. P. Rickman (New York, 1962); R. G. Collingwood, *The Idea of History* (Oxford, 1946); and Friedrich Meinecke, *Historicism: The Rise of a New Historical Outlook,* translated by J. E. Anderson (London, 1972).

2. Changed in 1946 to *Annales, Economique, Societes, Civilizations.*

L ITTRÉ, IN HIS DICTIONARY of 1873, calls civilization "the condition of that which is civilized; it is the body of opinions and customs formed by the interaction of technology, religion, arts and sciences." Civilization is a product: the product of moral, material, intellectual, and religious forces acting on the human consciousness in a given place and at a given time. Littré, in spite of the inelegance of his own definition, would certainly agree. Holding firmly to this idea, we shall in the pages to come by no

means attempt to examine or reconstruct "the body of opinions and customs" on which a society as varied and alive as that of early Renaissance
France was based. Nor shall we imitate the bustling host who does not let
his Sunday visitors leave before he has shown them every rabbit in the
hutch and each and every cabbage in the patch. We shall limit ourselves
to essentials, to what was truly characteristic of the highest and most original parts of that civilization which we still admire today. We shall seek
out all that which best defines the highest aspirations and commitments
of the people of that time, the people who lived through and made the
Renaissance, Humanism, and the Reformation, their strivings after
Knowledge, Beauty, and God. That will be the subject of this study.

All those admirable efforts share a common ground: man's image of
himself. History is the study of man. In his glorious *Introduction,* Michelet
congratulates himself for having given history so fine and firm a basis: the
earth. He was quite right. But on that foundation, as stable as it is varied,
we must set men. Renaissance, Humanism, Reformation are not mere abstractions, personifications wandering over the heavens where the Chi-
mera chases Transcendent Ideals. To understand these great changes we
must recreate for ourselves the habits of mind of the people who brought
them about.

Were those minds like our minds? I know that man's essential nature
is unchanging through time and space. I know that old tune. But that is
an assumption, and I might add, a worthless assumption for a historian.
For him, as for the geographer, as we have had occasion to remark earlier,
man does not exist, only men. His efforts are directed toward discerning
the particular originality, the distinguishing marks, all that in which and
by which those men differed from us, men who did not live or feel or behave as we do.

The men of the early sixteenth century must be the object of our attention if we wish to try to understand what the Renaissance was, what
the Reformation was. It would be an impossible task to try to "recreate"
them, to build them up into their real unity, an impossible task and an
unnecessary one. Let us be less ambitious. By way of introduction it
should be enough to evoke them, projecting onto the screen of our imaginations some typical silhouettes. Looking at these images now will prove
helpful later when, having seen, we try to understand.

Twentieth-century man, the Frenchman of the twentieth century,
can be defined in many ways, but essentially, taken in terms of his physical existence, his material life, three points stand out: he is urban, seden-

Reprinted by permission of the publisher. From Lucien Febvre, *Life in Renaissance France,* edited and
translated by Marian Rothstein (Cambridge, Mass. and London: Harvard University Press, 1977),
1–23. Copyright © 1977 by the President and Fellows of Harvard College.

tary, and refined. We are urban, living an urban life in the city, the modern big city which is not merely a place where there is a greater agglomeration of people more densely packed than elsewhere, but a place where man is not the same as elsewhere. Age distribution, for example, is not the same in the city as in the country. Proportionally there are fewer children and fewer old people than adults, who, having spent their childhood elsewhere, often leave the city in retirement, adults who come to the city to spend the strength of their youth and their maturity. All ties between us and the land have been broken, except perhaps for a short time during vacations. The land seen through urban eyes is a place of rest and relaxation and beauty rather than hard physical labor.

We are sedentary. We may talk much about travel and go rushing about by car or by plane; that is only further proof of our need to be sedentary. The ever-increasing speed of such machines, their flexibility, their ease of access, in fact, the comfort they provide, make it possible for us to take long trips without ever really leaving home. How rare it is nowadays to find the ordinary man more than two or three days' journey from his home.

Man has become urban, sedentary, and refined as well. What a large place the word "comfort" has come to occupy in our language, modern comfort in which we take such pride. What implications the word has, of convenience and material ease: a light turned on or off at the flick of a finger, an indoor temperature independent of the seasons, water ready to flow hot or cold, as we wish, anytime, anywhere. All these, and a thousand other marvels as well, fail to astonish us. Yet they affect the physical temper of our bodies, help us to avoid certain diseases and make us prey to others. They influence our work habits, our leisure time, our customs and conventions, and all the ways of thinking and feeling which are the result of these things. Can we really claim then that they are merely exterior, merely accident, not worth noting or discussing? We are tied to all this technology, it has a hold on us, it makes us serve it, odd, rooted spirits as we are. We are slaves three times over to the insatiable hungers we ourselves have created. In that sense, the men of the sixteenth century were free.

I

The people who lived in the sixteenth century, in the France of Charles VIII, of Louis XII, of François I, were not urban; they lived on the land. There were no big cities in the modern sense of the word. It is true that foreigners, and the French themselves, sang the praises of their cities. They spoke of Paris as one of the wonders of the world. Yet what were these cities really like? We see the sixteenth-century city laid out before us in old prints, in cosmographies, in collections of maps: Munster, Belleforest, Antoine du Pinet, Braun and Hogenberg. The city lay surrounded by crenelated walls, flanked by round towers. A sunken road led to the narrow gate protected by a drawbridge guarded night and day by watchful soldiers. To the right, a crude cross. Straight ahead on a hill top, a huge gibbet, pride of the citizens, where the bodies of hanged men were left to mummify. Often over the gate, impaled on a spike, hung a head or an arm or a leg, some hideous slice of human flesh carved by the hangman: justice at work in a thick-skinned society.

The sunken road leading to the gate was muddy. Past the gate the street widened as it followed a capricious route through the town. A filthy stream ran down its center, fed by rivulets of liquid manure seeping from nearby manure heaps. It was a muddy slough in the rain, a desert of choking dust in the heat of the sun, in which urchins, ducks, chickens, and dogs, even pigs in spite of repeated edicts to control them, all wallowed together.

Entering the city we see that each family has its own house, as in the country. As in the country, each house has a garden behind it, where boxwood borders mark out the vegetable patches. And again as in the country life, each house has an attic with a window for raising and storing hay, straw, grain, and all kinds of winter provisions. Each house has its oven where the mistress and the female servants bake every week. Each house has its press near the cellar, filled every October with the fumes of new wine. Finally, each house has its stable and saddle and draft horses, and its barn with cows and oxen and sheep, led away in the morning when the neighborhood shepherd blows his horn, and brought home again in the evening.

The city was permeated by the country. The country even penetrated into the houses. The city man received his country tenants in his home, peasants who came periodically, bringing their master what his land had produced, laying baskets heavy with their rustic bounty on the polished tiles of the floor. The lawyer received his clients in his study, their arms filled with hares and rabbits, chicken or ducks. The country penetrated city bedrooms in the summertime when the floor was strewn with flowers or leaves and the unused fireplaces were filled with greenery to keep the rooms cool and sweetsmelling. In the winter the floor tiles were covered with a thick layer of country straw to help keep men and animals warm. The country made its presence felt even in everyday language, which was filled with allusions to the fields. Seasons began with the singing of the cricket, the blooming of the violet, the ripening of the wheat. The city, filled with orchards, gardens, and green trees, was nothing but a slightly more densely populated countryside. Life there was scarcely more rushed or more complex than in the villages. The city had no hold on its inhabitants.

II

The great majority of people did not live in cities. Nor were all those who lived on the land peasants. All the noblemen of France in those days had homes in the country. Some of them lived in chateaux, often admirable buildings. But let us turn away for a moment from the classical facades, the sculptures, the finely carved marble, and look instead at these fine houses with the eye of a prospective tenant. Each room leads to the next, all huge, all monotonously square: a wall in front, a wall behind, windows in the left wall, windows in the right. To go from one end of the house to the other, one must pass in turn through all the rooms in the series. This was not only the case in France. In his diverting *Memoirs*, Benvenuto Cellini explains the rather colorful origin of the disfavor in which he tells us he was held by the Grand Duchess of Tuscany. When Cosimo dei Medici in his palace in Florence sent for his favorite sculptor, Benvenuto Cellini had to drop whatever he was doing and rush to his master. Quickly, nearly running, he would burst through the door and climb the stairs. On his way to see the Duke he would go from room to room, crossing each in turn. But these rooms were not all merely ceremonial chambers; there were also private ones, even very private ones used by the Grand Duchess herself. And from time to time it happened that these rooms were not empty when he passed through them, so that the artist was forced, in passing, to bow before some noble and powerful person whose attention at that moment was fully occupied with other things, and to whom the sudden appearance of the artist in these most private apartments must have seemed highly disagreeable. But Cellini had no choice; the Grand Duke was waiting and this was the only possible route.

That took place in Florence, in the Uffizi, in Florence which by comparison with France at the same time was a model of delicacy and refinement. Now consider what the real level of comfort in the French chateau must have been. For one thing, people must have lived through the winter shivering, their teeth chattering. We may admire the huge fireplaces which sometimes extend over the whole of one wall of the great square rooms, and we are quite right to do so. We are in a position to admire them, standing as tourists in the chateau where central heating has since been installed. In the sixteenth century they were also admired, but the people who did so kept their fur-lined coats and their warm hats on. In vain did an army of woodcarriers bring in load after load of branches and logs to be added to fire after fire. All the brightly burning (or smoking) fireplaces of Chambord or Blois would not meet the requirements of us modern sybarites. Far from the fire it was freezing; and when the flames crackled and rose, close to the fire it was hot enough to fry you. People were cold, always cold, even inside their homes.

Their homes were simply an extension of the countryside, without the sharp contrast of home's welcoming warmth. Can we really believe that the ideas of such people about home and hearth, about the family, would be the same as those held today by people drunk with warmth, slaves to central heating? Now try for a moment to imagine modern man without any ideas or feelings about his house, his home. What a void this would create! In fact, thinking about what those palaces were really like, one may find oneself, timidly, speaking the words of Brother Lardoon, the monk from Amiens who went to Florence with Epistemon: "These things carved from marble and prophyry are beautiful; I have nothing against them. But the pastries of Amiens, the old roast shops with the mouthwatering odors, and, yes, even the girls there. . . ." Those good everyday, useful, comfortable things have their worth after all, a very considerable one.

III

In any case, the list of such chateaux is short: Blois, Chenonceaux, Azay, Amboise, Oiron, Bonnivet. They are the exception. The ordinary dwelling for the gentleman who was not a prince was a manor house. And in the manor, people spent most of their time in a single room, the kitchen. Generally, meals were eaten there. (French houses almost never had a special room for dining until the eighteenth century. Even Louis XIV, on ordinary occasions, ate his meals at a square table placed in front of the window in his bedroom. The noblemen of the sixteenth century, having fewer pretentions, generally ate in the kitchen). This room is called, in the dialect of some provinces, the "heater." That is the giveaway. It was warm in the kitchen, or at least, less cold than elsewhere. There was always a fire. The aromatic steam coming from the stew-pot made the air a bit heavy perhaps, but warm, and all told, welcoming. Fresh straw spread on the floor kept people's feet warm. People gathered in the kitchen where they lived elbow to elbow, and they relished this kind of closeness. Like all peasants, they hated to be alone. The more the merrier. The sixteenth century did not have our modesty. It knew nothing of our need to be alone. The beds of the day are evidence of this, great big things in which several people would sleep at once without embarrassment or scruples. Individual bedrooms are a modern idea. "Whatever for?" our forefathers would have asked. Setting apart a room for each activity is another modern notion. The kitchen was the gathering place for everyone, and everything, or almost everything, was done there.

The lord of the manor and his wife were there in their high-backed wooden chairs next to the fire. Their children, both boys and girls, sat on benches. Their guests were received there, the parish priest, their tenants, and their servants. Bustling servants laid or cleared the table under the vigilant eye of their mistress. Farmers, plowmen, day laborers coming in from the fields at day's end heavy with fatigue and with mud, sank into their seats to eat their meager fare. Adding to the confusion were the animals: chickens and ducks who made their home beneath the table, hunting birds perched on the shoulders of the hunters, dogs crouched at their masters' feet, grooming themselves as they lay stretched out in the straw or searching out their fleas under the cover of the women's skirts or roasting themselves before the fire.

Slowly, methodically, respectfully, people ate the coarse food put before them. Bread was rarely made from wheat. Thick floury soup, mush made of millet or groats were served in place of potatoes or pasta. Generally each person at the table was given a large thick slice of somewhat stale dense bread. On this, using three fingers, the diner scooped up whatever he might choose from the central serving dish. Very little red meat was eaten except at weddings and other special occasions. Salt pork appeared from time to time, but there were many meatless days, and fast days, and days of abstinence, and Lent so well, so strictly observed that people often undermined their health. When there was meat it was game or fowl. The sixteenth century did not know the stimulation provoked by red meat, by flesh food accompanied by alcohol and wine; it did not know the illusion of strength and power which modern man obtains from his usual food, nor the instant stimulation of the nervous system which, thanks to coffee, even the most humble know today. The closest equivalent in the sixteenth century was spices, whose use was limited only by their enormous cost. People who used neither alcohol nor tobacco nor coffee nor tea and who only rarely ate red meat got their stimulation from spices, setting themselves aflame with ginger and pepper and nutmeg and carefully concocted mustards.

All told, people spent very little time in the house. They came to eat or to take refuge when life and work in the fields was cut short by a heavy rain, and at night. Night too was different; man had not yet learned to conquer the darkness. The kitchen and bedrooms were lit most usually by the dancing flames in the fireplace. Lamps were, in general, nasty, sooty little things which sputtered or smoked and spread their stench through the room. We can scarcely imagine what one of those big kitchens must have been like after three or four hours of habitation by twenty or so people still in work clothes, not to count the animals who lived there. The room would fill with musty, lingering odors of men and beasts and past meals, the acrid odor of sputtering wicks and the smell of muck-spattered leggings drying in front of the fire. Imagine a boy who wants to settle in his nook to read or to study under such conditions. How can he admidst all this disorder? The kitchen is not for reading except maybe for four or five times a year when it is raining hard and no one knows what else to do. As a last resort someone reads aloud a few chapters from an old romance. From time to time, late in the evening when everyone else is in bed, the master brings his account book up-to-date, carefully detailing what was owed him as well as his expenses. Real life for this man and those like him was life out-of-doors, riding over the fields and vineyards, the meadows and woods. They oversaw their land while they hunted or hunted while overseeing their land. Real life was going to a fair or a market, exchanging a few words with the peasants there in a shared language about shared interests which, needless to say, were neither political nor metaphysical. On Sundays and holidays the lord, who considered from a certain point of view was nothing but a kind of superior peasant, started the dance by taking the girls once around the floor, and if need be played at bowls, archery, or wrestling.

IV

But what about the court, you will ask, the brilliant court of François I, if not earlier, that of Charles VIII or Louis XII? Let us have a look at the court. The word itself is impressive, evolving magnificent visions: great gilded rooms glowing with the light of a thousand candles, filled with lords and ladies who themselves live in sumptuous chateaux. It matters little whether we imagine the Louvre, Saint-Germain, Fontainebleau, Chambord, or later, Versailles. Only the outward setting and the fashions change. But the court surely always remains just that, the court, a place of privilege above all, and display, where powerful people, whose every costume costs a fortune, gather to live in ostentatious luxury and comfort in the midst of a continual whirl of banquets, receptions, and other entertainments. Lazy and useless lives no doubt, yet not totally free of all signs of wit, clever remarks, now and then, little verses or biting epigrams.

Very well. But against this image must be set the work of patient scholars who have gathered and classified the letters and documents of the royal chancellery. From these we can reconstruct, day by day, for all the thirty years of the reign of François I, the activities of the sovereign. Suppose we open the collection at random to 1533. The king was just over forty. He was already starting to turn gray; his eyes were becoming heavy; his nose was growing longer. The ladies of Paris and elsewhere had left a heavy mark on the king. And the earlier misfortune of Pavia had broken many an enchantment.

On the first of January, 1533, François I was in Paris, at the Louvre. He had spent all of December there. He was to spend all of January and February there. Three months in the same place! That was most unlike the king's usual habits. He soon reverted to another pattern. In March the king set off. First he made a tour of the Valois and the Soissonais. On the seventh of March he was at La Ferté-Milon; on the ninth at the Abbey of Longpont; on the tenth, at Fère-en-Tarendois; on the fifteenth at Soissons; on the seventeenth at Coucy. Then he turned northward. Francois spent the twentieth at Marle and la Fère; the twenty-first at Ribemont; the twenty-second at Guise; the twenty-fourth at Marle again. Then he turned toward Champagne. On the twenty-eight he arrived at Saint-Marcoul de Corbeny; the next day he was at Cormicy, and the day following at Reims. That city, in which the kings of France were crowned, did not hold him long. By the third of April he had arrived in Château-Thierry by the way of Fère-en-Terendois. He stayed there for three days. By the seventh he was at Meaux, but by then it was Holy Week and the king remained at Meaux for the Easter celebrations. It was not until the nineteenth that he came to Fontainebleau to spend a week. On the twenty-sixth he was at Gien, having come by way of Montargis and Châtillon-sur-Loign. Then he set off toward Bourges, arriving on the second of May for three days, after which he set off again toward Moulins where he spent four days after touring the Bourbonnais: Issoudoun, Meillant, Cérilly, Bourbon-l' Archambault. With an intermediate stop at Roanne, the king made his way to Lyon by the twenty-sixth of May. And there he stopped. He spent a month in Lyon, not, of course, without making numerous excursions to other places nearby. At the end of June he left the city, crossed the Forez, and entered Clermont-Ferrand on July tenth. Next he wandered about the Auvergne from Riom to Issoire to Vic. A week later he was in Velay. By the seventeenth he had come as far as Polignac; by the eighteenth he was at le Puy for two days; the twenty-fourth at Rodez; the twenty-fifth on the road to Toulouse, the city where he spent the first week in August. By August ninth he was at Nîmes; on the twenty-ninth he began a twelve-day stay at Avignon; by September fifteenth he was in Arles; the twenty-first at Martigues; the twenty-second at Marignane. On the fourth of October he entered Marseilles. We need follow him no further; it is clear that we shall have had more than enough of these endless lists of dates and places long before Francois I had his fill of travel. Was this the life of a king or of a knight-errant, wandering always, up hill and down dale? Or a revision of *Don Quixote* by the Flying Dutchman?

The court followed the king. It followed him on the highway, through the woods, along the rivers and across the fields, more like a train of perpetual tourists than a court. Or, more exactly, it was like a troop doing a day's march. The advance party would move out ahead to set up "camp" before the king arrived: the quartermaster, the official charged with finding and allocating housing for everyone; and a whole tribe of cooks, specialists in sauces, roasts, and pastries. Riding old nags usually acquired through the generosity of the king, they hurried through the dawn to that night's stopping place. It might be a simple village house, a gentleman's manor, or the palace of some important nobleman. Or, if need be, from time to time the king would be content to spend the night in the big tent which a sturdy mule bore on its back, following all the peregrinations of the king. The tent might be set up anywhere, in a clearing, in the midst of the fields or meadows, as the whims of the master dictated.

Once the advance party had moved out, the body of the court began to leave also. First the king and his guards, officers, and gentlemen of his household: as he passed through a village the church bells would ring, and the priests would come running to the roadside. The peasants who saw the royal cortege approach from the distance as they worked in the fields would run toward it. There, in the midst of a splendid group of mounted men, they saw the king, either on horseback himself or riding in a litter that lurched with each step taken by the stout mules drawing it. Behind the king came the ladies of the court, ladies who did a day's march alongside the men. Following the example of the king, they too lived like soldiers on a campaign. Constant travel may eventually become a way of life which one comes to enjoy or even to feel a kind of nostalgia for; nonetheless it is not an easy life or a restful one, not suited to frail women of delicate constitution.

The ladies of the court were not frail. Their portraits have been preserved for us thanks to the popularity of pencil drawings in the sixteenth century. Collections of these portraits, especially those of the most beautiful and powerful figures of the court, drawn with varying degrees of skill, are to be found in the most far-flung lands. What disappointments await us in the pages of such collections. The written words of contemporaries are filled with a thousand sincere-sounding compliments. And here are the ladies of unparalleled beauty preserved, for example, in the Montmor collection in the Library at Aix-en-Provence, once attributed to Madame de Boissy, wife of the head of the king's household. The portraits have manuscript captions. First we come to Madame de Chateaubriand, mistress of the king, of Bonnivet, and others too, none of whom was ashamed of the association. She was the devoted sister of Lescun, Lesparre, and of the ill-starred Lautrec. Looking at the portrait of so famous a beauty we find a rather fleshy blond woman with a wide, flat face and rather ordinary shoulders. The caption leaves us with a shred of hope: "Formed better by nature than by pencil," it says. We find Madame de l'Estrange. Her name in the madrigals of the day inevitably rhymed with "face d'Ange" (angel face); her face now seems to have been whittled from some cheap, intractable wood. And Diane de Poitiers, who was the delight of the son, Henri II, after having been the joy of the father, François I, surely must have been an extraordinary woman to be able to extend her reign from one sovereign to the next, especially when the two men were so unlike one another. "A beautiful sight, an honest companion," says the caption under her portrait in the Montmor collection. No doubt she was honest, at least in Brantôme's sense. As for her looks, however, we see an astute face with a sharp nose, premature bags under the eyes, and a wide, thin-lipped mouth. This is the evidence not merely of one portrait, but of five of six drawn between 1525 and 1550, so that no effort of the will can make our own esthetic sense coincide with that of our ancestors: for us that face holds neither charm nor distinction nor grace nor beauty.

It is odd that these depictions of great ladies or princesses or court favorites almost never convey a sense of breeding or nobility. Or perhaps what breeding there is seems surprisingly rustic and casual. But in all fairness, how could they have refined their features or simply preserved the freshness of their looks while exposing themselves constantly, on horseback, to the out-of-doors, to the cutting wind, to the driving rain and snow, traveling for weeks and weeks without real rest, without anything more than improvised lodgings? The ladies of the court were a sad sight as they followed the king; the oldest dozing in their litters, the others rocked by the rhythmic step of their mares or packed into wagons without springs so that the wheels transmitted every bump in the road. Relief might come when they all piled into a rented or borrowed barge, to drift between the flat banks of some river or stream.

Twelve thousand horses, three or four thousand men, not counting the women (who were by no means all of the respectable sort): the court was like a little army, privately outfitted, self-sufficient, living an independent existence. It brought its own merchants of all sorts, protected and regulated by the chief provost, granted the sole right to supply the courtiers. There were butchers and poultrymen, fishmongers and greengrocers, fruiterers and bakers; wine merchants prepared to sell both wholesale and retail; purveyors of hay and straw and oats. There was a whole tribe of servants to aid in the hunt: to care for the dogs and falcons; to see to the nets and traps. Another group was needed to see to the feeding of the court: two mares carrying bottles of wine intended for the king's table and that of his chamberlains and the head of his household; cooks and their apprentices who on certain days established by tradition would entertain the king with dances. And there were the couriers and fast riders, hardy horsemen who were always ready to ride at top speed to the nearest coast from the depths of Auvergne or Burgundy, seeking oysters or mussels or fish for the king's table on meatless days.

Ambassadors were brought to despair by the unsettled life of the court. One of them, Mariano Giustiniano, was ambassador in 1535, that is, two years after the period we have just been examining in detail. To the Senate in Venice he wrote the following report: "My tenure as ambassador lasted forty-five months . . . I traveled constantly . . . Never during that time did the court remain the same place for as long as two weeks." It should be said that of all those who followed the peregrinations of the court, the diplomats suffered the most. The king did his best to avoid contact with these observers, interested by profession in unearthing hidden secrets, and he led them a merry chase in doing so. He was careful never to inform them of the court's itinerary; he would invent a hunt or a sudden excursion as an excuse to flee their company. They, on the other hand, were professionally obliged to be as close as possible to the person of the king.

The nobles were less assiduous. Those who followed the royal party for more than a month or two were rare indeed. Most of those who already belonged to the world of the court came each year to spend a few weeks with the king. They left their land and their homes intending to return, and in fact, they did so as soon as they could. There they recovered and settled once more into a familiar society, while from the north to the south, from the east to the west, from the Ardennes to Provence, from Brittany to Lorraine, the king of France, on horseback, continued his rounds, begun at his coronation and ended by his death.

V

What has been said so far has brought us to no conclusion. No conclusion is wanted, for the aim of these pages has been to present to the reader, by way of introduction, a few images of life in sixteenth century France, images of the time of Louis XII and François I, striking images. They show us in action, so to speak, people performing timeless acts, going through the eternal circle of all human life. But if I am not entirely mistaken, the reader has also seen, and I suppose felt, as he was reading, that this eternal circle did not follow quite the same course in the sixteenth century as it does today.

Was man in the abstract the same? Possibly. I know nothing about him. He and the historian have little contact, for the historian is concerned with reality rather than abstractions. Concrete man, living man, man in flesh and blood living in the sixteenth century and modern man do not much resemble each other. He was a country man, a nomad, a rustic, and in all these we are far from him. When we see him before us in the strength of his manhood at the age of forty, what dangers has he not surmounted, what challenges has he not overcome? Above all, he survived. He lived through his first sixteen years during which, regularly, at the very least half of all children died. Family account books yield an eloquent record of this grim fact. They are punctuated nearly every three lines by the death of a child, like the tolling of a funeral bell. Later, our sixteenth century man escaped death by that combination of mortal scourges known in a word as the plague, which killed several thousand people each year, spreading occasionally to epidemic proportions when it would decimate entire populations.

However middle class, however bourgeois, we may assume him to be, however far by profession from arms and the military, he had nonetheless risked his life a hundred times as a soldier. When the enemy was at the gates of his city about to besiege it, he ran to the ramparts with his halberd and his helmet to fight alongside the others. He risked his life equally when he traveled, as all men of the sixteenth century did, whether they were lawyers or merchants or journeymen making their tour of the kingdom, or students heading across the Alps to the schools of Padua or Pavia. They all wrote their wills before leaving home. As he approached the nearby woods, the traveler would observe the dark copse spreading up the hillside, offering a hiding place for the brigand waiting for the opportunity to attack the unaccompanied or unarmed as they passed. In the wretched inn which he reached just as night fell, the exhausted traveler found sinister vagrants and black-handed charcoal burners; men whose motions were brusque and whose faces gave rise to disquieting suspicions came stealthily into the room to drink themselves sodden. The traveler spent the night standing guard in his miserable room, without fire or lamp to give him light, his sword unsheathed and placed across the crude wooden table he had pushed against the door to keep it closed. By dawn he had had enough; he fled without further ado, pleased to find that thieves had not made off with his horse.

Life was a perpetual combat to be waged against man, the seasons, and a hostile and ill-controlled nature. A person who was a victor in such a combat, who arrived at maturity without too many accidents or misadventures, had a tough skin, a thick hide, literally as well as figuratively. If a vein of great sensitivity or delicacy lay hidden beneath the surface toughness we have no way of knowing it. History must limit itself to recording appearances. In the sixteenth century, appearances are neither gracious nor soft. One, two, five children in a family died in infancy, carried off by unknown diseases ill-distinguished or ill-diagnosed and generally ill-cared-for. The family record book simply notes the deaths and the date. Then the writer, father of the child, passes on to more notable events: a hard frost in April killing the autumn's fruit in the bud, an earthquake signaling great catastrophes. His wife might be respected for her virtue and her fecundity, and praised, perhaps, for the skill with which she ran the home. But when she died, leaving her husband too few children, five or six at most, he married again as soon as he could because it was important to have a dozen, more if possible. On the other hand, if a peasant in the country had been left a widow and remarried, she would not take her children by the first marriage; they were left to shift for themselves as servants or beggars by the roadside.

Thomas Platter, in his memoirs, evokes a life enormously far from our own although we are separated from him by scarcely more than seven or eight normal lifetimes. Thomas Platter tells us, as though he were speaking of something entirely ordinary, without registering the least surprise, that as his father died when he was still an infant, his mother remarried soon thereafter. This caused the immediate dispersion of her children, so that Platter simply did not know how many brothers and sisters he had. With efforts he could recall the names of two sisters and three brothers and something of what became of them. About the others he remembered nothing. He himself was taken in by an aunt. He never again heard from his mother. This was, no doubt, the behavior of the people in the wild Valais. But there is nothing which suggests that the customs of people elsewhere were any less harsh.

Indeed, the things which are nearest and dearest to us today—home, hearth, wife, and children—seem to have been regarded by the man of the sixteenth century as merely transitory goods which he was always prepared to renounce. On occasion he would renounce them without any real or serious reason for doing so, impelled by an unconscious need to wander, the sprouting of seeds planted by generations of crusading and errancy. One of the constant companions of any historian of the sixteenth century is the *Colloquies* of Erasmus, a small but rich mirror of the times. In it we find scenes such as this: Four men are sitting at a table. They are middle-class, peaceful, sedentary, married, well-established men who have come together as old friends to share a glass of wine. Perhaps they have shared a glass too many and the wine has gone to their heads. One of them suddenly bursts out: "Any friend of mine will follow me; I'm going on a pilgrimage to Santiago de Compostella." A drunken impulse. The second man speaks in turn: "As for me, I'm not going to Santiago, I'll go all the way to Rome." The third and fourth friends make peace in the group, suggesting a compromise. First they will go to Santiago and then, from there, to Rome. All four of them will go, and they pass a glass of wine to drink to their pilgrimage. The pact has been sealed, the vows made. There is no going back on it, so they leave. One of the pilgrims dies in Spain; the second in Italy. The third is left dying in Florence by the fourth who returns home alone a year later, worn out, prematurely aged and ruined. The story is not fiction; it depicts the customs of a time which is no longer ours.

These are the things we should try to remember when we wish to understand the "things of the sixteenth century." We must remember that we are all, like it or not, hothouse products; the man of the sixteenth century grew in the open air.

Bibliography

Braudel, Fernand. "Lucien Febvre." In *International Encyclopedia of the Social Sciences,* vol. 5, edited by David L. Sills, 348–50. New York, 1968–79.

Braudel, Fernand. "Personal Testimony." *Journal of Modern History,* 44 (December 1972): 448–67.

Burke, Peter, ed. *A New Kind of History: From the Writings of Lucien Febvre.* New York, 1973.

Burke, Peter, ed. *Economy and Society in Early Modern Europe: Essays from "Annales".* New York, 1972.

Ferro, Marc, ed. *Social Historians in Contemporary France: Essays from Annales.* New York, 1972.

Hughes, H. Stuart. *The Obstructed Path: French Social Thought in the Years of Desperation, 1930–1960.* New York, 1968.

Iggers, Georg. *New Directions in European Historiography.* Middletown, Conn., 1975.

Shafer, Boyd C., ed. *Historical Study in the West.* New York, 1968.

Throop, Palmer A. "Lucien Febvre, 1878–1956." In *Some 20th Century Historians, Essays on Eminent Europeans,* edited by S. William Halperin. Chicago, 1961.

CHAPTER 19

Crane Brinton

The Anatomy of Revolution

(1938)

"Who now would dare model himself on Thucydides—even without the speeches?" Thus, in a single stroke, Crane Brinton (1898–1968) dismissed the long tradition of narrative history. The quotation is from his first major book, *The Jacobins, An Essay in the New History* (1930), the methodological implications of which—"the new history"—were as significant in his mind as the book's substantive findings, for Crane Brinton was announcing himself a social scientist. To historicists concerned with preserving a sense of the uniqueness and incomparability of events and people, he replied that exceptional individuals interested the new historian "only as the freak interests the biologist." The goal of history was to seek generalizations "which will have as much as possible the force of scientific laws." *The Jacobins* aimed at discovering the motivations of radical French revolutionaries as possible predictors for the behavior of other revolutionaries. The book comes up puzzlingly short of its goal, but in *The Anatomy of Revolution* eight years later, Brinton, undaunted, went on to seek the laws of revolution in general.

Brinton was born in 1898 in Winsted, Connecticut, and remained a New Englander his life long. He graduated from Harvard University in 1919, and after study at Oxford University as a Rhodes Scholar, completing his doctorate in 1923, returned to join the faculty at Harvard and taught there until his death in 1968. He developed intellectually between two poles: the influence of his Harvard tutor, the left-leaning political philosopher, Harold Laski; and the conservative exponent of the "New Humanism," Irving Babbit. Thus, as he put it himself in the 1940s, "In 1919 I thought of myself as a Liberal with at least an initial capital. I now think of myself as a liberal with inverted commas," so far had his innocent rationalism been tempered by a sense of people's passions and prejudices.

But he took seriously the possibility of a social science with emphasis on "science." Besides writing history from that point of view himself, he chaired Harvard's "Society of Fellows," which encouraged interdisciplinary and comparative studies and supported students of specially flexible mind in the search for laws of human development. (Thomas S. Kuhns, who wrote *The*

311

Structure of Scientific Revolutions [1962], was a product of the society. His classic work might profitably be read with Brinton's *Anatomy of Revolution*).

Brinton's parallel interest was intellectual history. The rise of Fascism, the outbreak of the Second World War, and the persistence of authoritarianism in the postwar world drew him to write a series of books in the 1940s and 1950s in which he interpreted democratic ideals to a popular readership in hopes of preserving them.

His earlier research had been supported by a grant from the Social Science Research Council (SSRC), which was formed in 1923 by scholars who, like Brinton, wanted to discover the laws of social behavior. The 1920s were the years in which sociologists, psychologists, and political scientists began to have a sense of the empirical base of their study that would help them replace mere history as a guide for statesmen. However, the SSRC invited historians to participate in its coordination of research efforts, and the reports of its Committee on Historiography in 1945, 1946, 1954, and 1963 are worth reading even if the advances they claim are modest. (They are listed in the bibliography at the end of this chapter as are other books and collections that argue for history as a social science.)

Brinton's *Anatomy of Revolution* describes and sees uniformities in four modern revolutions: the seventeenth-century Puritan Revolution in England, the American Revolution, the French Revolution, and the Russian Revolution. His introduction states the scientific ideal as it can apply to history and offers the pathological metaphor of a "fever" as the conceptual scheme within which revolution can be understood: first symptoms of disturbance, onset of the disease, crisis (analogous to the Reign of Terror), convalescence, and return to health. These opening remarks are full of disclaimers about what may be supposed to be the author's antirevolutionary bias represented in the metaphor, but his earlier book, *The Jacobins,* suggested that "if we can . . . establish the laws under which revolutions run their course, we can possibly prevent revolution. . . ." In any case, *Anatomy of Revolution* is a less belligerent work than *The Jacobins.* Brinton compares his revolutions to reveal uniqueness as well as uniformity. In a small way, his style preserves the distinction between his roles as historian and as social scientist: he uses verbs in the past tense for events that actually happened and present tense for events that *tend* to happen.

Here is Brinton's comparative discussion of how revolutions begin.

I. THE ETERNAL FIGARO

THERE IS in the *Marriage of Figaro* of Beaumarchais, first performed at Paris in 1784, a famous soliloquy by Figaro in which much of what we have laboriously analyzed in the previous chapter is dramatically focused in a few pages. Figaro himself is the able young man unjustly kept down by the pressure of a social system built on privilege. As the scene opens he is waiting in the darkness to surprise in an assignation his bride and his master, the Count Almaviva. His first reflections on feminine inconstancy pass over very rapidly into a violent attack on his noble master. "Because you are a great lord, you think you are a great genius! . . . nobility, fortune, rank, appointments; all this makes a man so proud! But what have you done to deserve so many good things? You took the trouble to get born!" Then he looks back on the struggles that have filled his life—his obscure birth, his education in chemistry, pharmacy, surgery, all barely sufficing, because of his lack of high birth, to give him the privilege of practicing veterinary medicine; his venture in playwrighting, and his inevitable clash with the censor; his turn to writing on state finance, and the resulting prison term; another essay in literature, this time in journalism, and another suppression; rejection as candidate for a government job, since unfortunately he was fitted for the post; a turn as gambler, when his noble patrons took most of his profits; and his final return to his old trade as barber-surgeon.

Scattered throughout the soliloquy are a train of epigrams which delighted fashionable audiences in the old regime, and were taken up throughout the country. Indeed, families would come up to Paris chiefly to see the *Marriage of Figaro,* and hear French wit at its best directed against a wicked government. Here are a few of Beaumarchais' most famous jibes: "Not being able to degrade the human spirit, they get revenge by mistreating it." "Only little men fear little writings." "For the job an accountant was necessary; a dancer got it." "To get on in this world, *savoir faire* is worth more than *savoir.*" And, of course, that bitter jibe at the Count's attainments—"qu'avezvous fait pour tant de biens? *vous vous êtes donné la peine de naître.''* Here in this one speech are so many indications of the coming revolution that, with the wisdom of after-the-fact that comes so naturally to the historian, we can say the revolution is already almost full-blown in Figaro. Including, of course, the fact that, after a long vacillation, the censor *did not stop* Beaumarchais' play.

The years just preceding the actual outbreak of revolution witness a crescendo of protests against the tyranny of the government, a hail of pamphlets, plays, addresses, an outburst of activity on the part of interested pressure groups. Facing all this, the government certainly does not live up to the reputation its opponents seek to make for it. Its tyrannous attempts at suppressing the rebellious opposition may perhaps fail because that opposition is too strong, resourceful, and virtuous; or its attempts

Reprinted by permission of Prentice-Hall, Inc., from Crane Brinton, *The Anatomy of Revolution* (New York: Norton, 1938), 82–112. Copyright © 1938, 1952 by Prentice-Hall, Inc. Englewood Cliffs, N.J.

may fail because they are carried out half-heartedly and inefficiently by governmental agents more than half won over to the opposition. The fact remains that they do fail.

Even the period of the personal rule of Charles I which preceded the English revolution was not altogether as quiet and successful as it seemed on the surface to be. Many Puritan divines escaped Laud's attempt to drive them from the Established Church, and the others found plenty of independent pulpits and printing presses. Strafford might write in 1638 that "the People are in great quietness and, if I be not much mistaken, well-satisfied if not delighted with his Majesty's gracious government and protection"; but he was much mistaken. At the very least these eleven years of personal government were but the calm before the storm.

In our other three societies we do not even find this deceptive calm, but a steady growth of revolutionary agitation. In America hardly a colony escaped some form of rioting in the period between the Stamp Act and Lexington, and all of them saw a steady growth of agitation through merchants' committees, correspondence committees, Sons of Liberty, and similar groups. The French government in the 1780's drew nearer and nearer to bankruptcy, and with each expedient to avoid bankruptcy brought nearer the calling of the Estates-General and the signal for revolution. As for Russia, it was a society strikingly conscious of the possibilities of revolution. Upper-class Russians had for more than a generation been turning their uneasiness into the smooth coin of conversation: "sitting upon a volcano," "after us the deluge," "the storm is rising." In 1905 and 1906, under pressure of defeat by the Japanese, a kind of dress rehearsal of the great revolution took place. The patriotic enthusiasms of 1914 for a while stilled conspicuous preparation for revolution, but military defeat in 1915 and 1916 brought back conditions that grew daily more and more like those of 1905.

II. THE EVENTS OF THE FIRST STAGES

The Russian revolution began more dramatically and definitely with a single event—street riots in Petrograd in 1917—than did any of our other revolutions. Yet even in Russia it took four or five days for the revolutionists themselves to realize that the confused milling around of Petrograd crowds might bring about the fall of the Romanovs. History and patriotic ritual have singled out dramatic episodes—the battles at Lexington and Concord, the fall of the Bastille—as beginning revolutions. But though contemporaries were aware of the dramatic quality of such events, they were not always sure that they had turned revolutionary agitation into revolution. The first steps in revolution are by no means always clear to the revolutionists themselves, and the transition from agitation to action is rarely a sudden and definite thing.

Charles I came to the throne in 1624, and almost immediately found himself engaged with the House of Commons in a struggle chiefly over taxes. Out of the conflict there emerged the Petition of Right of 1628, in which the Commons forced the King's consent to a statement of definite limitations on the royal power: Charles promised not to raise forced loans, not to quarter soldiers on unwilling householders, not to permit officers to exercise martial law in time of peace, not to send anyone to prison without showing cause why he had done so. Emboldened by this success, the Commons under the leadership of the emotional Sir John Eliot went on to refuse to grant the King the usual form of customs' revenue—tonnage and poundage—and to insist in an aggressive and indeed revolutionary way on their privileges. At a final debate on March 2, 1629, two men, Denzil Holles and Valentine, held down the Speaker in his chair by force while Eliot proposed a ringing declaration on the illegality of paying tonnage and poundage without a grant from Parliament. Conservatives pushed forward to free the Speaker. There followed a riotous debate fully worthy of the standards set later by the National Assembly in France, but somehow or other in the confusion Eliot's resolutions were put through before the royal order dissolving the Parliament could be carried out. The parliamentarians had made a grand gesture of protest. From that day, no Parliament met in England for eleven years. Eliot, jailed for rioting, maintained that the King had no power over a member of the House of Commons. He died a most effective martyr in 1632.

In the years of personal rule Charles, aided by his two great supporters, Strafford and Laud, did his best to organize the government of England in accordance with notions of efficient centralization and expert rule which were the chief political heritage of the Renaissance. He did a job in some ways surprisingly good. But he may, as nineteenth-century liberal historians fondly believed, have been going against the basic grain of the English character and the basic mold of English institutions; he was most certainly going bankrupt. A clash with the Scotch Presbyterians probably merely hastened the inevitable. Charles called a Parliament in the spring of 1640, but dissolved it after less than a month. A Scotch army now invaded England, and Charles had to buy it off. To get money he had to call another Parliament. The Short Parliament was, therefore, but a breaking of the ground for the Long Parliament, which met on November 3, 1640, was dissolved on April 20, 1653, and was brought briefly to life again in 1659, just before the restoration of the Stuarts. The life of this extraordinary assembly thus spans almost completely the twenty years of the English revolution.

The Long Parliament got to work at once, for on November 11, 1640, a week after it first met, Pym moved the impeachment of Strafford for high treason. The impeachment, held up by the more conservative House of Lords, was turned early in 1641 into a bill of attainder. Impeachment involved at least the forms of judicial action, whereas attainder was a simple legislative act. The Lords were willing enough to abandon Strafford, if not to try him, and on May 12th he fell under the executioner's ax. Less than eight years later that ax was to reach his royal master.

Actual outbreak of armed hostilities between Charles and the Parliament was not to come for another year. Parliament voted by a majority of eleven the Grand Remonstrance, a long summing-up of all the grievances accumulated against the King in the seventeen years of his reign. Charles replied to this vote of want of confidence by attempting to arrest six members of Parliament, Lord Kimbolton in the Lords, Pym, Hampden, Haselrig, Holles, and Strode in the Commons, who had compromised themselves by entering into technically treasonous negotiations with the invading Scotch army. Charles rashly came down to the House of Commons himself with armed men and attempted to seize the members. He was met with something of the kind of passive resistance the French Third Estate displayed at the royal session of June 17, 1789, when Louis XVI ordered them to give up attempting to form a National Assembly. The threatened members fled to the City of London, and Charles was again checkmated. The Commons were now so aggressively successful that they decided to take over the military by naming officers in the militia and trainbands. Charles, in turn, began to build up his own army, and set up his standard at Nottingham in August, 1642. The Civil War had begun.

Where in this long and closely knit series of events you wish to say the English revolution fairly began is partly a subjective matter. Somewhere between the calling of the Long Parliament in 1640, and the outbreak of the war two years later, the first critical steps in the revolution were undertaken. Perhaps the execution of Strafford is a good dramatic date, or Charles' futile attempt to seize the five members in the Commons. At any rate, by the summer of 1642 the English revolution had taken on unmistakable form.

Events in America moved hardly more rapidly. In a sense, you can maintain that the American revolution really began in 1765 with the Stamp Act; or at any rate that the agitation which culminated in the repeal of that Act was a kind of rehearsal for the great movement of the seventies. The imperial government was determined to do something about the American colonists, and Townshend's mild duties on tea, glass, lead and a few other articles imported into America were accompanied by an attempt to collect them in an efficient modern way. Under Townshend's act His majesty's customs houses in America were equipped with a hopeful and willing bureaucracy. The result was a series of clashes with increasingly well-organized groups of Americans. Tarring and feathering of informers, stealing sequestered goods from under the noses of customs officers, jeering at British troops, led up to the more dramatic incidents enshrined in the textbooks: the seizure of the *Gaspee* at Providence, the Boston Massacre of 1770, the Boston Tea Party, the burning of the *Peggy Stewart* at Annapolis.

The closing of the port of Boston, the dispatch of Gage and his troops to Massachusetts, the Quebec Act itself, were all really measures taken by the imperial government against colonies already in revolt. You may, if you are interested in such matters, discuss at length the question as to just when the American revolution is to be considered as formally beginning. You may go as late as the first Continental Congress in 1774, or the battles of Lexington and Concord in 1775, or even the most famous Fourth of July in 1776. But the complex group struggles out of which revolutions actually grow only later turn into formal sources for patriotic ritual. The first steps in the American revolution were many and spread over something like a decade. Only an absolutist mind could insist that out of this long process a given detail be isolated as the beginning of the American revolution.

The French revolution of 1789 may be said to have been incubating for several decades. Overt and definite resistance to the royal government, as in the parliaments of Charles I and in the American colonial assemblies, is not to be found in France, which was wholly without such representative bodies. The nearest thing to such a body was the *parlement de Paris*, a kind of supreme court composed of judges who were nobles and held their positions by heredity. It was precisely this *parlement*, followed by the provincial *parlements*, that began in the 1780's an open quarrel with the Crown, which culminated in a dramatic defiance of royal power and the forced exile of the judges. Popular opinion, at least in Paris, was overwhelmingly with the judges, and privileged nobles though they were, they became heroes and martyrs for a day.

Meanwhile, approaching bankruptcy had forced the King to call in 1787 an Assembly of Notables, a kind of hastily gathered special commission of prominent nobles, from whom Louis XVI in good eighteenth-century style no doubt expected enlightenment. This he certainly obtained, for the Assembly contained many upper-class intellectuals, like Lafayette, who were convinced that France must cease to be a "despotism," must endow itself with an up-to-date constitution of the kind the new states of the American union were making fashionable. The Assembly of Notables was accordingly very divided and doubtful about ways of filling the empty treasury, but clear that further consultation with the nation was necessary. The Crown finally yielded, brought back into the government the Swiss commoner, Necker, who had a reputation as a financial wizard, and summoned a meeting of the Estates-General for the spring of 1789.

This Estates-General had last met in 1614, and there was some uncertainty as to how one went about electing it. The antiquarians came to the rescue, however, and three hundred representatives of the First Estate, or clergy, three hundred of the Second, or nobility, and six hundred of the Third, or commons, were chosen, practically in time for the first meeting. The double representation of the Third Estate had no precedent in 1614 or earlier. It was, in fact, a revolutionary step, a concession wrung from the King, an admission that in some way or another the Third Estate was more important than the others. In the old constitution, however, final decisions were made by the orders as units; that is, if the Clergy and the Nobles as separate houses agreed on a policy, they could carry it, two to one, even against the dissenting Third Estate. When the Estates met in May, 1789, the great question was whether to follow the old constitution and vote by orders, or to vote in one great assembly of twelve hundred members in which the doubled Third Estate, plus the "liberals" among the other two orders, would have a clear majority. Louis had characteristically permitted this problem to remain vague and unsettled, and only after the Third Estate had insisted on one great assembly did he royally insist on three separate ones.

The issue out of which the French revolution formally grew was this simple one of vote by orders or vote by individuals in one assembly. The Third Estate stood pat, and refused to transact any business until the other orders joined it in what was to be called—and the name was a sound piece of propaganda for the revolutionists—the National Assembly. There are certain dramatic moments in a two-months' struggle which was essentially parliamentary and lacking in the more physical kinds of violence. Shut out by a royal blunder from their usual meeting place, the Third Estate on June 20, 1789, met hastily in a large indoor tennis court, and swore not to disperse until they had endowed France with a constitution.

Thanks partly to David's famous painting, which is more symbolic than realistic, this episode is now second only to the taking of the Bastille in the patriotic ritual of the present Third French Republic. Actually more important was the glowering defiance of the Third Estate when in a plenary royal session of June 23rd the King called on all the prestige and pageantry of the Crown to enforce voting by separate orders. At this session the Third Estate remained behind after the King's withdrawal, and Mirabeau is said to have made his famous reply to a request from the King's Grand Master of Ceremonies that they in turn withdraw: "We are assembled here by the will of the nation, and we will not leave except by force." Shortly afterwards the King yielded, though probably not to Mirabeau's rhetoric. By the beginning of July the National Assembly had been duly constituted, and was ready to put the Enlightenment, so long in

France a matter of theory, into practice. The first steps in the French revolution had been taken.

Those who insist that you must have violence before you can label revolution as begun will date the great French revolution from July 14, 1789, when a Paris mob, aided by soldiers who had gone over to the popular side, took the gloomy fortress-prison of the Bastille on the eastern edge of the city. Bastille Day is the French republican Fourth of July, a great holy day in one of the best organized of our contemporary nationalist religions. As such it has been surrounded by legends, endowed with a martyrology, safely withdrawn from the unedifying touch of history. To an outsider, the taking of the Bastille seems an involved and confusing process, at least as much the result of the weakness of the royal governor, De Launay, as of the strength of the besiegers. What is important for us is that Paris was in the hands of a mob for three days, and that this mob was clearly shouting against the King, shouting for the National Assembly. After the rioting had died down, the National Assembly—or rather, the revolutionary majority in the Assembly—could proceed in the useful assurance that the people were on its side, could feel that it had *carte blanche* to neglect royal protests as it went about its task of remaking France.

The revolution in Russia got under way with great speed. As we have seen in a previous chapter, there were plenty of precedents for a Russian uprising, and several generations of Russians had been discussing the inevitable coming of the storm. The first steps which led up to the February revolution of 1917, however, took even advanced leaders like Kerensky somewhat by surprise. Socialist parties the world over had been used to celebrating March 8th as Women's Day. On that day—February 23rd of the old Russian calendar, whence the name, February revolution, by which it has gone down in history—crowds of women workers from the factory districts poured into the streets calling for bread. Each day thereafter crowds increased. Orators of the radical group harangued at street corners. Soldiers from the large Petrograd wartime garrison mingled with the crowds, seemed indeed to sympathize with them. Even the Cossacks were not hostile to the people, or at any rate, seemed to lack stomach for fighting.

Meanwhile the authorities were consulting, and as piecemeal measures failed to work, they decided on March 11th to repress the troubles in accordance with a fine, neat plan already drawn up on paper for just such emergency. But the plan didn't work. The soldiers of the garrison, anxious not to be sent to the front, began to waver. On March 12th the first of the mutinies broke out, and one after another the famous regiments of the Imperial Army poured out of the barracks, but to join, not to shoot on, the crowds. Obscure leaders, sergeants, factory foremen and the like arose and directed their little groups at strategic points. Out of all the confusion and madness which makes the detailed record of events in this week the despair of the historian, one clear fact came out. There was no imperial government left in the capital, no formal government at all. Gradually there emerged the nucleus of the Soviet government to come, organized through trade unions, Socialist groups, and other workingclass sources. The Czar and his advisers, too bewildered and incompetent to control the movement, did prevent the legal Duma from taking control. Instead, moderates of all sorts got together to form the nucleus of the provisional government to come. In such a chaotic condition, indeed, it would seem that the action of the moderates is a uniformity of revolutions. Their sentiments and training impel them to try and put a stop to disorder, to salvage what they can of established routines.

Socialists and liberals alike were agreed that the Czar must abdicate. Nicholas himself had started from Headquarters for his palace at Tsarskoe Selo near Petrograd, but was held up at Pskov by the increasing disorders. Here, on March 15th, he decided to abdicate in favor of his brother, the Grand Duke Michael. What centralized power there was in Russia seems to have been in the hands of a committee of the Duma, and this committee waited on Michael in person. Kerensky, who was on the committee, seems at this juncture to have been as neurotically dramatic as usual; at Michael's refusal to accept the Crown he went into a transport of delight. Russia was to be a republic. Michael's own decision to refuse seems to have been dictated by personal cowardice. One of the nice problems of history in the conditional centers around the question of what would have happened had this Romanov been a man of courage, decision, and ability. No one can say, but the question reminds us that even in its most sociological moments, history cannot neglect the drama of personality and chance.

With Michael's abdication on March 16, 1917, the Russian revolution had clearly begun. There were repercussions in the provinces, and in some remote spots the fall of the Romanovs was not realized for weeks. But the work of those eight days had destroyed a centralized bureaucratic government at its most vital point—its head and nerve-center. Much in Russia was unchanged by the February revolution, but politically a week had done what it had taken years to do in England and France. The Romanovs had gone much more rapidly than the Stuarts and the Bourbons.

III. SPONTANEITY OR PLANNING?

Even from the foregoing sketch of the first steps in four revolutions, it should be clear that to the narrative historian the differences in the four are striking. The English revolution was begun in one of the oldest, best established of representative bodies; the American revolution began chiefly in New England, among people used to town meetings and colonial legislatures; the French revolution developed out of the meetings of a legislative body with no immediate precedents, staffed by men unused to parliamentary life; the Russian revolution started in street riots in the capital city, and went on without benefit of any parliamentary body, since even the old Duma met only through an emergency committee. There are differences of personality, differences of time and place. Charles raising his standard in hope at Nottingham in 1642 seems worlds apart from the abject Nicholas, buffeted about the northern plains in a railroad train at the mercy of striking workers and troops in revolt, drearily abdicating in the provincial gloom of Pskov. There may even be racial differences. The orderly and almost chivalrous Civil War of the English seems at first sight something quite unlike the madness of July 14th, or the tragicomic spectacle of metropolitan Petrograd in the hands of a mob without even a good slogan.

Yet this last should give us pause. At the informal level of mere dramatic or narrative likenesses, these early stages of revolution have similarities as striking as their differences. Speaker Lenthall defying Charles come to seize the five members, Mirabeau thundering his challenge to the bewildered Grand Master of Ceremonies at the royal session of June 23rd, Patrick Henry warning a king of the unfortunate fate of certain other rulers—these seem to be speaking the same language, assuming the same effective postures. The English House of Commons in the pandemonium of its final session in 1629 seems much like the French National Assembly during its frequent heated moments, and not worlds apart from certain important sessions of the Petrograd soviet.

For the emotions of men in groups, and the rhetoric and gestures necessary to bring out and make effective for action these emotions, are more uniform than the rationalist likes to think them. Any representative body of several hundred responds in definite ways to certain definite stimuli, and it does this the more certainly and invariably because it cannot respond to logic, cannot confront a new situation with complete experimental freedom. Especially are excited representative bodies much alike, whether they are composed of "irresponsible" Russians, "excitable" Frenchmen, or "sensible" Englishmen. We need not be surprised if in these early stages of revolution there are clear parallels in the behavior of men in such groups.

It is, however, more important for us to see whether there are not in these four revolutions uniformities which can be grouped together, related to the whole course of the movements, given a place in our conceptual scheme of the fever. What evidence have we here that we are dealing with a process which has definite and common stages? Do these first steps in revolution take place under conditions sociologically similar even if dramatically dissimilar?

One uniformity is crystal-clear. In all four of our societies, the existing government attempted to collect monies from people who refused to pay. All four of our revolutions started among people who objected to certain taxes, who organized to protest them, and who finally reached the point of agitating for the elimination and replacement of the existing government. This does not necessarily mean that those who resisted taxation foresaw or wished a radical revolution. It does mean that the transition from talking about necessary great changes—for in all our societies, as we have seen, something was in the air—to concrete action, was made under the stimulus of an unpopular form of taxation.

A second uniformity is quite as clear, though the consequences that derive from it are much more obscure. The events in this stage, these first steps in revolution, do most certainly bring out of the confused discontents of the old regime two parties into clear opposition, and indeed into preliminary violence. These parties we may call briefly the party of the old regime and the party of the revolution. Moreover, by the end of this period of the first stages, the party of the revolution has won. The muddy waters of doubt and debate are momentarily cleared. The revolution, hardly begun, seems over. In England after the Long Parliament had disposed of Strafford and wrung concessions from the King, in America after Concord, and that greatest of moral victories, Bunker Hill, in France after the fall of the Bastille, in Russia after the abdication, there is a brief period of joy and hope, the illusory but charming honeymoon of that impossible pair, the Real and the Ideal.

That our four revolutions ran through some such early stage as this, in which the opposition between old and new crystallized dramatically, and the new won a striking victory, is too evident for the most old-fashioned narrative historian to deny. Over the reasons why this stage developed as it did, however, there is still a running dispute among writers who concern themselves with such matters—historians, political theorists, sociologists, essayists. The heart of the dispute is a matter which must be got straight before anything like a sociology of revolutions is possible. Briefly, one set of disputants maintains that these glorious first steps in revolution are taken almost spontaneously by a united nation rising in its might and virtue to check its oppressors; another maintains that these first steps are the fruition of a series of interlocking plots initiated by small but determined groups of malcontents. By and large the first view is that taken by persons favorable to a given revolution, the second by persons hostile to it, or at least loyal to the memory of the old regime. There are, however, all sorts of variations on the theme, and different commentators have differently balanced these elements of spontaneity and planning.

This opposition is clearest, and in some ways quite adequately typical for our purpose, in the historiography of the French revolution. Augustin

Cochin used to describe this opposition as that between the *thèse des circonstances* and the *thèse du complot*, the explanation by circumstances and the explanation by plot. Those who on the whole regarded the revolution as a good thing maintained that the people of France, and especially the people of Paris, were goaded into revolt by the oppression of king and court, that the circumstances of their social, political, and economic life in 1789 are in themselves adequate explanation of what happened. Given such circumstances, and men and women of French blood, and you have revolution as naturally, as *automatically*, in a sense, as you have an explosion when a spark strikes gunpowder.

This figure may be applied to specific steps in the revolutionary process. The Bastille riots, for instance, were not planned in any sense. Paris heard of the dismissal of Necker, noted that the King was concentrating troops around Paris, and in a million forgotten conversations spread the fear that the King and his party were about to dismiss the revolutionary National Assembly and rule by armed force. Paris therefore rose in its might, and with a sure instinct seized on the Bastille as a symbol of the hated old regime, and destroyed it. The sovereign people were self-guided in all this, moved if you like by a natural force, by a hatred of injustice, and were led by hundreds of small men, by noncommissioned officers of the revolution, but not by any general staff, not by any small group who had deliberately planned an aggression.

The opposite theory maintains that the whole revolutionary movement in France was the work of a scheming and unprincipled minority, freemasons, *philosophes*, professional agitators. These people in the second half of the eighteenth century got control of the press and the platform, and persistently indoctrinated the literate part of France with a hatred for established institutions, and especially for the Church. As the government found itself in increasingly bad financial straits, these plotters wormed their way into its councils, and finally secured the promise of an Estates-General. By clever electioneering in a populace not used to representative assemblies, they filled the Third Estate with members of their sect, and succeeded in penetrating even the ranks of the First and Second Estates. They had been used to working together, and thanks to years of discussion of political reform, they knew what they wanted. The more determined and initiated of these plotters could therefore control the actions of the large and shapeless National Assembly, though they were a minority of its twelve hundred members.

Bastille Day seems very different to the writers of this school. Louis was concentrating troops to protect, not to dissolve, the National Assembly, to protect it from the minority of wild radicals who were abusing its machinery. Fearing defeat, these radicals stirred up Paris in a hundred ways: they sent orators to street corners and cafés; they distributed radical news-sheets and pamphlets; they sent agents to spread discontent among the royal troops, and especially among the French Guard; they even subsidized prostitutes to get at the soldiers more effectively. Everything was planned ahead for a more propitious moment, and when the dismissal of Necker afforded that moment, the signal was given and Paris rose. But not spontaneously. Somewhere a general staff—Mirabeau was on it, and most of the popular figures in the National Assembly—was working, carefully sowing the seeds of rebellion.

With the appropriate changes, this sort of opposition can be made out in all our revolutions. To the Stuart partisans—and they still find their way into print—the Great Rebellion was an unhappily successful conspiracy of gloomy money-grubbing Calvinists against the Merrie England of tradition. More commonly, since the Whigs gave the tone to modern England, the Parliamentarians are seen as liberty-loving children of Magna Charta, who rose quite naturally and spontaneously against unbearable Stuart tyranny. American Loyalists always maintained that the best of the country was with them, that the Whigs had won by superior organization and chicanery. Most of us, of course, were brought up to regard George III as a personal tyrant, a hirer of Hessians, a man who wished to grind the Americans into unmanly submission. The American revolution was to us the spontaneous reply of injured freemen to British insolence.

Finally, some Russian émigrés still seem to believe that a minority of unscrupulous Bolsheviks somehow engineered both the February and the October revolutions. Marxism attaches no shame to revolution, and admits the importance of planning and leadership in revolutionary movements. Therefore, though official Communist explanations by no means soft-pedal Czarist guilt and oppression, though they insist that the people of Russia in February, 1917, wholeheartedly and nearly unanimously rose against the Czar, still they admit, and indeed glory in, the role of leaders consciously planning a revolution. At least, this was the explanation accepted in orthodox Marxist circles, and it is classically stated in the first volume of Trotsky's *History of the Russian Revolution*. There are signs in Stalinite Russia of a reversion to something analogous to an American schoolbook explanation of our own revolution; Czarist tyranny and the spontaneous popular uprising are emphasized, the tactics of a revolutionary minority minimized.

Indeed, that these two conflicting, and in their exaggerated forms antithetical, explanations of the first steps in revolution should arise is in itself a clear uniformity to be got from the comparative study of revolutions. Very early indeed these two interpretations arise, the victorious revolutionists attributing their success to the rise of the many against intolerable tyranny, the defeated supporters of the old regime attributing their failure to the unscrupulous tactics of a minority of clever, wicked men. Neither explanation is interested primarily in facts or the scientific interpretation of facts; both are aimed at satisfying human sentiments. It is interesting to note that even the revolutionists' explanation seeks to gloss over violence, seems in a way ashamed of the fact of revolution. This again is perfectly natural, since once in power the revolutionists wish to stay in power. A useful help to this end is a general feeling among the governed that it is wrong to resist those in authority. By and large, successful revolutionists do not often subscribe to Jefferson's desire to see a revolution every twenty years or so; rather, they endeavor to create a myth of their own revolution, which becomes the last one necessary. Marxist theory even anticipates this, since the proletarian revolution ushers in the classless society, where there will be no class struggle, and no need for revolution.

It is, however, possible for us to go further than simply noting this division of opinion among the lovers and the haters of a given revolution. We may venture the generalization that there is some truth in both the explanation by circumstances and the explanation by plot. This may seem to many in 1938 a characteristically liberal and wishy-washy solution, a stupid adhesion to an outdated notion of a golden mean. But it does seem to have a more satisfactory relation with the facts than either extreme explanation.

Bastille Day may again serve as an example. There is plenty of evidence that organized groups did help stir up trouble in Paris in those July days. We know that the radical groups, the "patriots" in the Assembly at Versailles, had close connections with Paris politicians. A kind of skeletal political organization had been left over from the Paris elections to the Third Estate, and these Parisian electors helped greatly to bring a new municipal organization, and a new National Guard, out of the confusion of the riots. Most of the Royalist description of agents circulating in the crowds, of inflammatory pamphleteering, even perhaps of subsidized prostitutes, is substantially true. What is not true is that these elements of planning can be traced to any one or two small plotting groups, to the Duc d'Orléans, or to a few freemasons. The word "plot" is indeed a bad one—except for the purposes of Rightist propaganda, where it proves very useful indeed. Rather we must say that there is evidence of the activities of a number of groups of the kind any careful observer of societies knows well—pressure groups, embryo political parties, semi-religious sects, gatherings on the lunatic fringe. There is, however, no evidence that these very dissimilar groups were in July, 1789, managed from any one center, controlled by a small scheming directorate.

On the contrary, there is every evidence that once the dismissal of Necker got these various groups excited, what followed was in a sense spontaneous mob action. No one has yet said the final word on the psychology of crowds, but it is fairly well accepted that the behavior of crowds cannot be completely gauged in advance by the cleverest of mob leaders. Actually it is clear that in Paris in those days there was not one mob, but at least several dozens. People came out in the street because their neighbors were already out. They paraded up and down, shouting and singing, stopping now and then for another drink, or to hear another street-corner orator. Self-constituted leaders of little groups certainly supplemented any planned action. The decision to march on the Bastille seems to have been taken independently in several quarters. No one knows for sure who first had the brilliant idea of going to the Invalides Hospital to secure small arms. The rioting seems to have died out less because the Bastille fell than because the rioters were tired out. Three days is a long time to be riotous, or drunk, or both.

What holds for the taking of the Bastille holds for the general preparatory work and the first stages of revolutions as we have discussed them in this chapter. The Russian February revolution centered in Petrograd in one week and seems like the Bastille riots on a larger scale. Trotsky has done some of his best writing in his description of the February revolution and in his balanced accounting of what must be considered spontaneous popular risings and what must be attributed to conscious revolutionary tactics. Kerensky writes flatly that the revolution "came of its own accord, unengineered by anyone, born in the chaos of the collapse of Tsardom." Trotsky admits that no one planned or expected the revolution when it did come, that it developed out of ordinary Socialist manifestations and a mild bread-riot. But that development, he adds, was led by "conscious and tempered workers, educated for the most part by the party of Lenin." We may question the last part of this statement, but there can be no doubt that in the last few days of the Petrograd riots leaders of the coming soviet and leaders of the coming provisional government combined to force out the Czarist government.

The role of the pressure group is especially conspicuous in the early stages of the American revolution. As early as April, 1763, the merchants of Boston organized a "Society for Encouraging Trade and Commerce with the Province of Massachusetts Bay" with a standing committee of fifteen to watch trade affairs and call meetings. Accounts of their activities were sent to merchants in other colonies. To combat the Stamp Act the radicals organized themselves as "Sons of Liberty," a mass organization which met at times openly, at times secretly, to promote the work of revolution. Their vigilance committees "maintained a sort of Holy Inquisition with the sales and purchases of every man of business, into the outgoings and incomings of private households, and with the reported opinions of individuals." Town and county in the North, the county in the South, provided a framework for public meetings and resolutions. The Committees of Correspondence, organized originally as private pressure groups, were later skillfully manipulated by Sam Adams until they had partly supplanted the more conservative town meetings. Adams called into meeting in 1773 a joint committee for Boston, Dorchester, Roxbury, Brookline, and Cambridge which was able to swamp the now fairly conservative merchant vote. Throughout the movement, violence was employed whenever it seemed necessary, from grand affairs like the Boston Tea Party to isolated beating of Tories.

Yet the most realistic of our modern historians will hardly go so far as to assert that the American revolution was plotted by a tiny minority. The net effect of a dozen years of British mistakes, of concessions and retractions, blowings-hot and blowings-cold, together with a great variety of American agitation, was to produce in 1775 a widespread popular backing for the Continental Congress in its resistance to George III. It is quite impossible to say how many Whigs, how many Tories, and how many indifferent or neutral persons there in the thirteen colonies at the outbreak of armed hostilities. Probably there were proportionately more Tories than there were extreme Royalists in France in 1789 and many more than there were Czarists in Russia in 1917; and there were probably fewer Tories in revolutionary America than partisans of the Stuarts in England in 1642. But in all these cases it is a matter of proportion. The American revolution was, like the others, in part the result of an active, able, and far from infinitesimal minority working on a large majority group with grievances enough to be stirred up effectively when the right time came.

To sum the matter up in a metaphor: the school of circumstances regards revolutions as a wild and natural growth, its seeds sown among tyranny and corruption, its development wholly determined by forces outside itself or at any rate outside human planning; the school of plot regards revolutions as a forced and artificial growth, its seeds carefully planted in soil worked over and fertilized by the gardener-revolutionists, mysteriously brought to maturity by these same gardeners against the forces of nature. Actually, we must reject both extremes, for they are nonsense, and hold that revolutions do grow from seeds sown by men who want change, and that these men do do a lot of skillful gardening; but that the gardeners are not working against Nature, but rather in soil and in a climate propitious to their work; and that the final fruits represent a collaboration between men and Nature.

IV. THE ROLE OF FORCE

A final uniformity to be discerned in these first stages of our revolutions is perhaps the clearest and most important of all. In each revolution there is a point, or several points, where constituted authority is challenged by the illegal acts of revolutionists. In such instances, the routine response of any authority is to have recourse to force, police or military. Our authorities made such a response, *but in each case with a striking lack of success*. Those of the ruling class responsible for such responses in all our societies proved signally unable to make adequate use of force. Let us first look at the facts.

In England there was no considerable standing army, and of course nothing like a modern police force. Indeed, the question of control over what standing army there was had been one of the big issues between the first two Stuarts and their Parliaments. The Crown had been obliged to quarter its soldiers on private citizens in order to keep any kind of army together, and this quartering was one of the grievances most strongly held against Charles I. When a Scotch army crossed the border, Charles was obliged to call the Long Parliament to get money to buy this armed force off. When the actual break between Royalists and Parliamentarians drew near, both sides tried to constitute an armed force. Charles had the benefit of a devoted noble officer-class, and enough tenant-followers of noblemen and gentry to constitute what was by far the strongest armed force controlled by the government, or conservatives, or party-in-power side in any of our four revolutions. Yet the Civil War proved that he didn't have enough good soldiers, in comparison with the human resources available to the Parliament. Charles was beaten in the first instance because he lacked decisive military power.

Similarly in the American revolution, neither the American Tories nor the British armies were quite strong enough, as in the actual event they used their armed strength to suppress the revolutionists. Notably in the earlier stages, the British undertook to introduce what they knew to be unpopular governmental changes with what now seems an amazing disregard of police necessities. No doubt the long tradition of British loyal self-government made it hard for a British colonial administrator to conceive of any other methods. But the fact remains that these forces in North America in 1775 were quite inadequate to enforce authority. How many more men than Gage actually did have would have been necessary to keep royal order in Massachusetts Bay is a matter of guesswork, of perhaps unprofitable history-in-the-conditional. It is, however, unduly complimentary to rugged Yankee love of independence to suppose that no armed force could have been large enough to have controlled Massachusetts. Had there been a Napoleon instead of a Gage, there would perhaps have been a different end to the fighting. Whether such a policy of repression would not ultimately have produced a successful revolution anyway is a matter we are not called upon to discuss. What does concern us is the simple fact that in America also an important initial failure of the government was its failure to use force adequately and skillfully.

Louis XVI had in 1789 a fairly trustworthy armed force. His French troops were perhaps open to propaganda by the patriots. But he had important household troops, mercenaries recruited from foreign peoples, chiefly Swiss and German, and not accessible to French agitators. That the Swiss would die for him, or for their duty, was proved three years later at the storming of the Tuileries. He had, especially in the artillery, a capable set of officers, most of whom could be relied upon at this stage. Yet at the decisive moment, the rioting in Paris in July, he and his advisers failed to use the military. Again we edge into history-in-the-conditional, but one cannot avoid wondering what would have happened had a few disciplined troops with street guns attempted the reduction of Paris in July, 1789. Napoleon was later to show that such a force could readily beat down civilian resistance, and this fact was to be amply confirmed in 1848 and 1871. Louis might have failed. But the point is that he didn't even try. Once again a government has failed to make adequate use of force.

Petrograd in 1917 is the most perfect example of this important role of the military and the police. Everyone, from Czarist to Trotskyite, admits that what turned somewhat chaotic and aimless street demonstrations into a revolution was the failure of the elaborate government plan to restore order in Petrograd. And that plan failed because at the critical moment the soldiers refused to march against the people, but regiment by regiment came over instead to join them. Again, such is the advantage which a disciplined force with modern artillery possesses over even the most inspired civilian revolutionists, there can be little doubt that if the Cossacks and a few of the famous regiments of the line, the Preobrazhensky, for instance, had been warmly loyal to the government, even the somewhat incompetent rulers of Petrograd could probably have put down the disturbance. Whether another and worse riot was not inevitable within a few months under existing conditions of failure in war is not a matter that concerns us here.

This striking failure on the part of the rulers to use force successfully is not, however, likely to be an isolated and chance phenomenon. Indeed, it seems intimately bound up with that general ineptness and failure of the ruling class we have noticed in a previous chapter. Long years of decline have undermined the discipline of the troops, bad treatment has given the private soldiers a common cause with civilians, the officers have lost faith in the conventional and stupid military virtues. There is no co-ordinating command, no confidence, no desire for action. Or if there are some of these things, they exist only in isolated individuals, and are lost among the general incompetence, irresolution, and pessimism. The conservative cause—even the cause of Charles I—seems a lost cause from the start. The American case is somewhat different. Here we have an inept *colonial* government, but not an inept native ruling class.

We can then with some confidence attribute the failure of the conservatives to use force skillfully to the decadence of a ruling class. After all, we are dealing with fairly large groups of the kind we are accustomed to treating as subjects for sociological generalization. When, however, we attempt to bring the four crowned heads of our societies under some such general rule, we can hardly help feeling that we have no adequate statistical basis. Yet Charles I, George III, Louis XVI, and Nicholas II display such remarkable similarities that one hesitates to call in chance as an explanation. Trotsky confidently asserts that a decaying society will inevitably head up into the kind of incompetence displayed by these monarchs. We dare not display quite as much confidence, but we must bring forward these uniformities in the behavior of four men as a valid part of our observed uniformities. At any rate their being what they were had an important part in that process through which the revolutionists won their preliminary and decisive victories over incompetent authority.

At the very least, one can discern in all these monarchs mistakes which point to their lack of a reasonably objective thing, the technical skill necessary to rule men. If a baseball player strikes out consistently over a long stretch of games, and fields badly, it may be because of poor eyesight, or family troubles, or a lot of other reasons, but the simple fact remains that he is a poor ball-player. Our four kings were poor kings, though they were all good family men, men on the whole whom we should probably list as good, or at least as well-meaning. Nicholas was petty and jealous, as well as ignorant and superstitious, and by conventional Christian moral standards probably the worst of the lot. But he was far from being a cruel tyrant. Louis was kindly, well-meaning, but singularly unsuited to affairs of state. Both men were deficient intellectually, were very much under the domination of determined, passionate, proud, and ignorant wives, and both have left diaries which display amazing parallels in obtuseness. Louis went hunting on Bastille Day and in his diary records "Nothing"; Nicholas in a similar crisis records "Walked long and killed two crows; had tea by daylight."

We cannot here go into the fascinating subject of the personalities of all these monarchs. George III was high-minded, stupid, and stubborn, which is a very bad combination indeed in a ruler. Charles is humanly the most attractive of the four; there is a sound basis for the romantic legend woven around him. But he was a bad king for a number of reasons, of which the chief were perhaps first an almost complete inability to understand what was going on in the hearts and heads of those of his subjects commonly called Puritans—and this emphatically includes the Scotch Calvinists—and, second, a tendency to high-minded intrigue. In politics, high-mindedness and intrigue are much safer if kept decently apart. This much, in summary, we may conclude about our kings. However much they differed as men, they were alike in being wholly unable to make effective use of force, even had they possessed it, at the first stages of the revolution.

For our revolutions, then, we may put this last uniformity very simply: they were successful in their first stages; they became actual revolutions instead of mere discussions, complaints, and riotings, only after revolutionists had beaten, or won over, the armed forces of the government. We cannot attempt to erect uniformities for other revolutions or for revolutions in general. But we may here suggest in very tentative and hypothetical form the generalization that no government has ever fallen before revolutionists until it has lost control over its armed forces or lost the ability to use them effectively; and conversely that no revolutionists have ever succeeded until they have got a predominance of effective armed force on their side.

V. THE HONEYMOON

The first stage of revolution ends in all four of our societies with the victory of the revolutionists after what is rather dramatic than serious bloodshed. The hated old regime has been conquered so easily! The way is open to the regeneration men have been so long talking about, so long hoping for. Even the Russian February revolution, though it broke out in the midst of the misery and shame of defeat at the hands of Germans and Austrians, was cradled in the hope and joy that seems a natural heritage of revolutions. Russians all over the world heard the good news with delight. Liberals were as happy as their ancestors had been in '76 and '89. Now Russia was washed clean of the stain of absolutism, could take her place with confidence in the ranks of her sister democracies of the West, join with a new effectiveness in the crusade against the sole remaining forces of darkness, the Hohenzollerns and the Hapsburgs.

The honeymoon stage of revolution is most perfectly developed in France, where the revolution came in peacetime, and at the end of a great intellectual movement called the Enlightenment which had prepared men's minds for a new and practical miracle. Wordsworth's lines are familiar:

> France standing on the top of golden hours,
> And human nature seeming born again.

But poets in a dozen languages set to work to celebrate the regeneration of France and of mankind. And not only poets. Sober business men, professional men, country gentlemen, people who in the twentieth century tend to regard revolution with horror, joined in the rejoicing. Far away in unenlightened Russia noblemen illuminated their houses in honor of the fall of the Bastille. Americans and Englishmen rejoiced that the ancient enemy had come to join the self-governing peoples. Frenchmen themselves were for a brief happy moment almost unanimous. The King had seen the error of his ways, had embraced the paladin Lafayette, had come freely to his good city of Paris to hear the cheers of the heroes of the Bastille.

Yet the honeymoon period even in France was brief, briefer yet in Russia, in England and in America never quite so clear and so definite. In the first stages, and at the critical moment when the test of force comes, the old regime is faced by a solid opposition. The opposition is indeed composed of various groups, is never that myth a "united people." But it is welded by the necessity of effectively opposing the government into a genuine political unit, into something more than a chance coalition of contradictory elements. Its victory is, if we are willing to take the terms critically and not sentimentally, the victory of the "people" over its "oppressors." It has shown itself stronger and abler than the old government in this time of crisis. It has now become the government, and is facing a new set of problems. When it actually gets to work on those problems the honeymoon is soon over.

Bibliography

Altman, Elizabeth G. "C. Cane Brinton." In *International Encyclopedia of the Social Sciences,* 18 vols., edited by David L. Sills. New York, 1968–79. Vol.18: 72–750.

Berkhofer, Robert F., Jr. *A Behavioral Approach to Historical Analysis.* New York, 1969.

Davies, James C. "Toward a Theory of Revolution." *American Sociological Review,* 27(February 1962): 5–19.

Gottschalk, Louis; Clyde Kluckhohn; and Robert Angell, eds. *The Use of Personal Documents in History, Anthropology, and Sociology.* New York, 1945. (Social Science Research Council Bulletin 53).

Gottschalk, Louis, ed. *Generalization in the Writing of History.* Chicago, 1963.

Hofstadter, Richard. "History and the Social Sciences." In *The Varieties of History,* 2d ed., edited by Fritz Stern. New York, 1973.

Landes, David S., and Charles Tilly, eds. *History as Social Science.* Englewood Cliffs, N.J., 1971.

Merriman, Roger B. *Six Contemporaneous Revolutions.* Oxford, 1938. [Published the same year as Brinton, but stresses uniqueness.]

Saveth, Edward N., ed. *American History and the Social Sciences.* New York, 1964.

Social Science Research Council. Bulletin 64, *The Social Sciences in Historical Study: A Report of the Committee on Historiography.* New York, 1954.

Social Science Research Council. Bulletin 54, *Theory and Practice of Historical Study: A Report of the Committee on Historiography.* New York, 1946.

CHAPTER 20

William O. Aydelotte

"Voting Patterns in the British House of Commons in the 1840s"

(1963)

The emergence of quantification in history cannot be so easily documented by reference to a single paradigmatic figure as some other changes in historical writing can. It may be useful to observe, however, that Lucien Febvre's successors turned the Annalist school rather sharply in a statistical direction following the Second World War and that Crane Brinton's social science (note especially *The Jacobins*) used statistical analysis to document generalizations about revolutionary character. William O. Aydelotte's work is simply plucked from that of a group of scholars in America who challenged their colleagues to abandon generalizations based upon impressions of a few cases and turn instead to computer-analyzed data. If they could not produce final, scientific answers, they would at least force historians to discipline their thinking. The challenge revived the old debate between the historicists and the social scientists concerning the idiographic or nomothetic character of history. Carl Bridenbaugh, president of the American Historical Association in 1962, warned historians not "to worship at the shrine of that bitch-goddess QUANTIFICATION," while Robert Fogel, a pioneer in "econometrics," was equally confident that the future of history lay in numbers.

Amidst a heated controversy in the 1960s, Aydelotte's voice was a voice of moderation. A historian to whose own work computer analysis was central, he published a review and criticism of the new history in 1966 that dwelled as much on the limitations of quantification as on its prospects. His commentary, listed in the bibliography for this chapter, quickly became a standard introduction to the discussion for students.

Though quantification seemed the special province of "younger historians'' in the 1960s, William Aydelotte was already fifty-six years old when his critical essay established his place in the debate. He was born in Indiana in 1910 and educated at Harvard University (A.B., 1931) and Cambridge University (Ph.D., 1934). Following two years' government service as an administrator in a New Deal agency, Aydelotte began a teaching career that would take him from the University of Minnesota in 1937 to Trinity College, Smith College, and finally to the University of Iowa, where he taught from 1947 to his retirement in 1978. His first book, *Bismarck and British Colonial Policy* (1937), employed a fairly standard methodology, and not until he published studies of British Parliamentary politics in the 1960s did his work begin to demonstrate what quantification could contribute to the understanding of the past.

Aydelotte defines quantification as "the numerical summary of comparable data," which is, perhaps, too simple, since the word has come to mean different things to different historians. It may refer only to techniques of statistical analysis, such as Aydelotte's use of a "scalogram" in the article reprinted here, or it may mean the sweeping reduction of history to econometrics, in which models and theoretical constructs of modern political economy are filled in with historical instead of current data. Thus, Robert Fogel in *Railroads and American Economic Growth* (1964) theorized what history would have been like without railroads to determine how important they were to economic growth in the late nineteenth century. His work involved positing a "counterfactual" world of roads and canals that never existed outside his mathematical model. Or quantification can mean "serial history," which the Annalist historian François Furet defines as "forming historical fact into temporal series of homogenous and comparable units, so that evolution can be measured in terms of fixed intervals." Thus, changes in and correlations among series on agricultural production, climate, population growth, and so on can be studied to reveal unique configurations for a few years or trends over many years. Furet's concession to historicism is small, of course, for he insists on repetition of occurrences and says that the credibility and significance of a piece of information comes from its relation to other elements forward and backward in the series rather than from other sources within its own time.

The compatibility of quantification with historicism is still an open question. By recognizing its limitations, Aydelotte's critique of 1966 went some way toward allaying the suspicions of many historians that quantification could produce a scientifically knowable past only by defining much of historical experience out of existence. But one should still read the more radical criticism in Jacques Barzun's *Clio and the Doctors* (1974). "In the end," Barzun, an eminent cultural historian, writes, "multiplicity defeats regularity and no one can turn from the record or the history feeling that 'now he knows.' Truth is a relative term, here as always, an abbreviation for truthfulness."

Reprinted here is a portion of Aydelotte's article, "Voting Patterns in the

British House of Commons in the 1840s." His own description of the "scalo-gram" (pp.337-38) needs no amplification here. But note that this statistical ranking of votes on various subjects in Parliament reveals relationships and linkages among men and events that could not be known without the proce-dure. The results are unexpected and cry out for explanation. Aydelotte's in-terpretation, which takes up the bulk of the essay, is based on his awareness of the character of Victorian England—including an historicist's sense of the unique possibilities and likelihoods of the time—drawn from more traditional ways of studying history.

The original documentation has been omitted here, but Aydelotte makes frequent reference to G. Kitson Clark, *The Making of Victorian England* (Lon-don, 1962); readers not familiar with men and events brought up in the article may find this standard work useful.

IN THE 1840s, the time of Sir Robert Peel's great ministry, the British House of Commons debated and voted upon a number of substantial political issues. The Parliament of 1841-47 not only repealed the Corn Laws; it also placed on the statute books important legislation regulating factories, banks, railways and mines. It approved the income tax, reintro-duced by Peel in 1842, and the Poor Law, which was renewed in 1842 and again in 1847. It discussed and voted upon, though it was far from approv-ing, proposals for the extension of the franchise, the adoption of the secret ballot and the restriction of the special legal privileges of landowners. There were divisions as well on various aspects of the Irish question, reli-gious questions and the position of the Church of England, army reform, fiscal reform and other matters.

The magnitude of these questions, the richness of content of the poli-tics of the 1840s, make this decade of exceptional interest for the study of the development of modern political attitudes. Many of the most signifi-cant issues that arose as a consequence of Britain's transformation from an agricultural to an industrial state were raised, even if only in a prelimi-nary form, in the debates in this Parliament. The relations between these questions constitute a problem of historical interpretation of great inter-est. This problem, the general character of the ideological patterns of the period has, however, been relatively little studied in detail.

Yet there exists a source, a body of materials, on this subject which is

Reprinted by permission of the publisher from William O. Aydelotte, "Voting Patterns in the British House of Commons in the 1840's," *Comparative Studies in Society and History* 5 (Jan. 1963), 134-55, 161-63. Copyright © 1963 by Cambridge University Press.

not only readily available but is also fuller and more reliable than most sources which historians have at their disposal. This is the division lists in Hansard. The peculiar value of these lists is that they contain expressions of opinion upon important subjects from men who are no longer available for questioning. It does not strain terms too much to say that, imaginatively used, they can constitute a kind of questionnaire which we may submit to the dead and on which they will give us their replies. Further, the information about the votes of members of Parliament is perhaps more complete and more certain than anything else that is known about them. Their social background, their economic interests and their relations with their constituents can be studied with profit, but on such matters the information is and always will be fragmentary and there are nuances which it is difficult now to recapture. By contrast, the stands which these men publicly adopted on the major issues of the day are documented by the division lists with a wealth of detail, repeated corroboration and, I have reason to believe, a relatively high degree of accuracy.

It is important, also, that the division lists give information for all the men in Parliament, so far as they voted in the issues in question. Doubtless the opinions of a limited number of prominent individuals could be gleaned from their biographies or private papers; this would not, however, be possible for more than a small fraction of the group since, for the majority, detailed biographical materials are not available. Yet one may not generalize about a large group of men on the basis of a few individual cases, and an undue concentration on the principal characters may be misleading about the rank and file. Dr. G. Kitson Clark rightly criticizes the facile generalizations and oversimplified stereotypes about the opinions of the governing class in some of the older works on this period, and asserts that: "The old bland confident general statements about whole groups of men, or classes, or nations ought to disappear from history." To say this, however, is not to say that the ideas and opinions of the governing class cannot be investigated. The point is that we must make sure of our ground, and base generalizations about a group upon information that applies to all members of it, so far as such information exists. It is in this context that the division lists appear to be a source of peculiar interest and value. Their merit is that they yield information, and comparable information for the entire group.

The division lists have never been fully exploited. Whatever may be the reasons for this, certainly the bulk and the complexity of the materials make them difficult to use. It is hard to see the wood for the trees or to obtain a general view that will at the same time do justice to the richness of the information. Most members of Parliament did not vote consistently "liberal" or consistently "conservative" on all issues; only a small minority, those on the extreme left and the extreme right did this; the great majority approved of reform on some questions and disapproved of it on others. Nor were all men "liberal" or "conservative" in the same sense: some (though by no means all) of those liberal in the sense of supporting free trade were conservative in the sense of opposing factory legislation; some (though by no means all) of those conservative in the sense of opposing free trade were liberal in the sense of supporting factory legislation. It seems hard to make sense out of all this, and these complexities have been more fully appreciated as the period has come to be studied more carefully. Writers of some of the older texts sought to interpret the political history of the time in terms of some "angle," some general principle that would tie together a number of diverse happenings. Early Victorian politics have been variously explained as a battle between the poor and the rich, between agriculture and industry or between the principles of laissez-faire and state intervention. As our knowledge has increased these general schemes have come somewhat under a cloud—though one still hears of them—and they have been replaced by a new realization of the complexity of events and by a scepticism about the possibility of describing what happened in any readily intelligible pattern of formula. This feeling of scepticism is one that I myself shared until recently. As I wrote in an earlier article, "the prevailing social and political objectives of this age form a rich and complex pattern which is as stimulating to study as it is difficult to characterize." My views on this subject have changed, however, and I now think that I can begin to characterize it.

By borrowing a technique worked out in a different field for a different purpose I have been able to find patterns that embrace a large amount of this material and, I believe, aid substantially in its interpretation. I had glimmerings of such a pattern some years ago when I observed a relationship between votes on several issues in the House of Commons: I found that some men supported all three; others opposed the first but supported the second and third; others opposed the first and second but supported the third; while a fourth group opposed all three proposals. Although I did not know it, I had stumbled upon a central feature of the Guttman scale. At that time, I lacked both the technical skills and the theoretical knowledge to proceed further, and I did not appreciate the significance of what I had found; I dropped the subject and turned to other matters. Some years later, as a result of a suggestion made by a colleague in another department I decided to try a Guttman scalogram analysis on my data, not with great hope of profit, but as an experiment to see what would happen. To my surprise a pattern emerged which even at the first attempt could be clearly distinguished, and which much further work has now brought into sharply defined focus.

The basic property of a Guttman scale is that it ranks in cumulative order two things: the issues voted upon and the men voting upon them, and, furthermore, ranks each of these terms in terms of the other. The issues that fit a scale may be ordered according to the proportion of favorable votes each received, the one having the least support—i.e., the hardest to vote for, the most radical proposal—coming first, and the one having the most support coming last. The men are then ranked according to the number of issues each supported, those voting positive or "liberal" on all being placed at the top, and those against everything at the bottom. It is by no means a foregone conclusion that these procedures will create a scale: the technique is, properly speaking, not a means of establishing a scale but a means of testing for the existence of one, discovering whether such a pattern is intrinsic in the material. If a scale does exist, however, this double ranking should produce a reasonably consistent pattern in which all persons voting positively on a given issue will prove to have voted positively on all issues lower in the scale and will also have higher ranks than all those who voted on this same issue negatively. By the same token, all those voting negatively on a given issue will prove to have voted negatively on all issues higher in the scale and will have lower ranks than all those who voted on this issue positively. In a perfect Guttman scale every fourfold table showing the relation between two items in the scale has an empty cell, since no one who responds negatively to the more popular or lower item will respond positively to the less popular or higher item.

The scheme can be readily understood from Table 1. This table compares the votes in five divisions with each other and shows how those voting positively or negatively in each one voted in each of the other four. The selection and ordering of the issues were determined only after considerable investigation. A comparison of these five issues with each other produces ten fourfold tables. If the issues are arranged in the order indicated, it turns out that those who voted positively on the first item also voted positively on the remaining four, so far as they voted on them at all. Those voting positively on the second item also vote positively on the last three, though they were divided on the first item, 37 of them being for it and 26 against it. The remaining items fall into a similar pattern. Each of the ten fourfold tables contains one cell that is empty or almost empty, this being the upper right-hand cell in every case. In the ten fourfold tables shown in Table I the upper right-hand cell is completely empty in two cases, it is less than one-half of one percent in four others, and it is 2% or less in two others. The upper right-hand figures in the last two tables, 19 and 15, look somewhat larger but on a percentage basis they are also insignificant, 4% and 3% respectively, a relatively trifling proportion of exceptions to the general pattern.

Not all issues will fit together in a cumulative scale of this kind. Thus, for example, a man's vote on the Corn Law motion of 1846 tells nothing

TABLE I. FIRST SCALE

		Chartism, 1842		Corn Laws, 1843		Income Tax, 1842		Corn Laws, 1846		Duty on Livestock, 1842	
		+	−	+	−	+	−	+	−	+	−
Chartist petition 3 May 1842	+	51	0	37	2	43	2	40	0	32	1
	−	0	289	26	224	48	195	117	111	197	62
Repeal of Corn Laws, 15 May 1843	+			127	0	93	4	111	0	94	2
	−			0	383	31	247	119	194	209	98
Opposition to Income Tax Bill, First Reading, 18 April 1842	+					190	0	146	8	126	19
	−					0	287	87	138	183	63
Corn Law Repeal Bill, 3rd Reading 15 May 1846	+							349	0	223	15
	−							0	251	91	78
Rejection of proposal that duty on imported livestock be taken by weight, 23 May 1842	+									115	0
	−									0	382

about his vote on the Ten Hours division of 1844; votes in the two divisions are quite irregular with each other. (The figures are given in Table IV [omitted].) If, however, such cumulative patterns can be found, as I have found them in great quantity here, a scalogram analysis can be useful in that it reveals a relation between a number of different questions, some of which received very different degrees of support. It thus incorporates into a single intelligible scheme a far larger amount of information than could be brought together by a simpler method, and points the way to generalizations based not on votes in one division or on one issue only but on much wider information, on a number of issues considered together in terms of their relationship with each other. This is, I think, the particular interest of scalogram analysis: that it permits the continuation of the search of uniformities, for wider patterns, on a reasonably secure foundation of accuracy and reliability. The result of detailed research can be disheartening: it often destroys existing theories without offering anything to replace them. What is useful about sealogram analysis is that it helps to reverse this trend. It makes possible a concrete, precise and detailed description of the larger patterns of voting behavior and political choice in this Parliament and it may also, by revealing these patterns, suggest some insights into the ideas, preconceptions or working political assumptions that underlay them.

The operations performed in preparation for this report may be briefly summarized as follows:

(1) The votes cast by the 815 men who sat in the House of Commons between the general elections of 1841 and 1847 in a total of 114 divisions were recorded on IBM cards. Recording and checking this information, which comprised nearly 93,000 items of data (92,910, to be exact) proved a formidable task involving several years work and the help of a number of assistants. Every division was checked at least three times; some had to be checked as many as ten times to run down all discrepancies. I am satisfied that the information now on my cards is substantially correct. No formal sampling procedure was used in the selection of issues. I simply tried to get in at least one division on each of what seemed the most important questions, and tried also to cover more thoroughly certain highly controversial subjects of particular interest by including a considerable number of divisions on each. These last included such topics as: political reform, free trade, the Poor Law, the income tax, Irish questions, religious questions and the regulation of working hours in factories. Most of the divisions tabulated took place during the lifetime of the Parliament of 1841–47, but I included a number from earlier and later Parliaments as well.

(2) A conjunction count was made on a 650 IBM machine showing the relation of the votes cast by men in the Parliament of 1841–47 in each of these 114 divisions to their votes in each of the others. In other words, a set of fourfold tables was prepared showing the extent to which those who voted positively or negatively in each division voted positively or negatively in each of the others. This resulted in a total of 6,441 fourfold tables, each of which was punched on a separate card which gave the frequencies, marginals, totals and percentages. This seems like a wholly unmanageable amount of information; however, I had the tables classified mechanically and then printed up in a form in which it was not too difficult to do a good deal of work with them manually. These procedures necessitated the invention of a certain number of techniques on which I will not elaborate here. It should be made clear, however, that the method I have used for deriving scales is that of paired comparisons, rather than any other of the variety of means that have been suggested for scaling. My method differs from those employed by others also in the point that I have not used a single group or sample of the individuals in the population throughout the operation. I have, on the contrary, included in each paired comparison all the men who voted on both the issues in question. This meant using not one sample but as many samples as I had pairs, or a total of

6,441, though probably a number of them included nearly the same men. Though this procedure may appear unconventional it has the advantage that it permits the use, for each paired comparison, of all the evidence available.

(3) From an inspection of these tables I attempted to build such scales as the evidence permitted. The method was to begin with two divisions that stood in a scale relationship to each other in the sense that the four-fold table comparing the votes in the two divisions had an "empty" cell in the upper right-hand or lower left-hand corner. An "empty cell" was defined, after a certain amount of experimentation, as one containing less than 6% of the total of the figures in the four cells put together. It was also a criterion of a scale relationship that each of the figures in the other three cells should be 6% or more and that each should be more than twice as large as the figure in the "empty" cell. Two items that proved to be related in this way could then be shown to be related to a third, and so on, and a scale could be built up. These steps may sound more elaborate in description than they proved in execution: I was able to devise a number of short cuts by which the work could be expedited. . . .

The procedure described here is more empirical than that ordinarily followed. It is more usual to start with a hypothesis and then verify it; to define, on the basis of an inspection of the subject-matter of the items, a "universe of content" and then to test whether the items that seem to belong to it fall into a scale. I have, however, gone at the problem in the opposite way. I obtained my scales first, from the paired comparisons, without regard to my own notions of which items belonged together and which did not, and then considered whether these relationships could be explained by postulating a "universe of content" to which all the items in a given scale might plausibly be supposed to belong. Doubtless some hypothesizing was implicit in the original selection of divisions for analysis, but this was only of a very general kind.

The proper defense of an empiricism so strict as this is that it helps to emancipate the student from his own preconceptions. This seems particularly advantageous when one is attempting to describe the attitudes of a body of men removed at some distance in time and whose political assumptions, as the following discussion will show in detail, were rather different from those prevailing today. It is only too easy to misinterpret the views of men living a century ago, to believe that what seems important or what seems reasonable to us must have appeared in the same light to them and to read our own assumptions or prejudices into the past. A quantitative analysis of attitudes serves to bring out the discrepancies between present and past opinions, and gives a means of evaluating issues which, a hundred years ago, could have had a very different meaning from what they do now. It brings out connections that one might not have expected

TABLE II. SECOND SCALE

		Poor Law, 1847		Lace Factories Bill, 1846		Ten Hours, 1844		Ten Hours, 1847		Roebuck's resolution, May 1844	
		+	−	+	−	+	−	+	−	+	−
Vote against 2nd Reading of Poor Law Bill, 21 May 1847	+	44	0	17	69	22	7	26	1	24	3
	−	0	220	23	1	64	62	71	46	88	40
Duncombe's Lace Factories Bill, 20 May 1846	+			68	0	37	6	48	0	40	2
	−			0	153	24	73	20	52	65	33
Ten Hours, 1844: clause 8 of bill specifying "12 hours" per day, 22 March 1844	+					194	0	104	6	109	5
	−					0	191	13	48	94	41
Ten Hours, 1847: rejection of Hume's proposal for postponement, 17 Feb. 1847	+							197	0	105	6
	−							0	89	24	35
Rejection of Roebuck's resolution against interference with contractual power of adult labourers, 3 May 1844	+									284	0
	−									0	78

and also reveals that some connections that one might have expected did not in fact exist. The difficulty of comprehending the opinions of men in the past century, whose ideas were in many ways so like ours but in many ways so different, suggests that it is advisable to lean as far as possible in the direction of objectivity and empiricism. In dealing with problems and with a body of materials which are so complex and about which so much is still unknown, there would seem to be a strong case for making the original investigation an exploratory one.

From this analysis there emerged a great number of different scales. What also emerged, however, and what makes it possible to present in an article a general view of the results of a rather complicated investigation, was the fact that many of these scales coincided with one another. Voting patterns in the British House of Commons in the mid-nineteenth century were, in striking contrast to those revealed by studies of the United States and France in the mid-twentieth century, relatively simple, regular and comprehensive. What I have found is that the great majority of the divisions analysed, over four-fifths, belonged to one or the other of two principal scale patterns. These two scales are illustrated in Tables I and II. It will be noted that, in each, the proportion of votes that do not fit the scale—the figures in the upper-right corners of the fourfold tables—is extremely small.

Table I contains 2,989 pieces of information; of these, 2,939 or 98.3% fit the pattern. In Table II, of the 1,554 pieces of information presented, 1,517 or 97.6% fit the pattern. It will be observed also that it is possible for two divisions on the same subject, at two different dates, to fit at different points in the same scale. Those supporting Corn Law repeal in 1843 continued to support it in 1846, but by then they had been joined by others and the 1846 Corn Law vote, in which a considerably larger proportion favored repeal, comes at a lower point in the scale. A similar change took place on the Ten Hours question between 1844 and 1847.

It turned out, however, that many other divisions belonged to one or the other of these two patterns. Each item in each of the two illustrations was selected out of a number of possible alternatives, any of which could have been substituted for it without impairing the symmetry of the scale. Instead of using the division on the Chartist petition as the first item on the first scale, it would have been possible to use the division on Roebuck's motion to exclude earned incomes from the income tax on 17 February 1845, or the division on the motion to abolish parliamentary oaths on 30 March 1843, or Roebuck's motion against the privileged status of Irish landowners of 8 March 1847. A positive vote in any of these three divisions predicts a positive vote on all four of the other divisions used in the illustration. Similar substitutions could have been made at other points on both scales. The exact figures are as follows. An analysis was made of a total of 114 divisions. Four of these could not be used for scaling, since the votes on only one side were recorded. Of the 110 usable divisions, 72 or 65.5% fit the first scale and 28 or 25.5% fit the second. For the most part the scales are quite unrelated, as appears from Table IV [omitted]; it turned out, however, that 11 items or 10% could be fitted into either scale, a curious fact to which I shall revert. Between them the two scales included a net total of 89 items or 81% of the usable divisions; 21 items or 19% did not fit either scale. . . .

The following remarks will deal principally with what seems the most interesting feature of the findings, the fact that divisions on different subjects occur together in the same scale. That a number of issues which seem to us unconnected should prove to be related may at first appear surprising. If all the items in a scale concerned one question only, the pattern would be easier to understand. If, for example, the central question in the scale had been the amount of duty on a given article of import, some would perhaps want a certain amount, others this much and more and so on, and there might be a regular progression through a number of steps. In the first scale, however, it turns out that divisions on very different subjects are brought together in this same intimate fashion. To take only the items used in the illustration, almost all those who voted for the Chartist petition favored Corn Law repeal so early as 1843, almost all those who voted for Corn Law repeal in 1843 opposed the income tax and so on. Votes on these different questions were associated together as they might have been if they had all been votes on the same question, and it is not easy to see why this should have been the case.

Yet these associations between diverse issues were actually far more extensive than is indicated by the illustrations given. The first scale, which is the more comprehensive of the two, includes divisions on, among other things: free trade, not merely in corn but also in articles like sugar and cattle; religious questions, such as the abolition of parliamentary oaths, the opening of public exhibitions on Sunday, the temporalities of the Church of Ireland, the Ecclesiastical Courts Bill of 1844, Roman Catholic Relief, and the removal of Jewish disabilities; Irish questions; the income tax; proposals affecting the status and privileges of landowners, such as Elphinstone's motion in 1842 that legacy and probate duties on the succession to real property be equated with those on the succession to personal property, or Roebuck's motion in March 1847 attacking the privileged status of Irish landlords; the abolition of flogging in the army; the reduction of the national debt; the Health of Towns Bill; Russell's education proposals in 1847; and the Masters and Servants Bill of 1844. These different topics seem to have been closely associated in the minds of men living at the time. Members of Parliament, though they disagreed as to the merits of these questions, yet apparently possessed a set of common views or shared assumptions regarding their relation to each other and the order in which they stood. The existence of these associations and their great extent constitute a principal finding of this investigation and present a difficult but challenging problem of historical interpretation.

Connections or relationships between some of these questions have been observed or at least surmised by other scholars. Some of these connections were also identified in debates in Parliament at the time: I have often noticed that a speech on one of the issues in the scale may bring in several of the others. Thus, for example, Sharman Crawford, speaking on reform of the representation, found occasion to mention also the national debt, the privileged legal position of the landowning class, the Corn Laws and the Irish question, and the context in which he introduced these subjects suggests that to him they were almost inseparable from one another. The scale, however, provides a more weighty demonstration than could be obtained from other sources of the connection of these questions in the minds of members of this Parliament and also a more exact account of which issues were related to each other and—what has proved very important—which ones were not related. Nor, I believe, has it been shown before what a number and variety of different questions were tied together in this general scheme.

The problem is to find a theory that will account for these relationships. The most plausible interpretation, and one that is commonly advanced for such findings, is that the items in the scale represented to the men who voted on them different aspects of or different ways of stating some larger general question. The usual interpretation of a scale is that it represents either a single variable or else several closely correlated ones. Although a scale is not regarded as necessarily demonstrating the existence of a single variable, it is consistent with this hypothesis, and to postulate such a variable may turn out to be the most reasonable and convincing way of accounting for the evidence. It seems difficult to explain the results except by assuming the existence of some more general question or issue which was reflected in or in some way related to all these divisions and which was also important enough so that it might plausibly be regarded as the determining consideration in the voting in each.

To suggest that the many subjects in the first scale all reflect a single variable or several closely correlated ones may appear to be an oversimplification. It might be objected that a vote or any other political choice is often a complex matter, perhaps a compromise between pressures pulling in different directions and, therefore, reflecting a number of different objectives. Doubtless this is often the case. Yet it is also possible that a single issue or a single variable may be reflected in men's votes on many questions, and the great number of issues that fit the first scale affords a strong presumption that this was the case here. A certain caution in regard to generalizations is right and proper, but it should not induce us to ignore uniformities in the evidence when they are handed to us on a silver platter. It may be instructive, then, to consider whether these issues have in any sense a common content or a common denominator that may account for the observed relationship between them. . . .

It is tempting to describe the first scale, by analogy to a scale that has appeared quite prominently in modern dimensional studies, as a rural-urban conflict. Or, perhaps, in the terms more commonly used in the 1840s, it might be described as a conflict between agricultural interests and business and professional interests, between the aristocracy and the "middle classes." This, of course, is not the kind of class controversy we think of in connection with modern politics, between rich and poor, but rather one between rich and rich, between the great landowners and the great merchants and industrialists, between the old and the new forms of wealth. Though I am not entirely happy about such an interpretation, for reasons which I will explain, there are certainly some features of the evidence that make it plausible.

It seems supported, in the first place, by an analysis of the content of a number of issues that belong in the first scale. Radical attacks by Roebuck or Elphinstone on the special privileges of the landowners fit the scheme easily enough. The free trade cause and particularly the movement for the repeal of the Corn Laws were regarded in many quarters at the time, whether rightly or wrongly, as directed against the interests of the landowners and as favoring the commercial and manufacturing interests. The moderate proposals for political reform in this decade could be regarded as designed to establish a reliably middle-class electorate and thus to increase the influence of the newer interests in the House of Commons.

Perhaps the many divisions relating to religious subjects and the Church of England and a number of the large divisions on certain aspects of the Irish question could also be comprehended in a scheme of this character. It is often said that the conflict between the Establishment and Dissent was as much a social question as a theological one. Admittedly the connection between religious and social questions was occasionally contrived as, for example, in the case of Cobden's success in enlisting the support of a large number of dissenting ministers for the anti-Corn Law cause. Yet the fact that such a maneuver was even feasible, that it was possible to line up religious sentiment behind a political objective of this kind, tells something about the associations of ideas that seem to have been acceptable at the time. As for the Irish question, it could be and apparently was regarded, by some at least, as a kind of paradigm of ideological and social questions in England, an area in which they could be fought out in a preliminary way. Irish problems were, in particular, closely related to two sensitive points of general controversy that the first scale seems to represent. They raised the question of the position of the landlords and constituted a field in which Radicals could pursue their attacks on the landed class, as Roebuck in fact did in his amendment to the Landed Property (Ireland) Bill on which a division took place on 8 March 1847. Religious issues also played a prominent part in Irish affairs and attacks on the Establishment could be carried on in debates over the position of the Church of Ireland, as for example in the debate over H. G. Ward's motion for a committee on the temporalities of the Church of Ireland, on which there was a division on 12 June 1844.

Furthermore, the notion that politics represented a general class controversy of this kind was widely held at the time, though just how widely I will not undertake to say. The class interpretation of early Victorian politics is not a theory imposed by historians at a later date but is derived from the opinions of contemporaries. The existence of such a controversy was an important part of the message of the classical economists. Class arguments were a commonplace of the political pamphlet literature of the 1830s and 1840s, as I have observed from my reading of this material in the collection at the Newberry Library. Propagandists for repeal of the Corn Laws played extensively on the theme. Class arguments frequently occurred in the debates in Parliament, and were used on both sides of the House. That they should have been found serviceable by the right as well as by the left is rather interesting, since it is generally said that class arguments are a more useful weapon for the left because the poorer or more underprivileged classes, to which the left appeals, are in a majority. Yet in Parliament in the 1840s it was apparently a powerful argument that a given proposal represented a threat to the landowning interest; the reason was, presumably, that at least four-fifths of the members of the House of Commons belonged to or were immediately related to the gentry, the baronetage or the peerage.

There is one obvious difficulty here which seems on consideration, however, to be without great weight. It may be objected that the conflict between the aristocracy and the "middle classes," whoever they were, is a *cliché* of the textbooks, a foggy generalization based on assumptions which, so far as they have any meaning at all, are untenable in the light of modern knowledge. The class concepts in terms of which the political history of this age has commonly been described are crude and unsatisfactory and have been energetically attacked by a number of recent students, myself included. It is better understood now than it used to be that class is a relative matter, that the boundaries between different social groups are not easy to ascertain, and that different indicants of status may cut across one another and divide a population in different ways. This is not to say that notions about class divisions are nonsense, but rather that these matters must be carefully investigated and statements about them cautiously formulated. Even if they were nonsense, however, this would be immaterial to the present argument, for the fact that an issue is unreal does not necessarily prevent its being a subject of political controversy, and would not exclude the possibility of its being the central variable in a scale. A scale is a psychological thing which reveals not the facts of social history but what men thought about them. That men believed one thing while the reality was apparently something rather different would be an interesting finding but not an incredible one, for there is no reason to suppose that men are never mistaken. Politics may and sometimes do revolve around an illusion. In the general confusion men may embrace a theory that seems to offer some insight into what is otherwise unintelligible, and they may particularly welcome a theory that provides a scapegoat, an en-

emy on whom their troubles may be blamed and against whom their energies may be concentrated. The idea of a controversy between aristocratic
and middle-class interests, even if the question was rather more complicated than is suggested by the polemical arguments at the time, apparently served for a number of contemporaries as a point of orientation of
this character. Why this was so, why class theories should have seemed
more plausible in the middle decades of the nineteenth century than they
did earlier, is an interesting question and one on which several historians
have already presented some suggestive evidence and comment.

The real difficulty about a class interpretation of the first scale is that
it fails to cover a certain amount of the evidence about the scale itself.
Though it seems persuasive to regard a class conflict of this kind as part of
the content of the first scale, it is difficult to regard it as the whole content.
A number of issues in the scale do not fit so neatly into such a scheme as
do those already mentioned. The income tax, for example, would, one
might suppose, have borne with equal severity upon all those who had
taxable incomes, and it is not easy to see at once why it should have been
more unwelcome to those whose incomes came from trade or industry
than to those whose incomes came from rents. One wonders whether the
county members who voted for it did not do so more out of a desire to
support a conservative government than out of consideration of the advantages of the tax for them or for their constituents; there is some evidence in the debates to show that they accepted the measure with reluctance. It may be forcing the evidence to fit even some of the questions just
discussed into a scheme of this kind. . . .

Beyond this, however, so simple an answer appears meagre and unsatisfactory in comparison to the richness of content revealed by the analysis. Though it is reasonable to suppose that class interests were involved
in some of the items in the scale, much more seems to have been involved
as well. To dismiss the results in a sterile and empty formula may be to
miss taking advantage of what is perhaps the most interesting aspect of the
findings, the elaborate interconnections that they reveal. What is striking
about the first scale is not that it makes everything simple but rather that
it shows the richness of the ideological pattern of mid-century politics and
the way in which this pattern was, so to speak, embroidered upon. It may
be more illuminating to regard the scale not as reducing many questions
to a common denominator but rather as showing the connection of these
questions with each other. There are, as has been mentioned, two common interpretations of a scale: that it reflects one variable, or that it reflects several closely correlated ones. The variety of subject matter in the
scale described here seems to make the second of these interpretations the
more reasonable one. To assign to this group of issues a single descriptive
name would be difficult and, indeed, misleading.

This view may appear overly conservative. That these questions were all tied together in this way is a striking finding: one might expect it, then, to lead to a new interpretation, a key to the period that would suddenly unlock its secrets. Scalogram analysis, however, is no gimmick to answer all questions. It is merely a means of placing in some kind of intelligible order a mass of evidence too profuse and too complex to be clearly observed without the aid of such a device. Further, as I have tried to insist, the interpretation of a scale is a controversial matter. A scale gives no ready answer to problems of historical interpretation; its function, rather, is to provide a concrete basis, a firm foundation, on which argument about these problems can be effectively carried forward. . . .

The issues in the first scale occupied a considerably larger share of the time and attention of Parliament than did the issues in the second, as will be discussed more fully below when the two scales are compared. The importance of the subject-matter of the first scale is also, however, underlined by another finding, which is that the issues contained in it were those around which party conflict tended to crystallize. . . .

It proves that party affiliation was closely related to votes in the divisions that fit the first scale. This does not mean, of course, that either party voted unanimously in all these divisions. If this had been the case, there would have been no point in a scalogram analysis, for there would have been only two possible ideological positions. There were, on the contrary, important cleavages of opinion within each of the two general party groups. Yet in a more general sense an unmistakable pattern does emerge. This consists in the fact that each party occupied a different section of the ideological spectrum defined by the scale. The five issues used in the scale divide the members of Parliament who voted on these questions into six scale-types. It turns out that almost all those in the first three scale-types, i.e., those voting positive on the first, second or third items, belonged to the Liberal group; while almost all those in the last three scale-types, i.e. voting negative on the third, fourth or fifth items, were Conservatives. The break between Liberals and Conservatives comes at a clearly defined point on the scale, and the ideological gamuts of opinion in each party radiate away from this central point: the Liberals in one direction and the Conservatives in the other. Some questions, such as the income tax bill of 1842 in the illustration given, were voted upon almost exactly according to party lines. Other questions, such as the first two in the illustration, split the Liberals and on these some Liberals voted with the Conservatives. Still others, such as the last two in the illustration, split the Conservatives, and on these some Conservatives voted with the Liberals. However, questions in the scale that divided one party never divided the other. On the first two items, as will be seen from Table III, the Liberals disagreed but the Conservatives were unanimously negative; on the last

TABLE III. PARTY VOTES ON ISSUES IN BOTH SCALES

	Liberals		Conservatives	
	+	−	+	−
First Scale:				
1. Chartism, 1842	51	68	0	221
2. Corn Laws, 1843	127	52	0	331
3. Income Tax, 1842	186	6	4	279
4. Corn Laws, 1846	235	10	114	241
5. Live Cattle, 1842	169	29	213	86
Second Scale:				
1. Poor Law, 1847	11	120	33	100
2. Lace Factories Bill, 1846	16	64	52	89
3. Ten Hours, 1844	94	56	100	135
4. Ten Hours, 1847	77	55	120	34
5. Roebuck's resolution, 1844	56	13	228	5

two the Conservatives disagreed but the Liberals were almost unanimously positive.

Thus, in terms of the divisions in the first scale, the conflict between the two main party groups clearly had an ideological content. Despite their internal differences of opinion parties did, in the sense described here, differ substantially on major questions of the day, and can be clearly distinguished from each other in terms of program, in terms of the causes they supported or opposed. The main line of political cleavage and the main line of ideological cleavage in this Parliament appear to have been closely related to each other, and it was in terms of the issue or nexus of issues in the first scale that the principal lines of political battle were drawn.

This finding may seem to suggest a simpler interpretation of the scale. This is that the relationship between these issues can most easily be accounted for not in terms of their substantive content but in terms of party maneuver and political opportunism: that the content of the scale, the central variable, consisted not in the subject-matter of the issues or connections that we now believe we can see between them, but in political objectives quite unrelated to them. This view, which is certainly accepted to a considerable extent by students of party history, implies an instrumental interpretation of issues: they are to be regarded not as ends in themselves but as means by which political leaders and politically active groups seek to promote their own interests: to build majorities, to retain power or to secure it and to mobilize support behind them for these purposes. Issues, then, need have no logical connection except for their convenience in serving the purposes of party politics. Attitudes on them might be determined by the political exigencies of the moment, party coalitions and alliances, efforts of the government to secure its position or efforts of the opposition to obtain a majority against the government. By this view, any general ideological scheme such as might be inferred and frequently was inferred from the group of causes supported by a particular party might be not an animating principle but an improvised rationale devised after the event, an attempt to bring into a coherent plan, as plausibly as the circumstances permitted, a variety of matters that had no logical connection apart from the fact that they had all proved politically serviceable.

Such a view is in many ways attractive. It would be idle to deny the presence of opportunism in the politics of Early Victorian England. Cases can be cited readily enough where the struggle for political advantage appears to have dictated both the selection of issues to debate and the positions taken on them. I doubt, however, that anyone who has read widely in the debates in Hansard would regard opportunism as the whole story. It would be difficult to credit that the animated and acrimonious discussion of the various measures proposed, and the way in which they might be expected to affect the interests of different groups in the community, was nothing more than an external facade. It is also relevant here that, as mentioned earlier, the scales proved to be relatively stable and did not greatly change with changes of government, as might have been expected if nothing more than opportunism was involved. Doubtless, also, motives may be mixed, and men may pursue at the same time both their own advantage and what they conceive to be the public good, and these objectives may be combined in different proportions in different individuals in a way that it would be difficult now to disentangle. I cannot in any case discuss the question of motives here, since I am not presenting evidence on correlations between political choice and personal or political background.

The point to make here is, rather, that the argument about political opportunism does not necessarily refute the suggestion already made about the content of the scale and about the relationships between the issues that make it up. One may admit, and must admit in part, that political leaders made use for political purposes of issues or causes to which they were personally indifferent or even hostile. To concede this, however, is not to concede that these causes were a matter of indifference to everybody. Exactly the opposite is the case. A completely instrumental theory of issues, that they served no other purpose than that of rallying men to the support of a party or coalition, runs up against the difficulty that issues can be offered as a kind of political bait only to those who take them seriously. It would be useless for party leaders to take up causes out of strategy unless others were ready to support them out of conviction. Even if it is admitted that political stands were often taken for reasons of opportunism or demagoguery, it would have to be admitted at the same time that there were groups in the political community, whether in the electorate or in Parliament, who supported these causes for their own sakes. Otherwise the "opportunism" would be pointless or useless. The very fact that issues could be used for opportunistic purposes by some implies that they served substantive purposes for others. Whether these substantive goals were real or fictitious, whether men's reasons for wanting a particular measure were good or bad, intelligent or silly, based on a reasoned calculation or on a neurotic compulsion unrelated to reality, is irrelevant. The point is that it would be useless for a politician to make an instrumental use of an issue unless it represented something that a considerable group of the electorate or of Parliament wanted. In view of this, it is clearly unsatisfactory to propose an explanation in terms of what might be called a "vulgar" opportunism: i.e., a theory that the connection of issues in the scale and the votes of members of Parliament on these issues can be explained exclusively in terms of competition for office and majority-building, or that the connection between these issues was wholly unrelated to their content or to the expressed interests or desires of anybody in the political community.

The point can be put even more strongly. If politicians adopt a certain policy it may make little difference in practice whether they do so from conviction or because they realize that there is no political future for those who continue to oppose it. Even if politicians are wholly opportunistic, pressing certain causes exclusively for political advantage, to gain support in the electorate or in Parliament, they may still be very much concerned with the merits of these questions, and may argue strenuously about their details and their anticipated impact on the interests to which the politicians wish to make their appeals. Even if attitudes were manipulative, arguments could still be about content. To say that politicians were opportunist—which may or may not be true, but was very likely true in part—has no bearing on the question whether the issues in the scale were related in their substantive content. . . .

I wish, finally, to suggest how a multi-dimensional analysis can throw light on a problem that has bothered some students of the period: the fact that men who were radical in some respects were not radical in others. As the complexity of the period has been more clearly perceived it has led, as I mentioned at the outset, to a scepticism about the possibility of reducing these varieties of political choice to any intelligible pattern. One sophisticated modern critic has put the problem as follows:

> Political spectrum-making on the basis of programmes is invariably plagued by difficulties. Shaftesbury, Oastler, and Peel, Newman and Blomfield, Disraeli and Cecil make unmanageable gaps in Conservatism; Owen and Mc-

Culloch, Fielden and Bright, Mill and Martineau make a meaningless hodge-podge of Radicalism. What can one do about Cobbett or Feargus O'Connor? One must either suppose a capricious incidence of radicalism or resort to what Professor Hexter in another connection has called "apologetic epicycles"—Tory Radicals, Radical Conservatives, breeds of Chartists—to save the appearances. The polarities of conservative and radical are better used to describe tempers or approaches. To classify (for what it is worth) by approach rather than programme, if it does not solve the problem entirely, at least simplifies it. [R. K. Webb, *Harriet Martineau* (London, 1960)]

I believe, however, that for the 1840s at least these difficulties are not so formidable as this quotation would suggest. Actually it is perfectly easy to meet this problem if we think of the men who sat in this Parliament as being divided not by one issue but by two or several, and if we think of not one radical-conservative dimension but two or more. By this means it is quite possible to define radicals and conservatives not in terms of approaches but in terms of concrete political objectives. The use of two scales as alternative and unrelated dimensions provides a conceptual framework in which it is possible to take account of men who were "radical" or "conservative" in different ways and on different issues, and replaces the apparently chaotic picture of political attitudes with a reasonably simple and comprehensive scheme. What emerges is not an unmanageable multiplicity of different attitudes but a simpler pattern: only two kinds of behavior, or a small number, which are unrelated, but which taken together offer an entirely adequate description of the evidence. The argument that radicals and conservatives cannot be described in terms of program presupposes that only a single dimension exists. If this assumption is abandoned the problem is readily resolved.

The existence of unrelated political dimensions both operating at the same time has been frequently observed in studies of twentieth-century politics. In the United States at the present day, for example, it has been found that economic "liberalism" does not always coincide with "liberalism" in the sense of support for civil liberties, that often the two causes are supported by quite different kinds of people, and that some individuals are both economic liberals and extreme segregationists. . . .

Actually it was demonstrated long before. Here, as perhaps in other cases, one can find in the nineteenth century political phenomena sometimes alleged to be peculiar to the twentieth. The two scales presented here constitute an example of unrelated "liberal" dimensions in the mid-nineteenth century; and I have found evidence pointing to additional examples in later decades, on which I hope to report separately. In this manner, multi-scale analysis does, I believe, change our thinking about the period and make clear things that were not clear before. Not merely does it provide a technique for identifying the dimensions and sorting out which items belong to which, but it also helps to make sense out of these cross-currents and provides a scheme in which they can be intelligibly explained.

Bibliography

Aydelotte, William O. "Quantification in History." *American Historical Review,* 71 (April 1966): 803–25.

Barzun, Jacques. *Clio and the Doctors: Psycho-History, Quanto-History and History.* Chicago, Ill., 1974.

Beringer, Richard E., ed. *Historical Analysis: Contemporary Approaches to Clio's Craft.* New York, 1978.

Berkhofer, Robert F. *A Behavioral Approach to Historical Analysis.* Glencoe, Ill., 1968.

Bridenbaugh, Carl. "The Great Mutation." *American Historical Review,* 68 (January 1963): 315–31.

Dollar, Charles M., and Richard J. Jensen. *Historian's Guide to Statistics: Quantitative Analysis and Historical Research.* New York, 1971.

Floud, Roderick. *An Introduction to Quantitative Methods for Historians.* Princeton, N.J., 1973.

Fogel, Robert W. *Railroads and American Economic Growth: Essays in Econometric History.* New Haven, Conn., 1964.

Fogel, Robert W., and G. R. Elton. *Which Road to the Past? Two Views of History.* New Haven, Conn., 1983.

Fogel, Robert W., and Stanley L. Engerman. *Time on the Cross: The Economics of American Negro Slavery.* 2 vols. Boston, Mass., 1974.

Furet, François. "Quantitative History." In *Historical Studies Today,* edited by Felix Gilbert and Stephen R. Graubard. New York, 1972.

Gutman, Herbert. *Slavery and the Numbers Game: A Critique of Time on the Cross.* Urbana, Ill., 1975.

Kousser, J. Morgan. "Quantitative Social-Scientific History." In *The Past Before Us: Contemporary Historical Writing in the United States,* edited by Michael Kammen. Ithaca, N.Y., and London, 1980.

Rowney, Don K., and James Q. Graham, eds. *Quantitative History: Selected Readings in the Quantitative Analysis of Historical Data.* Homewood, Ill., 1969.

Schlesinger, Arthur M., Jr. "The Humanist Looks at Empirical Social Research." *American Sociological Review,* 27 (December 1962): 768–71.

CHAPTER 21

William L. Langer
"The Next Assignment"
(1958)

William L. Langer (1896–1977) was best known for his extensive work in diplomatic history and for his editorship of "The Rise of Modern Europe," a popular series of books by various scholars that synthesized recent scholarship in European history from 1250 to 1945. In 1957, when he was elected president of the American Historical Association, he was, at sixty-one years old, among the most distinguished historians in the United States. Up to that time his approach to history had been quite traditional, but his presidential address summoned his fellow scholars to a new approach: the use of psychoanalysis in history. Many who heard or later read "The Next Assignment," which Langer offered more as an agenda for the next generation than as a definitive statement of possibilities, must have known that his proposal was not entirely new. Sigmund Freud himself, the founder of psychoanalysis, wrote interpretations of Leonardo da Vinci and Fyodor Dostoevsky, and figures like Martin Luther had been the subject of modern psychological studies, including one by Lucien Febvre. Indeed, the printed version of Langer's address was heavily documented with footnote citations revealing the large bibliography already extant in "psychohistory." Yet not until a figure of Langer's stature took up the cause could the new approach even begin to achieve some legitimacy in the profession as a whole. Like Turner's "Significance of the Frontier," Beard's "Written History as an Act of Faith," and Aydelotte's "Quantification in History," Langer's "Next Assignment" became a controlling document for its time.

Langer was born in Boston in 1896 to German immigrant parents. He worked his way through Boston Latin School and Harvard University, showing special interest in languages and literature. His military experience in the First World War pushed his interest towards history, so that on being mustered out of service in 1919, he returned to Harvard for graduate studies that led to a Ph.D. in history in 1923. He earned a national reputation for his work in European diplomatic history, though only his brief study of popular fantasies about imperialism in chapter 3 of his otherwise traditional *Diplomacy of Imperialism, 1890–1902* (1935) suggested the possibilities of psychology.

The small interest was increased, however, by his own happy experience in 1938 with psychoanalysis, which he sought in the midst of repeated episodes of paranoia. He thought further about psychology during his service in World War II as an intelligence analyst for the Office of Strategic Services (OSS), prompted, no doubt, by the work of his brother, Walter C. Langer, a psychiatrist, who prepared a psychological portrait of Adolph Hitler for the OSS. Still he took no steps to incorporate psychology in his historical writing. Known as a traditional historian, the only controversy Langer attracted was the charge from Charles Beard and others that his books, *Our Vichy Gamble* (1947), *The Challenge to Isolation, 1937–1940* (1952), and *The Undeclared War, 1940–1941* (1953), which were based on his privileged access to secret government archives and which defended America's entry into the Second World War, were "court history" and lacked objectivity. His election as president of the American Historical Association in 1957 amounted to a vote of confidence by the professional establishment. Yet the establishment, which considered Langer one of its own, was hardly prepared for his controversial presidential address in which he urged his colleagues to take up psychohistory.

Langer focuses on mass psychology, using Freudian concepts of repressed anxiety, guilt feelings, and regression to infantile behavior in order to explain the psychological reaction to the Black Plague of 1349, a traumatic disaster that wiped out perhaps a third of the European population. But, as with quantification, psychohistory has different meanings for different historians. To some, like Freud himself, it meant psychobiography, like the malicious study he wrote with William C. Bullitt of Woodrow Wilson, composed about 1932 but not published until 1967. In it, Wilson's assumed presidential obsessions are rooted in childhood relations with his father. Psychobiography remains the dominant theme in psychohistory, but most writers prefer the more flexible scheme of Erik Erikson, who posits eight stages individuals go through from birth to death and the crises associated with each. Erikson's own *Young Man Luther* (1958) and *Gandhi's Truth* (1969) are respected reconstructions of two great figures' lives in accordance with some of his categories.

Social psychology is another theme in psychohistory, as exemplified by Stanley Elkins' *Slavery* (1959), which, in part, offered a stimulating and much criticized comparison of Black American slavery with Nazi concentration camps to reveal how a closed society in each case produced the "Sambo" personality among Negroes and Jews, respectively. Further, David Brion Davis used the Freudian theory of projection to explain how some groups in nineteenth century America imputed their own repressed desires to others they saw as enemies, like Catholics, Masons, and Mormons. Finally, the theory of cognitive dissonance, first elaborated by Leon Festinger in 1957, has been used by historians to explain why people seem to act contrary to their own best interests. Cognitive dissonance occurs when one's knowledge or opinion (cognition) of reality is in conflict with one's behavior; yet, instead of changing behavior, a person may "change" reality by imaginatively reconstructing it to fit the original behavior. Richard E. Beringer's *Historical Analysis,* cited in the bibliography below, discusses this and other psychological theories and reprints R. C. Raak's "When Plans Fail," an application of cognitive dissonance to a failed Prussian conspiracy against Napoleon in 1808.

Does psychohistory bring history closer to social science or does it offer a return to historicism? Perhaps a little of both. On the one hand, psychoanalysis, whether Freudian or Eriksonian, assumes developmental categories that are universal to all times and cultures. It would seem logical, then, that a total psychohistorical explanation of human experience is, in theory, possible. In company with social science historians, psychohistorians could identify the laws of human development. On the other hand, psychobiography, at least, returns to an exploration of the individual. Just as the historicists claimed that historians must rethink the thoughts of the individuals who wrote the documents, so the psychoanalyst tries to re-create in his or her own mind the experience of the patient or historical subject. Of course, there are differences, among them the important one that historicism involves conscious thoughts whereas psychohistorians explore the unconscious. Yet, despite that, psychohistory, still in its infancy, may offer a road back to historicism.

A NYONE WHO, LIKE MYSELF, has the honor to serve as president of this association and to address it on the occasion of its annual meeting may be presumed to have devoted many years to the historical profession, to have taught many successive college generations, to have trained numerous young scholars, and to have written at least some books and articles. The chances are great that he has reached those exalted levels of the academic life which involve so many administrative and advisory duties, as well as such expenditure of time and energy in seeing people, in writing recommendations, and in reading the writings of others that he is most unlikely ever again to have much time to pursue his own researches. Nonetheless, his long and varied experience and his ever broadening contacts with others working in many diverse fields have probably sharpened his understanding of the problems of his own profession and enhanced his

Reprinted by permission of Leonard C. Langer, executor of the estate of William L. Langer, "The Next Assignment," *American Historical Review* 63 (Jan. 1958), 283–304. Copyright © 1958 by William L. Langer.

awareness of the many lacunae in our knowledge of the world and mankind, both in the past and in the present. It would seem altogether fitting, therefore, that I, for one, should make use of this occasion not so much for reflection on the past achievements of the profession (which is what might be expected of a historian), as for speculation about its needs and its future—that is, about the directions which historical study might profitably take in the years to come.

I am sure to sense, at this juncture, a certain uneasiness in my audience, for historians, having dedicated their lives to the exploration and understanding of the past, are apt to be suspicious of novelty and ill-disposed toward crystal-gazing. In the words of my distinguished predecessor, they lack the "speculative audacity" of the natural scientists, those artisans of brave hypotheses. This tendency on the part of historians to become buried in their own conservatism strikes me as truly regrettable. What basically may be a virtue tends to become a vice, locking our intellectual faculties in the molds of the past and preventing us from opening new horizons as our cousins in the natural sciences are constantly doing. If progress is to be made we must certainly have new ideas, new points of view, and new techniques. We must be ready, from time to time, to take flyers into the unknown, even though some of them may prove wide of the mark. Like the scientists, we can learn a lot from our own mistakes, and the chances are that, if we persist, each successive attempt may take us closer to the target. I should therefore like to ask myself this evening what direction, if I were a younger man, would claim my interest and attention; in short, what might be the historian's "next assignment."

We are all keenly aware of the fact that during the past half century the scope of historical study has been vastly extended. The traditional political-military history has become more comprehensive and more analytical and has been reinforced by researches into the social, economic, intellectual, scientific, and other aspects of the past, some of them truly remote from what used to be considered history. So far has this development gone that I find it difficult to envisage much further horizontal expansion of the area of investigation.

There is, however, still ample scope for penetration in depth and I, personally, have no doubt that the "newest history" will be more intensive and probably less extensive. I refer more specifically to the urgently needed deepening of our historical understanding through exploitation of the concepts and findings of modern psychology. And by this, may I add, I do not refer to classical or academic psychology which, so far as I can detect, has little bearing on historical problems, but rather to psychoanalysis and its later developments and variations as included in the terms "dynamic" or "depth psychology."

In the course of my reading over the years I have been much impressed by the prodigious impact of psychoanalytic doctrine on many, not to say most, fields of human study and expression. Of Freud himself it has been said that "he has in large part created the intellectual climate of our time." "Almost alone," remarks a recent writer in the *Times Literary Supplement,* "he revealed the deepest sources of human endeavor and remorselessly pursued their implications for the individual and society." Once the initial resistance to the recognition of unconscious, irrational forces in human nature was overcome, psychoanalysis quickly became a dominant influence in psychiatry, in abnormal psychology, and in personality study. The field of medicine is feeling its impact not only in the area of psychosomatic illness, but in the understanding of the doctor-patient relationship. Our whole educational system and the methods of child-training have been modified in the light of its findings. For anthropology it has opened new and wider vistas by providing for the first time "a theory of raw human nature" and by suggesting an explanation of otherwise incomprehensible cultural traits and practices. It has done much also to revise established notions about religion and has given a great impetus to pastoral care and social work. The problems of mythology and sociology have been illuminated by its insights, and more recently its influence has been strongly felt in penology, in political science, and even in economics, while in the arts almost every major figure of the past generation has been in some measure affected by it.

Despite this general and often profound intellectual and artistic reorientation since Freud published his first epoch-making works sixty years ago, historians have, as a group, maintained an almost completely negative attitude toward the teachings of psychoanalysis. Their lack of response has been due, I should think, less to constitutional obscurantism than to the fact that historians, as disciples of Thucydides, have habitually thought of themselves as psychologists in their own right. They have indulged freely in psychological interpretation, and many no doubt have shared the fear that the humanistic appreciation of personality, as in poetry or drama, might be irretrievably lost through the application of a coldly penetrating calculus. Many considered the whole psychoanalytic doctrine too biological and too deterministic, as well as too conjectural, and they were, furthermore, reluctant to recognize and deal with unconscious motives and irrational forces. Psychoanalysis, on the other hand, was still a young science and therefore lacked the prestige to make historians acquire a guilt-complex about not being more fully initiated into its mysteries. Almost without exception, then, they have stuck to the approach and methods of historicism, restricting themselves to recorded fact and to strictly rational motivation. So impervious was the profession as a whole to the new teaching that an inquiry into the influence of psychoanalysis on modern thought, written a few years ago, made no mention whatever of history.

This is as remarkable as it is lamentable, for, on the very face of it, psychoanalysis would seem to have much to contribute to the solution of historical problems. Many years of clinical work by hundreds of trained analysts have by now fortified and refined Freud's original theory of human drives, the conflicts to which they give rise, and the methods by which they are repressed or diverted. Psychoanalysis has long since ceased being merely a therapy and has been generally recognized as a theory basic to the study of the human personality. How can it be that the historian, who must be as much or more concerned with human beings and their motivation than with impersonal forces and causation, has failed to make use of these findings? Viewed in the light of modern depth psychology, the homespun, common-sense psychological interpretations of past historians, even some of the greatest, seem woefully inadequate, not to say naïve. Clearly the time has come for us to reckon with a doctrine that strikes so close to the heart of our own discipline.

Since psychoanalysis is concerned primarily with the emotional life of the individual, its most immediate application is in the field of biography. Freud himself here showed the way, first in his essay on Leonardo da Vinci (1910) and later in his analytical study of Dostoevsky (1928). He was initially impressed by the similarity between some of the material produced by a patient in analysis and the only recorded childhood recollection of the Italian artist. With his fragmentary memory as a starting point, Freud studied the writings and artistic productions of Leonardo and demonstrated how much light could be shed on his creative and scientific life through the methods of analysis. No doubt he erred with respect to certain points of art history. Quite possibly some of his deductions were unnecessarily involved or farfetched. Nonetheless, recent critics have testified that he was able, "thanks to his theory and method, and perhaps even more to his deep sympathy for the tragic and the problematic in Leonardo, to pose altogether new and important questions about his personality, questions which were unsuspected by earlier writers and to which no better answer than Freud's has yet been given."

The striking novelty and the startling conclusions of Freud's essay on Leonardo had much to do with precipitating the flood of psychoanalytic or, better, pseudo-psychoanalytic biographical writing during the 1920's. Almost all of this was of such a low order—ill-informed, sensational, scandalizing—that it brought the entire Freudian approach into disrepute. I have no doubt that this, in turn, discouraged serious scholars—the historians among them—from really examining the possibilities of the new teachings. Only within the last generation has the situation begun to change. The basic concepts of psychoanalysis, such as the processes of repression, identification, projection, reaction formation, substitution, displacement, and sublimation, have become more firmly established through clinical work and have at the same time increasingly become part of our thinking. Meanwhile, concerted efforts have been made to build up systematic personality and character study on a psychoanalytic basis and the so-called neo-Freudians, advancing beyond the narrowly environmental factors, have done much to develop the significance of constitutional and cultural influences.

While recognized scholars in related fields, notably in political science, have begun to apply psychoanalytic principles to the study of personality types and their social role, historians have for the most part approved of the iron curtain between their own profession and that of the dynamic psychologists. It is, indeed, still professionally dangerous to admit any addiction to such unorthodox doctrine. Even those who are in general intrigued by the potentialities of psychoanalysis are inclined to argue against its application to historical problems. They point out that evidence on the crucial early years of an individual's life is rarely available and that, unlike the practicing analyst, the historian cannot turn to his subject and help him revive memories of specific events and relationships. To this it may be answered that the historian, on whatever basis he is operating, is always suffering from lack of data. Actually there is often considerable information about the family background of prominent historical personalities and the sum total of evidence about their careers is in some cases enormous. Furthermore, the experiences of earliest childhood are no longer rated as important for later development as was once the case, and the historian, if he cannot deal with his subject as man to man, at least has the advantage of surveying his whole career and being able to observe the functioning of significant forces. In any event we historians must, if we are to retain our self-respect, believe that we can do better with the available evidence than the untrained popular biographer to whom we have so largely abandoned the field.

The historian is, of course, less interested in the individual as such than in the impact of certain individuals upon the society of their time and, beyond that, in the behavior of men as members of the group, society, or culture. This leads us into the domain of social or collective psychology, a subject on which much has been written during the past twenty-five years, especially in this country, but in which progress continues to be slight because of the difficulty of distinguishing satisfactorily between large groups and small groups, between organized and unorganized aggregations, between such vague collectivities as the crowd, the mob, and the mass. Much certainly remains to be done in this area, especially in the elaboration of a theory to bridge the gap between individual and collective psychology.

Freud himself became convinced, at an early date, that his theories might have a certain applicability to historical and cultural problems. He accepted the conclusions of Gustave Le Bon's well-known study of the psychology of crowds (1895) and recognized that a group may develop "a sort of collective mind." As the years went by, his clinical work led him to the conclusion that there were close parallels between the development of the individual and of the race. Thus, the individual's unconscious mind was, in a sense, the repository of the past experiences of his society, if not of mankind. In his most daring and provocative works, *Totem and Taboo* (1913) and his last book, *Moses and Monotheism* (1939), Freud tried to determine the effect of group experience on the formation of a collective group mind.

Anthropologists, like historians, will probably continue to reject Freud's historical ventures as too extravagantly speculative, but the fact remains that anthropological and sociological researches suggest ever more definitely that certain basic drives and impulses, as identified by Freud, appear in all cultures and that the differences between cultures derive largely from varying methods of dealing with these drives. Furthermore, social psychologists are increasingly aware of the similarity in the operation of irrational forces in the individual and in society. Everett D. Martin, an early but unusually discerning student of the subject, noted in 1920 that the crowd, like our dream life, provides an outlet for repressed emotions: "It is as if all at once an unspoken agreement were entered into whereby each member might let himself go, on condition that he approved the same thing in all the rest." A crowd, according to Martin, "is a device for indulging ourselves in a kind of temporary insanity by all going crazy together." Similarly, Freud's erstwhile disciple, C. G. Jung, has characterized recent political mass movements as "psychic epidemics, i.e. mass psychoses," and others have noted that the fears and rages of mass movements are clearly the residue of childish emotions.

All this, as aforesaid, still requires further exploration. It does seem, however, that we shall have to learn to reckon with the concept of "collective mentality," even on the unconscious level, and that the traits of that mentality—normally submerged and operative only in association with others or in specific settings—can best be studied as a part of, or extension of, individual psychology. That is to say that progress in social psychology probably depends on ever more highly refined analysis of the individual—his basic motivations, his attitudes, beliefs, hopes, fears, and aspirations.

Perhaps I may digress at this point to remind you of Georges Lefebvre's long-standing interest and concern with the character and role of mobs and crowds in the French Revolution, and especially of his impressive study of the mass hysteria of 1789 known as "The Great Fear." Although Lefebvre thought Le Bon superficial and confused, he was convinced by his own researches that there was such a thing as a "collective mentality." Indeed, he considered it the true causal link between the origins and the effects of major crises. Without specific reference to psychoanalytic concepts, Lefebvre arrived at conclusions altogether consonant with those of modern psychology. His truly impressive studies in a sense prefaced the more recent analyses of totalitarian movements which, in my estimation, have so clearly demonstrated the vast possibilities that have been opened to social scientists by the finding of dynamic psychology.

As historians we must be particularly concerned with the problem whether major changes in the psychology of a society or culture can be traced, even in part, to some severe trauma suffered in common, that is, with the question whether whole communities, like individuals, can be profoundly affected by some shattering experience. If it is indeed true that every society or culture has a "unique psychological fabric," deriving at least in part from past common experiences and attitudes, it seems reasonable to suppose that any great crisis, such as famine, pestilence, natural disaster, or war, should leave its mark on the group, the intensity and duration of the impact depending, of course, on the nature and magnitude of the crisis. I hasten to say in advance that I do not, of course, imagine the psychological impact of such crises to be uniform for all members of the population, for if modern psychology has demonstrated anything it is the proposition that in any given situation individuals will react in widely diverse ways, depending on their constitution, their family background, their early experiences, and other factors. But these varying responses are apt to be reflected chiefly in the immediate effects of the catastrophe. Over the long term (which is of greater interest to the historian) it seems likely that the group would react in a manner most nearly corresponding to the underlying requirements of the majority of its members, in other words, that despite great variations as between individuals there would be a dominant attitudinal pattern.

I admit that all this is hypothetical and that we are here moving into unexplored territory, but allow me to examine a specific problem which, though remote from the area of my special competence, is nevertheless one to which I have devoted much study and thought. Perhaps I may begin by recalling Freud's observation that contemporary man, living in a scientific age in which epidemic disease is understood and to a large extent controlled, is apt to lose appreciation of the enormous, uncomprehended losses of life in past generations, to say nothing of the prolonged and widespread emotional strain occasioned by such disasters. Some exception must be made here for historians of the ancient world who, since the days of Niebuhr, have concerned themselves with the possible effects of widespread disease and high mortality on the fate of the Mediterranean civilizations. Some have made a strong case for the proposition that malaria, which seems to have first appeared in Greece and Italy in the fourth or fifth centuries B.C., soon became endemic and led on the one hand to serious debilitation, sloth, and unwillingness to work, and on the other to excitability, brutality, and general degradation. Recent researches suggest that malaria may have been one of the main causes of the collapse of the Etruscan civilization and may have accounted, at least in part, for the change in Greek character after the fourth century, especially for the growing lack of initiative, the prevalent cowardice, and the increasing trend toward cruelty. With reference to the fate of the Roman Empire, Professor Arthur Boak has recently reexamined the striking loss of population in the third and fourth centuries A.D. and has attributed it largely to the great epidemics of A.D. 165–180 and 250–280, thus reaffirming the view of Niebuhr and others that the Empire never really recovered from these tragic visitations.

The literature on these and subsequent epidemics is, however, devoted largely to their medical and sanitational aspects, or at most to their economic and social effects. My primary interest, as I have said, is with the possible long-range psychological repercussions. To study these I think we may well pass over the great plague of Athens in 430 B.C., so vividly reported by Thucydides, and the so-called plague of Justinian of the sixth century A.D., not because they were unimportant but because there is much more voluminous and instructive information about the Black Death of 1348–1349 and the ensuing period of devastating disease.

Western Europe seems to have been relatively free from major epidemics in the period from the sixth to the fourteenth century and it may well be that the revival of trade and the growth of towns, with their congestion and lack of sanitation, had much to do with the spread and establishment of the great mortal diseases like plague, typhus, syphilis, and influenza. At any rate, the Black Death was worse than anything experienced prior to that time and was, in all probability, the greatest single disaster that has ever befallen European mankind. In most localities a third or even a half of the population was lost within the space of a few months, and it is important to remember that the great visitation of 1348–1349 was only the beginning of a period of pandemic disease with a continuing frightful drain of population. It is hardly an exaggeration to say that for three hundred years Europe was ravaged by one disease or another, or more usually by several simultaneously, the serious outbreaks coming generally at intervals of five to ten years. Professor Lynn Thorndike, who thirty years ago wrote in the *American Historical Review* of the blight of pestilence on early modern civilization, pointed out that the period of greatest affliction was that of the Renaissance, and especially the years from about 1480 until 1540, during which period frequent severe outbreaks of bubonic plague were reinforced by attacks of typhus fever and by the onset of the great epidemic of syphilis, to say nothing of the English Sweat (probably influenza) which repeatedly devastated England before invading the Continent in 1529. The bubonic plague began to die out in Western Europe only in the late seventeenth century, to disappear almost completely after the violent outbreak at Marseilles in 1720. But the Balkans and Middle East continued to suffer from it until well into the nineteenth century and the pandemic that broke out in India in the 1890's was evidently comparable to the Black Death in terms of mortality and duration.

The extensive records of the Black Death have been long and carefully studied, not only with reference to their medical aspects, but also in connection with the economic and social effects of so sudden and substantial a loss of population. The English population is estimated to have fallen from 3,700,000 in 1348 to 2,100,000 in 1400, the mortality rates of the period 1348–1375 far exceeding those of modern India. While the figures for continental countries are less complete, the available data suggests that the losses were comparable. Cities and towns suffered particularly, but in some areas as many as 40 percent of the villages and hamlets were abandoned, the survivors joining with those of other settlements or moving to the depopulated towns where opportunity beckoned. Although a generation ago there was a tendency, especially among English historians, to minimize the social effects of the Black Death, more recent writers like G. G. Coulton, for example, acknowledge that the great epidemic, if it did not evoke entirely new forces, did vastly accelerate those already operative. The economic progress of Europe, which had been phenomenal in the thirteenth century, came to a halt and was soon followed by a prolonged depression lasting until the mid-fifteenth century and in a sense even into the seventeenth.

I make only the most fleeting reference to these questions, because my chief concern, as I have said, is to determine, if possible, what the long-term psychological effects of this age of disease may have been. The immediate horrors of great epidemics have been vividly described by eminent writers from Thucydides to Albert Camus and have been pictured on canvas by famous artists like Raphael and Delacroix. At news of the approach of the disease a haunting terror seizes the population, in the Middle Ages leading on the one hand to great upsurges of repentance in the form of flagellant processions and on the other to a mad search for scapegoats, eventuating in large-scale pogroms of the Jews. The most striking feature of such visitations has always been the precipitate flight from the cities, in which not only the wealthier classes but also town officials, professors and teachers, clergy, and even physicians took part. The majority of the population, taking the disaster as an expression of God's wrath, devoted itself to penitential exercises, to merciful occupations, and to such good works as the repair of churches and the founding of religious houses. On the other hand, the horror and confusion in many places brought general demoralization and social breakdown. Criminal elements were quick to take over, looting the deserted houses and even murdering the sick in order to rob them of their jewels. Many, despairing of the goodness and mercy of God, gave themselves over to riotous living, resolved, as Thucydides says, "to get out of life the pleasures which could be had speedily and which would satisfy their lusts, regarding their bodies and their wealth alike as transitory." Drunkenness and sexual immorality were the order of the day. "In one house," reported an observer of the London plague of 1665, "you might hear them roaring under the pangs of death, in the next tippling, whoring and belching out blasphemies against God."

The vivid description of the Black Death in Florence, in the introduction to Boccaccio's *Decameron,* is so familiar that further details about the immediate consequences may be dispensed with. Unfortunately neither the sources nor later historians tell us much of the long-range effects excepting that in the late nineteenth century a school of British writers traced to the Black Death fundamental changes in the agrarian system and indeed in the entire social order; the English prelate-historian, Francis Cardinal Gasquet, maintained that the Black Death, with its admittedly high mortality among the clergy, served to disrupt the whole religious establishment and thereby set the scene for the Protestant Reformation. Though this thesis is undoubtedly exaggerated, it does seem likely that the loss of clergy, especially in the higher ranks, the consequent growth of pluralities, the inevitable appointment of some who proved to be "clerical scamps" (Jessopp), and the vast enrichment of the Church through the legacies of the pious, all taken together played a significant role in the religious development of the later Middle Ages.

But again, these are essentially institutional problems which may reflect but do not explain the underlying psychological forces. That unusual forces of this kind were operative in the later Middle Ages seems highly probable. Indeed, a number of eminent historians have in recent years expatiated on the special character of this period. I will not attempt even to summarize the various interpretations of the temper of that age which have been advanced on one side or the other. None of the commentators, so far as I can see, have traced or determined the connection between the great and constantly recurring epidemics and the state of mind of much of Europe at that time. Yet this relationship would seem to leap to the eye. The age was marked, as all admit, by a mood of misery, depression, and anxiety, and by a general sense of impending doom. Numerous writers in widely varying fields have commented on the morbid preoccupation with death, the macabre interest in tombs, the gruesome predilection for the human corpse. Among painters the favorite themes were Christ's passion, the terrors of the Last Judgment, and the tortures of Hell, all depicted with ruthless realism and with an almost loving devotion to each repulsive detail. Altogether characteristic was the immense popularity of the Dance of Death woodcuts and murals, with appropriate verses, which appeared soon after the Black Death and which, it is agreed, expressed the sense of the immediacy of death and the dread of dying unshriven. Throughout the fifteenth and sixteenth centuries these pitilessly naturalistic pictures ensured man's constant realization of his imminent fate.

The origins of the Dance of Death theme have been generally traced to the Black Death and subsequent epidemics, culminating in the terror brought on by the outbreak of syphilis at the end of the fifteenth century. Is it unreasonable, then, to suppose that many of the other phenomena I have mentioned might be explained, at least in part, in the same way? We all recognize the late Middle Ages as a period of popular religious excitement or overexcitement, of pilgrimages and penitential processions, of mass preaching, of veneration of relics and adoration of saints, of lay piety and popular mysticism. It was apparently also a period of unusual immorality and shockingly loose living, which we must take as the continuation of the "devil-may-care" attitude of one part of the population. This the psychologists explain as the repression of unbearable feelings by accentuating the value of a diametrically opposed set of feelings and then behaving as though the latter were the real feelings. But the most striking feature of the age was an exceptionally strong sense of guilt and a truly dreadful fear of retribution, seeking expression in a passionate longing for effective intercession and in a craving for direct, personal experience of the Deity, as well as in a corresponding dissatisfaction with the Church and with the mechanization of the means of salvation as reflected, for example, in the traffic in indulgences.

These attitudes, along with the great interest in astrology, the increased resort to magic, and the startling spread of witchcraft and Satanism in the fifteenth century were, according to the precepts of modern psychology, normal reactions to the sufferings to which mankind in that period was subjected. It must be remembered that the Middle Ages, ignoring the teachings of the Greek physicians and relying entirely upon Scripture and the writings of the Church fathers, considered disease the scourge of God upon a sinful people. All men, as individuals, carry within themselves a burden of unconscious guilt and a fear of retribution which apparently go back to the curbing and repression of sexual and aggressive drives in childhood and the emergence of death wishes directed against the parents. This sense of sin, which is fundamental to all religion, is naturally enhanced by the impact of vast unaccountable and uncontrollable forces threatening the existence of each and every one. Whether or not there is also a primordial racial sense of guilt, as Freud argued in his *Totem and Taboo* (1913), it is perfectly clear that disaster and death threatening the entire community will bring on a mass emotional disturbance, based on a feeling of helpless exposure, disorientation, and common guilt. Furthermore, it seems altogether plausible to suppose that children, having experienced the terror of their parents and the panic of the community, will react to succeeding crises in a similar but even more intense manner. In other words, the anxiety and fear are transmitted from one generation to another, constantly aggravated.

Now it has long been recognized by psychologists that man, when crushed by unfathomable powers, tends to regress to infantile concepts and that, like his predecessor in primitive times, he has recourse to magic in his efforts to ward off evil and appease the angry deity. It is generally agreed that magic and religion are closely related, both deriving from fear of unknown forces and especially of death, and both reflecting an effort to ensure the preservation of the individual and the community from disease and other afflictions. Death-dealing epidemics like those of the late Middle Ages were bound to produce a religious revival, the more so as the established Church was proving itself ever less able to satisfy the yearning for more effective intercession and for a more personal relationship to God. Wyclif, himself a survivor of the Black Death, is supposed to have been deeply affected by his gruelling experience, and there is nothing implausible in the suggestion that Lollardy was a reaction to the shortcomings of the Church in that great crisis. In this connection it is also worth remarking that the first expression of Zwingli's reformed faith was his *Song of Prayer in Time of Plague*.

Most striking, however, is the case of the greatest of the reformers, Martin Luther, who seems to me to reflect clearly the reaction of the individual to the situation I have been sketching. Luther left behind almost a hundred volumes of writings, thousands of letters, and very voluminous table-talk, suggesting an unusually self-analytical and self-critical personality. From all this material it has long been clear that he suffered from an abnormally strong sense of sin and of the immediacy of death and damnation. Tortured by the temptations of the flesh and repeatedly in conflict with a personalized demon, he was chronically oppressed by a pathological feeling of guilt and lived in constant terror of God's judgment. So striking were these traits that some of Luther's biographers have questioned his sanity.

Here it is interesting to recall that one of our own colleagues, the late Professor Preserved Smith, as long ago as 1913, attacked the problem in an article entitled "Luther's Early Development in the Light of Psychoanalysis." Smith, who was remarkably conversant with Freudian teaching when psychoanalysis was still in its early stage of development, considered Luther highly neurotic—probably driven to enter the monastery by the hope of finding a refuge from temptation and an escape from damnation, and eventually arriving at the doctrine of salvation by faith alone only after he had convinced himself of the impossibility of conquering temptation by doing penance. It may well be that Smith overdid his thesis, but the fact remains that his article was treated with great respect by Dr. Paul J. Reiter, who later published a huge and greatly detailed study of Luther's personality. Reiter reached the conclusion, already suggested by Adolf Hausrath in 1905, that the great reformer suffered from a manic-depressive psychosis, which, frequently associated with genius, involved a constant struggle with, and victory over, enormous psychological pressures. The point of mentioning all this is to suggest that Luther's trials were typical of his time. In any event, it is inconceivable that he should have evoked so great a popular response unless he had succeeded in expressing the underlying, unconscious sentiments of large numbers of people and in providing them with an acceptable solution to their religious problem.

I must apologize for having raised so lugubrious a subject on so festive an occasion, but I could not resist the feeling that the problems presented by the later Middle Ages are exactly of the type that might be illuminated by modern psychology. I do not claim that the psychological aspects of this apocalyptic age have been entirely neglected by other students. Indeed, Millard Meiss, a historian of art, has written a most impressive study of Florentine and Sienese painting in the second half of the fourteenth century in which he has analyzed the many and varied effects of the Black Death, including the bearing of that great catastrophe on the further development of the religious situation. But no one, to my knowledge, has undertaken to fathom the psychological crisis provoked by the chronic, large-scale loss of life and the attendant sense of impending doom.

I would not, of course, argue that psychological doctrine, even if it were more advanced and more generally accepted than it is, would resolve all the perplexities of the historian. Better than most scholars, the historian knows that human motivation, like causation, is a complex and elusive process. In view of the fact that we cannot hope here to have complete evidence on any historical problem, it seems unlikely that we shall ever have definitive answers. But I am sure you will agree that there are still possibilities of enriching our understanding of the past and that it is our responsibility, as historians, to leave none of these possibilities unexplored. I call your attention to the fact that for many years young scholars in anthropology, sociology, religion, literature, education, and other fields have gone to psychoanalytic institutes for special training, and I suggest that some of our own younger men might seek the same equipment. For of this I have no doubt, that modern psychology is bound to play an ever greater role in historical interpretation. For some time now there has been a marked trend toward recognition of the irrational factors in human development, and it is interesting to observe the increased emphasis being laid on psychological forces. May I recall that perhaps the most stimulating non-Marxist interpretation of imperialism, that of the late Joseph Schumpeter, which goes back to 1918, rests squarely on a psychological base? Or need I point out that recent treatments of such forces as totalitarianism and nationalism lay great stress on psychological factors? Indeed, within the past year two books have appeared which have a direct bearing on my argument. One is T. D. Kendrick's *The Lisbon Earthquake*, which is devoted to a study of the effects of that disaster of 1755 upon the whole attitude and thought of the later eighteenth century. The other is Norman Cohn's *The Pursuit of the Millenium*, which reviews the chiliastic movements of the Middle Ages and comes to the conclusion that almost every major disaster, be it famine, plague, or war, produced some such movement and that only analysis of their psychic content will help us to explain them.

Aldous Huxley, in one of his essays, discusses the failure of historians to devote sufficient attention to the great ebb and flow of population and its effect on human development. He complains that while Arnold Toynbee concerned himself so largely with pressures and responses, there is in the index of his first six volumes no entry for "population," though there are five references to Popilius Laenas and two of Porphyry of Batamaea. To this I might add that the same index contains no reference to pestilence, plague, epidemics, or Black Death. This, I submit, is mildly shocking and should remind us, as historians, that we cannot rest upon past achievements but must constantly seek wider horizons and deeper insights. We find ourselves in the midst of the International Geophysical Year, and we all know that scientists entertain high hopes of enlarging through cooperation their understanding as well as their knowledge of the universe. It is quite possible that they may throw further light on such problems as the influence of sunspots on terrestrial life and the effects of weather on the conduct of human affairs. We may, for all we know, be on the threshold of a new era when the historian will have to think in larger, perhaps even in cosmic, terms.

Bibliography

Barzun, Jacques. *Clio and the Doctors: Psycho-History, Quanto-History and History.* Chicago, Ill., 1974.

Beringer, Richard E., ed. *Historical Analysis: Contemporary Approaches to Clio's Craft.* New York, 1978.

Davis, David Brion. "Some Themes of Counter-Subversion: An Analysis of Anti-Masonic, Anti-Catholic, and Anti-Mormon Literature." *Mississippi Valley Historical Review,* 47 (September 1960): 205–24.

Elkins, Stanley. *Slavery: A Problem in American Institutional and Intellectual Life.* Chicago, Ill., 1959.

Erikson, Erik H. *Gandhi's Truth.* New York, 1969.

Erikson, Erik H. *Young Man Luther: A Study in Psychoanalysis and History.* New York, 1958.

Freud, Sigmund, and William C. Bullitt. *Thomas Woodrow Wilson: Twenty-eighth President of the United States: A Psychological Study.* Boston, Mass., 1967.

Langer, William L. *In and Out of the Ivory Tower.* New York, 1977.

Lowenberg, Peter. "Psychohistory." In *The Past Before Us: Contemporary Historical Writing in the United States,* edited by Michael Kammen. Ithaca, N.Y., and London, 1980.

Mazlish, Bruce. "Freud." In *The Riddle of History: The Great Speculators from Vico to Freud.* New York, 1966.

Meyer, Donald. Review of Erikson, *Young Man Luther. History and Theory,* 1 (1961): 291-97.

Meyerhoff, Hans. "On Psychoanalysis and History." *Psychoanalysis and Psychoanalytic Review,* 49 (1962): 3-20.

Raak. R. C. "When Plans Fail: Small Group Behavior and Decision-making in the Conspiracy of 1808 in Germany." *Journal of Conflict Resolution,* 14 (March 1970): 3-17.

Schorske, Carl E. "William L. Langer." In *International Encyclopedia of the Social Sciences,* 18 vols., edited by David L. Sills. New York, 1968-79. vol. 18: 402-5.

Sinofsky, Faye; John J. Fitzpatrick; Louis W. Potts; and Lloyd deMause. "A Bibliography of Psychohistory." *History of Childhood Quarterly,* 2 (1975): 517-62.